MARTIN
AMIS
THE BIOGRAPHY

MARTIN AMIS

THE BIOGRAPHY

RICHARD BRADFORD

PEGASUS BOOKS

NEW YORK LONDON

MARTIN AMIS

Pegasus Books LLC
80 Broad Street, 5th Floor
New York, NY 10004

Library of Congress Cataloging-in-Publication Data is available.

ISBN: 978-1-60598-385-1

10 9 8 7 6 5 4 3 2 1

Printed in the United States of America
Distributed by W. W. Norton & Company, Inc.
www.pegasusbooks.us

For Ames and Harry.

And with thanks to Helen and Gerard Burns.

Contents

Acknowledgements   *ix*
Introduction   *xi*
Preface   *xv*

1 Before He Left   1
2 Wild Times   43
3 Oxford   70
4 The Novelist   92
5 The Seventies   121
6 Paris   175
7 America, Kingsley and Bellow   192
8 Self, Marriage, Children   218
9 Dystopian Visions   255
10 The Break-Up and *The Information*   287
11 A Gallery of Traumas   320
12 Novelist and Commentator   351
13 Significance: Is He a Great Writer?   409

Notes   *427*
Bibliography   *435*
Index   *439*

Acknowledgements

Thanks are due principally to Martin Amis for cooperating with my research. All potential interviewees were encouraged to approach him for reassurance that he had no objections to the project, and he generously agreed to five lengthy interviews with me. Also, he was good enough to permit quotations from both his own writing and his father's. Isabel Fonseca provided assistance with the preparation of the work.

I am immensely grateful to the following for their time and help: Rosie Boycott; Angela Gorgas; Anthony Howard; Bruce Page; Francis Wheen; Rt Hon. Nicholas Soames MP; Sargy Mann; Frances Mann; Colin Howard; Elizabeth Jane Howard; Will Self; Alan Jenkins; Clive James; Anthony Thwaite; Ann Thwaite; Professor Zachary Leader; Patricia Parkin; Anthony Blond; Laura Hesketh; Dannie Abse; Eric Jacobs; Christopher Hitchens; Alexandra ('Gully') Wells; Professor David Papineau; Andy Hislop; Chris Mitas; John Walsh; Professor John Carey; D. J. Taylor; Esmond Cleary; Sam Dawson; Roger Lewis; Steve Foster. Unless otherwise indicated, quotations are from interviews conducted with the above for this book.

Thanks are due also to the Huntington Library, California and the Bodleian Library, Oxford for their assistance with my research.

The book could not have been written without the time

allowed for my research and writing through my appointment as Research Professor of English at the University of Ulster.

Roger Lewis was generous with his time and help, and the assistance of my agent, the incomparable Leslie Gardner, was invaluable.

I am grateful to Andreas Campomar of Constable and Robinson for his advice, encouraging comments and patience, and to Angela Martin for handling the publicity.

Rosemary Savage provided careful and reliable assistance.

A grant from the British Academy enabled me to visit various libraries and conduct interviews in the UK, Continental Europe and the US.

Finally, enormous thanks are due to Dr Amy Burns, without whom this book could not have been written.

Reference details of quoted works are provided in brackets in the main text. The bibliography is made up solely of works by Martin Amis. The following abbreviations are used: '*TWAC*', *The War Against Cliché*; '*VMN*', *Visiting Mrs Nabokov*; '*TSP*', *The Second Plane*; '*TMI*', *The Moronic Inferno*.

Introduction

I was on a plane somewhere above Continental Europe and a man, a seat away, was reading a book while sipping his something-and-tonic. I thought he was trying to control a hiccup or a sneeze but then his whole upper body began to shake and he appeared, to my alarm, to be battling with some sort of seizure. Soon after that the contents of his nose and throat left for various destinations on his trousers, tray and glass. He was now growling, screaming with previously suppressed laughter. The book, I noted from the cover, was *Money*. It was, I thought, odd. Nothing wrong with laughing in public, surely? But later I began to understand the poor man's problem. He didn't care what *anyone else* felt; *he* felt ashamed of what *he* was doing. The book makes you feel complicit with the narrator, the hilarious (the sexist, obese, partially deranged, pornographer hero) John Self. Self isn't simply a one-off, a grotesque; he is an unapologetic representative of what Martin Amis calls the 'background'. And when you follow him there you feel uneasy about enjoying what, outside the book, you might profess to treat with disdain, or pretend to ignore. 'Suspending disbelief' is a familiar cliché. Upending, smothering disbelief, denying us a complacent immunity from the background is something else, something few writers can achieve. I'd met Martin several times already but it was then, in his absence, that I became particularly fascinated by the relationship between the man and his work and decided to write this book.

Unfortunately – at least for fans of celebrity biography – there are no extraordinary, portentous, shameful, let alone monstrous, aspects of Martin Amis to be discovered. If there is a mystery about him it comes from the anomalous relationship between his public persona, driven by his writing, and the private individual. It is almost as though he is the mirror image of his father, with everything in reverse. Kingsley's work is magnificently ecumenical; all human life is there but throughout there are sustaining verities. By contrast, Kingsley himself was a mass of fears and dilemmas, sometimes hurtfully unpredictable. His fiction was his refuge.

Martin projects his perplexities and horrors on to the fictional canvas, but not to dispose of them. He feels he has a duty to his audience, to challenge, infuriate, entertain, but not to use his work as a clearing house for his personal fallibilities and crises. His fiction is an index of his honesty. If in life he is confronted by moral and emotional perplexities – and there have been quite a number – he will not, like many intellectuals, smother pain with ideas. And this refusal to make sense of unkempt reality is the keynote of his novels. The retching man on the aeroplane reminded me of what he does indeed have in common with his father, something that has guaranteed for both a great deal of critical ire. Kingsley put it well: 'The rewards for being sane are not many but knowing what's funny is one of them. And that's an end of the matter.'

Martin certainly knows what's funny, which will not be a surprise to readers of his work. 'But,' asked a friend of mine – we'd been admirers though certainly not unreserved fans of his fiction since the 1970s – 'but . . . what's he *really* like?' I have known him for twelve years but I refer to him throughout this book by his first name for the simple fact that I need to

distinguish him from Amis Snr, not because we are close
friends. We have talked one-to-one at very great length, for
which I thank him; we have talked about everything, laughed
about his father's inimitable manner as a letter writer, argued
over nuclear weapons, global warming and *Ulysses* (I advocate
retention of the second, mock doom-evangelists of the third and
am bored senseless by the fourth, and he despises my opinions
accordingly). He has told me of his childhood, his various
families, friends and peers, of how he writes, what he writes;
and I have interviewed friends, lovers, intimates. But can I claim
knowledge of what he's '*really* like'? I doubt it.

Preface
for the American Edition

Martin Amis is probably the most transatlantic of all British novelists. Aside from a disastrous summer with his parents and siblings in Portugal, farcically recorded in his father's novel *I Like it Here* (1958), his first experience of anywhere other than the dull monochrome atmosphere of 1950s Britain was when Kingsley was invited to Princeton in 1958 as a Visiting Fellow. Martin was only nine years old when they arrived but the year there would have an enduring effect on his sense of where he came from and where he felt he belonged. Hilly, his mother, had shared with her children a delight in all aspects of popular culture that carried the imprint of America, which included everything from Westerns and crime movies to comic books and cartoons. Now, suddenly, images that seemed to belong in a separate universe had become part of their daily lives. Martin and his brother devised American names for themselves. 'Mine was Marty. Adapting one of his middle names [Nichol], Philip had come up with Nick Junior.' His remark that he and Philip 'picked up a new language' seems a reference to their juvenile diversions but it foreshadows a key aspect of his writing.

During the early 1980s Martin Amis earned far more from journalism than fiction, and for several London broadsheet newspapers and magazines he presented wry portraits of the personae and opinions of prominent US writers and politicians, making regular visits to do interviews and cover newsworthy events. He was based mainly in London and out of this double perspective evolved one of his most striking creations, the narrator of *Money* (1984), John Self. Self is a grotesque version of that very English stereotype, the loud, vulgar, working-class self-made man. His appetite for every kind of indulgence – a spectrum involving pornography, economically purchased sex, and the artery clogging consumption of food and alcohol – is phenomenal, verging upon the preposterous, but his preferred landscape of New York City lends the book a correlate sense of urgency and impatience. Most of his novels involve a divided allegiance; England is never quite something he seems able to fully contemplate without inviting some kind of comparison with the place across the Atlantic.

In *London Fields* (1989) Self is reincarnated, and plunged even further down-market, as Keith Talent, but Talent's London, also involving sex-crazed temptresses and pitiable aristocrats, would seem hardly credible were it not shown to us via the perspective of an uneasy outsider, the American writer Sam Young. The two writers, Richard Tull and Gwyn Barry, who in *The Information* (1995) epitomise the most repulsive aspects of literary culture – combining narcissism, envy, and an outrageous potential for self-aggrandisement – again carry with them a quintessential brand of Englishness, something rather pompous that overrides their differences. Amis seems dissatisfied with this. It is as if, despite their already unenviable personalities, they deserve a special form of levelling. So he despatches them to America on a shared book-promotion tour and allows the unforgiving change of context to exact a special form of revenge.

Amis's preoccupation with America reaches beyond representational stereotypes. It is surely no coincidence that both of his wives, divorced and current, are American. His closest friend, the late Christopher Hitchens, became a permanent resident of the US, and he and Amis came to treat the country from the early 80s onwards as, by parts, their playground and a blank space for their exploration of ideas that seemed stifled by their home environment in Britain. One feature of his involvement with the country that he would be unlikely to admit to involves his relationship with his father. More specifically, Martin Amis, while respecting Kingsley's achievements without reservation, has always feared that his own writing would be more an invitation for comparison than something that should be judged by its own qualities. Kingsley Amis's reputation as a stalwart of the 1950s generation of anti-modernists – variously the Movement and the Angry Young Men – was a gross simplification of his versatility but it endured and carried with it the notion of these British post-war figures as innately provincial in their concerns, treating a taste for 'foreign' culture as the badge of pretension. It is not therefore entirely improbable that his son's cultivation of himself as a literary hybrid, neither owing full allegiance to the land of his birth nor to the one that fascinated him, was in some degree motivated by a long-term strategy of discouraging attempts to treat him as inheritor of his father's alleged tendencies. Indeed, his perception of Saul Bellow as his true 'literary' father might in this respect be seen more as calculated gesture than a process of discovery.

In the light of all this it is somewhat ironic that he published his most unapologetic vision of England and Englishness a year after he, his wife Isabel Fonseca, and their two daughters had moved permanently to America from London. *Lionel Asbo* (2012) invites comparisons with Dickens; indeed Amis himself issues such invitations via allusions in the book itself and generously distributed prompters in interviews. The parallels are, however, overwhelmed by the disparities. Dickens' novels about his home city are characterized and some might argue weakened by his habitual exaggerations. Nasty figures are made slightly less depressing through being touched by farce, and victims doused with bathos immunise us from a proper sense of horror. Perhaps he had one eye on the delicate sensibilities of his middle-class readership or maybe his own experiences of the terrors of Victorian London made him reluctant to revisit them in fiction, at least in unadulterated form. Neither of these motives can be claimed by Martin Amis as justification for what he does in *Lionel Asbo*. The eponymous Lionel changes his surname from Pepperdine by deed-poll to honour his status as a career thug (ASBO refers to 'Anti-Social Behaviour Order', a status accorded to habitual criminals as, in effect, social outcasts). As a presentation of the proud arrogance of low-life existence; so far, so good.

Beyond this, however, one begins to detect a sense of calculated distancing, a desire to make Lionel and his fellow denizens of the horrible East London borough of Diston so grotesque, so removed from the world we live in, as to provoke by equal degrees lurid fascination and relief – the kind of relief that carries the less than compassionate, snobbish note of 'at least I'll never be like that'. Lionel is guardian and 'uncle' to Desmond Pepperdine and six years his senior, a vision of family spirit that begins to spin out of control when we learn not only that Lionel is 'a heavily weathered twenty-one' and that the otherwise sane Desmond contrives to have sex with Grace, Lionel's thirty-nine-year-old mother (a case of statutory rape). Lionel himself has won £139,999,999.50

on the National Lottery. In normal circumstances we would envy Lionel's good fortune, but as Amis demonstrates, persons of this level of imbecility are not even worthy of the jealousy of their betters. Lionel's bank balance might have improved but this cannot drag him out of the wretched class where he and his like appear to relish intemperate vileness. Lionel becomes a low-life celebrity, reinforcing the suspicion that Amis treats figures such as this as belonging in the ghetto of their own making: unity in grossness and vulgarity. He takes on a lover called Threnody, a soft porn model with expanded breasts. These portraits are often hilarious but far too cartoonish and preposterous to be treated as caricature or satire. Threnody divides her time between posing before the camera and her other vocation, poetry, and she is bitterly disappointed when denied the T. S. Eliot prize.

How should we react to this? Laughing at people in novels who fully deserve ridicule is one thing but it is not so easy to connive in the mockery of those who have been made very easy targets. Amis has always treated England as a rich source of raw material for his work, without really showing much affection for the place. Perhaps his act of distancing – residential and literary – has prompted him to explore his true feelings.

—Richard Bradford, August 2012

1

Before He Left

What makes a writer? Being born into what would strike most as a scenario suitable only for fiction might play some part. Martin Louis Amis came into this world on 25 August 1949 at Radcliffe Maternity Hospital, Oxford. His father Kingsley reported the next day to his closest friend Philip Larkin that Martin 'was as blond as P [Philip, his elder brother by a year] and less horrifying in appearance'. His mother, Hilary Amis (née Bardwell), was just twenty. She was as Larkin would later remark, 'The most beautiful woman I have ever seen without being the least pretty', a woman, some would say girl, who had encountered as much in her teens as most of her peers would experience in a lifetime. A scion of comfortably middle-class Home Counties stock – her father was a senior civil servant at the Ministry of Agriculture with a taste for madrigals, folk dancing and 'traditional' English culture – she had been sent first to a St Trinian's-style boarding school for girls in North Wales (Dr Williams's School for Young Ladies) from which she frequently absconded, and after that to the more respectable Bedales where she was bullied and which she left, by mutual consent, after less than a year. She completed her education at Beltrane, Wiltshire, departing aged fifteen with no qualifications. She then worked, as general helper, with board and lodgings, at a dog kennel in Bracknell run by two amiable lesbians, a period she enjoyed greatly. Aged sixteen Hilly enrolled at the Ruskin School of Drawing and Fine Art in Oxford and after six months, bored with her course, gave up the study of art to become their 'head model'. This, literally, meant that her head was the subject of paintings and sketches. Soon, however, she was posing in the nude, with little embarrassment or concern except for the draughty ill-heated studios where she was asked to sit for most of the day.

Kingsley was at this time in the third year of his degree in English, having returned to St John's after war service with the Royal Corps of Signals. In 1947 he gained a first, an achievement which he greeted with unconvincingly modest surprise. He had, he knew, a razor-sharp critical intelligence and his only flaw was a tendency to allow derision to intrude upon measured evaluation.

They met in 1946, via mutual friends, in a tea shop in the Cornmarket. Kingsley had noticed her before on several occasions, assumed she was an undergraduate and was mildly unsettled to learn that she was just seventeen 'and hence not nearly so depraved as I had hoped', he reported to Larkin. Within a year Hilly was pregnant and Kingsley, determined upon a literary or academic career, greeted the prospect of family life with horror. Hilly felt trapped and confused, pregnant by a man she had known for only twelve months, whose magnetic amusing social persona belied a well-protected seam of hapless despondency. At Kingsley's apologetic promptings they went in search of an abortion: not a locally sourced back-street termination endured by those with no alternative, but the more expensive, almost legal services provided by indulgent, venal practitioners in West London. The operation was booked with a 'Central European Private Practitioner' who asked them for £100 in advance. Only after taking advice from a GP, a friend of his old army comrade Frank Coles, that such procedures even when practised by trained gynaecologists could be 'brutal and dangerous' and with no legal protection, did Kingsley decide that Hilly's welfare should be given precedence. So began the brief, one-month, engagement of Kingsley Amis and Hilly Bardwell. Their marriage in the Oxford Town Hall Register Office was attended by both sets of parents but only after Kingsley's mother had persuaded her husband and the Bardwells to lift their horror-stricken boycott. Nick Russel, a fellow undergraduate at St John's and the only other guest, treated the couple to dinner in The George, a nearby pub. Both sets of parents departed separately as soon as the brief ceremony was concluded. On the morning of his wedding day Kingsley composed a letter of application for admission as a B.Litt research student. He would for the time being survive on a grant in the hope that he would eventually obtain an academic post. The couple first took a flat in Norham Road but by the time Martin was born they had moved into a quiet nineteenth-century terrace house in Banbury called Marriner's Cottage.

In letters to Larkin written during this period Kingsley professes his happiness at being with Hilly, complaining only that marriage obliged him to spend inordinate and unendurably boring periods in the presence of his in-laws. What he also discloses without explanation or contrition is the Kingsley Amis he would have been had a combination of fate and social convention not contrived to turn him into a married father of two, desperately seeking regular employment. In one letter he offers an ardently detailed report on a dark-haired, slim, sullen-looking girl with 'notice-able breasts' who returned his stare 'disinterestedly, half-closing her eyes'. His prose discharges a hint of something much more intimate than glances exchanged in a dance hall, but most striking of all is the fact that Hilly was alongside him when this occurred. She knew nothing of it but the frisson of sharing this secret with his friend, fuelled both by guilt and excitement, would set the tone for much of their subsequent correspondence during Kingsley's marriage to Hilly.

Marriage and children created two versions of Kingsley Amis and by the end of the 1950s he would often allow them to coalesce. He had by then grown tired of the ritual of deceit which in any event he practised with little competence. He frequently used Robert Conquest and even Larkin as bearers of alibis for his adulterous excursions, but Hilly too had become aware that her husband and the father of their children lived in a manner that any good-looking lecherous bachelor would envy. Despite an extramarital affair of her own – begun much later and somewhat despairingly – and Kingsley's seemingly ingenuous apologies, Hilly never countenanced an open marriage. The dinner party at their Swansea house when Kingsley went into the garden three times to have sex with each of the women guests is a verified fact yet the implication that the non-participating observers were indulgent debauchees-by-association is inaccurate. Hilly struggled to control her distress. Martin: 'Hilly, a virgin when she met Kingsley, was a very reluctant "swinger", and never stopped minding the other women *a lot.*'

Even after much of the lying and secrecy was undone there remained in Kingsley's psyche, and certainly in his writing, a propensity towards guile and doubling. Whether his unplanned early marriage was the cause or a symptom of this is a matter for psychoanalysts but what is certain is that throughout his adulthood there was never one Kingsley Amis. He became a cabinet of gestures – some genuine, others fabricated – and release mechanisms, the latter allowing him to simultaneously advance and retreat from the same position. Friends, interviewers, critics; all would for a moment seem to gain knowledge of the essential Kingsley Amis only to have the illusion dispelled by an act or statement variously moving, candid or quixotic, and on further inspection anomalous.

Martin was of course far too young to have knowledge of this aspect of his father's personality in the 1950s but later when he too had become a writer the past began to interweave with the present: he saw in Kingsley things that he recognized and wished if possible to suppress in himself. He succeeded only partially and his endeavours would certainly leave an imprint on his work.

During the summer holiday of 1949 Kingsley, faced with a second child to support, scoured the *Times Educational Supplement* for any university jobs in English, anywhere. Prague and Buenos Aires turned him down, as did Bristol, King's College, London, Manchester and Durham. Then, on 23 September he was invited for interview at University College, Swansea and subsequently offered an Assistant Lectureship with the salary of £300 per year. He left Oxford within a week, alone, to begin work and search for accommodation while Hilly, Philip and Martin stayed with his parents. Impatient and anxious, Hilly joined him, with Martin, in mid-November and found a flat within two days of her arrival. On 16 December she set off in a rented van with all of their possessions and two noisy infants to join her husband in the cramped second-floor flat of 82 Vivian Road, Swansea.

It is significant to note that Kingsley played hardly any part in the move, having spent two months searching unsuccessfully for a suitable residence. He commented to Larkin that 'I need all the time I can get for *house hunting*, and thinking about house hunting'. The placing of this activity in italics, and the droll coda in which he admits to giving as much time to contemplating the task as executing it are revealing. Hilly stated to Zachary Leader that he was 'totally impractical': a somewhat generous abridgement to what in truth was a predilection for selfishness. It was not that he did not love his wife and children, simply that for the time being he took every opportunity to postpone the tiresome responsibilities that came with them. Kingsley's salary was pitiable and Hilly, as well as looking after the children, worked part-time five days a week in the local cinema and later at a fish and chip shop in the Mumbles, whose leftovers were frequently brought home for family suppers. Nevertheless, Hilly later recalled the period as probably the most blissful of their marriage. 'We were perfectly happy. We saw the funny side of it.'

The death of Hilly's mother followed by an endowment in her will enabled the Amises to move from the cramped flat in Vivian Road – where the two baby boys were bathed in the kitchen sink, recorded in the first ever photograph of Martin – to a house, 24 The Grove, for which they paid £2,400.

Even before *Lucky Jim* brought him fame Kingsley was treated at Swansea as a minor celebrity: still in his twenties, a first from Oxford, handsome and as a lecturer like no one that his students, colleagues or, to their unease, his seniors had previously encountered. He taught the canon but encouraged his students to question the apparently inviolable qualities of great authors. One of his first students, Mavis Nicholson, remembers his disparaging remarks on Keats – 'self-indulgent and impenetrable' – along with his dashing appearance at his first lecture, when he strolled on stage with his 'chic' overcoat hung over his shoulders and a lock of hair falling distractedly across his forehead. 'There's talent,' she commented to a friend.

Although he was not conscious of the parallels, Kingsley was during this period becoming an almost exact version of the man who in 1954 would cause a minor earthquake in the otherwise torpid zone of English domestic fiction, Jim Dixon. The feature of Jim and indeed his quiet accomplice the narrator that made him so popular, particularly for those looking for something both unorthodox and selfishly optimistic in the still gloomy aftermath of 1945, was the fact that he was a magnificent fraud. He was an academic who loathed the pretensions of academia and most of all he was much cleverer, and indeed more cunning, than he pretended to be. The subtle alliance between Jim's sardonic, cutting private ruminations and the merciless orchestrations of the narrator was a kind of revenge against fate. He detested the provincial world in which the need to earn a living had placed him, treated those similarly grounded with a mixture of pity and scorn and dreaded the prospect of ending up in a long-term relationship, marriage, with the leech-like Margaret – a thinly disguised version of Monica Jones, with whom Larkin had recently begun a relationship in Leicester. The novel's conclusion was for some of its more scrupulous admirers its only weakness; even John Betjeman, hardly an advocate of harsh realism, found it slightly implausible. Suddenly, Jim's dismal existence is exchanged for the realization of his fantasies. He is offered a job in London by a wealthy entrepreneur – well paid but with no onerous duties – and the girl of his dreams, the magnificently busty Christine, leaves with him arm in arm on the train for the capital. His loathsome Head of Department and his son – based respectively upon Hilly's father and her brother with some swipes at academic posturing and aggrandizement thrown in – are left standing, enraged and humiliated, on the platform.

Christine was a compromise. In part she was Hilly, the innocent but outstandingly sexy girl he had come across in Oxford, and married. She was also a fantasy endemic to maleness, the kind of woman that men long for but with whom they don't necessarily wish to have children and spend the rest of their lives.

He wrote to Larkin only six months after his arrival in Swansea to report on the weekend he had spent in London with his friend James Michie 'where I drank a lot, and talked to sweet ladies, and smoked a lot of cigarettes, and spent some money on myself'.[1] Already, it seems, the exercise in wish fulfilment so brilliantly realized in the novel four years hence was being played out in Amis's sullen frustrated disclosures to Larkin. He goes on:

> As I came back on the train on Sunday evening, sinking as I did so into a curious trance-like state of depression, some ideas began clarifying in my mind:
> (a) The proportion of attractive women in London and Swansea is 100:1 or more – this is a sober estimate;
> (b) Nobody in Swansea really amuses me;
> (c) Children are not worth the trouble;
> (d) I would rather live in London, than I would live in Swansea;
> (e) Consequently the best thing I can do in Swansea is to keep on shutting myself up on my own and writing poems and a novel . . .

A more exact moment of gestation for his first novel cannot be located. Jim's constant sense of inhibition and infuriation, his irritation at having to spend his time in a place and with people he dislikes and the prevailing mood of having failed to secure the lifestyle and career he genuinely wished for: all are present in Kingsley's list. Just as significantly he betrays, no doubt unwittingly, a key aspect of himself post-*Lucky Jim*. There is no evidence that he disliked his children nor even resented their intrusion upon his battles against thwarted ambition, quite the contrary, yet at the same time he rationed the time he felt it necessary to spend with them. His university job was moderately demanding, though by today's standards it seems as much a salaried hobby as a profession, and the rest of his days involved the realization of his 1950 objective to '[shut] myself up on my own . . . writing poems and a novel'.

Martin recalls the mid-1950s in Swansea as a happy time. When he was not at school Hilly would during summer evenings and weekends take the children to the beach or the cinema or just for rides in the Morris 1000 Traveller. Nothing was planned or well organized and that, wittingly or not, suited the two young boys, Martin and Philip, very well indeed. She wasn't negligent, simply as innocent as her wards, according to Martin. What occurred to him later was that his father appeared biddably yet only partially present. 'She [Hilly] let us do anything . . . everything . . . he wouldn't need to be consulted about a matter to do with the open air. He was in his study. He was always in his study.' The parallels between Martin's recollection and Kingsley's letter to Larkin, particularly involving points (c) and (e), are striking and slightly eerie.

Kingsley's friends from Oxford – Michie, Larkin and Bruce Montgomery in particular – provided him pre-1954 with some relief, albeit experienced temporarily or vicariously, from his life in Swansea. After *Lucky Jim* the Amis house became a magnet for visitors both from the Home Counties literary circuit and those based locally who were fascinated by the prospect of socializing with an officially designated danger to public morality (Somerset Maugham in a famous article on Amis in the *Sunday Times* had cited *Lucky Jim* as a licence for mass degeneracy).

Kingsley and Hilly held parties in which they seemed intent on reclaiming the opportunities for youthful irresponsibility which pregnancy had denied them at Oxford almost a decade earlier. Hilly's endowment and Kingsley's new source of income, boosted by an advance for *That Uncertain Feeling* (1955), enabled them to take on regular domestic help in the form of Eva Garcia, a woman of mixed Celtic/Iberian stock married to the similarly provenanced Joe, a solidly built hard-drinking steel-rigger. Eva's principal duties involved repairing the post-party damage – according to Philip the house smelled for most of the time 'like a pub' – but she also took over tasks routinely undertaken by the woman of the house. She looked after the children, who now included Sally, born in 1954. The Garcias were genuinely and unapologetically working-class, unawed by and indifferent to the mannerisms and cultural prestige of their employers. Kingsley was amused and there is evidence that he drew upon them as sources for the thread of South Wales kitchen-sink realism detectable in *That Uncertain Feeling*.

'It was', recalls Martin, 'incredibly dissolute, at least by the standards of middle-class Swansea.' Following all-night parties good-natured but otherwise bleary guests could be found recovering among the debris of ashtrays, bottles, half-empty glasses and records. 'Sometimes we'd be dragged along to Kingsley's colleagues' houses, to have tea, cakes, jelly. I'd go to theirs and sometimes they'd come to me and there was a huge contrast . . . Children are so conventional, and I could see they were surprised and I couldn't see that mine was about ten thousand times nicer than theirs, but it was. When I brought friends home Mum would be there with her feet on the table, shoes off and music in the background, probably jazz. And my friends thought it was so great. Phil said once, "Ah breakfast in the wine shop." Mum might greet us, or guests, slightly hung-over and as we sat down to our cornflakes . . . well, the milk jug would be surrounded by half-empty wine bottles . . . Far more boho than everybody else.' They began to wonder if anyone else lived in quite the way they did. Esmond Cleary, one of Kingsley's colleagues and recently married to Jean, sometimes looked after the children at their house or visited the Amises for parties. Cleary: 'Everyone seemed to look on The Grove with a mixture of envy and bafflement. The children were happy, bright, quite well behaved but the place was wonderfully disorganized, an endless cocktail party. A strange combination. You have to remember that this was provincial Britain in the fifties, everything seemed hopelessly dreary, but Kingsley, Hilly and the children were determined to enjoy themselves. Don't misunderstand me, they weren't irresponsible hedonists. The children were loved and cared for ... yet there was an energy and optimism about the house that was at odds with the time and the area.'

The Garcias provided a further unaccountable twist to the children's already peculiar journey towards adolescence. In April 1956 the Amises moved from The Grove to 53 Glanmore Road, Uplands, the latter a spacious, handsome Edwardian house retaining most of its original features. Kingsley would now have a study, to which he could constantly retire, which was roughly the same size as their previous sitting room. Each of the children had a bedroom to themselves and the rear garden was private and mature. Instead of selling 24 The Grove they arranged to let it to the Garcias, who had two children, Michael and Hilary. The precise reason for this is lost in the mists of rumour that surround the Amis family of the mid-1950s. The rent would barely cover the upkeep of the property, but Hilly's and Kingsley's motive would seem apparent from subsequent events. For long weekends or mid-week evenings when one or both of their parents were mysteriously elsewhere the children would go to the Garcias, and each year for five years Martin, Philip and Sally spent four to five weeks with Eva and Joe as their unofficial foster children.

The effect of this upon the two brothers can be gleaned from their contrasting accounts. Martin describes Joe as 'a cuboid, semi-literate grafter who seemed actually taller sitting down than standing up. To adults he would probably have appeared as menacing ... For us he was a fascinating addition to our extended family of curiosities ... Eva was terrible and great ... one of the divinities of my childhood.' He recalls her as a mixture of striking and rather grotesque images, singing as she made the tea, with 'delight in her Hispanic eyes', the romance of her red bandana and shiny black hair undone by the 'slab' of the orthopaedic boot on which she was obliged to swivel. He fixes also upon a particular incident when the family with Eva and Sally in the back seat of the car passed the scene of an apparently fatal accident. Eva seemed to feel it her duty to have her charge, then barely three, behold the sight of a man lying on the pavement, soaked in blood and twitching either from terrible pain or as a last concession to mortal existence. She announced, '*Look* at him, Sal. *Writhing in agony* he is.' According to Philip their periods with the Garcias were 'bloody awful ... I hated it. But we were forced to do it because Kingsley and Hilly were having such a wild time.' He remembers Joe as far more gigantic and intimidating than any adult he had previously encountered and the prospect of having to share bedrooms with the Garcias' children, plus the experience of Joe's regular drunkenness, and the ingrained habits of a family unused to routines of personal or domestic hygiene struck him as 'horrible ... incredibly primitive'. Surely, he thought, Kingsley's and Hilly's commitments, whatever they were, did not merit them being put through something so apparently punitive as this. Sally, he recalls, was even more upset, having no understanding of why she seemed to have been abandoned by her mother and father and on one occasion having to endure several weeks in the much rougher and even less familiar council house of friends of the Garcias, an exigency that Eva and Joe did not bother to explain to Kingsley and Hilly.

Martin again: 'Joe. He was illiterate too. He'd get out his packet of ten Player's and with great concentration he'd write on it the names of the horses he'd want to bet on. And the "c"s and the "d"s would be the wrong way round. It was amazing, I thought, that a man couldn't write.

'It was egg and chips every night, meat on Sundays, and every evening ended with a huge plate of buttered toast and mugs of tea.

'Eva could be terrifying. She said, "You 'ave six stars in 'eaven and ev'ry time you tell a lie, one a' them goes out. And when they're *all* gone out – you *die*." That one had me sobbing with terror. And once, I asked for a glass of milk with my lunch. She couldn't be bothered to get it, so she fixed me with a stare and said, "I knew a man used to drink milk with his lunch . . . He *died*." I didn't drink milk for about five years after that.'

In terms purely of facts Martin and Philip do not diverge greatly but what is most striking is the enormous disparity between the apparent effects of these experiences upon each of them. It could of course be contended that Martin's account is more mature and indulgent than his brother's given that he bestows upon Eva and Joe an energy, even a uniqueness that belies their status as a class beneath the Amises. But it should also be remembered that both men were recalling events that occurred virtually half a century earlier. Recovered or even personal memories are notoriously partial but I would argue that Philip comes closest to the truth. Philip's recollections are unmalicious, he is not attempting some vengeful recompense for childhood maltreatment and indeed his occasional inconsistencies – he is terrified and appalled by people who also, he states, had 'hearts of gold' – testify to his honesty: he seems to have carried into middle age the sense of confusion and indecision that beset much of his childhood. Martin, however, takes a more positive view. 'I suppose,' he reflects, 'the difference between Phil and me is that I always thought of it [their time with the Garcias] as enriching in some ways. It was a new world, completely different from anything I'd experienced before.' The Garcias do indeed bear a close resemblance to the assembly of mostly working-class grotesques who populate much of his fiction. Did his time with them instigate this fascination? 'Probably.'

Becoming a full-time novelist has no predictable effect upon one's psyche but it is not too absurd to contend that since we elect to spend much of our conscious existence filtering perception and reality through an oblique variant upon language, a good deal of what we routinely apprehend and recollect is touched by our stock in trade of conceits and distortions. Martin was certainly not being dishonest regarding his presentation of the Garcias but, as all writers are aware, honesty is as much a device as a principle.

'What are your prevailing memories of the Swansea years?' I ask him. 'Was it a happy childhood?'

'Happy? Yes, I think it was, yes certainly. The stories told by Zach [in the 2006 biography] are true enough . . . the fights, the parties, the occasional sense of imminent catastrophe, that is, of break-up. We were aware of it all but it didn't register as anything very important. For all we knew every family was like that and it didn't seem to affect Hilly and Kingsley. It was part of their routine and that's how we saw it too. Nothing to be particularly concerned about.'

From *Experience* and other accounts one gets the impression that the family existed in something of a cocoon. Apart from the faintly bizarre experiences of living with the Garcias the children didn't seem to mix with others in the locality.

'Actually we did. We'd have cricket matches in the garden at Glanmore Road and the whole place would be full of kids of about the same age. Hilly would provide sweets and pop but we were otherwise unsupervised. And of course the house and garden were full of dogs, which Hilly loved. She'd take in strays or abandoned litters of puppies and put them up in the garage. Ten, sometimes twenty dogs of various ages and shapes would be wandering round the house at any given time. They weren't quite pets; lodgers I suppose. Hilly would always find homes for them.'

Sam Dawson, two years younger than Kingsley, was his most recent colleague in the English Department. 'Hilly was extra-ordinary. Sweet-natured, spirited yet in many ways more mature than Kingsley. She was of a mercurial nature . . . in a plodding world. The house was famously disorganized, but they [Hilly and Kingsley] weren't irresponsible. She particularly wanted a good life for the kids. They never missed school, and she fretted about their health. At the same time she wanted them to be happy, free to enjoy themselves.' Martin: 'The more I return to the Swansea years the more I *can* remember. But the point is they are memories without labels, such as regret, or disappointment or relief. Everything just seemed as it was, good. Down the road there was a park, Cwmdonkin Park – yes Dylan Thomas's house was close by but I didn't know that then . . . and groups of us would just play there, make up games, climb trees. Sometimes there'd by fights but no one ever seemed to get hurt . . .

'My primary school was like any other. I had crushes on a variety of girls but I fantasized most about my RK [Religious Knowledge] teacher . . . Miss Penellis. She was a witch. The more she preached a typically Welsh Chapel-style adherence to doctrine the more I was certain she was an agent of Satan.'

How old were you?

'Ten, nine perhaps.'

Precocious lust, then?

'No. There were teachers I fancied, but Miss Penellis was outstandingly ugly; fat, with black straw-like hair – that's where the witch aspect came in – but she would recite passages from the Old Testament in a way that was hypnotic.

'It was then that I went through my one "religious phase".'

Best to get rid of it early?

'Yes, by the time we left Swansea for Cambridge I was a proselytizing atheist, but for a while in Swansea I went through a bizarre and very private religious phase. I had several Bibles and I wrote all sorts of things in the margins. Sometimes, I performed black masses in my bedroom. You see, we had no idea whatsoever about God or faith. Certainly, there was the feeling that we weren't like a regular family. Most of my friends went to church or chapel, and Sunday school. I went a few times, to Sunday school, but for tea and blancmange. I liked the parables. No one cared about Sundays in the Amis house. So what I call my religious phase was actually a bout of early imaginative excess – inspired by that fact that we were a godless household and Miss Penellis was magnetically grotesque – a woman who seemed to have *powers*.

'I was six or seven years old, and filling out a school registration form, and I came to the disquieting question, which seemed to visit me from a different world. I ran into the hall and shouted up the stairs, "Mum! What religion are we?" There was a long silence, then: "Uh ... Church of England!" Yes, thank God for the Church of England, it didn't commit you to anything at all. In truth, though, "Church of England" was a mortal lie. We weren't even that.

'It was only much later, in the States, that I actually entered a church with friends of the family, and I had a wafer put into my *mouth*. It seemed grotesque. Even as a child I felt that religion *encroached* upon me, and I couldn't believe that so many others *believed* in it. Even during my Bible period, I was more a bibliophile than anything else. What it *said* was a mere curiosity. I liked the gold edging on the book. I was repelled by *worship*. As Kingsley said – I think someone was heckling him at an event in the sixties – you can believe what you like, "but do it in your *own time*, in private", like masturbation.' He pauses, as if about to qualify what he has said. So I ask.

'No, I'm no longer a "proselytizing atheist". Being an atheist is an irrational position. It is presumptuous, and crabbed. The right place to be is on the very brink of agnosticism, about to tumble into . . . atheism. About to but . . . We need to know more about the Universe, because to human beings the Universe is still very mysterious. I was talking recently to a friend of mine, the philosopher and scientist Colin McGinn, and he said, "We don't even know what *electricity* is". We certainly don't know how galaxies are formed, why they don't fly apart. We're still ten Einsteins away from even a *basic* understanding of the Universe.

'So, to say "I am an atheist" is a bit previous, isn't it? I mean, the basic fact is that the Universe is much more intelligent than we are. So that gives you pause, I think.' How very different, I comment, from the inflexible atheism of his closest friend Christopher Hitchens. Is Hitchens's position 'irrational – crabbed'? 'We have disagreed on many things. We do still.'

The impression Martin gives of life in Swansea is of a family who did not need faith or any other kind of doctrinal support. They just enjoyed life, and each other. There was the incident with the canoe, when Martin and Philip aged respectively nine and ten – or so he half recalls – were provided by Hilly with a rather flimsy vessel and allowed to set off from Swansea Bay west to Pembroke Bay where their mother would collect them at some vaguely estimated time. None of them had properly calculated the distance, nor indeed taken any account of weather conditions or currents. 'The Swansea *Evening Post*', says Martin, 'eventually reported that my act of heroism, getting ashore and summoning the coastguard, had saved my brother's life. Actually, he'd paddled back before I'd been washed up on the beach and was drinking Tango in a seafront café trying to remember our home phone number while the coastguards scoured the area.' Martin recalls his mother's carefree regime with a mixture of amused admiration and disbelief. 'My mother was made up of extremes. She was outstandingly compassionate, kind, shrewd and in other ways she kept the sheen of guileless irresponsibility that probably attracted Kingsley to her in the first place. I remember, after Sally was born – she'd be about four or five – being driven back from the beach in the dark, with the three of us, Phil and me either side and Sal in the middle, on the roof-rack. The only light came from the full moon and the headlamps. It felt as though we were flying. None of us felt nervous because at that age you don't recognize danger – I suppose we had much in common with our mother despite the age difference.' One suspects also that much later, when he became a father himself, the romantic tinge of his childhood recollections became the cause of an almost neurotic sense of protectiveness.

Around 1956–7 Martin's parents' marriage came close to collapse, due primarily to Hilly's affair with the journalist Henry Fairlie. Fairlie resembled the sort of character played by Leslie Phillips or Terry-Thomas in Ealing comedies, but while they were barely credible caricatures of the charming bounder he was a far more unsettling package of contrasts and anomalies. The Amises had got to know him during one of their trips to London and at first it seemed to Kingsley that he had come face to face with a man who was both his replica and his nemesis. Just as Kingsley regarded any of the attractive wives and girlfriends of those he knew as fair game – it was, as he saw it, their decision – so Fairlie seemed to regard himself as answerable to only one imperative, the word 'no'. Yet beneath their predatory personae could be found two very different individuals. Kingsley, though unswervingly polite in his dealings with his girlfriends, was also a ruthless opportunist; the best they could hope for was an extended, albeit clandestine, affair, such as the one with his ex-student Mavis Nicholson. No spurious affirmations of commitment or promises of endurance would be forthcoming or expected. Fairlie, however, was a true romantic. He once had a taxi-load of flowers delivered to the flat of an inamorata and would regularly spend a week's salary on absurdly lavish dinners at Claridge's as part of his ostentatious campaigns of seduction. But by all accounts he was sincere, at least to the extent that he could conjure sincerity from an untidy catalogue of conflicted interests. He was promiscuous and unfaithful but none of his women ever doubted his kindness. He was the ideal lover, with the proviso that he might well sustain this ideal for two or even three different women simultaneously, not forgetting his wife.

Kingsley knew of Fairlie's reputation in advance of becoming acquainted with him personally and then he witnessed the equivalent of what he had visited upon many others: he watched his wife become gradually enraptured by the attentions of someone else. At first he suspected that this was Hilly's act of vengeance, a suitably just experience of atonement he assumed would be brief. But to his surprise, and horror, Hilly announced that she and Fairlie had discussed a permanent relationship. As he put it to Larkin, 'on Friday a verbal statement was made to me by my wife by which I was given to understand that, far from just having an affair with Henry Fairlie, she is in love with him and he with her. The topic of divorce from the married state was raised, and no decision

19

reached.' The letter deviates from the blend of backbiting, satirical glee and self-caricature with which he and Larkin routinely communicated. The performer's mask has slipped and Kingsley cannot disguise a genuine sense of fear.

> I think . . . that my marriage has about one chance in four of surviving till next summer. If I do get a divorce, it means presumably that the children, about whom I feel strongly, will accompany their mother to her new home. But that isn't the same as having them in your home all the time, you see . . . Having one's wife fucked is one thing; having her taken away from you, plus your children, is another, I find.[2]

I asked Martin now if he recalls anything of the near break-up. 'Two things come to mind. I remember Henry Fairlie because he visited Swansea several times, and we had no cause to regard him as different from the other figures who would stay for weekends. Philip [Larkin], who did his duty as Phil's godfather, let's say he was thrifty, Lenten, with gifts. Unlike Bruce Montgomery, my godfather, generous, bountiful, who would drive down in his Bentley. George and Pat Gale were regulars, and there was Bob [Conquest] and John Wain and the Powells. We were children and we knew their names but we had no interest in what they actually *did*.

'I didn't know of the affair until the sixties when, very briefly, he [Fairlie] and Hilly got back together. She always reserved a special affection for him.

'But in Swansea . . . well at that age you don't articulate it to yourself. Subconsciously, you're uneasy. There was one absolutely terrifying row. We were, both brothers and sister, sitting on the stairs and they were screaming at each other. And next morning, Kingsley went up with a breakfast tray and shot back down again, having gym shoes and ornaments hurled at him. And we didn't say anything to each other, but it was pretty clear something serious was wrong. But you're thinking . . . what can *that* be? Probably your subconscious is coming to a conclusion but you don't really understand *that* at all. When you're told about the sexual act, told in the school yard, your first response is absolute outrage that your father could do that to your mother. I talked openly about it [sex] with Kingsley later – he made a point of this because his father and mother were obsessively secretive – but for us in Swansea, yes we knew something was *wrong*. It's all inklings and intuitions and subconscious conclusions but they're never articulated. Looking back it probably did have something to do with Fairlie.'

In December 1956 Fairlie was summoned to appear in court on bankruptcy charges and spent a brief period in Brixton prison. He made a good living as one of the most esteemed serious journalists of the day, but his profligate habits, and generosity, ruined him financially. He was serious in his proposal to leave his wife and set up home with Hilly and her children and she, to Kingsley's trepidation, was on the brink of a decision. His bankruptcy obviated the latter and up until her death she remained uncertain of what she would have done had fate not intervened.

In March 1957 Kingsley's mother died suddenly of a stroke. Kingsley helped his father with the practicalities and displayed due solemnity at the funeral but beyond that there is no evidence in correspondence or elsewhere that Rose's departure caused him great emotional distress. The effects on the family as a whole, however, were considerable. In November of the previous year, during the Fairlie crisis, Sally had suffered a severe head injury, a fractured skull, after falling from a garden table. She was unconscious for two days and doctors in the Swansea hospital warned that although there were no immediate symptoms of brain damage such injuries to a three-year-old child could result in later psychological and neurological problems. One can, therefore, only speculate on the consequences of what happened five months later. Sally was staying with her paternal grandparents and Rose suffered her fatal stroke little more than an hour after William, Kingsley's father, had departed for work. Sally was alone with the body of her grandmother for more than seven hours and at one point applied lipstick and face powder to her pale gaunt features in an attempt to restore to her some semblance of life. For years afterwards, and well into adolescence, Sally would exhibit an almost hysterical fear of witnessing anyone asleep, often attended by a pathological urge to wake them up.

Sally's unsteady childhood could well have contributed to her descent towards alcoholism in her twenties but it was significant also for its influence upon the hierarchy of the Amis siblings. Martin certainly did not seek any special role, let alone position of responsibility, but circumstances conferred both upon him. Hilly remembers that the night when Sally was born Kingsley had to rush to a callbox to telephone the midwife, a stressful yet fairly straightforward operation, but before leaving the house he rushed upstairs, grabbed the sleeping Martin and carried him with him up the street. It was not that his four-year-old son was any better equipped than he was to dial the correct number and feed the coins into the slots in the right order – or at least Martin modestly denies such precocity – but Martin had already become for his father a talisman of calm and stability. Hilly recalls that the incident of the phone call was not unusual. 'When he was anxious [at all] he'd go for Martin because Martin was the calmest of the three ... Philip [that night] would have been more startled at being woken up ... Martin was far more relaxed.' For a six-year period following Rose's death and until his own demise, William Amis became the sixth permanent member of the Amis household and Kingsley very much resented his father's presence. In a letter to Larkin he proffers a catalogue of habits that would to most seem harmless eccentricities – a tendency to slip French or German commonplaces into conversation and in particular a predisposition to chat with Amis's friends as if they were not a generation younger than himself – but which aroused in Kingsley bitterness, even loathing: 'Why doesn't he go away for good? Failing that, why can't he go away for a very long time and then go away again as soon as he has come back?'[3] There is no obvious explanation for this, given that William had grown used to those aspects of his son's personality he once found unacceptable and was by all accounts a grateful, unobtrusive guest. However, there is a passage in Martin's *Experience* which causes one to suspect that Kingsley's sense of unease and resentment was fuelled in part by envy.

He [William] spent a good part of his widowhood [. . .] keenly and inventively and rather sternly playing with my brother and me. I admit without reservation that he was one of the grand passions of my childhood – so much so that he once reduced me to a tantrum of misery when he found himself maintaining that it was 'natural' to have 'more feeling as a grandfather' for the first-born son. As far as I was concerned it wasn't a question of what was *natural*. This was a question of love: of insufficiently requited love. He tried to soften it but he wouldn't unsay it; he wouldn't bend to the severity of my distress . . .[4]

Martin's disclosure of his affection for William is as sincere as Kingsley's sense of displeasure, except that while the latter is nuanced and ambiguous the former is transparent. What was it about William that inspired his 'grand passion', his 'love'? 'He did seem incongruous, and pleasantly so. The Garcias came from a different world, and that distressed Phil, but Daddy A, our grandfather, was different in a way that was more benign and hospitable.'

The whole period was full of contrasts and paradoxes. 'In Kingsley's relationship with Daddy A, even there some resentment was tangible but he loved him too. There was an immense amount of love in the household despite the chaos. For example, one aspect of our life in Swansea that has gone unrecorded, was the orphanage . . . Every Saturday or perhaps Sunday we would go in the car to an orphanage just down the coast towards the Mumbles peninsula. This was when I was, oh six or seven I think, and we would pick up a boy called Andrew – I can't remember his surname, in fact I don't think we, the children, were ever told it. He was about Philip's age, maybe a little older and if it was summer we'd spend the afternoon on the beach or in a park where Kingsley would make his only attempts at ball games, cricket mainly, and various diversions were organized if the weather was bad and we had to drive around in the car; "I spy with my little eye" – that sort of thing. My parents did their best to make him feel part of the family but he seemed intimidated and apprehensive. Sometimes we'd go to museums or market towns, maybe the cinema. He never really relaxed. I found it slightly arduous, uneasy. I didn't understand at the time *why* we were doing this, it was just part of our life.'

The arrangement continued until the family left for Princeton in 1958 and as far as Martin can recall from later conversations his parents' arrangement with the orphanage was unsolicited. They knew of the place and simply wanted to offer a child something of the cosy family routine enjoyed by the Amis youngsters. It seems to go against the notion of Hilly and Kingsley as rather dissolute bohemians and the image of Kingsley in particular as solipsistic, for which he makes no excuses in his letters. Was Kingsley the more reluctant partner in this exercise in altruism? 'No, not at all. In fact I think it was his idea. You see my parents, despite their problems, were compatible in that they matched each other in unpredictability. The orphanage visits, trips out with Andrew, I know it all sounds curious but we, the kids, didn't think so at the time. They would have blazing rows and, as I learned later, there were affairs, but the most enduring memory was of their tangible, sometimes embarrassing affection for each other.'

Kingsley was invited by R. P. Blackmur to become Lecturer and Resident Fellow in Creative Writing at Princeton University for the 1958–9 academic year. The family were booked to sail for New York on the *Queen Elizabeth* – Kingsley would not countenance the thought of flying across the Channel let alone the Atlantic – but only Kingsley, his father and the two boys boarded the ship. Hilly followed several weeks later with Sally who had been diagnosed with a benign tumour in her thigh which required surgery.

Their house was in a characteristically middle-class suburban avenue called Edgerstoune Road, two miles from the Princeton campus and within commuting distance by train to Manhattan where most of the residents worked. For various reasons each of the Amises felt they had gone quite suddenly from stagnation to nirvana. The houses were copies of the inauthentic 'ranches' in which Hollywood frontiersmen spent their lives. These however were fitted with every modern convenience – kitchens with formica and stainless-steel units, spacious bathrooms plus walk-in shower cubicles, sitting rooms which gave on to the quarter-acre lawn via windows that stretched from floor to ceiling. Almost all the families on Edgerstoune Road were close to the Amises' age, some were academics and the rest earned comfortable livings from the law, journalism, advertising or management. Their lifestyle bore no relation whatsoever to the existence of even the comfortably off residents of Swansea. When the men were not at work the entire area seemed committed to a round of barbecues, cocktail parties, relaxed open-invitation dinners or games of baseball accompanied by chilled beer and wine. The spacious gardens were bordered by woodland in which deer could often be glimpsed and the children of the road – calculated to be sixty in number aged between six and sixteen – roamed around, happily unsupervised in what seemed like a giant playground. Martin: 'I think my mother felt she'd come home. I have vivid memories of Swansea when she would pick up Phil and me from primary school. The rest of the mothers would be dressed as you'd expect from films of the fifties; smart but rather dull skirts and jackets, nice shoes and usually, *hats*, with miniature flower and fruit arrangements attached. Hilly would turn up for us in jeans, flipflops in good weather, an open-necked shirt and blond hair all over the place. The other mothers would whisper things about her being a "beatnik", and if there were men around, well they just stared longingly. There, she was a misfit but in Princeton she fitted in perfectly.'

The famously dissolute parties hosted by the Amises in Swansea, provoking by degrees outrage, envy and gratitude among Kingsley's colleagues, now found concord in this world of US middle-class hedonism. Martin and Philip spent their time with children very much like themselves, inured to the relaxed open manner of the way their parents lived. The Amises' closest friends in the locality were the McAndrews, who lived two doors down. John McAndrew worked in advertising and Jean, like Hilly, took care of the house and the children; the McAndrews had six girls aged between four and sixteen. 'We [he and Philip] renamed ourselves Marty and Nick Jr and the girls in the US were a lot more outgoing and well, classy, than their Swansea counterparts. Nothing happened, of course.' Within months of their arrival Kingsley was having an affair with Jean McAndrew. It lasted for the duration of the visit and Hilly was caused to wonder yet again about trusting her husband's promise to at least try to forgo further extra-marital excursions. She began a relationship with John, prompted in part by despair and a desire for revenge. Kingsley supplemented his fling with Jean with a sequence of poorly concealed affairs with wives of Faculty members, students and anyone else who came within range at Princeton or his guest lectures in Chicago, New York, Washington DC, Harvard and Yale.

'There was a gruesome irony in all this,' observes Martin, 'because while we knew very little of what was happening with our mother and father, I was provided with a foul introduction to sex by two guests from one of the late-night parties.' A man and woman entered his bedroom; the former claimed to be a doctor and asked if he could 'examine' Martin, which he did, though in a manner he had never previously envisioned. Did it, I ask him, leave any sort of psychological scar? 'No, I don't think so. It was unpleasant, I knew that, but I didn't really understand why. That would come later.' This goes some way to explain the character of the passage in *Experience*. He wraps the episode in prose that is fastidiously detailed – he seems to recall exactly the posture, dress and demeanour of the two people – yet elegant and impersonal. It is a horrible incident, beautifully transposed. Nabokov comes to mind, but not *Lolita*; rather the more disturbing *The Enchanter* where the paedophile narrator cannot cite precocious sexuality as an excuse for his behaviour. He is unapologetically evil and calculating, and he fascinates Martin.[5] The US – its authors, its sheer exhausting excess – has for some time been a cynosure for Martin's fiction.

One suspects that his preoccupation with the place predates his emergence as a writer. 'It was as though we were being given remission from ordinary life. School in Princeton was a form of relaxation. At Bryn-Mawr in Swansea we were taught by rote, the distinction between verbs, nouns and adjectives, long division and multiplication, equations. American schools at that level were unbelievably far behind British schools. Probably more then than now. I went from doing long division of pounds, shillings and pence when I was eight to doing eight plus six equals fourteen a year later. In America we weren't obliged to do anything much, add up figures in columns, draw pictures . . . It was very enjoyable but had disastrous consequences when we got home. I was ten so I had a year to catch up for the eleven-plus but Phil took the exam soon after we got back – and failed it. Being in the American system was the equivalent of taking a year off. The country itself offered me a flavour of what I'd want more of ten, fifteen years later but at the time the school system was disastrous.'

He pauses. 'Back then, of course, it seemed of no great importance but America was my first real experience of a different world, where people behaved differently, and the way they spoke, talked, was part of that. I imitated US speech, but something stayed with me. I learned another language.' Does he mean that his famed ability to bridge the Atlantic in a single novel originated during his first, childhood visit? 'Yeah, it did. It's an odd thing. Brits and US writers should, you'd imagine, be able to think themselves into each other's idioms. But it's not as straightforward as that. Habits of speech are part of our disposition. It is difficult to borrow someone else's, and even Philip Roth, with his superlative ear, can't do ordinary spoken English, London English, in his novels. But I learned "American" as a child. It was easy.'

Martin passed the eleven-plus. 'I went to grammar school but

Phil went to a secondary modern, which meant that while I was faced with academic streaming for O-levels he was expected to leave at fifteen or possibly sixteen with CSEs, exams for the trades or manual labour.' Was he resentful? 'It was a horrible moment. They divided the boys in the playground. Passes to the right, fails to the left. It was traumatic, for him.'

At grammar school Martin was caned twice by the head-master, once for writing obscenities in the margin of his classmate's pocket diary and again for an act of truancy. He had played and greatly enjoyed rugby union at primary school. 'Saturday mornings, in Swansea, it was rugby. Yeah, I wasn't really up to snuff by Welsh standards. I rarely made the first fifteen and it was a thrill when I did. But in Cambridge [where they moved to after Swansea] I was considered really quite good, mainly because the standard was so much lower than in Wales. I played wing forward for a while and then became half back. Then came the moment . . . interesting moment, wonder how many people have gone through it . . . when you look into the ruck and everyone's gouging, punching, elbowing. There was nothing I liked more than diving in and coming out covered in blood. Now I looked into it and thought, "Don't fancy that." There's a line in Kafka, I can't remember where it's from. Talking about a certain point in your life when you realize that everything is needed and nothing is *renewed*. And thinking about it later, *that* was boys' stuff. And, by Cambridge, I was getting more interested in girls' stuff. I went on playing till I was fifteen or sixteen but with much less bottle from fourteen onwards.'

One element of Martin's childhood in Swansea that went unrecorded before his nuanced references to it in *Experience* was his relationship with the Partingtons, specifically Hilly's sister Margaret ('Miggy'), her husband Roger and their son David, who was close to Martin's age. The Partington house in

Gloucestershire often served as an idyllic alternative to the Garcias'. It was the rural England of the 1950s much as the country presented itself in contemporary cinema, particularly in films such as *The Titfield Thunderbolt*. Martin loved it, but it was only much later, in the 1990s, that he came to fully appreciate the rarity and value of such experiences of unsullied innocence.

The journalist George Gale had become one of the Amises' London friends in the early 1950s. Gale had contacts in Peterhouse, Cambridge, and when in early 1961 a new post of Fellow and Tutor in English was created by the college he orchestrated contacts between Amis and Peterhouse's Master, Herbert Butterfield. Butterfield was fully aware of Peterhouse's reputation as the most conservative, anachronistic of the Cambridge colleges – Tom Sharpe's *Porterhouse Blue* was comprised partly of stories, many accurate, of the bizarre, ritualistic archaisms of the place. Amis was interviewed for the Fellowship in March 1961. Some Fellows had never previously heard of him, and others were unsettled by the prospect of bringing in someone who was as much a celebrity as a scholar. But Butterfield wanted to modernize the college, and his preference for Amis held sway. He was elected and would take up the appointment of Official Fellow and Tutor in English in October 1961, Peterhouse's first. Amis resigned from Swansea, and the college provided the family with a quaint converted mill cottage in West Wratting. Soon after that they purchased a spacious, mid-Victorian house in Madingley Road, Cambridge. Kingsley and Hilly would turn this into a version of Glanmore Road, Swansea, with regular, now more convenient visits from friends in London.

If Swansea had seemed charmingly dissolute, Cambridge had an air of self-destructive decadence about it. Hilly maintained her tenderness for stray dogs and these were now supplemented by Debbie the donkey who lived in a shed outside the back door. Guests would be encouraged to ride her around the lawn or, as Martin recalls, through the kitchen and sitting room. The house had eight bedrooms, one bathroom and three reception rooms, each of the latter almost the size of the ground floor at Swansea. The only other permanent resident was Nickie who, recalls Martin, 'was a non-paying guest originally brought in to deal with the forbidding proportions of the house'.

She was, by consensus, very attractive, seemingly in her early thirties with a young child 'being looked after' by unspecified benefactors and if her accent, manner and general demeanour were anything to go by, insouciantly upper-class. Philip, with a hint of pity and unease, casts her as 'a sort of posh slave' while Martin's recollection differs somewhat. 'She seemed to spend most of her time as a louche social secretary, telephoning those coming up for weekend parties, fixing cocktails at dos, chatting to everyone without actually doing anything. My mother would be responsible for most of the day-to-day jobs, cooking, cleaning and clearing up the after-party debris.' Nickie also felt it her responsibility to set the moral tone for life at 9 Madingley Road. She had sex with Bill Rukeyser, a Princeton student now in Cambridge at whose recent marriage Kingsley had been best man, several other of Kingsley's friends and the occasional undergraduate reading English at Peterhouse. Showing no bias for age or experience she also slept with Kingsley himself and would eventually relieve Philip, aged fourteen, of his virginity. Nickie's long-term admirer was 'Bummer' Scott, who would arrive regularly in a decrepit saloon, perhaps take part in whatever jollities might be occurring at the time or disappear with Nickie for no more than an evening. He appeared at least three decades older than his paramour and, by the way he spoke and disported himself, was of the same quintessentially English class. Kingsley recommended Bummer to his sons as an exemplar of good spoken English, even when drunk, which he seemed to be for most of his waking existence. The well-battered saloon acquired fresh dents after his every departure.

On the margins of the household was the part-time barmaid at the nearby Merton Arms to which the Amises and guests would repair for a hair of the dog, following an arduous evening at home; the landlord, an indulgent sort, observed no regulated opening hours for thirsty regulars. Kingsley began a daylight-only affair with the barmaid, conducted in one of the empty back rooms of the pub. Rarely was she admitted to Madingley Road despite her habit, in drink, of standing beneath what she believed to be the Amises' bedroom window and keening for another encounter with 'Billy', Kingsley's middle name, a relic from his army days. Apparently she never learned his given name and was happily indifferent to his eminence. Martin, now in his early teens, was still only half aware of what was going on around him. 'It did not seem', he reflects, 'all that different from Swansea. But there was *more* of it, pursued with apparently greater energy.'

It is difficult to conceive of a more dissipated milieu than Madingley Road but such imaginings are superfluous thanks to George and Pat Gale, occasional visitors at Swansea and now regulars at Cambridge. Gale, staunch Tory and then at the *Daily Express*, lived in Staines. Despite being extremely well paid his baronial ambitions were constrained by the enduring and punitive tax regime of the post-war Labour government and he had to make do with one half of a gigantic Victorian-Gothic pile, albeit the part which, to his great satisfaction, included an absurdly vast ballroom. There was a regular, indeed incessant, counter flow of revellers between Staines and Cambridge, guests at both locations playing the double role of participant and scrutineer, assessing the relative levels of excess achieved by each. In truth there was no competition, with Gale able to outdo the Amises financially and offer a limitless supply of expensive drink and food. The Gales' house also had three more bedrooms, the ballroom was frequently the site for hand-to-hand combat – males only – and the Gales' non-paying guest, Ronnie, was the equal of Nickie as the house's faintly debauched social secretary.

Philip was absent for much of the Cambridge period, his precipitate encounter with Nickie taking place in Majorca. Kingsley and Hilly, despite their other failings, were conscientious parents and recognized that their elder son's time at secondary school in Swansea would frustrate any ambitions he might have beyond blue-collar work so they enrolled him as a boarder at the fee-paying Friends' School in Saffron Walden. Sally, aged eight when they moved to Cambridge, went to a local primary school, and infancy rendered her largely oblivious of the curiosities of her environment. Martin, however, arrived with the family aged twelve and was sent to the nearby grammar, Cambridgeshire High School for Boys. He was thus the only person – and the term is used with caution, given that the beginning of his teens involved the doorway to adulthood – who observed the Cambridge years without being a participant. According to Zachary Leader 'Martin liked talking to his father's students and friends and never seemed disturbed by the household's unconventional comings and goings'.[6] Which seems somewhat evasive and non-committal, given that it is difficult to imagine any precocious twelve- or thirteen-year-old remaining oblivious of a routine of Rabelaisianism. He had, for example, accompanied the family on excursions to the Gales' mansion. Had he, I ask him now, at least some sense of living in a world completely detached, say, from that of his peers at Cambridgeshire High School? 'Children can be very censorial, by which I mean that even if they are aware of everything happening around them they instinctively edit out parts of it that seem, well, unsuitable. Then, at Cambridge, I knew about sex and I knew that the adults around me were probably having sex. But it would be a year or two before Philip and I became coarsely energetic about it. So, since we had no experience of the real thing, it didn't matter much to us what others got up to.'

So you were by turns aware of what was happening at Cambridge and wilfully ignorant of it?

'Well I suppose so. By the time I was in my early twenties and talking to Hilly and Kingsley about their marriage I wasn't particularly surprised by what they had to say. And I remember during my first visit to the US in the 1970s I stayed with Bill Rukeyser who was very candid about Cambridge, he was part of it all of course. I was fascinated, shocked, to hear a detailed account but at the same time it seemed as though I already knew what he was telling me.' In *Experience* Martin reports a conversation with Sir Richard Eyre, when the latter was director of the National Theatre. Three decades earlier he had been one of Kingsley's tutorial students at Peterhouse and a regular visitor at Madingley Road. 'We must have come across each other back then,' observes Martin.

'Oh yes. You were so unhappy.'
'Was I?'
'You were *so* unhappy.'[7]

Martin claims to have no recollection of what Eyre perceived as a state of desolation. '*Was* I? I was unlucky thirteen, overweight and undersized.' One student showed him his recently purchased Burton's black velvet suit – very Beatles-era, early-1960s couture, apparently. Martin bought one and was informed by the student: 'You're too fat for that suit, Mart,' and he found an entry in Philip's diary which read, 'Mum told me she found

Mart crying in the night about the size of his bum. I do feel sorry for him but (a) it *is* enormous, and (b) it's not going to go away.'

The image that remains is perplexing and multilayered. Is the self-caricature, replayed in *Experience*, only a version of the truth, intended to blur a more vivid portrait of a household consumed by hedonism and to which, despite himself, he was a more observant witness than he cares to admit?

The question might remain unanswered were it not for the striking parallels between Madingley Road and his most unrelentingly morbid novel. *Dead Babies* (1975) is his second work of fiction, written little more than a decade after the Cambridge house had broken up and during the period when his teenage memories, his 'inklings, intuitions and subconscious imaginings' came face to face with personal experience. Martin claims that the raw material for the work – the casual sex, the post-1960s cynicism and lazy self-interest – originated from the year in Oxford when he moved out of college and shared a house. The figures who drift through Appleseed Rectory are, he points out, variously more feral, sadistic, pitiable and irredeemable than anyone he had actually met, and what he did in the book, in his own words, was to 'blend the image of Charles Manson and his acolytes with supine Englishness'. The novel does indeed appear to be a confection of mid-1970s archetypes that are too grotesque to be true. Read it alongside what we know of Madingley Road, however, and we suspect that its genesis predates the 1970s and is far more private. In terms of concrete events – notably the fact that each participant is murdered by the soulless, aloof Quentin Villiers – fiction certainly displaces muted recollection but there is something about the temper of the novel that captures perfectly and unnervingly the atmosphere of that period between 1961 and 1963. He begins the book with a list of its principal characters, including a précis of their physical characteristics and inclinations, rather as might be found in an early-seventeenth-century Revenge Tragedy in which fate and temperament conspire to visit ruination on all involved. Each has features that recommend them to the other – wealth, good looks, intelligence – and flaws that elicit vengeful or sadistic inclinations among their peers. All except Keith Whitehead, the feckless victim of the piece, introduced as 'very tiny, very fat – court dwarf to Appleseed Rectory'. Martin's account of his alleged teenage fatness is an exaggeration. 'Well, I was called "Fatboy" at school. Once.' All photographs of the period, however, show him to be unremarkably normal in stature. He did feel like an outsider, but for other reasons. He watched, fascinated but faintly baffled.

Reviewing *Dead Babies* Elaine Feinstein remarked that 'I hope for society that this is no true prophecy, I hope for Martin Amis that the nightmare of this vision will rapidly become part of his past.' Unintended irony can be the most arresting and in this instance Martin was darkly amused. When he put it into words the 'vision' was already part of his past.

> Everyone is always blacking out . . . and they can't remember farther back than a few days . . . Everything is out of whack . . . Appleseed Rectory is a place of shifting outlines and imploding vacuums; it is a place of lagging time and false memory, a place of street sadness, night fatigue and cancelled sex.[8]

There are of course obvious differences between the Rectory and Cambridge: heroin and other hard drugs were not part of the latter and Martin, unlike poor Whitehead, was never 'fist fucked' by one of the athletic undergraduates who treated the house as a licence for unrestraint. Yet the feature of the novel, indeed the engine of its narrative, that would one assumes disqualify it completely as a personal allegory is also that which binds it to Martin's unique, very private experience as a boy on the precarious brink of adulthood. The Appleseeders are, one by one, murdered – or at least their demise is meticulously assisted – by an undisclosed presence who eventually turns out to be their aloof, dispassionate host, the Hon. Quentin Villiers. No motive is ever indicated but throughout the book Martin sews into the dialogue and third-person narrative moments which blend resignation and disquiet. Everyone is at some point alert to a premonitory feeling of grim and ineluctable closure. They know it will end, in all likelihood unpleasantly, but none seems inclined to arrest this descent to oblivion.

The disintegration of Madingley Road was brought about not by homicide but, for the central characters involved, something comparably shocking and intemperate. Kingsley Amis met Elizabeth Jane Howard at the Cheltenham Literature Festival in October 1962. She was, that year, director of the event. Its theme was 'Sex in Literature', drawing in such luminaries as Joseph Heller and Carson McCullers and encouraging flirtatious banter between all involved. Kingsley and Jane Howard had met, briefly, on several occasions before but during the three days he spent at Cheltenham their mutual attraction progressed to discreet promises; there would be phone calls – involving purely literary matters if anyone enquired – and clandestine assignations arranged for London. Within a month of the festival they were having an affair but this one was unlike the earlier serial infidelities that had attended Kingsley's fifteen years of marriage to Hilly. Previously he had wished to sate his desire for gloriously uncommitted sex while remaining with his beloved family. Now, suddenly, he was writing ruefully candid letters to Jane which could have come from a precocious fifteen-year-old, desperately in love.

Hilly found one of Jane's equally consummate replies in his jacket pocket and although the discovery was not exactly shocking, given that she was fully aware of his taste for adultery, something about the temper of the letter unsettled her. It was the beginning of the end of their marriage. Villiers ends everything at the Rectory, despatching all its personnel to oblivion, his family included, without explanation. For those who treated the equally anarchic set-up at Madingley Road as an extension of its host, Kingsley – and here you can include his family – his act of dispersal, obliteration, would have seemed very similar.

A year earlier the family had visited Majorca, stayed with Robert Graves and his family, and Kingsley had decided to give up academia for good. He could exist comfortably on his advances and royalties, particularly in a place where the cost of living was approximately one-third that of the UK. By spring 1963 he was behaving like someone whose grasp upon reality had been displaced by wild prevarication. On the one hand he was promising Jane that their relationship would endure while at the same time pressing forward with plans made a year earlier, including his resignation from Peterhouse and arrangements for the rental of a property in Soller, Majorca, for himself, Hilly and the three children. No one involved is certain of when the final break-up occurred; there seemed to be a sequence of equally precipitate moments of disintegration until suddenly it was all over. Leader's biography lays out all accounts by living participants, plus circumstantial details from Kingsley's unpublished letters, but any attempt to pick through this evidence and recover a chronology results in sometimes absurd contradictions and anomalies. It is almost certain that he left Madingley Road, with a suitcase, either on 20 or 21 July and took a taxi for the station. Later, and again no one is certain of when, he met Jane in London and they took the boat train to

Paris and then on to Barcelona. They stayed in Spain for at least three weeks, perhaps as long as seven, and the uncertainty here might just be explained by the fact that when Kingsley eventually returned to Madingley Road the house was empty, with only furniture remaining. He had a notorious fear of staying in empty houses and this, plus the shocking discovery that his wife, with their children, had left *him*, accounts for there being no record made by Kingsley of these events, and thus no dates. Also, no one is clear about how exactly Hilly learned that Kingsley and Jane had gone to Sitges. A *Daily Express* reporter had discovered their location but the story was, apparently, spiked following orders from the editor George Gale. Whether Gale was prevailed upon to do so or whether he took matters into his own hands to spare his friends from vulgar public exposure is another mystery. It seems likely, however, that he was responsible for informing Hilly that her husband was involved in something other than one of his habitual flings.

For the facts go to Leader,[9] but even more fascinating and puzzling is the absence of any comment by Leader or the participants on a quite bizarre occurrence. The latter agree that Kingsley left, with a suitcase, to spend a number of weeks away but no one seems to recall, or felt it necessary to recall, an account by him of where, supposedly, he was going for such a length of time. It was not, as Hilly later insisted, 'an open marriage' in that she never indulged his continuous adulteries; to get away with them he had to cover them up. So we can rule out completely a confession-before-the-event on his part. It would have ended the marriage and this was not his intention. When he eventually returned to Cambridge he expected to find his family waiting for him. Moreover, the sale of the house was in the hands of the solicitors, travel arrangements were arranged and paid for, as were plans for a school in Palma which took the children of English-speaking expatriates. The more one reflects upon this series of occurrences the more peculiar they become. For a man so neurotic about travel and being left for long periods on his own Kingsley must surely have supplied elaborate and plausible details of his planned absence – irrespective of his reason for going – including phone numbers. He left for an unspecified destination, the purpose of his visit was not volunteered by him or apparently enquired into by his family and the duration of his departure was equally vague.

According to Martin it was only with the arrival of Eva Garcia 'for a visit' from Swansea that the children learned something of what was happening. Eva announced across the breakfast table that Kingsley had 'a fancy woman' in London and was living with her. Had Eva been appointed by Hilly as the grim messenger or was it simply that she had found a suitable topic for her delight in the sharing of morbid facts? Martin has never been certain, but her description of the then unnamed Jane stuck in his mind because it seemed ridiculously archaic: 'It brought to mind the image of a louche chorus girl from a film about the underside of Victoriana or the Folies-Bergère.' Did Hilly, I ask him, talk to them about what had happened? 'She didn't talk about it. She told me about it. We were driving to school and she said – I can't remember her words exactly – that she and Kingsley were breaking up. She was smoking a Consulate and she left me at the school gates.'

The weird inconsistencies and gaping lacunae that attend the different versions of the break-up again bring to mind the eerie temper of *Dead Babies*. It is as though the inhabitants of Madingley Road, like Martin's creations, are sleepwalking towards a predetermined fate. Cause and effect, attention to detail, appear to have been abandoned in favour of a wilful disinclination to notice what is happening.

In *Experience* the most memorable passage tells us as much through what it does not say as what it does. Martin recalls how his father 'left the house in Madingley Road, Cambridge. He was carrying a suitcase. A taxi waited . . . I am a good three or four inches shorter than my father, but our bodies are similarly disproportionate, with a low centre of gravity [. . .] Such legs are *made* for scuttling. He was en route from one reality to another; that taxi was part of a tunnel to a different world.'[10]

Throughout, Martin dwells on the term 'scuttling', a memory it seems of something guilty and secretive about his father's departure; the sound of his feet on the gravel drive emphasizes this impression. Can we believe that a thirteen-year-old could intuit all of this, sense that his father was 'en route from one reality to another'? No, because memory works gradually by augmentation. We don't change the original image but what we learn later of its potential significance becomes part of it. Martin did not, as he watched his father walk down the path, know even where he was going but within a matter of weeks the moment would begin to resonate with significance. Weeks later, as Martin would eventually learn, his father would walk back down the same path to find the house empty. This moment, which Martin could only imagine, bears remarkable resemblance to the description of Keith's return to Appleseed Rectory, the closing passage of *Dead Babies*. It reads rather like the account in *Experience* of Kingsley's departure played backwards.

> Keith limped steadily over the bridge. He paused at the opening of the drive. Appleseed Rectory stole out from under the morning shadows. Keith blinked. Was it really there? For an agitated moment he thought of turning back, of running away. But then he smiled at his own foreboding. It's all over now, he thought, stepping on the damp gravel.[11]

Keith and Kingsley have nothing in common of course, except that they seem to share the sense of absence and loneliness that accompanies a transition to the unknown. Later in *Experience* Martin joins them, telling of how he felt after his mother 'deliver[ed] the news'.

> It took me only a few seconds to leave the weightlessness, the zero gravity of childhood and feel the true mass of the world. Thinking something like, 'Yes, the easy bit's over. I've done the easy bit.' I moved into the yard with my satchel and cap.[12]

The imagination, deployed both for fiction and memoirs, preys partly upon events and partly upon the residue of emotion and trauma that stay with us long afterwards.

'We left, as planned, for Majorca – I think in August – and it was all extremely bizarre because we were following a schedule that had been shaped entirely by my father's decision to leave academia and England, but he was no longer there.' The journey to Majorca was a strange experience. Hilly drove, as she always did, and Martin and Philip took turns as front-seat passenger, where Kingsley should have been. Aged only eight, Sally remained largely immune from the strangeness of these events and indeed the atmosphere. 'It is difficult to remember exactly what happened,' Martin reflects. 'Hilly was calm but it was as though she had no idea what to do without him.'

2

Wild Times

In other circumstances Majorca would have been an idyll. Their house was in Soller, the island's second-largest town, but still untouched by its burgeoning tourist economy. Philip and Martin would take a daily train from Soller to the International School in Palma. 'It was a forty- or fifty-minute journey, twice a day. It was a beautiful little train, lovely countryside. The school was full of enviable curiosities, kids of the sort we'd never met before. They were the sons and daughters of wealthy expatriates, the girls were confident and mostly very attractive. On the whole they treated us as interlopers.' What did your mother do? I ask. 'Nothing. Looking back she was in a state of limbo. Nickie [of Madingley Road] had come over too. (She lived with us.) She and Phil had an affair. I was very shocked and very envious.' Martin and Philip also had access to a pair of 1950s motor scooters which they would ride to the station in Soller to meet the train. No one seemed concerned about their age and if licences to ride these machines were required, such regulations appeared to obtain only in cities on the mainland.

'I don't know what we'd have done without the bikes,' Martin recalls. 'We really had no idea about how to ride safely and we could probably have killed ourselves, but when we had the time we would just take off, sometimes to the coast. None of us spoke of how we felt but we would all become unusually alert to the sound of the postman's motorbike. We waited every day. We were waiting for something from Kingsley. He sent money for Hilly, certainly, but we wanted words, a postcard, anything.' Did they arrive? 'Not often. Anyone (particularly if they lived in Britain) would have envied our situation. We could do what we liked, go where we wanted. We seemed magically detached from the demands of ordinary life. Except that we were confused and depressed. We didn't talk about what had happened, but it was becoming clear to us that we were deluding ourselves. It was wonderful, yet it was also, we knew, temporary and pointless.'

Hilly returned with the children to London in January 1964, having arranged to rent a flat in Ovington Gardens, Knightsbridge. They stayed there for only six months and then moved on to a rented house, 128 Fulham Road, Chelsea. Accounts of what occurred there vary, but only in terms of the specifics of the indulgences allowed and practised. Martin enrolled at Battersea Grammar School – 'certainly the roughest school I'd ever been to' – and immediately began a regime of truancy. 'I would attend three or perhaps four days a week.' Philip had returned to his boarding school and although Sally was now the only one of the children who needed her mother's help and attention – Martin having opted for feckless independence – Hilly seemed to lapse into a state of depressed inertia. 'The only time she seemed to revive,' recalls Martin, 'was after she got in touch with Henry Fairlie again. He became a regular visitor, for maybe a month to six weeks, at Ovington Gardens, and they restarted their relationship. Henry was concerned for her and they appeared happy. I liked him, got on with him. We would play chess in the evenings and sometimes he'd talk about politics. I don't know why it cooled off but it did, and soon after that Mum went even further downhill. I'd been out but I saw her being taken away, to hospital.' He is referring to a night in June 1964 when she telephoned her friend Mavis Nicholson, repeating the phrase 'We're all disposable, darling' and sounding to Mavis close to collapse. Everything else she said was slurred and incoherent. Mavis called back and was eventually answered by a hysterical Sally. Her mother, she screamed, would not wake up. Mavis knew of how Sally had spent a day alone with the body of Kingsley's mother, attempting to restore to her some vestige of life with make-up and lipstick. Sally was now ten and the parallels would have been terrifying. That night Sally went to the Nicholsons' and because of her distressed state Mavis insisted on staying with her in the spare room. Sally did not sleep and would fly into a state of panic when Mavis, succumbing to exhaustion, closed her eyes.

Hilly had been drinking earlier that evening with a friend, had continued when her guest left and by the time she telephoned Mavis had supplemented alcohol with a dangerous amount of sleeping tablets. Martin thinks it likely that she had indeed attempted suicide, yet she was allowed to leave hospital the following day.

After summoning an ambulance Mavis telephoned Kingsley, who had spent most of the evening with Jane's brother Colin, drinking. Though unsettled by the news he seemed infuriated by Mavis's suggestion that he should go immediately to the hospital: 'Why do I have to?' he repeated, as much to himself as to Mavis. But he did so next morning and visited upon the semi-comatose Hilly an outpouring of invective for what she had done. Whether he was genuinely angry with Hilly or whether he was turning his own feelings of guilt and distress against her is unclear.

He was living the fantasy that all of his male characters since Jim Dixon had privately, sometimes bitterly, cultivated. Each of them had faced an inhibiting package of circumstances – involving, worst of all, monogamous commitment – and only Jim in his closing paragraph had opened the door upon pure escapism: a life with the girl of his dreams while seemingly excused such onerous matters as family, work and responsibility. Kingsley's arrangement with Jane Howard, in Blomfield Road, Little Venice, fell only just short of this in that he continued with a painstaking schedule, producing on average a thousand words per day. But he had never treated fiction writing as work. It meant the expenditure of enormous effort and skill but not of the kind that he resented, such as teaching, marking and administration let alone the demands of running a household. Writing fiction involved a world that was exclusively his own, one he could shape and control as he wished while of course taking pride in its formal design. It is evident from the letters he wrote to Jane in the year before he left Hilly that he had turned himself into a character born of his own imagination, a figure who became increasingly less credible as he exempted himself from a commitment to reality.

Martin holds that his father never planned to despatch the family to a form of emotional oblivion – 'He was far more sensitive and affectionate than the average, male, parent of his generation' – but he does not dispute the contention that during 1963–5 he immunized himself from the practical consequences of his actions.

The day she was released from hospital Hilly telephoned Jane and stated, curtly though not impolitely, that she was 'off' and now 'it's all up to you'. Jane was not sure what this meant until two days later she received a message from George Gale. Hilly and Sally were now, he announced, staying with them in Wivenhoe, Essex. He added that he had been down to the

Fulham Road house to collect some bags and found the place in an appalling state; empty bottles were all over the place, pots unwashed, nothing but a few decaying remnants of food in the fridge. Martin: 'The house was full of girls and some of my friends. Phil was out, but I didn't know where.' Gale reported to Jane that as far as he was aware Hilly had given Jane and Kingsley clear notice of her intention to leave for the country (it was evident to all that she was suffering from severe stress), which they had elected to ignore or deliberately misinterpret.

When Colin and Jane eventually arrived to inspect the house they found that, if anything, Gale had understated the dire conditions in which the boys were living. After cleaning the kitchen, bathroom and living room they realized that Martin and Philip certainly could not be allowed to remain there. Blomfield Road was too small so they decided to completely refurbish the Fulham Road house with a view to at least having the place presentable for Hilly following what they assumed would be her return and in the interim look for somewhere more spacious and permanent for themselves, Kingsley and the two boys. Martin's and Philip's initial encounter with Jane occurred shortly after their return from Majorca and is described in *Experience*, rather as if a piece by Iris Murdoch had been rewritten by a copy-editor with some thought for the real world. 'You know I'm not alone,' announces Kingsley as he opens the door. He is in striped pyjamas, Jane in the background 'in her white towel bathrobe, with her waist-long fair hair, tall, serious, worldly . . .' It was not, observes Martin, 'that he was surprised to see us. He was horrified to see us. We had busted him *in flagrante*.' At Fulham Road, the Howards had in little more than one week replaced all the unwashed, and unwashable, bedclothes, sanded the wood floors and repainted the walls. Martin observed all of this with studied detachment and when Philip arrived back from wherever his inclinations had taken him he too treated Colin and Jane as though they were tradesmen. Neither of the boys enquired as to the absence of their father. 'I was told later,' states Martin, 'that during the clean-up Jane told Kingsley that in her view it would all happen again. She and Kingsley decided that Philip and I would live with them. That is why the renovation of the bigger house [108 Maida Vale] took so long. It would need at least five bedrooms.'

In preparation for this Jane tried to persuade Kingsley that it would be both pragmatic and from his point of view responsible for the two of them to move temporarily to the refurbished Fulham Road house to keep an eye on the boys. He disagreed. During the short period that they had actually lived together Kingsley had dispelled most of the illusions that she might have entertained regarding his sense of responsibility, but surely, she thought, if some degree of respect and affection were to be restored in his sons' perception of him then an experiment in domestic proximity must be at least attempted. This would remain a hypothesis given that Martin only ever returned to the house to eat and sleep and Philip similarly only when on summer holiday from boarding school in Saffron Walden. Their sullen distaste for the arrangement was reflected by Philip's habit of addressing his father as a 'cunt' and ignoring Jane completely. By the end of summer 1964 an arrangement had been reached so that Philip and Martin would spend only weekends at Fulham Road with Hilly and the rest of the week at 108 Maida Vale. The changeover times were flexible enough for both to maintain their regime of unaccountable absences.

Jane's meeting in July with her old acquaintance Alexander Mackendrick, doyen of such Ealing classics as *The Lady Killers* and *Whisky Galore*, was pure coincidence but during their conversation on his forthcoming production she began to nurture ideas. *A High Wind in Jamaica* was to be shot on the eponymous Caribbean island later that summer and he was still casting children and adolescents. Martin: 'I was sent for screen tests at Pinewood Studios. Overall it took about three weeks. There were other candidates.' He looked a good three years younger than fifteen and was taken on. Hilly enjoyed innocuous yet glamorous dates with the good-looking support actors and stuntmen while Martin pursued Beverly Baxter, elder sister of the precocious fourteen-year-old lead Deborah. Most evenings he was left in charge of eight-year-old Karen Flack, another of the leads, who, Hilly advised him, was destined for stardom. She told him to share the huge double bed with her so that in years to come he could claim truthfully that he had slept with the delectable Miss Flack. Martin recalls the remark because it revealed to him, probably for the first time, how much his father and mother had in common: 'Kingsley would have loved it'. And Jane? 'Indulged it, yes, but with reserve.'

They had flown out first-class with BOAC, Martin's first experience of air travel, but shortly before proceedings were completed in the Caribbean Hilly decided to cash in their tickets for a cheaper, tourist return. The difference apparently was considerable and they remained in Jamaica for two months. She could for a while become again the fun-loving mother of the Swansea years. The rest of the film was made in Pinewood to which Martin travelled by chauffeured car, and by the time it was completed he was already two weeks into the new school term.

On the day of his return to Sir Walter St John's Grammar, Battersea, Martin, dressed in a brand-new uniform, found that his name did not appear on any of the registration lists in classes for which he had previously been enrolled (to state that he 'attended' them would be generous) before the summer break. He was not so much summoned to the headmaster's office as referred there by a sequence of form teachers who seemed by turns embarrassed and impatient with a superfluous pupil. The head glanced at his uniform and noted with undisguised weariness that he seemed to believe that he belonged there. Martin had brought a letter from his mother, plus a cover note from Mackendrick himself, explaining the delay in his return and asking for allowance to be made, given his significant contribution to the cinema arts. The note was, he was informed, irrelevant since two months earlier a letter had already been despatched to his home address informing his parents or guardians that he was henceforth expelled for persistent and unexplained truancy. No one is certain if the letter was lost, ignored or destroyed in the massive clean-up, but from autumn until Christmas Martin pretended to all who took an interest to be enrolled at Sir Walter St John's, while spending most of this time as an adolescent non-person, absent from the records of any educational institution.

Colin Howard: 'It is difficult to recall that time exactly, before Martin "moved in" properly. Jane and Kingsley seemed constantly busy, away quite regularly, and Martin . . . well he seemed to pass through. He was, to me at least, amiable but a little sanguine beyond his years – what was he, fifteen? As if he had tired of everything before he knew anything.'

By now Hilly was taking in lodgers to supplement her meagre wages. Following her return from Jamaica she had found a job in the Battersea Dogs' Home and Animal Refuge, an institution that took care of abandoned or maltreated domestic pets and curious urban strays such as donkeys, sheep and goats. Martin: 'Hilly always loved animals and the job in Battersea made her feel nostalgic. It reminded her of the time just before she met my father. But it gave her something to do, took her mind off what she still could not come to terms with.' Kingsley was still paying the rent for Fulham Road and on the advice of Jane agreed to supplement this with fees for a private day school. This was Martin's O-level year. Philip had already failed all of his and moved to Davies, Laing and Dick, a crammer in Notting Hill. Legally crammers fed upon those who had, post-sixteen, failed examinations in full-time, state or private schools though by some sleight of hand Martin, then only fifteen and technically an absconder from the education system, was enrolled with his elder brother. Martin: 'It was that sort of place, for upper-class drop-outs.' Some parts of Notting Hill itself were still downmarket but most of it had been reclaimed by the West London middle classes. Davies, Laing and Dick fed on this. 'The place appears in *The Rachel Papers*, undisguised. I found it fascinating because for the first time I came across that very English thing, class. The day I left Sir Walter St John's the other boys offered respectful nods and grins. My accent [very RP with even then a slight drawl] had previously marked me as posh and weak, but now I'd been thrown out and for a brief moment I became faintly villainous.'

At the crammer Martin was still perceived as solidly middle-class but this time by those who despised such people for their vulgar ambitions. 'The girls were what are still in some places called "County", girls who travelled, magnificent and unapproachable. The boys were straight out of Waugh or Wodehouse, without the compensating humour. Guys with lots of titles. I met Rob [Henderson] there. In the novel I fill the place with grotesques, teachers and pupils included.' There is certainly a good deal of merciless caricature, fuelled by resentment on Charles's part, and one suspects his creator's.

I knew the kind of punks that went to this kind of place. Cuntish public-school drop-outs, dropped out for being too thick, having long hair or dirty boaters, unseaming new boys in multiple buggery, getting caught too many times with an impermissible number of hockey sticks up their bums . . .

A tall ginger-haired boy in green tweed moved gracefully down the steps. He looked at me as if I were a gang of skinheads: not with fear (because the fellows are quite tractable really) but with disapproval. Behind him at a trot came two lantern-jawed girls, calling 'Jamie . . . *Jamie*'. Jamie swivelled elegantly.

'Angelica, I'm not *going* to the Imbenkment. Gregory shall have to take you.'

'But Gregory's in *Scotland*,' one said.

'I can't help thet.' The ginger boy disappeared into an old-fashioned sports car.[1]

'My concession to fact is that in both places [fictional and real] no one stood the faintest chance of passing exams, me included.' Philip retook his O-levels the same year that Martin sat them for the first time. 'We came out with three each. I failed English.'

By spring 1965 Fulham Road had fallen into a state of dilapidation even worse than the period before Hilly's overdose. She worked hard at the animal centre and some nights during the week she held parties for friends or went out to pubs and restaurants. Almost every weekend she left London to stay with the Gales in Essex. According to one of her occasional lodgers, Penny Jones, Martin and Philip 'never went to school . . . were heavy on drugs . . . were bonking every female they could get their hands on'.[2] Used condoms were, she reported, draped ostentatiously on the railings of the balcony, not through carelessness or for reasons of unhygienic economy but as notices of the rule of anarchy and hedonism. Similarly a pot labelled 'LSD' was placed in the fridge alongside similar vessels containing hummus or olives. Martin: 'Perhaps we were feckless. But there were no hard drugs. It's possible we did the labels, as a joke. The drugs didn't exist. Phil took some dope, but nothing heavy. I didn't drink till I was twenty.'

There is no record of Kingsley ever visiting the house (he supplemented the rent by banker's orders) and nor did he show any particular interest in the behaviour and educational progress of Martin and Philip. George Gale, as he had previously, acted as intermediary and informed Jane that Hilly was in a state of inertia. He did not accuse her of irresponsibility but he made it clear that she was finding herself emotionally incapable of dealing with the family she once shared with Kingsley, even though the boys were present only at weekends. Jane had made preparation for what she saw as inevitable and in April 1965 Martin and Philip moved in officially to 108 Maida Vale with Kingsley, Jane and Colin. For most of the subsequent six months both teenagers involved themselves in a regime of absorbed epicureanism and apathy. The episode described by Martin in *Experience* in which Jane and, reluctantly, Kingsley confront the brothers regarding their drug taking is characteristically wry and dexterous in its avoidance of the apportioning of blame. The characters strut marionette-style through a darkly comic performance of unhappy families with Martin, in early middle age when he wrote it, choreographing the act and recycling memories. Kingsley and Jane's horrified suspicion that they might be harbouring drug addicts opens out into the farcical disclosure of Philip's 'stash', a box on open display in his bedroom with two words painted garishly on the lid: 'Phil's Drugs'. Kingsley takes the sixteen-year-old Martin out to Biagi's, a nearby Italian restaurant, and instructs him on how the descent of contemporary youth into drug-induced torpor is part of an International Communist plot to undermine Western democracy. 'He was drunk, and he was working on probably his most ridiculous book, *Colonel Sun*, which involved his reading a large number of James Bond novels.'

In *Experience* Martin writes of his father and his soon-to-be stepmother with the kind of charitable concern, which raises the question of how exactly he felt at the time. 'It's hard to say. My memories of Jane during those first months are softened by what would happen later, most obviously with the help she gave with my education.' Did he share some of the resentment that Philip more conspicuously displayed? 'Yes. Very likely.'

Philip even today maintains that Jane, albeit in a haughtily diplomatic style that would have been alien to Hilly, indicated that the two of them were an onerous but unavoidable burden, part of the contract that would allow her a permanent relationship with Kingsley. Indeed in *Slipstream* she too hints that her development as a writer was hindered significantly by the events of 1963–6. Once she had finished one of her finest novels, *After Julius* (completed early 1964, published 1965) it would be four years before she would again work full-time on another piece of fiction. In Philip's account of things the atmosphere in the Maida Vale house was a confection of mutual antagonism and diplomacy: Jane took it upon herself both to alert Kingsley to problems he would prefer to ignore while making ostentatious attempts to offer advice and instruction to a pair of hooligans. Martin: 'Philip became a Mod. He bought a Lambretta scooter. The colour of his socks changed daily. Eventually we both took drugs. I smoked dope and occasionally took some speed. We associated booze with the lifestyle of Kingsley and his generation and hardly touched it. It had to be illegal to be interesting.'

Within two months Philip had left the Notting Hill crammer – not officially, he had simply ceased to turn up – found a girlfriend and in early 1966 he moved with her into a squat. Jane showed concern, token concern in Philip's opinion, and Colin – the only adult in whom Martin and Philip could confide – asked him without success to reconsider his decision. Kingsley, while of course not oblivious of events, neither attempted to persuade his eldest to stay on nor displayed any obvious concern for his well-being. Relations between them would remain fraught, verging upon bitter, for most of the subsequent decade. As Martin puts it, he 'never came back as a child of the house. He was gone.' Contrast this with Colin Howard's comments. '"Gone" in the sense that he rarely stayed for more than a night or two, but he made his presence felt. When they [Martin and Philip] were together they were formidable . . . Perhaps Kingsley and Jane would have got on better, in the end, if it hadn't been for the boys. No one could blame them, but Kingsley managed to avoid most of their wrath.' Both had inherited from their father a talent for mimicry and Jane's verbal mannerisms – unselfconsciously upper class – along with her postures and head movements were gradually assimilated and malevolently reproduced, particularly when responding to her complaints about their behaviour and suggestions as to how they might improve themselves. All accounts of the period present Martin and Philip as equally hostile to Jane and shrewd in their handling of Kingsley.

Colin's close friend the artist Sargy Mann became a more frequent visitor and moved in full-time in 1967. Aside from Martin, only Colin remained in regular contact with Philip after he left. He introduced Philip to Sargy who encouraged his nascent interest in painting and advised him to enrol at the Camberwell School of Art. 'I remember,' Sargy Mann observes, 'some time after Philip had enrolled at Camberwell, Kingsley asked him what he was *doing* – and I don't know if he was feigning ignorance or really knew nothing of his son's activities. Anyway Philip told him and he grimaced and said, "But painting, visual arts . . . it's all very second-rate, isn't it?" Maybe he was joking, it was difficult to tell with Kingsley, but I thought it one of the most hurtful, poisonous things I'd heard him say. He could make fun of people without being vitriolic but this upset Philip greatly.' I ask Martin now if he thinks that Philip was the instigator of much of the hostility. 'No, no, we were equally responsible.' Then why, I wonder, did the household become more relaxed and untroubled after Philip chose to stay away for longer periods? 'I was, what, coming close to seventeen and there seemed little point in continuing to make life difficult.' His response is candid enough but it involves a half truth. He was certainly causing fewer problems in the house, but elsewhere he maintained the lifestyle of the King's Road hippie.

Martin was in 1966 still enrolled at Davies, Laing and Dick, retaking the five failed O-levels from his previous year. On average he would turn up for two days per week while the rest of the time he spent largely in the company of Rob Henderson, also doing resits. 'Rob and I looked very similar, skinny and infuriatingly short. He sounded as though he came from minor nobility – he'd also been expelled, but from Westminster. We shared enthusiasms. We were both lazy. Neither of us could stand the sort of activity that involved effort and concentration, let alone mental commitment.' It would be wrong to say that Rob took over from Philip as Martin's mentor in insouciance but the two of them certainly enjoyed an attraction to fecklessness. They spent most of the period between autumn 1966 and summer 1967 in coffee bars on the King's Road venturing out only in pursuit of girls who had fallen prey to their inept but cautiously planned introductions, or to nearby bookies to place bets; 'only on the dogs' insists Martin. Their reluctance to countenance horse racing reflected their down-market affectations. They wore skin-tight velvet trousers – jeans were still at the time exclusively denim – and jackets of fashionably loud colouration. A café called The Picasso was a particular favourite, owned and run by an East End slum landlord and frequented by secretaries from nearby offices. 'Trying to get girls was all we ever did, so naturally we had some successes. I don't know about Rob, but love was always the quest for me. I fell in love there in 1967 with "Rachel", of the novel.'

Much has been written of the closing years of the 1960s, particularly 1967 when allegedly Europe and the US were seized by various states of transformative zeal, from hedonism disguised as political activism to rare examples of commitment and courage. Did he notice? 'Before the age of sixteen I had lived in the provinces. I had no reason to assume that London in the late 1960s was any different from the way it had always been. But there was an unmistakable loosening in the air. Only later did it become clear that some kind of cultural convulsion had taken place.'

Kingsley and Jane had married in June 1965, with a civil ceremony in Marylebone followed by a short honeymoon in Brighton. The location was convenient for the London-based media: for the subsequent week the press was full of reports and pictures of the two photogenic literary superstars. The publicity had been orchestrated by Kingsley's editor at Cape, Tom Maschler, who also arranged a lavish party at the Cape office for the couple on their return to London. Hilly had no illusions about a reconciliation but to witness Kingsley and Jane disporting themselves in the newspapers as a mature yet romantically besotted couple – there were accounts of their favourite restaurants, choices of wine and even on which sides of the bed they had elected to sleep – was especially distressing. They lived only two miles away and within a month Hilly had decided to remove herself and Sally from London. She enjoyed Wivenhoe, the small coastal village where she spent regular weekends at the Gales' house, according to Peregrine Worsthorne 'part baronial pile, part gin palace'. Within a few weeks she had found something more modest for herself and her daughter, a new semi-detached which Kingsley paid for. By early 1966 she had formed an attachment with D. R. Shackleton Bailey, occasional visitor at the Gales' and a Cambridge don. If one were tasked to imagine an embodiment of everything that Kingsley was not, Shackleton Bailey would have been it. He was a modest imbiber of alcohol and humourless observer of mankind's various foibles which he felt largely undeserving of his comments. These he preserved for his academic interests, particularly Cicero and the language and culture of Tibet, of which he was Cambridge's only specialist. Rumour had it that Hilly was his first 'girlfriend', though the term seems inappropriate for two people well into their forties. Martin remembers him with a mixture of civility and disbelief. 'Yes,' he says, 'I think she wanted someone so unlike my father that she ended up with his polar opposite.' They married in September 1967.

On the surface, then, the destructive effects of the break-up had been repaired, with the two previous partners remarried and comfortably resettled forty miles apart. Philip, now living separately and enrolled for courses at Camberwell, kept in occasional touch with his mother but retained only formal contacts with Jane and his father, most specifically in relation to his allowance of £55 per month. Martin too was provided with generous funding for clothes and other unaccounted purchases and he would set off daily for further resits, now alongside A-levels, at Notting Hill. In Maida Vale, dinner parties and other civilized gatherings had replaced the raucous indulgences of Swansea and Cambridge and this seemed to have a collateral effect upon the second son whose behaviour, at least indoors, was orderly and not unlike the reformed, almost decorous version of Kingsley which had evolved through his relationship with Jane. By mid-1967, Martin had come to resemble the standard model of the dutiful middle-class stepson.

Once beyond the front door, however, he spent virtually all of his time with Rob. Unsurprisingly in 1967 he failed all of his

A-levels, having managed over the previous two years to acquire in total six middle-grade O-levels. Kingsley had shown no particular interest in Martin's, or for that matter Philip's, educational prospects and Jane, grateful for the newly pacific domestic atmosphere, thought it best not to provoke further discord with too many enquiries on his progress. The question that had hovered and would now have to be addressed was that of university entrance. Martin had, he informed them with casual indifference, filled in his UCCA forms, though he did not comment on where he hoped to gain entrance let alone what he had applied to read. (Today he claims to have no clear recollection of this first attempt, nor even of having posted the form.)

A small conference was convened involving Jane, Colin and with some reluctance Kingsley. Martin, now eighteen, had shown little interest in high culture. 'Every now and then I read something like C. S. Forester's *Brown on Resolution*. And that was all. And I studied the set texts for O- and A-level. As for Kingsley . . . Well, I knew what he did for a living, that he was a writer, but I didn't know what *kind* of writer he was. For all I knew he could've been producing Westerns.' According to Jane she had in summer 1966 tentatively asked him what he wanted to do and he had answered, to her astonishment, 'Become a writer'. He confirms this: 'Yes, I was serious, though given my circumstances at the time it seemed absurd. All adolescents want to become writers, don't they?' Nevertheless Jane encouraged him to read Jane Austen's *Pride and Prejudice* which he claims to have enjoyed, though this brief introduction to serious fiction had no discernible effect upon his, as he puts it, 'lazy and easily distracted' approach to A-level English.

At the post-A-level (failed) meeting in 1967 Martin's grand vocational ambitions were sidelined by more immediate questions; specifically, did he seriously intend to try for university?

He replied that he did, though again without indicating preference for a particular subject. Jane said that she knew of a crammer that was far more distinguished and efficient than the Notting Hill institution. It was called Sussex Tutors, based in Brighton, and over the next few weeks she telephoned and wrote to Mr Ardagh, Senior Tutor for Arts and Humanities A-levels. She name-dropped and convinced him that Martin, despite his dismal record, had potential. Given that money was now available in abundance (it should be pointed out that Kingsley was now richer than he had ever previously been; along with solid royalties from his earlier Gollancz novels his advances from Cape were considerable) Martin was enrolled. He would go to Brighton in late August and in the interim Jane and Colin, suspecting that his extra-curricular activities had contributed to his dismal academic performance, arranged for him some part-time office work. In his spare time and for the remainder of the summer he and Rob resumed their odyssey of dope and chasing girls.

Martin, in *Experience*, presents his year in Brighton with the kind of faux embarrassment granted by fame and maturity, in which the slothful teenager toys pretentiously with intellectual aspiration. In truth, however, the period was far more transitional and formative than that. Sussex Tutors was, as Jane promised, efficient and productive, assessing the intellectual capabilities of new entrants before allocating appropriate courses and modes of instruction. Mr Ardagh was in charge of English and Jane travelled to Brighton to meet him in August 1967. Kingsley, while aware of the new arrangement and prepared to cover the fees, showed no great interest in what it would actually involve; his wife went to Brighton alone. She and Ardagh agreed that Martin was gifted with a natural intelligence which belied his poor examination performances. He was witty and linguistically far more adept than the vast majority of eighteen-year-olds. Ardagh found him slightly unnerving given that he had never before met someone so bright who had also consistently avoided any formal acquaintance with knowledge or learning. Ardagh and his colleagues had of course some vicarious notion of the Romantic idiot savant, uncorrupted by burdensome culture, but Martin was clearly not one of those. He could write sentences that turned eloquently upon their subject and he was ruthlessly articulate, able to diminish the confidence of other speakers simply by saying something.

The agreed objective would be to turn Martin into a suitable candidate for university entry in 1968 which, for someone who had spent the previous thirteen years resolutely apathetic to standard routines of memorizing anything, seemed an absurd ambition. But once Martin had decided to learn by rote and assimilation he acquired two further O-levels and passed three A-levels – at grades A, B and D. One O-level was in Latin, undertaken at Ardagh's advice as a necessary requirement for Oxbridge entrance. He was also being tutored by Ardagh for the Oxford entrance examination. Martin spoke occasionally to Jane about his aims. He had decided that he wanted to read English and mentioned that he had been thinking about Exeter and Durham universities.

Martin's year in Brighton was significant in another way too. 'I was eighteen and I started with *Lucky Jim*. The novel was part of our lives but I didn't actually read it until then. When I first arrived in Brighton I stayed at the school, a slight improvement upon a hostel, and the boy in the room next door asked me if I was related to the famous novelist. I said that I was and lent him my copy of *Lucky Jim*. I knew it was funny, and more than that, and what really, perhaps subconsciously, made me aware of what I liked about it was the sound that came from the room next door. His laughter came in painful bursts . . . he was trying to control himself but couldn't.'

Lucky Jim is far more than the prototype comic campus novel. It was a triumph of mischievous coercion, dividing readers between those who loved it and those, ridiculously, who saw it as presaging the decline of modern civilization. The novel is undoubtedly dominated by Jim's presence and outlook, but this figure who is so resolutely set against the intelligentsia is clearly the product of an immensely intelligent literary craftsman. After reading it, did Martin see his father differently? 'Yes, and no. As a man he was like a novel, simultaneously functioning at different levels, each slightly at odds with the others.'

At school and at Oxford Kingsley became famous and notorious as an imitator. He could reproduce the often eccentric locutionary habits of dons and other students and his alertness to the gap between what a person appears to be and what they are went further than a talent for entertainment. It was the subject for his, failed, postgraduate thesis and became the engine for the novel that would launch his career and dog his reputation as a major writer: the literary establishment would never fully accept a man who seemed to perceive everything as open to caricature and ridicule. Although Martin is nowhere near as adept as his father at impersonation, he had by his early teens developed a comparable talent for caricature, particularly in his ability to prey upon the guileless speech habits of others and present them as intellectual blemishes. Jane's brother Colin Howard recalls that 'his powers of detection were extraordinarily well developed. He could descry the subtlest weaknesses or peculiarities in people intuitively, and sometimes find a way of recreating them. It was not a vindictive quality, though rather unnerving.' Just as Kingsley had created an interplay between his disrespect for anything that made claims upon seriousness and the demands of writing fiction, so Martin in Brighton began to display something similar which would emerge again in the style of his own early novels. The most telling record of this is in the letters he wrote to Jane and his father during his twelve months on the Sussex coast. Thirty-five years later the letters between Amis senior and Philip Larkin would be published and recognized as the most outrageous epistolary novel ever, but written by very real correspondents. In the late 1960s no one apart from Kingsley and Larkin themselves had seen them, but there are quite remarkable parallels between Martin's letters to his father and stepmother and Kingsley's to his closest friend. Martin closes one of his first with an appraisal of authors encountered both on the A-level syllabus and recommended by Ardagh as supplements to impress interviewers. He now 'feels qualified to say why Lawrence's *The Rainbore* – is no good'. *War and Peace* and *Daniel Deronda* present him with no great misgivings and he ventures:

More light[n]ing opinions –
Ezra Pound   –   Trendy little ponce
Auden   –   Good but I feel he *must* be an awful old crap
Hopkins   –   Great fun to read, but doesn't stand up to any analysis
Donne   –   Very splendid
Marvell   –   „   „
Keats   –   All right when he's not saying 'I'm a poet. Got that?' 'La Belle Dame Sans Merci' – almost my favourite poem.

His comments are unsubstantiated by argument but this is where the resemblances between him and his father, circa 1946, are all the more striking. Typically: 'Now I must go and get some books out of the library to write an essay on "Spenser and the New Poetry". I'M NOT INTERESTED IN THAT.'

Spenser, monarch of the Renaissance English canon, features prominently in Kingsley's complaints simply because he is sacrosanct and compulsory, and Chaucer is subjected to caricature and derision for the same reason: the academic powers-that-be have elected a hierarchy of figures and will countenance no disfavour from those whom they are supposedly encouraging to think independently.

When Kingsley became a lecturer he maintained his tirades against literary icons, especially those he was obliged to teach, and his antipathies, and preferences, closely resemble his son's. In a letter to Larkin, he finds Keats 'a boring, conceited, self-pitying, self-indulgent silly little fool . . . incompetent, uninteresting, affected, non-visualizing'.[3] Martin at least thought 'La Belle Dame' a redeeming piece and enjoyed reading Hopkins despite the fact that under analysis he seemed incomprehensible. Kingsley, almost twenty years earlier in another letter to Larkin, had been less charitable: 'his silly private language annoys me – "what I am in the habit of calling *inscape*" *wellgetoutofthehabitthen* . . . I find him a bad poet . . . Though I can see why people like him.'[4] Pound was at the top of Martin's list of miscreants and after teaching a class on 'EP' Kingsley complained to Larkin that *'I can't see what people mean* who say he's good. I mean, good *in any way at all*. Just can't see anything in him, what?' And what is more, he had 'said as much to the class'.[5] Kingsley's favourites, pre-twentieth century, were Donne, whose muscular lyricism his own verse recalls, and Marvell. He wrote to Larkin praising a draft of his friend's 'If, My Darling': 'it has the ironic ambiguous feeling about it I admire in such as Marvell, as if you were pretending to be serious when really amused'.[6] According to Martin both Donne and Marvell are 'Very splendid'. More as confirmation than genuine enquiry, I ask if prior to then he had discussed poetry with his father. 'Never, no. Nor with anyone else for that matter.' What about D. H. Lawrence, for whom Kingsley reserved a lifetime of unqualified contempt? 'No, not even Lawrence.'

There are obvious differences, of course; principally Martin is either too in awe of the canon or lacking in confidence to turn intuition into vilification. Either way his inhibitions would soon be dispersed. It is astonishing that within four years of his having first properly encountered literature per se Martin would be writing pieces for the *TLS*, the *New Statesman* and *Observer* that caused great trepidation among the most established writers with books out for review.

Aside from their shared tastes and literary predispositions one other parallel is striking. This was the first time that Martin had written letters to anyone. In *Experience* he calls the exercise 'my half of this embarrassing correspondence',[7] which is part honest self-deprecation, part false modesty. Composing a letter to an intimate friend, a lover or a relative is the closest in real life that we come to writing fiction. In both instances we concern ourselves with marshalling our untidy wealth of activities, information and emotions into a coherent narrative, one that will by degrees convince, engage or entertain the reader. Some letter writers are embarrassingly or shamelessly ingenuous and one could find counterparts in fiction in Mr Pooter or Bridget Jones. The Amises, however, like to amuse their correspondents and, to an extent, indulge themselves, with admirably wrought tales. They don't dispense with authenticity – what they write is based principally on what they feel – but both enjoy the opportunity to fabricate, to create worlds in miniature from the raw material of otherwise dreary existence.

In his letters, particularly to Larkin and Robert Conquest, Kingsley freed himself from the confining routines of what could or could not be said. He confessed to everything, especially his extra-marital activities, but he also allowed the letter to become a conceit, a juggling act between report and ostentation. Imagine him as an eager novice. 'Sorry to hear you're not getting on too well with the colonials – are they *all* crappy. And you're working hard too. Still, you'll be back before you know it. Yes, that's when you'll be back.' This is the son, and there is something about the closing sentences – a self-conscious impatience with platitudes – that recalls the father perfectly. Within six months Martin was trying out virtuoso intolerance, setting up targets from his catalogue of peers and tutors.

> A pleasing extra is that the awful little Hun called Schicht, with whom I took the Latin exam, who got up after three quarters of an hour saying 'Interesting . . . interesting', *failed*. The Hobbiegobbie [Ardagh] himself has fixed me up with lessons once a week in Brighton. I go to an old shag called Mr Bethell who, I should say, is experiencing puberty for the second, or possibly the third time. This old dullard can speak seventeen languages fluently, including Latin, Ancient Greek, Welsh, Anglo-Saxon, Romney [*sic*], and the language of the tinkers. He says things like 'There are 140 first conjugation deponent verbs': I say 'Well I never' and he says 'They are Venor, Conor' and so on and on and on. He is also a high-priest of B.O. well versed in its most secret arts, and master of the most esoteric precepts of his craft. He still enjoys frequent use of his limbs although they taper off, after the second joint, to gangrenous supporating [*sic*] threads.[8]

In 1946 Kingsley explained to Larkin why he enjoyed writing to him . . . 'because I never feel I am giving myself away and so can admit to shady, dishonest, crawling, cowardly, brutal, unjust, arrogant, snobbish, lecherous, perverted and generally shameful feelings that I don't want anyone else to know about; but most of all because I am always on the verge of violent laughter'.[9] Kingsley and Jane were not Martin's confessors to the extent that Larkin was for Kingsley but they had unwittingly encouraged him to invest in letter writing that curious mixture of disclosure and performance that is the trademark of good fiction. Here is Kingsley:

> This is not going to be very long I am afraid as I have got to go out to tea with a young lady; so charming ('Like a picture, Herr Issyvoo'), whom I met this morning at her mother's instigation. Somehow I don't feel we are going to get along all that well: it was betrayed that I had literary ambitions, to which she remarked: 'I love arty people' er *awr* – ah-eeh mmm ooooh er-beeeeeeeee.[10]

And Martin:

> I met a fine girl called Charlotte a couple of weeks ago and I went round to her flat in Hamilton Terrace to take her out. I was introduced solemnly to her mother who, after asking if she could offer me a drink, expressed a desire to know where I lived. I told her and she exclaimed ecstatically: 'Oh! You must live near Elizabeth Jane Howard!' I calmly told her just how near Jane Howard I lived. She was suitably impressed and went on to eulogize 'After Julius'. As it happens, I went on to make Charlotte mine; a complement to an enjoyable evening.[11]

Kingsley, whatever he really felt about the arty young lady, was confiding to Larkin an early example of unfaithfulness; he was at the time going out with Hilly. Martin's 'fine girl called Charlotte' was real enough, though he did not have sex with her. Pretending that he had done, to Jane and his father, belonged in the same class of thrill as Kingsley's confidential story for his friend: for each of them truth was something to be manipulated and controlled. They even evolved exclusive, self-deprecating codes for their correspondents. Kingsley, after sending his regards to Larkin ('Yours etc. . . .') always finds space for 'bum', while Martin, more decorously, renames himself 'Osric' for all letters to his father and Jane.

The presence evoked by the Brighton letters would re-emerge, more polished and ruthless but essentially intact, as Charles Highway narrator of Martin's first novel *The Rachel Papers*. It is difficult to tell which of the passages below comes from the novel and which from the letters.

Don't I ever do anything else but take soulful walks down the Bayswater Road, I thought, as I walked soulfully down the Bayswater Road . . . Is *that* all it fucking is, I thought. For the question that interested me about this feeling was not 'What is it?' so much as 'Does it matter? Is it worth anything?' Because if there isn't a grain of genuine humility there, it's the electrodes for me.

We have had ten days of torrential rain punctuated with blizzards, hurricanes, whirlwinds, earthquakes, and like upheavals. My only comfort is indulgence in gruelling, man-of-the-elements walks through the blinding rain. I have also been known to look out of my window and silently determine, with haggard stoicism, that I shall wear white flannel trousers and walk upon the beach.

'Brighton', recalls Martin, 'was exhausting but also satisfying in a way. Very little happened. There was a calendar of deadlines for examinations and interview dates for university entrance. I went to Bristol and Durham, was accepted by both, but the Oxford Entrance seemed impossible. Ardagh fixed me up with a job at a prep school just outside Brighton where I taught everything that I wasn't studying, largely mathematics, and I was placed in charge of rugby training. I was rather good at that. I needed some money to show that I could look after myself, in the hope that Kingsley would chip in and help me rent a flat, well a bedsit, on Marine Parade away from the hostel. So yes I take your point. There is a remarkable contrast between the letters and my memories of that year.'

Were you amusing yourself, or trying to entertain or impress Jane and Kingsley?

'Both. Of course both.'

3

Oxford

Martin was interviewed at Oxford by John Carey, then Fellow in English at St John's and by Jonathan Wordsworth, the English don at Exeter, and accounts of what went on differ considerably, depending on their source. St John's was Martin's preferred college. His father and Philip Larkin had met and become friends there and according to Kingsley St John's, along with Balliol, Magdalen and Merton, maintained a special intellectual esteem. Undergraduates who went to these four were effortlessly clever. Everywhere else was full of strivers or throwbacks from Waugh's *Brideshead*, the latter again crowded conspicuously into Christ Church and Oriel. According to D. J. Taylor, St John's folklore has it that John Carey, a man of great probity and fairness, suffered something close to a crisis of conscience. 'He was determined not to allow the Amis lineage to affect the interview or his decision, yet he soon found himself doing battle with a precocious version of Martin's famously disputatious father.' Carey disliked the class-bound laziness of Oxford, the tendency to substitute rote-based intellectual conventions for thinking, but even he was unnerved by Martin who in the examination had been daring and unorthodox. In Martin's letter to Jane and his father he claims that Carey had turned him down for St John's because 'he was embarrassed by the state of my Latin'. Carey concurs. 'Yes. Well, it was more than forty years ago but I think that his second-language competence caused our only reservations – he was offering Latin. In any event neither of us doubted his suitability as an Oxford entrant. His exam papers on English poetry were extraordinary.' Did it not, I ask, seem odd that the son of a St John's alumnus should be sent somewhere else? Even during the sixties it was still a widely observed convention for sons to follow their distinguished fathers into the same college. 'Was it? Well perhaps. But we [St John's] certainly didn't turn him down because he wasn't good enough. I think we had reached our quota for English entrants that year.'

The most amusing account of his three days in Oxford is his rewriting of it for *The Rachel Papers*. Highway's experience seems very different from Martin's in that he is interviewed by a single tutor who, physically and temperamentally, precludes resemblances with Carey or Wordsworth. Knowd looks like a caricature of the radical late-sixties don: 'In urban-guerrilla dress; variegated, camouflage-conscious green and khaki canvas suit; beetle crusher, pig stomper boots; beret. Jack-Christ face and hair.'[1] Neither Carey nor Wordsworth dressed in this arch-revolutionary manner but the latter's interview technique – and indeed his routines as tutor for the subsequent three years – caused Martin to feel that he might have done. 'He was charmingly aloof, by which I mean that by instinct or design he gave the impression that what you said to him was acceptable but not quite up to his mandarin expectations. I suspect that for most of the time he just didn't care very much.' Carey on the other hand was chillingly erudite, encouraging Martin to revisit the attacks on orthodoxy of his exam papers but not as a reprimand; rather to remind him that if he did intend to maintain assaults upon the heavyweights of the canon he should at least arm himself with discernment. This is Knowd:

> For example. In the Literature paper you complain that Yeats and Eliot . . . 'In their later phases opted for the cold certainties that can work only outside the messiness of life. They prudently repaired to the artifice of eternity, etc., etc.' This then gives you a grand-sounding line on the 'faked inhumanity' of the seduction of the typists in *The Waste Land* – a point you owe to W. W. Clarke – which, it seems, is just a bit *too* messy all of a sudden.[2]

This figure combines the casual demeanour of Wordsworth with the intellectual acuity of Carey. The contrast between Carey, who showed him how far he would really have to push himself to close the gap between his aspirations and a good degree, and Wordsworth, the languid individual with whom he would have to spend most of his tutorials in Exeter College, amused him and in the novel he used his recollections to create Knowd. By the time he went up to Exeter his father had begun to tell him stories about his own experiences in Oxford. Kingsley admired most of all his undergraduate tutor at St John's, J. B. Leishman, one of the greatest mid-twentieth-century critics on Metaphysical Verse, which Amis enjoyed; when he began his thesis he was equally enthralled by encounters with F. W. Bateson, non-doctrinaire left-winger and founder of the then radical critical journal *Essays in Criticism*. At the other end of the spectrum was his first supervisor Lord David Cecil, whose lectures were musters of fatuity disguised as Wildean insights. Kingsley remembers him best for his absence; when sought for consultation Lord David was always apparently engaged with other undisclosed activities. Soon after his arrival in College Martin had confirmation of what his interview caused him to suspect: Jonathan Wordsworth was a late-twentieth-century version of Cecil. His habits – unfeigned or precious, no one could tell – included greeting his pre-luncheon tutees in his silk dressing gown, conducting part of the tutorial while he shaved in the adjoining bedroom and very often spending much of it discoursing on matters resolutely irrelevant to the designated topic, particularly the vintage and quality of the sherry and whisky he would dispense to all.

It is doubtful that Martin was confident or arrogant enough to foresee his Oxford years as the beginning of his ascent to success, but it is none the less intriguing that he elected to spend his last summer before going up revisiting the state of aimlessness that had stymied his prospects during his adolescence. It was as though he had decided to say goodbye to the fool he might have become, a fate that he had begun to suspect some of his peers, Rob Henderson in particular, would find difficult to avoid. He and Rob decided to drive through Europe to Spain and then take the ferry to Majorca to join Si and Fran (whom Martin still declines to identify) at Si's father's house near Soller. Martin had spent six weeks working in Colin Howard's hi-fi and record shop in Rickmansworth and had saved what he thought would be enough for food and occasional overnight accommodation. In any event the pound had recently been devalued and currency restrictions specified that a maximum of £50 could be taken abroad. Rob had attempted to raise cash for the trip by recklessly confident bouts of spread-betting on horses and greyhounds. Neither he nor Martin had made any profit from their exchanges with bookmakers and the difference between their preparations for the journey exemplifies the radical change that had occurred in Martin's approach to life in general. While he still regarded Rob as his closest friend there is evidence that he had begun to treat him also as a curiosity, a figure as endearingly capricious as ever but whose habits he now viewed with amusement and detachment.

They decided to drive. 'Rob's mum had a Mini and we borrowed that. We got the boat to Calais, drove through France and reached Spain without any problems. At Si's house there was a Mini Moke and the four of us used that for much of the stay.' Designed by British Leyland in a moment of cultural frivolity the Moke had a windscreen and a removable canvas top. It had four poorly upholstered seats and seemed by its nature to prefigure an endless summer through which lightly clad individuals would pass at little more than 30 mph. The 500 cc engine would by today's standards be the sort found on a ride-on lawnmower.

Martin had promised his companions an audience with England's most distinguished and hospitable expatriate writer, Robert Graves. He had first met him six years before when Kingsley and Hilly, still together and planning a shared future, had stayed with the Graveses and sought their advice on what it would be like to live permanently in either the Balearics or on the Spanish mainland. The Graveses, Robert and Beryl and their daughter Lucía, the latter roughly the same age as Martin, were used to unsolicited visits by writers, and the man himself had evolved a routine for dealing with petitioners. He would read their poetry and short extracts from their prose and offer honest advice. It was an immensely generous, altruistic regime but the arrival of Martin, Rob, Si and Fran perplexed Graves somewhat. Kingsley had asked Martin to pass on his regards – but he was used to studious, attentive would-be writers, not four nineteen-year-olds. The hilarious exchange between him and Rob, reported in *Experience*,[3] is according to Martin authentic. Rob was respectfully knowledgeable of Graves's reputation as

a poet but by the time he and Martin engaged him in
conversation the boundary between figurative excess and reality
had dissolved. Martin: 'I said [to Rob] "Pretend he's a god" so
Rob asked Graves to "Turn that mountain into a volcano, make
that mountain open up, make the cloud go away, summon a
tidal wave".'

Martin closes his description of the mildly surreal episode
with 'Robert got hold of Rob and roughly tickled him' and
follows up with an account of how they drove slowly down the
steep hill from the Graveses' house in the Moke with the
seventy-three-year-old writer following them on foot, arms
loaded with freshly baked bread and home-made pickles and
jam. It is a vintage example of dissolute yet respectful youth
making contact with a figure from an almost lost generation,
but it is more still than that. Martin shows an equal amount of
affection both for Graves and Rob, dispensing to the former
humble respect and the latter companionable amusement. It is
impossible to say for certain if the power relations that inform
the prose accurately reflect what really went on thirty years
earlier but we have no reason to assume that they do not. He
remembered Graves from 1962, particularly an evening when
Hilly and Kingsley had gone out for a meal and he and Philip
had been looked after by Robert and Beryl. Jollities involved a
culturally enriching game where the children would each
contribute a line to a collective improvised poem. The contrast
between this and soirées in the Amis literary household were
striking even for a thirteen-year-old. There was, however,
something about his father's visit to Graves that carried an air
of deference about it, as if the new boy was paying his dues to
one of the patriarchs of the establishment of which he was now
a member. Kingsley's inspiration as a novelist came from his
existence in a carefully constructed hall of mirrors, each
reflector telling an engaging version of the truth but none

making anything close to a proper claim upon candour. If there is any validity in the tempting thesis that the Amises father and son, embody a rare case of genetic literary inheritance then it is here that the link between them is most telling. The expedition to Europe was like the Osric letters, an experiment in control, a testament to his ability to be at once the hapless participant in a sequence of events and their detached observer, to make himself both the subject of the story and its choreographer.

Rob's mum's Mini broke down on the French side of the Pyrenees during their return journey, a wry echo of what had happened to Kingsley and family as they took the same route back from their visit to Majorca in 1962. Si and Fran remained in Spain. Martin and Rob had sufficient money to have the Mini towed a little closer to Perpignan but nowhere near enough to have the cylinder head gasket replaced. Martin was the first to telephone London to ask if Colin would be able to send them an international money order. Kingsley and Jane were in Nashville and Colin advised him to try to find a job, a prospect that seemed to him perplexing and faintly surreal. What form of labour could a nineteen-year-old Oxford entrance scholar expect to find in the still rather primitive region of south-west France? He and Rob were informed by forbiddingly confident, and enormous, Scandinavian backpackers that the docks in Barcelona had changed little since the Civil War and were always ready to employ manual labourers. Martin and his friend were roughly equal in height and they entertained only briefly the prospect of pitching in with hardened Catalans in an unmechanized dockyard. Rob decided to telephone his mother and ask her for help. There is no evidence that she had ever even met Colin Howard but her reply was identical: get a job. For several days they slept rough in parks and, briefly, in a rather sinister charity hostel. Eventually Colin telegraphed money to them – he admits now that he had always intended to do so yet delayed the draft as his personal contribution to Martin's 'coming of age'. Rob drove most of the way back through France after Martin's unfortunate experience of dropping a lit cigarette into the top of his hipster jeans which caused him to swerve into the path of an oncoming articulated lorry. Despite presenting himself and Rob as equally feckless in the episode of the broken-down Mini his coda in *Experience* discloses something closer to the truth:

> One day in 1978, in another car, Rob said to me as I dropped him off,
> – Sorry, Mart, but could you spare a tenner?
> I could, and usually I did. But this time I wouldn't.
> – A fiver. Okay a quid.
> – Okay. A quid.
> That week in Perpignan was my only experience of privation, of hunger. It would happen differently for Rob, who was no mere trier-out of hard times, and proved to have a genius for adversity.[4]

For Martin the 'privation', as he called it, of Perpignan was a brief digression from otherwise very promising forecasts: he was aware that there was no real danger of dying of exposure or starvation in a public park and that in a few months' time he would become a freshman and Exhibitioner at Exeter College, Oxford.

Exeter is one of the so-called 'Turl' Colleges, reached from the medieval street, or to be more accurate lane, of that name. Unlike grander houses it has no room for luxuriant expansive gardens and its vistas are limited to pockets of sky littered with spires, domes and battlements belonging to somewhere else. It is ancient, twelfth-century by record, but unlike many other colleges of that vintage it is not generously endowed with income from the post-Reformation estates of dissolved monastic orders. It has some distinction and eminence but not a great deal of room and thus Martin found himself in early October 1968, having been driven from London by Colin, with quarters that were spacious, at least compared with Brighton. The scout helped him upstairs with his luggage and his small but high-quality stereo. 'This', said the scout, 'is your study.' It was also apparently his living room and it would not even be his. 'Mr Marzys', the scout informed him, 'will be arriving later today.' 'It was', says Martin, 'a big comfortable room, with two small adjoining bedrooms.' There was a two-bar electric fire in what might once have been an ancient fireplace, now plastered over, and apart from a sofa and armchair the only pieces of furniture were adjoining desks and chairs beneath a large mullioned window which gave on to another roof.

Marzys was an Old Harrovian and well accustomed to the indignities of communal living but Martin disliked the prospect of sharing. Within a fortnight he had made friends with a freshman Classicist who had been allocated a study and bedroom to himself on a distant staircase. 'I didn't need to persuade him. He *wanted* to share. It would earn him a second year rooming in college.'

'Then I started to look around',[5] a moment he attempts to pass off as ingenuous but in truth he was not so much beguiled by his new environment as hungry for its opportunities. His tutor Jonathan Wordsworth was the poet's great-great-great-great-nephew and in case anyone suspected otherwise his rooms were generously decorated with 'family' memorabilia – prints, extracts from manuscripts, discreetly labelled items of clothing and pottery. He dressed, says Martin, 'casually and elegantly. Striking, shoulder-length dark hair.' He is best remembered for his manner in tutorials, frequently, indeed predictably, digressing from the alleged topic to matters not even of spurious relevance: including, for example, his puzzled reflections on the fact that his father, brother and mother were all 'queer'. He would reproach tutees for their rapt solemnity, particularly when it came to Blake. For those who had unquestioningly accepted that everything the latter produced was redolent of symbolism he declared: 'The burning tree [in *Songs of Experience*] is a burning tree, not an organ of procreation. Does *your* cock look like that?' Though the question was invalid for those from St Hilda's with which Exeter had a reciprocal teaching arrangement he continued to address it, eyebrow raised. 'It was', says Martin, 'an act. He was a good tutor. By the third year we had become friends.'

Mods were effectively a second entrance examination – without succeeding in them students could not proceed to the second and third years – and were comprised of ostentatiously difficult subjects. Old English Grammar and the Latin paper were the worst, the first involving the parsing of sentences from the likes of Aelfric and the latter translations from books of *The Aeneid*. Wordsworth was not a specialist in either but Martin was aware that their twice-weekly meetings were a vital investment. He had some basic Latin from his year at Brighton but he was nowhere near as familiar with the language as the public school peers who made up 60 per cent of the undergraduate intake and whose elite training the Oxford curriculum was designed to reflect. He needed Wordsworth and, despite his natural inclination towards caricature, indulged his, often ludicrous, affectations.

'Once you were used to his Country Squire drawl, and the rest, Wordsworth could be wonderful. Best of all he refused to allow the paraphernalia of criticism to get in the way of a direct response. He would sometimes say the unsayable, even on Shakespeare. He was superb on Shakespeare and he hated critical jargon. On that we certainly agreed.' There is one quote from Knowd in *The Rachel Papers* that might be treated as a thank-you note to Wordsworth from his erstwhile pupil: 'Stop reading critics, and for Christ's sake stop reading all this Structuralist stuff. Just read the poems and work out whether you like them, and why. Okay? The rest comes later – hopefully.'[6]

Martin claims, in *My Oxford*:

> [M]ost of my life [at Oxford] was to consist of me alone in a study, reading books pressed calmly out on the blotting paper, or writing malarial, pageant-like, all-night essays, or listening to records, or playing moronically simple forms of patience, or having soul-sessions, or having crying jags. And however self-pitying I was about it at the time, this segment of my life I regret not at all: a relative late-comer to literature, I was a contrite pilgrim on the path towards its discovery.[7]

He also allowed himself lengthy excursions to Blackwell's, where Jane had opened an account for him. He did so in the hope that if he loitered at the relevant shelves for long enough he might find a respectable pretext for beginning a conversation with someone, female, who had attended the same lectures. The experience was memorable enough for use in *The Rachel Papers*.

> She came on me from behind and poked me too hard in the ribs.
> 'Hello then. Wotcher reading?'
> 'Oh, hello,' I said, surprise borne out by the falsetto croak in my voice. But then I was off. 'Oh, you know, some tired old hack reproducing boiled-up earlier articles and pretending they form a unit.' I paused and made

(three) impatient gestures with my hand. 'He says they're all about "the problem of words".' I pointed to the subtitle on the cover, rich in adrenalin as a phrase from a novel took shape at the back of my mind. 'But what they're really about is him – his taste, his poise, and how much he likes money. Just look at the price.'[8]

The contrast between this and *My Oxford* is intriguing and of course raises the question of which comes closer to the real Martin: the 'crying jag' neurotic or a far more confident, rather louche presence? John Walsh: 'I was at Exeter and tutored by Jonathan Wordsworth, three or four years after Martin completed his degree, and he had bequeathed a small legend to the college, irrespective of the fact that he was already becoming known in London. Stories about "Mart" circulated, the girlishly handsome chap who shagged all night and spent all day in the library. I remember there was a copy of *The Rachel Papers* on Jonathan's desk, displayed more prominently than the family memorabilia and left open at the inscribed title page: "To Jonathan, My Star Tutor, With Thanks and Love, From Martin". Jonathan explained that even by the end of his first year there was a sense that Martin was part of the Elect, those who are inevitably destined for a First, prominence, esteem. Jonathan knew that Martin "belonged" and by his second year they had done a deal: if, a year after Finals, he had not completed a publishable novel he would come back and begin research. In college people even talked about his lethargic coolness, as if he'd been there only a few days before. He stayed on in anecdotes. For example, there was the story of the mock Mods exam set up by Jonathan and a part-time tutor as a rehearsal for the real thing. Exeter freshers were confined to a seminar room in College in exam conditions and asked to do a version of Old English. Apparently Martin sat staring at the paper, wrote three pages very rapidly, stretched and announced to everyone that he needed the loo, where was it? He was shown to a bathroom next door, came back ten minutes later and announced, "That room is an utter disgrace, there are pubic hairs as thick as pencil lead in the bath and the sink." The image was so vivid that no one else was able to finish the exam.'

During his first year he made friends with Tim Healey, who had just gone up to Balliol. They shared their respective fathers' inclinations towards wry cynicism. Denis Healey was a Labour Cabinet Minister and the fact that Martin and Tim had first met in London raises some doubts regarding the former's presentation of himself as detached from the various coteries that made up Oxford undergraduate life in the late sixties. In truth he did belong, but to an assembly that as yet had no defining features. Their parents would probably be seen as bourgeois but they themselves treated the conventions of the foregoing generation with indifference; they were unostentatious hedonists and they were ambitious. In much of Martin's fiction of the 1970s and 1980s they would occupy centre ground; in the real world, to their embarrassment, the Thatcher decade would provide them with a sympathetic milieu.

Tim Healey introduced Martin to Rosalind ('Ros') Hewer who became his regular girlfriend. She had a flat outside college where Martin would stay, Exeter still being monitored by scouts who relished the discovery of proscribed 'guests'. Martin now had his own car. 'A white Mini Cooper. I bought it with the money earned – £800 – from acting in the film in the Caribbean.' 'The Ashtray', as it would be dubbed by Philip, allowed Martin and Ros to graduate from occasional excursions to Cotswold pubs to weekends at 108 Maida Vale and the grander 'Lemmons' in Barnet to which the Amis entourage moved in March 1969. As Martin recalls there was no need for formal introductions or discreet enquiries regarding their sharing of a room and a bed. Ros was greeted in the congenial welcoming manner offered to all occasional visitors, irrespective of the nature of their relationship with the permanent residents, then consisting of Jane, Kingsley, Colin and Colin's friend, Sargy Mann. Martin also notes that his father was consistently engaging and companionable with all of his girlfriends, getting on with some better than others but doing his best to display no preference. 'There was no *effort*. He was like that. What lay behind it was the memory of what he had gone through with his own father, and of my grandfather's staid morality which drove them [Kingsley and his father] apart from the mid-forties onwards.'

The relationship with Ros lasted just over a year until late in Michaelmas term, November 1969. Martin claims to recall no particular cause for the break-up and although Alexandra 'Gully' Wells arrived at St Hilda's in October 1969 they did not begin a relationship until December. Gully and Martin had met three years earlier. Her mother, a friend of Jane's, was Dee Wells, American journalist and novelist, then married to the philosopher A. J. 'Freddie' Ayer, Gully's stepfather. Despite his presentation of himself as a recluse, Martin had by the end of his first year attained a certain degree of fame by association. Kingsley's 1950s reputation as a cultural reprobate had been exchanged for respectability and glamour, given his outspoken, conservative opinions on the arts and education, and the media attention – some coat-trailed and much unbidden – which followed his affair with and then marriage to Jane. Martin refers in *My Oxford* to the 'cool people . . . a recent type . . . the aloof, slightly moneyed, London-based, car-driving, party-throwing, even vaguely intellectual butterfly elite'.[9] Try as he might to make himself sound like the unassuming observer, by the end of his first year he had become part of that set. For example, when Edmund Blunden resigned as Oxford Professor of Poetry Yevgeny Yevtushenko was promoted by the leftist literary intelligentsia as his potential successor. Kingsley had been advised by Robert Conquest that despite the airbrushed profiles of Yevtushenko the dissident in the Western media, he was in fact a Kremlin puppet, cooperating with the Soviet authorities to sell the image of Moscow as tolerant of outspoken artists. Kingsley began a campaign in support of Roy Fuller who would eventually win the post – Professors of Poetry are elected by Oxford MAs – and in 1969 he set up headquarters at the house of Fuller's son John, then Fellow in English at Magdalen. On several occasions Kingsley, Jane and other London-based literary celebrities attended convivial meetings, including lunch and drinks, at John Fuller's house. The only undergraduates in attendance were Martin and Ros and James Fenton, then in his third year at Magdalen, son of the Canon of Christ Church and already a published poet. Fenton's acquaintanceship with Martin led to another introduction. Christopher Hitchens: 'I was walking down the Turl with James and he pointed out to me a couple coming towards us, the guy was small, blond, quite colourfully dressed, and James introduced us. "Son of . . . ?" I said. Yes, yes . . . That was all treated lightly. I was at my extreme SWP [Socialist Workers Party] stage and had little concern with Kingsley as a novelist; I was more interested in his support for the Vietnam War. Anyway the meeting with Martin was brief but we both recalled it a year or two later when we got to know each other properly in London.' Aside from the family association was he known in Oxford as a figure, a personality? 'James informed me that he was marked for a Starred First, and that he had a forbidding reputation for wit and hard work. One term, apparently, he'd never once signed out for lunch. Anything more than ten minutes between the library and hall would have disrupted his strict nine-hour daily routine. And the word was about that he wished to write, though no one was quite sure if he had designs upon a future as a poet or a novelist.'

During visits to London Martin would spend whole afternoons in the company of Gully's stepfather A. J. Ayer. They went to White Hart Lane to see Spurs and when Ayer was not watching football he would talk of philosophy 'casually but not patronizingly or exclusively, in the way that most of us discuss films, books, food or the weather' and they would play chess. Martin had become part of the cultural aristocracy. He and Gully met neither by accident nor through a more polished version of Martin's bookshop strategy. Their respective families, specifically Jane and Dee, arranged for them to get in touch at the beginning of the academic year. Martin remarked that his relationship with Gully 'lasted in its intermittent way about as long as the average marriage. Ten years?' He adds that 'we continued to spend – between our affairs with others – the occasional weekend together.'

Gully Wells herself has some interesting things to say about their time together. 'It was "arranged". Jane and my mother were friends and in a way conspired to make a couple of us. Martin at Oxford was much as he presents himself in that essay [*My Oxford*]. He didn't go to many parties, spend all night drinking or indulge in particularly bad behaviour, he *worked*. So did I, but I was fascinated and infuriated by him. I liked, enjoyed an active social life, but Martin didn't want to join in. He seemed to be pursuing an agenda. Commendable but a little sad. And yes, we did continue to see each other after the official break-up, not merely socially. Even if he was going out with someone else, or if I was, we'd just have sex for old times' sake. Ten years? Yes, from when we met in sixty-nine, about that.'

At the beginning of the summer holiday of 1970 Gully announced she had recently been in contact with a friend, Serena North, whose father owned a castle in Tuscany. Martin had made no plans for the vacation, apart from a rather desultory agreement with Rob to meet up in London for weekends of shiftless companionship. He would, he anticipated, spend most of his time at Lemmons and the prospect of six weeks in what Gully promised would be luxurious, ancient surroundings, plus guaranteed sunshine, brooked no hesitation. They flew to the castle via Florence and the place was, he recalls, even more preposterously grand than either of them had imagined, with their bedroom occupying the upper storey of a tower. Other parts of the rambling building dated from the twelfth to the nineteenth century and included an enormous library, a ballroom and a dining room the size of most houses, served by an appropriately gigantic kitchen. There was also a well-kept terraced garden and a swimming pool where as far as Martin remembers he and Gully spent most of their holiday. 'Nothing happened,' he muses 'nothing at all. We shared the place, sometimes, with other people, mostly friends of the family, people from the village, plus the ones who looked after the property would come up when necessary. Serena was there throughout. The visitors', he adds, 'came much, much later.' He refers here to *The Pregnant Widow* (2010), three-quarters of which is inspired by his 1970 summer with Gully. In the novel most of the 'visitors' are picked solicitously from the subsequent ten years of Martin's life and placed in a scenario that invites comparison with *Dead Babies* except that the host does not murder his guests. Keith Nearing keeps his promise to read every major novel in English from the eighteenth and nineteenth centuries, and so did his creator. Gully, according to Martin, was by turns astonished and irritated by his dedication. 'She was', he says, 'her stepfather's daughter, unpersuaded by the vulgar attractions of fantasy and imagination. Truth was her compass.' All of this is beguilingly disclosed in the novel.

After their return to Oxford Martin discovered – through

gossip from others who belonged to the 'cool' set – that Gully had begun to see someone else. In *My Oxford* he refers to this man as 'someone who everybody agreed was much nastier, thicker and uglier than me'. He was a journalist and political commentator, a man more suited to Gully's taste for rationalism over art. The fact that they resumed their relationship as if nothing much had happened sheds some light on how they also managed to sustain an amicable sex-without-commitment arrangement for much of the subsequent decade.

Martin spent much of the remainder of the summer with Rob in London in pursuit of any available female and on his return to Oxford he and Gully stuck with the agreement made before the previous June, to rent a cottage in the Cotswold village of Shilton, forty minutes' drive from the city. The Old Forge seemed in appearance to be unnervingly similar to Marriner's Cottage where Hilly and Kingsley had lived when Martin was born, but there the resemblance swiftly faded. The other residents – referred to as X, Y and Z in *Experience* and still unnameable for fear of causing offence or a possible libel action – spent most of the shortened six-week period of the rental in states that varied between fratricidal hostility and despair, involving two genuine attempts at suicide and one epileptic seizure induced by a drug overdose. Add to this a call by the police following an attempt by one of them to smash every piece of glass and pottery in the house, plus weekly visits from the unofficial lodger from London, Rob Henderson – who managed to seduce Z's girlfriend, in the house – and one had as Martin put it 'novel fodder' but not an environment in which one would actually wish to exist.

Gully: 'Martin's letter[10] does not do proper justice to the insanity of the place. "Z" who ended up sectioned was the victim of the piece, probably the originator of poor little Keith in *Dead Babies*. He slept under the stairs and his rather unbecoming appearance, he was squat and ugly, ensured that he never managed to persuade women to spend too much time in his company. He lacked self-confidence and had an ostentatiously regional accent, working-class I suppose. Martin, Rob and the other [unnamed male] teased him cruelly about all of this. I can see parallels with the novel, at least in terms of particular characters, but there are enormous differences too.'

Shortly before the end of term Martin and Gully left the Old Forge in the Mini at approximately 1 a.m. having earlier cached their clothes and belongings in the car. His claim that the darkly comic experiences in the Old Forge were the genesis for *Dead Babies* is credible but only partially. Certainly the personnel of the Forge are of roughly the same age and status as those in the book, with grotesquely exaggerated inclinations in the latter towards narcissism, self-loathing and murder. The novel's animus, however, comes from the carefully evoked sense of dread and resignation which each character seems to share. It is a community which for no apparent reason is obsessively preoccupied with staying together while being horribly alert to its collective demise, and Martin's cue for this came in part from his memories of Madingley Road, Cambridge.

Gully states that 'it was close to the Christmas break when we left the cottage and we agreed that for the remainder of the academic year, until he would finish his degree, we would live together in a small flat in the city. I found a place and busily acquired extra pots and pans and other less practical items. I can't remember exactly how Martin informed me that it was off, but it was not in person, and I took the train out to Lemmons where he explained to me, apologetically I suppose, that he had decided that his degree and whatever came after must be given priority. That there would be no distractions, such as relationships. I was very upset, and I recall vividly the fatherly, consoling presence of Kingsley. He took me into one of the sitting rooms, without Martin, gave me a hug and an enormous whisky and said . . . well I don't remember but he did his best to make me feel better. He was a very lovely man. As I say we "broke up" but not quite, hopping into bed together on occasions during the next decade. Freddie [A. J. Ayer], however, never forgave him. They had got on well, played chess, gone to see Spurs together, but Freddie refused to speak to him after that.'

In the second and third terms of his last year, after failing to obtain rooms in College, Martin moved into a dreary Edwardian terrace in Iffley Road, kept by Exeter to house its undergraduate overspill. The locality inspires rigour, being over the bridge from Magdalen and ten minutes walk from the British Leyland car plant. This suited Martin perfectly. He had decided that the remaining twelve weeks of his undergraduate career would be dedicated exclusively to hard work. He wanted a First.

Wordsworth had already stated that this was well within his grasp. Earlier he had nominated Martin as Exeter's representative at a year-long seminar run by a then Visiting Professor, Northrop Frye. Frye was an awesome figure, bestriding the chasm of quixotic impressionistic criticism and the rigours of the academy. Only thirty undergraduates, one from each college, were allowed to attend his seminars, a choice based partly on inter-collegiate etiquette and partly upon the meritocratic principle that of the three hundred or so reading for English only the top 10 per cent should benefit, and Martin certainly did. Like most major writers he rarely if ever admits to anything so compromising as influence but Frye can be treated as the first literary critic to hold his attention. Frye's trademark as teacher and critic was his wit and boldness. Allusions to and quotations from Frye feature like brief talismans in his own writing. Indeed the title itself of his controversial post-9/11 diatribe against organized religion 'The Voice of the Lonely Crowd' is borrowed from Frye and the phrase epitomizes Martin's affiliation to this distinguished, very unorthodox Canadian academic. Frye liked the intellectual challenge of systems but distrusted ideologies that claimed either to explain or incorporate their subject, be this literature or the meaning of life. The lonely crowd comprised those who sought collective abridgements of independent thought and individual responsibility.

For the time being, however, Martin knew that bursts of conjecture or iconoclasm must involve caution. His examiners would tolerate individuality only when grounded in a discernible accumulation of knowledge, so around the middle of his penultimate term he instituted a strict daily regime. Up by 7 a.m. at the latest, he walked to Exeter for breakfast and spent at least four hours in the college library followed by lunch, again at Exeter. He was back in the library no later than 2 p.m. and would return to Iffley Road at around 7 p.m. He prepared his own supper in the shared kitchen – 'Vesta curries or pasta' – and then returned to work in his room until a saturation of literary material caused him to lose any clear sense of focus or purpose. He would usually go to sleep at around 1 a.m. The routine would be broken only by impromptu tutorials with Wordsworth; the latter knew that this last lap before Finals would best be undertaken by someone like Martin with as little attention as possible to a regular timetable. 'He was available when I needed to talk with him,' says Martin, who had long since ceased to attend lectures. Some weekends would be spent at Lemmons, but he kept a diplomatic distance from Rob. He was still working as a studio-hand and general dogsbody in Soho, making low-budget films of limited quality. The friendship would be rekindled after Martin completed his degree but for the time being he had decided to forgo all potential temptations and indulgences and dedicate himself exclusively to a comprehensive mastery of English Literature from the twelfth to the twentieth century. The nine three-hour examinations were interleaved with at best no more than two half-day breaks, an Oxford convention that tests the endurance and psychological composure of students as much as their learning and intellect. He was called for a Viva, which could mean that he stood at the borderline between degree classifications and would be subjected to an interrogation to confirm either his promise or liabilities. Instead, however, this turned out to be the type where the dons simply congratulated him on achieving one of the most impressive Firsts of his year. In terms of the marks themselves he had come third. Did he think about an academic career, given that acceptance as a doctoral student at Oxford, including a reasonably generous government grant, would now be little more than a formality? 'Yes, and Jonathan Wordsworth had encouraged me to do so. We talked about a thesis on Shakespeare. Jonathan and I came to an agreement. If I hadn't finished a novel in a year – first draft – I'd come back and try for an academic career.' So if it were not for Rachel [real name Cynthia], Martin, like Kingsley, might have begun his literary life as a don.

4

The Novelist

Martin's mother's and father's circumstances had altered since he went up to Oxford. In 1968 Hilly had moved with her husband David Roy Shackleton Bailey to Ann Arbor, Michigan, where he had been appointed to a full professorship. Married only a year and remaining fond of Bailey, Hilly was beginning to recognize that she had been drawn to him mainly as an antidote to the exuberant, unpredictable and charming types – notably Fairlie and Amis – who had turned out to be too bad to be true. He was everything that they were not, studious, withdrawn and prudent, and as a somewhat futile attempt to revive their relationship Bailey and Hilly had decided to tour the Mediterranean coast from Rome to Spain. By the time they reached Ronda, inland from the Costa del Sol, Hilly had decided it was all over. Or to be more accurate her intuitions had been confirmed. She had become a close friend of Bailey's colleague Milton Cohen, sixty years old but refreshingly mischievous enough to remind her of the life and company she preferred. Cohen, at her request, had secretly arranged the rental for a flat in the town and when the time came for her to return to the US with Bailey she refused and moved into her new accommodation, followed shortly afterwards by Sally. Whether her friendship with Cohen would have developed into a relationship will remain a matter for speculation because within a week of Bailey's departure she had met Alastair Boyd, 7th Baron of Kilmarnock. If Bailey had appeared in a novel as the stereotypical bumbling don, Boyd could have joined him as a biddable down-at-heel aristocrat. All that was left of an impressive ancestry was the title. The baronetcy had once been an earldom which had been suspended completely in 1745, following the Earl of Kilmarnock's participation in the Jacobite rebellion and his subsequent beheading. It was revived in 1831, and Boyd was Seventh Baron of the demoted line. In 1970 he was running the Palacio de Mondragon Language School in Ronda, servicing both the sons and daughters of wealthy expatriate Britons and the children of middle-class locals. Hilly and Sally called in one day to see if work was available and Boyd was struck by Hilly's ageless vivacity. At forty-four she looked a decade younger and she was wearing a bright orange dress given to her by Gully Wells. Martin and Gully had flown to Ronda to spend a week with Hilly and the two women recognized traits in each other that ensured from the start a mutual affability. Both approached life with an intrepid casualness that could lead either to comedy or disaster. As soon as Hilly met Alastair Boyd something more than a working relationship was immediately intimated. Within a week they had begun an affair and by the end of the summer were living together.

For eight years from the beginning of 1969 Lemmons was a commune comprising Kingsley and Jane, Colin Howard and Sargy Mann. It was also Martin's permanent base until he moved into a flat in Belgravia with Rob in 1972 but even after that he used Lemmons as a reliable retreat from central London. When Kingsley and Jane purchased the property it was called Gladsmuir but Jane discovered its original name from the deeds and also that it had once been owned by Frances Trollope, mother of the more famous Anthony and herself a prodigious writer and literary hostess. It was a large detached Georgian house and to its front were the semi-rural vistas of Hertfordshire; at its back was London, and a twenty-minute walk would take you to a tube station. Its past association with two literary figures, one male and one female, seemed to Kingsley a good omen and his sense of optimism is reflected in a letter to Larkin: 'This is a bloody great mansion, in the depths of the country though only 15 miles from the centre, and with lots of room for you to come and spend the night.'[1] Jane had a study on the first floor, Kingsley's was on the floor below and Martin's spacious bedroom was directly above Kingsley's study. He too would work there when up from Oxford.

Following his graduation in late June 1971 Martin spent a month in Ronda with his mother and Boyd, accompanied for a week by Gully. Hilly was now working full-time with Boyd at his language school, an enterprise that remained in profit but only just enough to support their modest lifestyle in a country that had one of the lowest costs of living in Europe. Martin relaxed, cleared his head of the abundant desiccated material from his Finals and began to think about a project which he had nursed, privately, for a year but had set aside until after graduation: the novel. Its nature and temper were, as he now concedes, predetermined. Most writers begin their first attempts at fiction with the postulate that novels should be works of the imagination and not disguised autobiography but Martin – 'just feeling my way', as he puts it – spent his second and third years in Oxford making rough notes for a novel that would certainly reflect key aspects of his ongoing life. He began the first draft in

July 1970 in the room above where his father had just completed *Girl, 20* featuring Sir Roy Vandervane, a fifty-three-year-old composer and conductor and his friend and confidant Douglas Yandell, a music critic more than twenty years his junior, who tells the story. Their age difference functions as an autobiographical trick of the light because Kingsley carries forward to Vandervane many of the temperamental and behavioural features of himself from the mid-1950s: he is an irresponsible, egotistical lecher. Hence the manic determination of Vandervane to behave like a twenty-something libertine: he is no longer so much driven by lust as terrified by the prospect of what he might become without it. Yandell is a figure for whom hedonism, sex in particular, is a matter for dry contemplation and as a first-person narrator he is ill suited to his task, a detached saturnine presence, uncomfortable with the messy, visceral material of his account. Vandervane was Kingsley's non-literary reflection, a man whose epic libido might be restored by pills, psychology or sheer force of will, but with Yandell he raised a more troubling question: what will I be like as a writer if I lose interest in sex?

In a letter to Robert Conquest in 1991 Kingsley reflects on his separation from Jane '*8 years last Nov*': 'Now I wish it had happened in – well I suppose about 1970 would be right.' Martin in *Experience* comments, '1970? Surely not. But how would I know?'[2] His declared ignorance of his father's state of mind at that time is, he now admits, slightly feigned.

The most interesting if not particularly conspicuous character of *Girl, 20* is Christopher, Vandervane's son. He is the only one of the Vandervane family who has attained a sufficient degree of independence and self-sufficiency to feel confident enough to rebuke the patriarch. He acts as Vandervane's quiet conscience while the rest of his children have become feckless, sometimes tragic supplicants to his hedonistic example. Philip at this point was pursuing a career as a professional artist, an ambition he nurtured when he and Martin were occasional truants during the mid-1960s. According to Sargy Mann, himself a painter, Kingsley followed up his disparaging comments on Philip's decision to study art with equally dismissive opinions on what was now his profession. 'He thought the visual arts, painting particularly, should be classed as a recreation.' Philip responded with a mixture of distress and bitterness. Sally came to live in Lemmons in 1970 after a brief troubled period with her mother and Bailey in Michigan. She was sixteen but already had serious drink problems. Martin adds, 'She also took some drugs in the US, but stopped when she returned.' Penny, Vandervane's daughter, finds solace from her disjointed world in heroin and Ashley, his other son, frequently tells members of the family and visitors to 'fuck off', refuses to go to school and urinates regularly on the bathroom floor. Christopher, while remaining on good terms with his father – at least nominally, until he shops him to the papers – maintains a studied detachment from the maelstrom of despair and perplexity into which Vandervane seems to have dragged everyone close to him, his wife included. The Vandervane household was not a direct reflection of Kingsley Amis's family, but there is none the less a mixture of echoes and distortions. Christopher might have been Martin, except that the antagonism between him and Vandervane is the complete opposite of the growing sense of shared interests and mutual affection that many noted in the relationship between Martin and his father. Penny and Ashley also are grisly hypotheses; aspects of Sally and Philip are detectable in both but blurred by terrible speculations of what they might become.

Gully Wells recalls that during the eighteen months before their relationship officially ended her weekends at Lemmons were 'outstanding. A more hospitable household would be impossible to imagine; everyone was made welcome and guaranteed a wonderful time with limitless supplies of excellent food and drink. But with Kingsley and Jane the cracks were beginning to show. There were no dreadful public arguments but it was evident to all that something was wrong.' She does not remember if she and Martin spoke of this or whether he seemed alert to the tension between his father and stepmother sensed by others. 'What was clear, was that Kingsley enjoyed Martin's company immensely, they got on well and one could detect a feeling of pride in his [Kingsley's] dealing with him.' Martin had, since going up to Oxford, been admitted to the coterie of friends with whom Kingsley shared confidences, albeit sometimes tactically, and he could match their wry misanthropy with something similarly sharp and unindulgent. When guests such as Conquest, Larkin, Paul Fussell, Theo Richmond or George Gale joined Kingsley for after-dinner drinks – or to be more accurate a continuation of pre- and concurrent dinner drinks – the temper of the exchanges would be clubbish but with a competitive edge. Martin was by 1970 a respected contributor to these sessions and he also began to spend more time talking to his father one-to-one, something that neither of them had felt inclined to do before he gained his place at Exeter. 'He [Kingsley] was of course the same man with whom I'd spent most of my life but it was only then [at the end of the 1960s] that I started to get to know him . . .' Of all the autobiographical echoes that run through *The Rachel Papers* the only one that is entirely smothered involves The Father. The description of Gordon Highway at the beginning of the novel reads like a ceremony of exorcism. Highway senior 'gets fitter as he gets older'. Following his fairly recent acquisition of abundant wealth, source undisclosed, he has taken to playing tennis at weekends and squash three times a week at Hurling-ham. Moreover, he gives up smoking and forswears strong drink. Kingsley had avoided any form of exercise since leaving the army and at the time that Martin was writing the novel he was conducting what he called, gleefully and sardonically, 'research' for his next piece of non-fiction, *On Drink* (1972). The book is a magnificent culturally diverse invitation to cirrhosis of the liver. In preparing his recipes for devastating cocktails Kingsley never relied upon hypothesis and Martin recalls that Lemmons during 1970–1 became a test of endurance for even the most hardened drinker, with Kingsley holding court as chief experimenter. It sounds delightful but one suspects that Kingsley's encounters with these monstrous concoctions were touched with a sense of despair, a humorous pretext for simply getting drunk. The bizarre Dorian Gray figure of *The Rachel Papers* who seems to be magically regaining his youth obliterates any parallels with a very real man now approaching fifty for whom his wild past is irrecoverable.

The Rachel Papers took Martin approximately a year to write. He began in late summer 1971 after his return from Spain and completed the first draft in September 1972. Before leaving for another short visit to Spain, again with Gully, he placed the proof on the desk of his father's study with a note asking him what he thought of it. But surely he knew Martin was writing it? 'Yes of course he did. But we didn't speak of it when it was in progress.' And when he returned from holiday? 'He said it was good, and funny.' When did Martin first read *Girl, 20*: before or after he had completed *The Rachel Papers*? (Kingsley's novel came out approximately four months beforehand.) 'Afterwards, yes certainly afterwards.'

In the novel which launched Kingsley's career, Jim and the narrator reflect both versions of Kingsley: the one he allowed himself to be when off the leash, perhaps writing and talking with Philip Larkin, and the one burdened with obligations to family, job and so on, and not quite able to say, or do, as he wished. This technique of shared dissimulation, with two versions of Kingsley's personality cooperating yet remaining autonomous would become his trademark, a feature of all of his fiction. It emerges in the split perspective provided by Yandell the narrator and Vandervane his principal subject. It is painstakingly avoided in all of Martin's and here we begin to recognize the true significance of Charles Highway's 'Letter to My Father'. We learn nothing of its content because in truth the letter cautiously assembled by Charles and the novel written by Martin are the same thing. It was not that Martin had to dispense with key aspects of his own personality to step out of his father's shadow. Rather, he was politely moving Kingsley out of the picture – and the wry inversions of each aspect of his character indicate this – as a statement of intent. Charles is as much an extension of Martin as Jim was of Kingsley. The difference is that while Dixon and his narrator set a precedent for Kingsley's habit of using his work to hide or improve upon those aspects of his life that he did not like, Charles was an experiment in untrammelled self-scrutiny.

Colin Howard remembers Martin at various stages of his development from shiftless teenager to prodigious young novelist. 'Obviously the youth left with us [he and Sargy Mann] when Kingsley and Jane went to the States and the man with three dazzling novels to his name had undergone transform-ations, but the intervening period was barely ten years. And leaving aside the fact that he had succeeded, become famous, it was remarkable how many aspects of his personality endured. In the memoir in *My Oxford* he presents himself as a guileless unaffected sort, intellectually and as far as girls are concerned; this is very far from the truth.' Does he recognize Martin in Charles Highway? 'Oh yes. But the effect is curious because Charles speaks mainly to the reader. In Maida Vale and later in Lemmons Martin was generous with his drollery, not cruel you understand but everyone felt slightly guarded when talking with him. He was like Kingsley in that respect. You felt you had to monitor anything you said in case you ended up as the butt of a witticism.' This, presumably, was the confident post-Oxford Martin? 'More so, yes, but even as a seventeen-year-old he was dangerously sharp.'

I ask Colin Howard and Sargy Mann if the figure in *My Oxford*, ingenuously loitering in Blackwell's in the hope of striking up a conversation with a girl, evokes memories. They find this hilarious. Mann: 'In a way, but not as you might expect. I can imagine it as one of his strategies, presenting himself as diffident to gain the poor creature's confidence; a conceit if you like.' Colin Howard adds: 'During the couple of years before he went to Oxford there was a procession of girls through the house. You get to feel that even the title, *The Rachel Papers*, involves something close to modest self-deprecation given that I doubt if he could recall the names of his numerous conquests – Abigail, Jenny, Petra, Clarissa, Joan – I'm probably making them up – there were so many, but it's amusing to contrast Martin's busy lifestyle with Charles's apparent preoccupation with a particular girl.' Howard's use of 'apparent' is perceptive. Certainly Charles does not present himself as a rake, obsessed with Rachel only because she is the one female who appears immune to his charm, but this is more a matter of omission than probability. Rachel presents an oblique, arbitrary challenge and his desire for her is fed as much by confidence in his own ability to command and persuade as by such vagaries as sex or affection. Martin finds in Nabokov 'a certain Parnassian triumphalism' with the coda that this is a failing he greatly admires. Charles, like Nabokov, is unapologetic.

The parallels between Martin's and Kingsley's first novels are tempting and misleading. Dixon finds himself among a cabal of figures who are by equal degrees loathsome and farcical. We feel they are fully deserving of punishment by satire and that Jim's vituperative aspect will subside once he is among friends, notably Christine and someone like the reader who has laughed along with him and shared his fantasies for the duration of the novel. To admit that we like Charles, perhaps even envy his manipulative hypocrisy, is something that most of us would do only in private. Equally, few of us would dare articulate our abhorrence for him to anyone but ourselves for fear of seeming naïve or sanctimonious; he is, after all, only an invention.

Did Martin feel that Jim Dixon was sitting at his shoulder as he created Charles Highway? 'Obviously both were "coming of age" novels, and there was some of us in each of them [Charles and Jim].'

John Gross, then editor of the *TLS*, and guest at one of the numerous, informal gatherings at Lemmons, asked Martin if he had any interest in a full-time junior post. He did but asked if the appointment could be deferred for about six months. Did you explain why? 'No, I didn't. I don't think I was asked.' He was finishing his novel, still living at Lemmons and making occasional contributions to household expenses by putting in part-time hours first at an exclusive art gallery in Mayfair ('Very exclusive. On average one customer per day'), next as a trainee copywriter at the J. Walter Thompson Advertising Agency ('I was only there for a month or two') and occasionally in Colin Howard's electrical repair shop in Rickmansworth. Colin Howard: 'Oh yes. He did at least one day per month. He appeared busy with other things but he was simply taking time off from his real, if unofficial, occupation in the room above Kingsley. He spoke rarely of what he was doing but everyone knew and he was relentless, dedicated.' He began work officially at the *TLS* in March 1972 but he had already reviewed books for the *Daily Telegraph*, the *Observer* and the *Spectator*.

A contract for *The Rachel Papers* had been drawn up with Cape a month later after Kingsley's agent, Pat Kavanagh and Cape's chief commissioning editor Tom Maschler had dined at Lemmons. Both asked when he was likely to finish his novel, which he claims to find puzzling since he had not mentioned it to either of them. Of the jokes which circulated during Martin's period at the *New Statesman*, the most widely recalled involved the answer to a competition on who could come up with the unlikeliest book title. The winner, unanimously, was *Martin Amis: My Struggle*.

He left Lemmons in December 1972 shortly after delivering the final draft of *The Rachel Papers* and beginning work at the *TLS*. He shared a maisonette just off Pont Street, Belgravia with his old friend Rob Henderson and Rob's girlfriend Olivia. Rob had come into a modest inheritance, all of which he spent on the lease for the property ('He couldn't begin to afford to live there,' says Martin). Rob had now become a trainee film editor and apprentice set manager but his salary was largely unchanged. Rob and Martin would remain in close contact for the next two to three years, but the brief period in Belgravia marked something of a crossroads in their friendship. On the surface both appeared to have prospects, Martin among the literati with a contracted novel and a full-time job and Rob in film. But during Martin's period in Oxford those aspects of their temperaments that had secured the early friendship had evolved very differently. Unaccountability and irrational misbehaviour had for Martin become subordinate to a taste for control; matters he could by equal degrees contemplate and relish were no longer his animus or mood. Colin Howard remembers Rob at this stage as both unnerving and tragic. 'He and Martin both misbehaved when they used to hang around together during the Maida Vale years, but for Rob this gradually became more like dependency which, plus alcohol and drugs, could have unpleasant effects. He was once arrested for attacking his mother and although he was too slight of build to do anyone serious damage he could be alarming. I didn't know him that well but it was evident that he and Martin were growing apart, not that they quarrelled, as far as I know. I suspect that for his own sake, though, Martin began to keep him at arm's length.'

He was also, by now, beginning to mix with a very different set. His most enduring friendship has been with Christopher Hitchens, aka Hitch, and although they had overlapped at Oxford they first began to socialize regularly when Martin was completing *The Rachel Papers*.

Hitchens: 'You could tell that there was a shimmer of danger about him [Rob]. He got drunk quickly and very menacingly. I knew that he behaved badly to at least two girls who wouldn't sleep with him – this was when he was still with Olivia. Not nice at all. You could say that he was Martin's "low life guy" – he always liked to keep in touch with someone or something nasty and downmarket, and by the time I got to know Martin, Rob was in steep descent. And I think I deposed him as Mart's intimate – we'd talk about everything from the quality of women to our families. What cemented our friendship was the death of my mother. Martin didn't know her but the letter he sent me was far more sincere than anything else I received at the time. I wish I still had it.'

Martin: 'We didn't "first meet" at a particular place or time, but in my couple of years at the *TLS*, three or four men began to spend time together.' Clive James, apparently, gave the impression of having *lived*. He dressed in standard early-seventies gear – low-slung denims and leathers, notably – and looked like an extra from *Easy Rider*. He had only been in London for three years, but he seemed a generation ahead of the rest. 'He could be the funniest,' recalls Martin. 'I'd met Hitchens and James Fenton in Oxford but got to know them properly in 1972 or '73. I also met Julian [Barnes]. Most worked on the Staggers [*New Statesman*].'

The contrast between his new associates and Rob, who was frequently coming to remind him of the state of hapless inertia to which barely four years earlier they had both consigned themselves, influenced his decision to leave the Belgravia maisonette after less than a year. Shortly before he moved there was, however, time for a party. Martin explains the 'launch' of *The Rachel Papers*: 'That's the way it was in those days. A minority-interest field. All quiet. This was the seventies – no readings, no interviews, no parties. I gave the launch party myself.' Odd then that he should also recall, barely a fortnight later, a man of about his own age on the tube, holding a copy of his novel and shaking with laughter; not to mention the avalanche of reviews which had praised the emergence of a new unsparing satirist. 'Well,' he adds, 'it sold only fifteen hundred copies.' He does, in *Experience*, refer to one review, his worst, ironically by Peter Prince in the *New Statesman*, in which he is accused of indulging a tasteless schoolboyish brand of humour. The rest were unflinchingly complimentary, and it is a credit to the fair-mindedness of contemporary reviewers that none dwelt upon his family connection. Even Peter Ackroyd, tireless scourge of anything vaguely conventional, enjoyed this piece of mordant readability. Aside from Martin himself, eleven people attended the launch party: the Amis siblings, Philip and Sally, Martin's newest and soon to be most regular acquaintances, Hitchens and Clive James, Pat Kavanagh, the other residents Rob and Olivia, and Kingsley, accompanied by his old friend and mentor Bob Conquest.

Hitchens: 'God, yes, the launch. The flat, Belgravia somewhere, was comfortable enough, a little drab – though the places I kept at the time were probably much, much worse. There was some champagne, malt whisky from Kingsley I think, all manner of other poisons. Everyone was drunk very quickly. Martin said a few words and I chatted up his sister. We then slept together. No one felt this worth commenting upon. In retrospect, and given Sally's fate, there was something tragic about her. We were the last to leave the flat and I think that if it hadn't been me she would have gone with absolutely anyone. Very sad. I think it was company, even protection, she was looking for, not sex.'

Of the revellers as a whole it would be difficult to imagine a more unlikely combination of affinities and inclinations. Conquest in works such as *The Great Terror* was responsible for exposing to the liberal intelligentsia of Europe and the US the tyranny of Communism in practice and the gigantic scale of Stalin's genocide while Kingsley, in his Conservative Party pamphlet *Lucky Jim's Politics* (1968) had declared similarly that left-wing ideology was by its nature authoritarian. Hitchens was an unapologetic disciple of Trotsky, avowing that the drawbacks of Socialism in one country could be rectified only by global revolution and Communism for all. Clive James was his raffishly liberal associate, rather like Kingsley to Conquest. Martin was, at this point, enthusiastically indifferent but if pressed would probably have confessed to being centre-left.

Clive James: 'At the time of the launch I was spending a fair amount of time with Ian Hamilton of the *New Review*, as well as doing some work for the *Statesman*. It was a small group of people who in other circumstances would have had little reason to spend time together drinking, but that was Martin for you. It would be wrong to say he was the cause of unlikely friendships, but, well, perhaps he was. It was difficult to imagine how Hitch, Fenton, even Clive James, could have ended up as mates of Kingsley and his fellow Tories. Martin was the common factor. If you enjoy wit, sharpness, you forget

divisions. So maybe that night launched more than the novel.'
By midnight everyone was too drunk to recall how the evening
ended. Most took breakfast and lunch together and the fact that
Hitchens and Sally had shared a bed at the nearby Cadogan
Hotel was treated by her brother ('He only told me,' says
Martin) with polite amusement; he had almost been admitted
to the family. Martin recalls the evening with distracted
affection – 'Well, of course, I was happy about the novel. And
the next day we got together for lunch' – and there is a prescient
similarity between the launch party and Martin's journey
through the rest of what he calls 'the joke decade'. He was
usually at the centre of everything, emerging largely unaltered,
the cause of the event but not really *there*.

Little more than a fortnight later he moved west from
Belgravia to what was called a 'mansion flat' in one of the once
grand, late-Victorian terraces between Earl's Court and Crom-
well Road. 'Which', he adds, 'I shared with seven or eight
others. I had one room.' The £250 advance from Cape for *The
Rachel Papers* seems modest by today's standards but in the
early 1970s it was generous for a debut novel. Maschler's
estimation of his own critical acumen was grossly inflated but
he was adept at fostering new literary talent. He could spot a
marketable product and Pat Kavanagh, now Martin's agent,
had no difficulty in negotiating the advance, plus a favourable
deal on royalties and a contract with Cape for his second novel
prior to his first going into print. In the light of his relative
financial security his choice of a flat, indeed a street – called
appropriately Hogarth Road – that seemed to conserve aspects
of London from Patrick Hamilton's *Hangover Square* is
amusing.

Earl's Court at the turn of the 1960s was made up of mostly
white arrivistes from the Commonwealth, particularly Austra-
lians, and a bathetic scattering of the ailing bourgeoisie now

obliged to share their century-old terraces with bohemians, bankrupts and others who had known or hoped for better times. Socially and culturally the area was exquisitely baroque. The semi-retired general practitioner on the ground floor was, thinks Martin, the only occupant with some familial link with the building. They shared little more than the occasional greeting or brief exchange but the thought that this individual still dealt with patients somewhere else in London conjured up images both macabre and engrossing. He spent most of his hours doing little beyond carrying around half-empty bottles of spirits and fortified wines while dressed only in his filthy unbelted dressing gown and billowing grey Y-fronts. Tramps, also with bottles, repaired often to the foot of the basement steps but appeared only slightly less dishevelled than the other tenants.

The term 'sock' was Tina Brown's invention (though often, wrongly, attributed to Hitchens) but its inspiration came from Martin's rooms in Earl's Court where he would live for almost two years. Francis Wheen, who worked both with Martin and Hitchens on the *New Statesman* reflects: 'There was probably a slight hint of raillery in this. Hitch's own places in the mid-1970s were pretty dire but they suited his habits and his politics. With Martin, well, he seemed to take a certain morbid pleasure in hanging around among those who would most likely appear in his work as grotesques. Slumming, I suppose.' Whatever private indulgences were served by his fascination with living testaments to failure and degradation, their effects on his fiction are self-evident. The work that would eventually become *Dead Babies* was begun in Oxford, alongside his early drafts of *The Rachel Papers*. The latter subsequently occupied his attention for the simple reason that much of the narrative could be picked from experience; it was his obvious first novel. The former, however, was made up of a series of ghostly vignettes. Some were based on people he knew but in Martin's version the constitutional constraints, which tempered their more distressing or ghastly features, had been removed, revealing a cast of figures in various stages of nihilistic self-destruction. He states in *Experience* that the idea for the novel germinated in the anarchic assembly of the individuals with whom he shared a house in his third year at Oxford, but there is evidence that it drew inspiration from periods before that, partly Madingley Road but sometimes also from his shady London experiences. Colin Howard provides a vivid account of Martin's friends and associates from his profligate pre-Oxford years. 'Si was without doubt the most peculiar of that set. I only ever met him on one or two occasions and for a long period we supposed that he didn't really exist, a running practical joke by Mart. He would tell us long deadpan stories of what Si had got up to that day, or rather failed to get up to since he seemed hardly sentient, having taken or smoked anything available. The phone calls were, we thought, too hilarious to be true, brilliantly choreographed cameos. The phone would ring and he'd ask Martin for the address of Vanessa or someone. Martin would go to the address book and begin to read it out very slowly: "It's 38, yes 38, Crox . . . ton Road" – he'd enunciate every syllable carefully – "Just off . . ." Then we'd hear the dialtone and a couple of minutes later the phone would ring again and Martin would answer, "Vanessa, yes. Yes, she does live at 38 Croxton Road . . . But Si, why are you telling me this? *You* asked for *her* address." It was excellent entertainment but we assumed that someone so raddled with drugs was too bizarre to be credible. Until we met him, of course. It was curious because via Martin poor old Si was superbly entertaining. In person he was sad, tragic.' Martin describes him slightly differently. 'Well off. Very languid. He's a painter now. And clean.' He is defensive, perhaps uncomfortable at having made use of his friend for fiction, when he was more vulnerable and far less 'clean'.

Turn to Chapter 9 of *Dead Babies* in which the gin-soaked Giles Coldstream receives a phone call from his mother:

'Ah, no, now, today *isn't* a good day, actually. Oh, I've got lots of things I must do. Jolly busy indeed. And tomorrow, do you see, is Sunday, and one can't very well – If it were *Satur*day tomorrow then nothing would be simpler than to ... Are you sure?' Giles muffled the receiver and looked up groggily at Celia. 'Today wouldn't be Friday, would it? Oh dear.' He contemplated the telephone unhappily. 'What? Yes, mother, you were right.'[3]

'Yes,' says Colin Howard, 'that is most certainly Si.' Giles also incorporates a hint of authorial self-caricature, given that when he does find it possible to marshal his disintegrating faculties he is preoccupied exclusively with one subject: the state of his teeth.

Sargy Mann recalls that Rob Henderson often outdid even Martin as a poseur. 'They all wore the most fashionable clothes available. Purple velvet trousers, flowered shirts with enormous collars, dandified cowboy boots come to mind, but Rob carried himself with a kind of arrogant disdain, masculine but self-consciously pretty also. I know the comparison might not seem apt but he reminded me of the Great Gatsby, albeit a teenage, drugged version. He was incredibly amusing, and he had a reckless disregard for anything formal and conventional – I think this was fed by contempt for his prep school and public school background – but when you were with him you always suspected that something terrible and precipitate was about to occur.' Colin Howard agrees and adds, 'Gatsby, yes. Plus Jekyll and Hyde. He was self-destructive and dangerous, violent, to others. He could swing from being affable to psychotic for no evident reason.' When I first spoke to Sargy and Colin neither knew that Rob was dead. Both were saddened, but not at all surprised by the news. 'I suppose he epitomized the worst aspects of that period, uninhibited, hedonistic but not really content. Disaster was always not far from Rob.'

The characters in *Dead Babies* are hybridized versions of their actual counterparts. It would indeed be an insult to Martin's sleight of hand to expect otherwise. Yet with the more enthralling of them a particular imprint predominates and Rob finds his way into the book via Andy Adorno. As his surname indicates Andy is a magnificent specimen of highly sexed manhood, a living Adonis. He is also given to casual acts of violence, which for the women further enhances his attraction. I ask Martin if Rob was on his mind as the figure of Andy evolved. 'Rob came from a déclassé, establishment family. Andy is, was, working-class but makes himself classless by force of personality. And while Andy is sculptural, forbidding, Rob was about five foot seven and very slight. But let's put it this way, Andy was what Rob might have wanted to be.' Martin adds, 'You have to remember that it takes a long time, a very long time for a [fictional] character to mature. They might pick up things from one, two real people but once they reach the novel they have a life of their own.'

By the time he was writing regularly for the *New Statesman* Martin had begun to evolve in his non-fictional prose a stylistic temper that both reflected his personality and provided a neat counterpoint to his novels. But in the intervening period when he was preparing *Dead Babies* the contrast between him as creator of such grotesques as Keith and Andy and the demands of his day job at the *TLS* was notable and faintly amusing.

One of his earliest *TLS* reviews was of a selection of

Coleridge's verse edited by William Empson and David Pirie, which included a monograph-length introduction by Empson. To his credit Martin includes it in *The War Against Cliché* along with a footnote confessing that following Empson's letter to his editor (Arthur Crook), he, as 'Our Reviewer' had replied in print, apologetically. In the review he had accused Empson of transgressing the dated mantra of W. K. Wimsatt and Monroe Beardsley's 1946 essay 'The Intentional Fallacy', which derided the assumption that a poem, like a letter or an essay, contains a particular message. He adds, 'The apology was, principally, for a serious factual error.' He had his First, but he had yet to test his abilities in the world where ideas were no substitutes for insight. It would be four months before *The Rachel Papers* went into print, and Sargy Mann offers a very shrewd observation on Martin during these transformative years. 'What you have to remember is that unlike his father, who'd had a very orthodox, classical education, virtually from infancy, Martin became an autodidact and went from nowhere to an Oxford First in little more than three years. It was an extraordinary achievement, and reflected his natural intelligence and determination. At the same time I sometimes sensed that he felt slightly nervous, especially when his own set, Hitch, Fenton, sometimes Clive James and Julian Barnes, would come over to Lemmons. Kingsley himself was actually a shy man but once he started talking about matters he knew well, he was in his element; he held court. When they were all together it was frighteningly competitive and Martin was as sharp and erudite as anyone. But still – and maybe I'm wrong – you sensed that he was trying just a bit harder than the rest, perhaps conscious of the fact that, well, in simple terms, he'd started later than all of them, had a lot to make up for.'

His confidence was boosted when in autumn 1973 *The Rachel Papers* won him the Somerset Maugham Prize, which his father had been awarded for *Lucky Jim*. Colin Howard: 'Kingsley was delighted, and amused. I can't recall his exact words, but something like "Good that it's back in the family. It should keep the old prig turning in his grave."' Maugham, the award's patron, was alive in 1954 but an impartial panel of judges decided on its recipient. Kingsley's reference is to a *Sunday Times* article published several months after the panel's decision in which Maugham treated *Lucky Jim* as symptomatic of an imminent social and moral apocalypse.

Unlike *Lucky Jim*, the novel did not generate newspaper profiles of its author. Nonetheless, Martin was now shifting from a point in the literary in-crowd granted chiefly by association to one touched by genuine promise. It was this that earned him the attention of Tina Brown, an undergraduate at Oxford.

Debs' balls, weekends at the estate, Ascot and so on had since the 1950s become defunct or anachronistic as routes to social or sexual advancement, but the golden triangle of London and Oxbridge retained some magnetism even for scions of the conscience-ridden, Labour-voting middle classes. In *Experience* Martin presents Tina Brown as a late-twentieth-century Zuleika Dobson.

> As an undergraduate Tina was already famous (and this at a time when *no one* was famous): fringe playwright, journalist, looker, prodigy. To get to her room in college I would have to step over waiting TV crews, inter-viewers, profilists.[4]

In the summer of 1973 when *The Rachel Papers* came out Tina was nineteen, a second year at St Anne's, and Martin's description of her is certainly not hyperbole. That autumn, at the beginning of her third year, she won the Sunday Times

Drama Award for her one-act *Under the Bamboo Tree* and the Peckenham Award for Best Young Female Journalist. As well as contributing to *Isis* she had already written articles for the *New Statesman* and the *Sunday Times*, which would employ her on a freelance basis as soon as she graduated in 1974. Her father, George Hambley Brown, had made a small fortune from producing popular British films in the 1950s and 1960s, including the Miss Marple series starring Margaret Rutherford, and her mother had been Laurence Olivier's confidante and press agent. George's first marriage, in 1939, to Maureen O'Hara, had been brief and well publicized. Martin, understandably, is guarded about the exact nature of their affair, which lasted slightly less than a year, but his description of its effect is revealing. 'Before I met her I was beginning to understand what it must have been like to be Philip Larkin. A sense of grubbiness and exclusion, a combination of desire and resigned failure that women intuit and stay away from. Tina got that scent off me, gave me confidence. She banished that spell.'

While the comparison between him and Larkin sounds absurd – Martin was already a practised and effective seducer – Tina represented both a special challenge and an alluring prospect. Her background, combined with her good looks – 'compelling' is the term most of her acquaintances reach for – and self-confidence were impressive enough but they alone do not account for the effect she had on, mostly male, denizens of Oxford and London in the early 1970s. Zuleika, by comparison, was predictable. At the beginning of her second year Dudley Moore's chauffeur-driven limousine drew up outside St Anne's and Moore asked the porter to deliver a message to Miss Brown. Moore had never even seen a photograph of her but she had already achieved legendary status among the London social and cultural circuit. They began an affair the same day. Next in line was Auberon 'Bron' Waugh. Like Moore, Waugh arrived in Oxford unannounced, with no previous introduction and their relationship too began almost instantaneously. The weekend after they first met he invited her down to the Somerset manor house, Combe Florey, where his father Evelyn had held court and where Bron now resided, with his wife. How exactly he accounted for his 'guest' goes unrecorded but the fact that she inspired such acts in otherwise conservative figures testifies to her potency.

She first met Martin during her second year at a party in London. They got on, but their relationship did not begin properly until 1973 after Martin had published *The Rachel Papers*. Although he would not be taken on as a full-time salaried correspondent for the *New Statesman* until the end of that year he was already doing reviews and filing articles, notably as the pseudonymous researcher into pornography, Bruno Holbrook. Waugh, who according to Anthony Howard was 'still besotted with her despite her now being with Martin', also did occasional pieces for the *New Statesman*, though he was better known for his savage caricatures of the great and flamboyant in *Private Eye*. He persuaded Howard, then literary editor, to consider some articles by a 'brilliant' Oxford student (she would in fact get a very ordinary second). Howard, when first approached was one of the few people in London never to have heard of her. He consulted Martin who still had contacts in the university, and who did indeed know Miss Brown, rather well, and had dined once or twice at her parents' charming sixteenth-century house in Little Marlow. Howard's concern about her abilities as a journalist were quickly sidelined by Martin's portrait of her quixotic character and magnetism, which he provided without disclosing his personal involvement. 'It seemed', recalled Howard, 'like something from Tony Richardson's film of *Moll Flanders*.' So he commissioned her, first to do a piece on the Oxford and Cambridge Boat Race ('On the River', 8 June 1973), followed by an account of the festival of vulgar hedonism that had allegedly become a feature of the once select resorts on the Spanish Mediterranean coast. The result was 'On the Beach' (17 August 1973). Martin plays up his anxious unsuitability and Tina's magic because he is reluctant to admit that both of them, when they met, felt an equal sense of egotistic gratification. The 'grubbiness' had nothing to do with him but it was an accurate description of the state of England in the early 1970s, a country in a state of social, political and cultural inertia. 'Yes,' reflects Colin Howard, 'they did seem to come across as sublime alternatives to widespread drabness. Mind you, Mart treated it all with customary irony. Kingsley too. He [Kingsley] was most impressed by Tina. He liked her but I don't think he could quite take her seriously. She had insisted that Martin should be formally introduced to her parents, at tea at a rather grand hotel, and she was one of the few female visitors to Lemmons who felt confident enough to join in with the generally male-only exchanges, with Kingsley and Mart holding court. She was indulged, let us say, with amused fascination. She could indeed be unintentionally humorous. She telephoned once after a weekend at the house. I was alone there, answered and without asking who I was she said, "Is Martin there?" I replied he was not. "Well, what about Kingsley?" Sadly no. "Jane?" No, not Jane. There was a long pause. "Is *anybody* there?" We had met on a couple of occasions but I replied the house was empty, I was merely a disembodied presence, and I replaced the receiver. Her manner could be stentorian, especially for a twenty-year-old. Martin loved the story.'

One cannot ignore the resemblances between Tina and Diana Parry of *Dead Babies*. 'Diana's background may not in itself be illustrious, but it has an unquestionable lustre. Always she has mingled with the great.'[5] Like Tina's, Diana's experience of

115

wealth and high celebrity is built as much upon proxy and association as direct involvement. Their respective fathers work in the film industry, Tina's as a producer and Diana's as assistant chief casting director of Magnum Cinematic Promotions Ltd. Eleanor, Diana's mother, functions as an intermediary between the lives of the fashionably rich and those who wish to read about them, filing copy for 'Nell's Notebook' in the distinguished glossy *Euroscene*, an occupation not unlike that of Bettina Bohr, who skilfully choreographed media representations of Olivier and his set. Diana had a troubled school career – not unlike Tina who was expelled from two prestigious girls' schools – and on one occasion Eleanor feels it necessary to apologize to the parents of a fellow pupil: 'Then Bettina's *your* child. Oh dear. I'm afraid Diana must pester her dreadfully.'[6] The clues are proffered and playfully refashioned as a tentative signal of what would soon become his literary trademark.

Martin baulks at the idea that real people find their way unaltered into his fiction. 'From *The Rachel Papers* on I've never really written a naïve novel in the sense that the action is presented as actually happening, there's always a playful element, or a more than usually animated narrator hovering around.' By this he means that a second filter is always present, ensuring that anything that might be mistaken for a naturalistic, even autobiographical frame is distorted. Nevertheless, he does not wholly reject the notion of the playful, animated narrator being stimulated by raw material from the world of Martin Amis. Hitchens describes him as a 'meticulous observer', a 'collector' of foibles and minutiae. Martin adds, 'It's serendipitous. Phrases, images, anything that hangs around in my memory for a while can get in [to fiction].' But how does he select it for refashioning by the playful narrator? 'It must resonate with some experience. It has to make me ask, "What's it still doing in my mind?"' It therefore seems not unreasonable to assume that fragments of his experience with Rob and Tina, among others, will resurface in *Dead Babies*. Martin was not, of course, invoking parallels between the lifestyle and dreadful fate of the Appleseeders and those of people he knew. Fiction writing is not as straightforward as that.

Academic critics have routinely described Martin as a postmodernist, a writer who fidgets self-consciously with the processes of writing fiction, the most obvious example of this being the appearance of the somewhat gnomic writer Martin Amis in *Money*. This classification, like most of the tireless routines of academe, is lazy and misleading. Martin is not accountable to an 'ism'. His novels, indeed the very act of writing novels, unsettle him as much as they do the reader and in this respect he has more in common with Kingsley's closest friend Larkin than he does with his father. Larkin's verse contains kernels of self-loathing, depression, nihilism that, elsewhere, would be taken as evidence of imminent nervous collapse or at least the signs of an anti-social saturnine temperament. But his genius is affirmed by an ability to make beautiful poems from fragments of his personality. So too with Martin. Except that the novel is a mechanism quite different from the poem. For one thing fiction is crowded with characters who, like us, seem to have pasts, irritable and deniable compulsions, distracted ambitions. People Martin knew, knew well, fascinated him in a manner that was humane and sympathetic, yet at the same time he speculated on how they privately felt and perceived themselves. In his 1970s novels, he borrowed from them and left notes in the fabric of his work, but later he would begin to contemplate a far more complex dilemma, one that involved the prospect of accountability: with the writer as master of the characters' fate, yet hesitant – even regretful – in his actions.

A condition of the Somerset Maugham Award is that the prize money should be spent on a substantial period abroad. Its eponymous sponsor believed that all British writers, like himself, coveted the imaginative enlightenment promised by foreign parts. The farce visited upon Kingsley by this is recorded in his novel *I Like It Here*, an undisguised act of vengeance against his experience of a summer with his family in Portugal. Martin elected to visit a region once cherished by British and US bohemians and now attracting more profitable if less culturally ambitious visitors: southern Spain. He was fascinated by the anomalous combination of a military dictatorship which predated the Second World War and Blackpool-on-the-Mediterranean and he intended to spend much of the summer of 1974 with his mother and her new partner, Ali Boyd.

The language school which Hilly and Boyd hoped would provide a regular and respectable income had been an ambitious project, involving the leasing of property for classes in Seville, and had effectively gone bankrupt in 1971. They concentrated their remaining resources in Ronda, opening their handsome townhouse to paying guests and running art classes there. This lasted less than six months and by the time Martin arrived they had converted their basement into a bar and tapas restaurant.

Indulged by a relaxed hierarchy at the *TLS* Martin was allowed to draw his salary during his Maugham-sponsored sabbatical and Hilly persuaded Boyd to let him have, rent-free, a self-contained studio in the *palacio* adjacent to the main house with an airy sitting room overlooking the courtyard. Here he would spend two months working full time on finishing *Dead Babies* and have the novel ready for submission to Cape on his return to London in the autumn. When he arrived in Ronda the book was made up of a series of vignettes, individuals in settings that contemporary readers would find both familiar and nightmarish. His problem was of how to come up with a shaping trajectory or theme; without either, these miniatures would proceed with little purpose, an arbitrary patchwork of short stories. Spain, to his surprise, indicated a solution.

Martin recalls his visit as sepia-tinted and mildly surreal. He knew something of his mother and father's life in Marriner's Cottage, outside Oxford, but only vicariously through family lore. He, then, had been the same age as his new half-brother Jaime, born the year before his arrival, in 1973. Although in early middle age Hilly and Ali seemed to have taken on the busy, chaotic lifestyle of newlyweds (they would not actually marry for two years), lavishing attention upon the newborn and struggling with chaotic finances. 'Obviously,' muses Martin, 'I felt as though I was being shown a revised version of the past, events that had already shaped the lives of quite a few people, my own included.' His most enduring memory of his time there was when he and Hilly encountered Rafael, a convivial cripple, 'a spastic', in the main square. They were evidently on first-name terms. 'After he'd hobbled away, she turned to me and said, "I'm at home here. I love living in Spain. I now regard him as completely normal." She was forty-five but seemed like someone my age.' Was she happy? I ask him. 'With Ali, yes. He was the other love of her life. She sometimes worried a little about Jaime. Largely though, she was euphoric.'

Although neither Hilly nor Ali Boyd is even remotely connected with the characters in *Dead Babies*, the dreadful momentum of the narrative drew its impetus from Martin's period in Ronda. Seeing his mother projected back a quarter of a century prompted questions. Mainly, what would happen next? Of course he knew exactly what had happened in the first version. That had reached some kind of conclusion, involving Madingley Road. Could one person be held responsible for what happens to the others caught in the same web of events?

Martin certainly does not and did not then think of his father as wicked. 'Weak, vulnerable, capricious, but he meant no one any harm.' The fact was, however, that the people in his personal orbit were harmed. It is only in Part Three of *Dead Babies*, barely 1,500 words in length, that we learn that Johnny and The Hon. Quentin Villiers are the same person. The disclosure is as beguiling as a skilfully executed card trick: what once seemed an assembly of coincidences is suddenly revealed to be predetermined. The question which the novel leaves unanswered, indeed unaddressed, is how and why seemingly the most humane, cultivated figure in the book should turn out to be its most terrifying. Colin Howard: 'Kingsley was a lovely man, extraordinarily hospitable. Yes, certainly. But on occasions he could be cruel, very cruel. Even to those closest to him.' Which was closer to the real Kingsley Amis? 'That was the point. Both aspects of him were the real Kingsley Amis.'

5

The Seventies

While the 1960s are recollected by most with nostalgia or indifference, the 1970s tend to provoke embarrassment. Political and economic mismanagement, seemingly endless strikes, football hooliganism, crass popular culture – particularly in music and fashion – and the rise of the package tour all come to mind. As a decade it is by consensus a medley of the tasteless, the shambolic and clumsily hedonistic. Martin's experiences after *The Rachel Papers* were, however, enviable and would leave an indelible imprint upon his work.

Within a year of beginning his salaried junior post at the *TLS* he was filing copy for the *New Statesman*. The literary editor John Gross and deputy editor Anthony Howard were almost a generation older than Martin and they detected in him the same sort of energy that had prompted them to appoint Hitchens and Fenton, his near contemporaries at Oxford, something that would improve on the rather stern puritanical image of the magazine as the conscience of post-war Fabianism. Howard: 'We had asked Martin to think about a series of articles on what it was like to do jobs in central London, the sort of manual work that went on beneath the surface of the West End. I suppose the suggestion, inadvertently, contributed to the birth of a legend, given that "Coming in Handy" [14 December 1973] was his best-known piece.' Martin had stuck to the remit of his commission, but only just. The workers were those who serviced the booming pornography industry of Soho and the West End, and 'Coming in Handy' is a laconic survey of the new sub-genre of monthlies dedicated exclusively to photographs of naked women, perused, generally in solitude, by men. His title, of course, requires no elucidation. Martin produced three pieces, including accounts of strip clubs and call-girl agencies (see 'Fleshpots', 14 September 1973), under the pseudonym of Bruno Holbrook. This was carefully chosen. David Holbrook, poet and guardian of public morality, had contributed a vigorous anti-pornography chapter to *Pornography: The Longford Report* (1972), berating the *New Statesman* and similar left-leaning publications for conniving in the growth of the filth industry. To add authenticity Martin included a note beneath his byline: 'Bruno Holbrook is at present engaged in a study of Wayland Young' (author of *Eros Denied: Sex in Western Society*, 1964). Soon, speculation was rife as to the identity of the mysterious Bruno. Was he a relative of David, pornography being by implication a family interest? If Martin's creation had come across as a ranting puritan or even a louche apologist for men's magazines and strip clubs, he could have been dismissed as a spoof – the first wave of anti-establishment satire driven by *Private Eye* and *That Was The Week That Was* had after all only recently broken – but Bruno was much more effective, and for David Holbrook and those similarly inclined, infuriating. He is a figure who treats his subject with a certain amount of rueful distaste but more powerful than this is his sense of sexual connoisseurship: he assesses the relative quality of the material on offer and treats the customers as far more pitiable than the strippers and nude models. I, he implies, am content with an abundance of the real thing. And how prescient, for Bruno's creator, this would prove to be.

Before examining the literary and intellectual controversies that beset Martin during the 1970s it would perhaps be best to first offer a brief summary of his love life. The two narratives are intertwined and an appreciation of the former can only benefit from a preliminary account of the latter.

In a sardonic review of a book by Robert Bly[1] Martin ponders Bly's enthusiasm for 'male grandeur', for a revival of the seigneurial dominance that women love so much and which feminism, freakishly in Bly's opinion, had taken against. Martin does not need to undo Bly's thesis; rather he patrols its salient features and allows it to expose its preposterousness without his assistance. Nevertheless his piece does raise a question. Given that men have now been exposed as by turns unflinchingly repressive, predatory and self-absorbed, how should the more thoughtful members of this gender be best advised to behave in the continued dance to the music of sex? Such abstract hypotheses are of course difficult to take seriously without giving some consideration to particulars. If the male in question is an outstandingly ugly, tongue-tied dwarf then it does not really matter too much about how he behaves towards women with whom he might recently have become, or wish to be, acquainted. Most of them simply would not want to know. (This, I should add, is not an image conjured from my morbid imagination. Rather it derives from Gully Wells's witheringly vivid evocation of 'Z', the most pitiable tenant at 'The Old Forge' who stood as she puts it 'in cruel contrast to the handsome double act of Martin and Rob, as they never tired of reminding him'.) And so to Martin who, despite his faux-modest claims to the contrary, was possessed of effortless charm, even in his pre-Oxford years. Like most he did not live according to a conscious ordinance, but during the 1970s there is remarkable consistency in his behaviour, at least with regard to the women with whom he had relationships. Tamasin Day-Lewis was eighteen when her father, terminally ill, and mother moved into Lemmons in 1970. Jane Howard, despite having had an affair with C. Day-Lewis in the 1950s, remained a close friend of the poet and his wife Jill and offered the spacious house as a peaceful setting for his imminent demise. When Tamasin first met Martin he was still seeing Gully Wells but Gully was an occasional visitor, not always present when Tamasin stayed over at weekends. Colin Howard and Sargy Mann recall the liaison with wry amusement. Howard: 'Tammy was a terrific flirt but we didn't know anything was actually going on, at least at the time. I think Martin dropped a hint after it was all over. He probably kept it quiet because he was juggling trysts with Tammy against Gully's weekend visits. Such energy.' Frances Mann adds: 'Of course, the slightly macabre cameo in *Experience* where Martin describes them [himself and Tamasin] standing in the room with [Colin's] mother's body was wrong. It must have been Day-Lewis himself, since your mother outlived him by a couple of years.' 'Yes,' adds Howard, 'I wonder why he did that?'

During the week Tamasin divided her time between a pre-university London crammer and modelling assignments. Her combination of girlish innocence and sexual allure was the essence of the late-sixties/early-seventies media and advertising stereotype. She resembled Twiggy. According to Colin Howard she, at least in 1970, 'made the advances'. Martin responded as would most twenty-one-year-old men, but postponed a proper, albeit brief, relationship until after he had separated from Gully and his affair with Tamasin took place as he was finishing *The Rachel Papers* in Lemmons during 1972. According to Gully,

'He had his cake and ate it', but she does not intend this as a rebuke. He did, but he also tried to ensure that the untidy overlaps between his various encounters caused minimal discomfort for all involved. 'Even before he became a literary celebrity,' adds Colin Howard, 'women wanted him.'

In mid-June 1974 Tina Brown hosted a graduation party – for her own graduation – at her college's boathouse, involving a generous spread of expensive canapés, champagne, gin- and vodka-based cocktails, plus a small band. Martin was present, and from the London circuit Anthony Howard, Auberon Waugh, Anthony Holden, Hitchens and several other figures were also in attendance. Martin and Tina were still involved albeit informally but he did not mention to her that three months earlier he had begun an affair with Julie Kavanagh, twenty-one-year-old London editor of the US *Women's Wear Daily*; not the most prestigious publication and one whose title brings to mind the interests of male magazine purchasers depicted by Holbrook. She did, however, persuade her bosses that the readership, women of course, would be interested in a piece on London's newest novelist who bore a remarkable resemblance to Mick Jagger. She wrote the article without an interview but Martin and Julie met soon afterwards at one of the parties where, according to Hitch, 'I held the coats while Mart paired himself off with whoever was available, or on some occasions available while attached to someone else. Don't get me wrong, all this on his part involved no sense of industry or exertion. They came to him. So my task was not at all time-consuming.' Martin impressed Ms Kavanagh with meals in Knightsbridge brasseries followed by brief encounters in a nearby but less fashionable part of West London, specifically the flat in Pont Street still occupied by Rob and Olivia, and their first full night together was spent in an agreeable Cotswold hotel, the Sign of the Angel in Lacock, Wiltshire. In late 1974

Julie took a flat in Hugon Road. Martin had virtually completed the final draft of *Dead Babies* during his period in Ronda that summer and had invited Julie over for a week to meet his mother and Ali Kilmarnock. Hilly got on well with her – she was, indeed, well disposed to every girlfriend of Martin's she encountered.

The Hugon Road flat proved useful in several ways. He completed the last revisions to the novel there in a state of relative comfort; he enjoyed the solitary life but he was averse to anything that involved cleaning or cooking, another trait he shared with his father. From November 1974 he became a semi-permanent co-resident and his occasional overnight absences were accounted for as visits to Lemmons. In truth, they just as frequently involved excursions to Earl's Court, where, almost a year after meeting Julie, he would begin assignations with his boss at the *New Statesman*, Claire Tomalin, the then literary editor. Tomalin was recently widowed. Her husband Nick was a journalist who was killed in 1973 by a Syrian shell while reporting the conflict in the Golan Heights. They kept a house in North London and one in Kent but her busy schedule of literary parties and book launches often meant that she stayed over in London. Anthony Howard: 'Well, Martin was certainly epicurean in his tastes, also eclectic. He seemed to enjoy the companionship of mature women as much as those just out of their teens. There was Claire [Tomalin] of course, but I recall a garden party at someone's house in London. Paul Johnson [a regular contributor to the *New Statesman*] and his wife were there and she and Martin were clearly involved in an exchange of confidences. Of course I can't say for certain if they were having an affair but everyone assumed they were.' Martin adds: 'They were wrong.' 'But what you must remember,' comments Howard, 'was that Martin was never – well, as far as I could gather – never the initiator, at least when he began affairs with married women, often of course when he himself was going out with someone. This does not make a saint of him, but any male who claims he would refuse such unsolicited opportunities is a liar.' Howard remembers one day in the *New Statesman* office when Tomalin pleaded with him to find a way to 'have Martin sent on some roving reporter assignment or moved to another part of the building'. It was not, Howard explains, that they could no longer work together – the affair had recently concluded, and both were 'sanguine, civilized enough about that' – but rather that she now felt particularly 'embarrassed by the fact that she had started it'.

Hitchens reinforces Howard's impression of Martin as more the recipient of female attention than sexual predator. 'Things happened to him,' according to his friend, 'but the rest of us had to strive. Everyone was promiscuous but, for most, sex at least involved preliminaries, flattery, persuasion, rhetoric and came as part of the package that women wanted.' Martin introduced Julie Kavanagh to what was becoming the most fashionable literary set since the war, based on a kernel of *New Statesman* writers but with no unifying aesthetic or political mantra. The mainstays were Martin, Christopher Hitchens, James Fenton, Craig Raine and Clive James. Julian Barnes was a laconic occasional, to be joined later in the 1970s by Ian McEwan. Anthony Holden – aka Tony Hardon – was the principal poker fetishist, nurturing Martin's enduring fascination with the game in which he had first been coached by Colin Howard and Sargy Mann during Kingsley's and Jane's periods abroad. Francis Wheen arrived in 1975 and the artery-clogging food and drink sessions at the Bursa kebab house in Theobald's Road were often attended by Kingsley and Robert Conquest. Terry Kilmartin and Anthony Howard sometimes followed the out-of-office excursions, rather as amused observers than die-hard revellers. The women included Tina Brown, at least until she began her relationship with Harold Evans of the *Sunday Times*, Claire Tomalin and Lorna Sage. Martin had a brief affair with Sage which took place while he was juggling his encounters with Claire Tomalin against his apparently long-term commitment to Julie Kavanagh, and still this commendable performance was not complete. His liaison with Sage occurred during the early summer of 1975 and lasted little more than a week. In January, Julie had purchased a spacious second-floor flat in fashionable Pimlico and Martin, already her occasional live-in lover, spent even longer periods there each week as co-resident. Julie would now host parties and through these he became more acquainted with another stratum of the London social circuit, one that offered an amusing contrast to the *New Statesman* crowd and, as he would soon find, much else too. Martin describes Julie's set as 'high bohemian'. They did not in the 1970s merit much media attention – the apparently imminent collapse of the economy seemed more significant – but they were none the less Sloanes before their time, made up of sons and daughters from that grey area between the gentry and the second-generation nouveaux riches, for whom the notion of 'class' was never actually referred to while its absence in others was self-evident. One of Julie's pals from her teens, Emma Soames, was a regular caller at the Pimlico flat. In fact, Julie introduced her to Martin in February 1975 at a drinks party at which backgammon sessions predominated. Martin confessed to complete ignorance of the game and Emma agreed to meet him for lunch the next day to teach him the rules, which they both knew was a rather spurious pretext for a date.

The heightening of tension between Kingsley and Jane became the warrant for Martin's occasional overnight absences, allegedly in Barnet. But his eventual split with Julie was not, as he had promised Emma, amicable. One afternoon in the flat he was engaged in a hushed conversation, assuming Julie to be in the next room. On discovering she was standing behind him he slammed down the receiver and a moment worthy of Noël Coward's dramaturgy followed, with them both staring at the telephone number of Emma Soames displayed on the open page of Julie's address book. 'Yes,' reflects Hitchens, 'sometimes his seeming talent for legerdemain belied a rather disorganized streak.' He was obliged to leave the flat that same evening after also admitting that he had been having an irregular affair with one of Julie's closest friends, Victoria Rothschild, heiress to the wealthy banking family, plus a couple of encounters with his old flame from the Oxford years, Gully Wells. The only transgression Julie Kavanagh knew of before that was, curiously, the most brief and, for Martin, the most consequential. The circumstances were almost identical to those in which Martin had met Julie except that at this party she accompanied him as his partner and soon found herself waiting with Hitchens while their friend seemed, as Martin now admits, to be 'exchanging whispers' with a woman neither of them knew. She was Lamorna Seale and while nothing occurred at the party they found a personal empathy and attraction, and they agreed to meet again. Their relationship would be fleeting and two years later he would learn of its consequences, a daughter called Delilah.

His affair with Emma Soames lasted through 1976 and 1977, during which he enjoyed, accompanied by Hitchens and on at least three occasions his father, the antithesis of his recently acquired taste for slumming in the most unsavoury regions of the capital. Specifically he visited the Soameses' country residence where her parents – her mother was Churchill's daughter – indulged the epicurean loucheness of their children including their accompanying parties of associates, friends, lovers et al. More will be said on this, but rather than risk losing focus upon Martin's Olympian endeavour I shall for the time being concentrate simply upon the figures who made up the narrative.

Martin ended the relationship with Emma Soames in late summer 1977. Earlier that same year, in the spring, he had encountered a young woman of the same generation as Emma, Julie, Gully and Tina. He noticed her – and she was charismatically noticeable – at some social event attended by the first two in the quartet but they did not have the opportunity to speak. During the summer, however, they met in a different context, specifically a lunch party made up largely of those associated with Ian Hamilton's recently formed weekly, the *New Review*. Some, like Jeremy Treglown, worked mainly for the *TLS* whose list of part-time female staff would by the 1980s come to resemble an antechamber for Martin's love life: the magazine would play a bit-part in his earliest encounters with his first wife, Antonia Phillips and his present one, Isabel Fonseca.

Mary Furness, daughter of the late Robert Furness, Bt of Little Shelford, Cambridgeshire, scion of county lower-gentry was, according to accounts from all the men who met her, the most captivating female of her generation. One has the impression that all of the women in Martin's life so far were by turns either in awe of him or at least suborned by his combination of wit and charm, and this went back as far as Gully to his pre-*Rachel Papers* days. This was not the case with Mary Furness. She was beautiful, but carelessly so; if she was aware of the effect her mere physical presence had upon men then she showed no conscious recognition of this knowledge. She was dark-haired, with a sharp facial bone structure, and slightly taller than Martin. He was smitten. Their relationship predated his break-up with Emma Soames by about a month and was effectively its cause; it endured thereafter for almost a year. The collapse of his first marriage and his subsequent life with Isabel Fonseca were well publicized but were far less gripping than his largely unreported time with Mary Furness. She was, in the words of Hitchens, 'outrageously sexual and forbidding too. She drove men mad, partly because of the way she looked and held herself and, more so, because she was their intellectual equal. She was not a feminist, not in the dogmatic sense, but she unmanned men and, without apparent exertion, caused them to want her more than anything else and this made them feel inferior.' I put it to Hitchens that she was the model for Nicola Six in *London Fields*, a book written ten years later. 'Oh, yes. There are many striking parallels.'

Kingsley was egalitarian in his dealings with Martin's girlfriends but in this case he remained, as Martin puts it, 'loyal to Emma'. Hitchens again: 'She [Mary] was very often nuts, completely off the wall, prone to breaking the crockery, enraged, calamitous and at the same time very impressive in her command of language, even when completely drunk. Imagine Martin or Kingsley undergoing a sex change, but retaining the essentials of their personality, with an extra dose of unpredictability. That was Mary.' It could not, of course, last. Opposites might attract but oppositional equals constitute an explosive mixture. 'It was', reports Hitchens, 'one of those affairs made up of extremities. He hated the idea of losing her. In fact he proposed marriage to her, the first time he ever did so to anyone. She turned him down. He was grief-stricken, then relieved. It was a fascinating spectacle.' Curiously Martin brought their tempestuous relationship to a close, of sorts. By the end of 1977 he had begun to keep his distance, though not because he had found someone else. He felt threatened, a sensation that Martin had never previously experienced.

We will revisit this story in due course, and consider its impact upon Martin's career as a writer. In the meantime consider an observation from Clive James: 'Women just adored him, and as far as I am aware they were never disappointed. He enjoyed himself, of course, but he loved the company of women, was quietly attentive to anything they said and talked with them as if no one else was present. They were, as a consequence, even more captivated. Ah, it was all a bit rough if you were outside, male, with your nose pressed to the glass. I didn't die from envy, not quite, because I like him so much. But others? Well, it bred bitterness and resentment in some.' As in love so in life? 'Yes, I'd say so.' He continues: 'It should be said that Martin was rather chivalrous. He indulged women, even those he had never met before, and even if before this they had only vaguely fancied or admired him they'd soon take things a stage further. Just by being Martin he seduced them but it involved no industry on his part. It just happened.'

Hitchens's observation is equally telling. 'The impression left thirty years later, particularly lately in reports by some of the women, is of a rake, a young man enjoying what his father was obliged to practise surreptitiously. [Hitchens refers here to the stories sold to newspapers by three of Martin's ex-girlfriends.][2] But this is a misrepresentation of him. The facts are authentic enough but what should not be overlooked was that Martin never wished to wound.' He means that while Martin was not exactly an exemplar of morality, nor was he careless with the emotions of those who were in truth as much his pursuers as his prey. Hitchens: 'He was a success, but they, the women, were just as enthusiastic. It is spurious of them to present themselves as victims.' Gully Wells concurs. 'He dealt with our break-up rather clumsily, that is true, but neither of us was particularly mature despite our claims to cleverness. And I remember vividly the train journey to Lemmons and the evening there. To be honest he was as upset as I was but he faced a dilemma. If he told me the truth – that he didn't wish us to continue because he was committed to his work – he feared that I would feel cheapened, to say the least. So he had no choice but to pretend that things were simply coming to some sort of conclusion. I'd say it was confused compassion. He never wished to upset people. That's why I kept on our occasional liaisons – yes I did that – for another ten years.'

There are parallels between Martin the Lothario and Martin the novelist. His characters, especially in the early novels, leap from the page with Dickensian vibrancy yet he seems reluctant to impose upon them the restrictions of a story or an ethical boundary. He respects them – they are after all his creations – but he is reluctant to interfere with their private inclinations or puzzling volitional urges. Those, he seems to say, are their business. Or at least he creates the impression that they are. There is concern, puzzlement, sometimes morbid fascination, often regret, but not control. He reflects: 'Gully. We went on seeing each other throughout our twenties, frequently. But there it was. We saw each other when we were between other people or when things weren't going so well. It's not remembered how bruising a lot of that was, that period. I'm writing about it now [in *The Pregnant Widow*] because it was a revolution and suddenly, suddenly behaviour was different. There were various tenets in this revolutionary manifesto. There would be sex outside and before marriage. This, for some, had happened before but its openness was completely new. So for the previous generation there was much hatred and resentment and many of my friends felt trapped between parental in-dignation and peer pressure. They had terrible, laboured arguments with their parents. But it was all right for me. I never had that fight with my father. He had had that fight with his and he wanted to spare me that.' Martin insists that Kingsley had not encouraged him to be pro-miscuous; rather that his father, despite his own failings, had provided a point of relative stability in a period without any sort of moral compass. So, ironically, he caused Martin to be conscious of the dangerous potential in promiscuity? 'Yes, perhaps he did.'

'Another tenet was that girls had sexual appetite. They always did have, of course, but this was suddenly, openly acknowledged. And then there was the really difficult one . . . Much like the dissociation of sensibility [Eliot's diagnosis of seventeenth-century poetry]. In the seventies sex and love, sex and emotion were dissociable. People were hurt, badly.' He adds, 'Charles Highway [of *The Rachel Papers*] seems to be able to dissociate feeling from lust, but he can't. Highway's cleverness is an attempt to protect himself. He is terribly susceptible to love, and gratitude, but he finds it difficult to . . .' Difficult to accept this? 'Yes.'

Martin's reflections on the 1970s as a period of emotional and intellectual disconnection go further than the much-vaunted sexual revolution. He was also part of a generation, mostly those who had come down from university at the beginning of the decade, who began to feel that they belonged to a society that was coming adrift from the social and political consensus that had endured since the post-war Labour administration. Perceptions of where this would lead, let alone whether one had a particular role to play, depended as much upon temperament as ideological outlook.

Anthony Howard, then editor of the *New Statesman*: 'Fenton and Hitch were more concerned with the front part [social and political]. Despite the fact that James [Fenton] is now best known as a poet the two of them were then, ostensibly at least, concerned with politics. In their spare time they worked for the Socialist Workers Party, distributing pamphlets to the general public on the imminent demise of capitalism and the benefits of International Socialism, Trotskyism. The newcomers at the back end [arts and literature] were Martin and Julian Barnes. I felt rather sorry for Julian. He was a few years older than the rest, had spent some time working in the *OED* or something, and in many ways he seemed rather more considered, mature. Yet through the seventies he was always the sidekick, or second in line to the new boys. Clive James was part of the set, as was Craig Raine. I suspect that they saw themselves as comparable to the post-war fifties generation – Kingsley, Conquest and so on. Of course the seventies bunch were far less conservative on politics and literature but it was clear that they felt they could shape trends and opinions for a few decades.'

There are some similarities between Martin's experiences of the 1970s and early 1980s and his father's in the 1950s and 1960s, but not quite as Howard suggests. Father and son became chameleons, they absorbed the peculiarities and absurdities of their respective worlds, charmed others – particularly women – but begrudged commitment or affiliation.

When he first arrived at the *New Statesman* Martin was protective of his image as an emerging intellectual, maintaining close contact with figures such as Karl Miller and John Sturrock from the *TLS* and Terry Kilmartin of the *Observer*, but within a year he had become the fulcrum for a bizarre unprecedented transformation. 'It was not simply a matter of writing for the *New Statesman*,' reflects Francis Wheen. 'The place and those associated with it took on a kind of clubbishness, exclusive in the sense that you had to be clever and funny to become a member.'

Martin's and Barnes's shared interest in sport was in parts sincere and self-parodic. They set up a ping-pong table in the basement and what had once been the junk room for semi-discarded files, decrepit furniture and typewriters became the site for bi-weekly table-tennis tournaments. To compensate for the image of wholesome worthiness implied by all this it became the convention that smoking during matches, for spectators and competitors, was *de rigueur*, and as far as Martin was concerned a self-imposed obligation. 'There was also', recalls Wheen, 'a cricket and football team. Martin didn't play much cricket but at soccer he was rather a nippy winger. He preferred the ball delivered to him so he could make a brief, brilliantly nuanced pass rather than having to do a lot of work himself. My abiding memory is of him positioned close to the touchline viewing the progress of play with a roll-up hanging from his mouth.' Did he take it out after he received the ball? 'Not if he could help it, no.'

Hitchens: 'Just before Martin published *The Rachel Papers* Peter Ackroyd, then literary editor of the *Spectator*, said to me one day, "There's someone I'd like you to meet. I think the two of you will get on rather well." He told me his name and I mentioned that we'd met before, briefly, in Oxford but he introduced us properly in a place called the Bung Hole, a bar of questionable legality near the *New Statesman* offices – you could cash cheques there and depart the next day. We had an excellent evening, leaving Peter in the bar and going on to several other pubs. We knew it would be good, no *necessary*, to meet again.' Martin concurs, 'Yes, Hitchens was unstoppable. I'd never met anyone quite so energetic. Politically I was . . . well, let's say I didn't share his enthusiasms, but he is a great conversationalist. Politics was his concern, not literature, but he was a literary *presence*.' Hitchens: 'We got on immediately and I knew soon that it was not only banter. A few months after we met my mother died, unexpectedly, and I had to leave town. I didn't tell Martin, didn't really know him well enough, but on my return I found a very thoughtful letter. It was consoling and, well, impressive. People . . . of our age rarely tended to do that sort of thing in those days.' Martin knew James Fenton from Oxford but at this time he was away sending in copy to the *New Statesman* on the spread of the Vietnam conflict into neighbour-

136

ing Cambodia. 'Oddly,' reflects Hitchens, 'Martin became a supplement to James, for me. How can I put it? – with Martin we shifted between in-depth conversations on writing and life and discussing sex.'

Clive James recalls the 1970s with a mixture of hazy nostalgia and some pride: 'The *New Statesman* crew were nearly all Oxford. I was Cambridge and anyone who'd read English there left with an enduring wound caused by Leavis, even though he'd retired in 1962. His advocates still held that the London literary circuit was lightweight, modish, elitist – based on Leavis's hatred for Bloomsbury. So we decided that we'd create an alternative to academia, based in London, something made up of people who were writers *and* critics.' Who was the 'we'? I ask. 'Ian Hamilton was at the centre of things, at least as far as I was concerned. He'd founded the *New Review* [in 1974], but his head office was next door, a pub called the Pillars of Hercules. Editorial conferences took place there.' Both were in Greek Street, Soho, two doors down from the offices of *Private Eye*. Shortly before Hamilton set up the *New Review* the younger recruits to the *TLS* and the *Observer* began the so-called Friday lunch club at Motherunch's, which Hitchens describes as a 'villainous wine bar, under the Arches at Blackfriars. The early patrons were Russell Davies and the elder statesman Terry Kilmartin. Martin – and this was even before he published *The Rachel Papers* – was brought in as a feted, enormously promising man and was soon installed as chief whip. Put simply he was brilliant, and brilliantly amusing. Once James [Fenton] and I got to know Martin we would call in but by 1974 the centre of gravity moved to a place called the Bursa, a Turkish Cypriot kebab house in Theobald's Road.' Customers were offered shamelessly inauthentic Turkish dishes from 8 a.m. to midnight, served with flagons of red wine or whatever spirit the customer might request from the battery of cupboards and fridges. The Bursa, though not technically a wine bar, had declared independence from standard licensing regulations. Meals in haste were available at what the *New Statesman* staff referred to as 'the Caff', an establishment that changed hands so frequently as to merit anonymity. It was, however, the source of an enduring feature of *New Statesman* culture, the 'Yob's Breakfast' or 'YB'. In the office the declaration that 'we're off for a YB' meant that a glorious raid on the arteries was imminent, traditional British fare involving principally black and white pudding, bacon, sausages, baked beans, fried bread, eggs.

'There were not', Hitchens recalls 'two opposed groups, because in both places [the Pillars of Hercules and the Bursa] the personnel was largely the same, predominantly me, Martin, James, Julian, Clive and, a little later in the decade, Ian [McEwan], Russell [Davies], Piers Paul Read, Craig [Raine]. But the Pillars was Ian Hamilton's head office and it has to be said Martin predominated at the Bursa.' Clive James concurs. 'Martin, you must understand, was not an egotist. In no sense did he *attempt* to impose himself on a group. It was simply a matter of natural selection. His humour was unforced, and shot through with observations that seemed casual but were much more astute than could be found in the best prose. I'll say again, none of us felt intimidated, or second-rate. We just enjoyed listening. Fenton was brilliant, but taciturn. Julian, beyond taciturn. He made the statues on Easter Island seem garrulous, but when he spoke he was entrancing. Ian [McEwan] was hungry, hungry for material I mean. You had the impression of him hoovering up conversations, postures, atmosphere for his fiction . . . At the Pillars rules were observed. No anecdotes, no prepared jokes, long stories were forbidden. Well, Hitch was allowed stories because he told them so well, digressions included. No one had decided on these conventions. They evolved. A reflection of the mood of the place. There was much improvisation and combat by dialogue and Martin emerged as the star. Fenton said that Martin was "indispensable". If he wasn't there, something was missing. I would agree but qualify that. He and Ian [Hamilton] were equally impressive. Not competitively; they became very close friends, at least until they were attracted to the same woman.' For a précis of what if anything this shifting amorphous group of writers subscribed to, an observation from Hitchens will suffice. 'Ian Hamilton was marvellously entertaining, but for our generation Terry Kilmartin was the exemplar. Once, he was dealing with Gore Vidal [on an article for the *Observer*] and telegraphed him, apologetically, at his villa in Italy explaining that his piece was exceptional but too long, they simply couldn't fit it in, so he, Terry, had taken the liberty of editing it by about 150 words. Gore replied that he was powerless to overrule Kilmartin's decision but that he allowed no one to interfere with his work and would therefore never again write for or even communicate with the *Observer*. He later confessed to me that when he read the article he was astonished. It was much shorter but he could not detect the changes or cuts. And, he admitted ruefully, it was *better*. Terry was a brilliant editor and more than that he knew how prose works. He taught us more than we ever learned in university. He gave us a feel for the effect of language on the reader, how it should be used unselfishly and eloquently. Martin respected his father unreservedly but he was indebted to Terry too.' Each of the writers who spent their spare time in the Bursa or the Pillars assented to different generic demands and pursued varied ambitions, as reviewers, feature writers, political journalists, literary and television critics, poets, novelists et al. But if they can be said to share a collective mantra it was this: challenge, unsettle but certainly do not patronize or bore the reading public.

It was in the Bursa that two very different writers devised a bizarre narrative worthy of Swift and the Scriblerus Club. Martin and Barnes were responsible for the competition pages at the back of the literary and arts section and quite soon began to speculate on what kind of readers spent their time toiling over their literary crossword puzzles. Occasionally entries would be published from individuals who apparently preferred to be known only by their *noms de plume* – most memorably the in-house duo, Spiro Keates and Fat Jeff, pseudonyms for Martin – without causing a murmur of incredulity either from other readers or editorial staff. Emboldened, Martin and Barnes began to refer to the top floor of the *New Statesman* office as their new headquarters in which they, and others unnamed, devised and determined the future strategy of the competition. The 'Comp. Complex' was born and grew in intricacy week by week, mutating from a practical annex to the rest of the building into something far more exotic and durable. They debated at length the appropriateness of copper-plated bathroom fittings, the size of the bath itself and, most troubling of all, the spa – the *New Statesman* was still after all an organ of Socialist principle. There was even, very briefly, discussion of a helipad for the roof, mainly to service businessmen and certain Arab and South American diplomats who had of late become devoted connoisseurs of the Competition and wished to visit the Complex. There are some references to this fantastic location in the *New Statesman* itself but one is engrossed by its similarities to an equally bizarre place in Part One, Section 7 of *Dead Babies*. Penthouse Cloudscape 'is a top-floor Knightsbridge maisonette . . . not by any means an atypical household and we would do well to look at it closely'. It has, we are informed, 'luxury bathrooms', spacious communal quarters with continually flickering TVs and the only other disturbance of the pellucid calm comes from the rumble of arriving and departing helicopters. These deliver visitors to the penthouse. Three residents, Mitzi, Serena and Lucy, are high-order prostitutes. This trio were an invention of Martin's but as we shall see the mildly surreal subculture of the *New Statesman* often involved women, real and imagined, in a manner that would traumatize the most indulgent feminist.

Hitchens believes that this curious invention was inspired by a number of Martin's experiences at the magazine. 'Of course the "Comp. Complex" was more a state of mind than a place but gradually it turned into something concrete and disturbing. We would all set questions, largely requests for parodies or imitations of well-known writers or politicians – you know, "write a report on Crufts in the manner of Harold Wilson". We'd sign these requests with the nicknames we'd appended to each other. Obviously Mart was Little Keith, I was Hitch, Wheen took over as Fat Jeff, Sid ('Sydney') James was Clive and so on. But the trouble was that very often real contributors turned in stuff that wasn't usable, so frequently we ended up writing the answers to our own questions. But for those who *did* enter material we could use we'd have an end-of-year party, and, oh God, they were weirdoes, very bizarre individuals. They could sometimes be quite funny on paper but in person they were frighteningly odd. So, yes, perhaps we felt like Mitzi, Serena and Lucy, entertaining strange men. They were all men. And Martin was inordinately concerned with writing about dodgy sex. The Holbrook articles are well known but he was also writing under his own name as the reviewer of soft porn.'[3] Hitchens remembers a comment by Martin that never went into print. 'He said that in porn shops, the men standing before the racks, muttering and swaying, pulling out and replacing the mags, seemed to him like the "Wailing Wall".'

'There was', says Wheen, 'a competitive culture of what might be called cumulative impropriety, initiated mainly by

Martin and Hitch. Someone would spin a story out of a joke or a pun and it went without saying that this was a challenge to the rest to better it. The most notorious was the Tupper family tree, started off by Conquest who came with Kingsley and Martin to boozy lunches at the Casa Alpino – an Italian restaurant slightly more respectable than the Bursa – or Pillars. There was Woppy Tupper, who was rather shy with girls and his second cousin Julian Fawcett-Tupper, rake and hedonist. Woppy's brother had lost his part of the inheritance, ended up working in a sweet factory, and was thereafter known as Sticky Tupper. To take part you had to adopt a member of the family, describe their misbegotten lifestyle or dire fate and of course generate as much sexual innuendo as possible from the surnames. I remember once Martin and Hitchens sitting together and telling each other stories – and as you'll know Martin was a fine mimic, so was Hitch – and the whole thing had spiralled to the point where neither could control themselves. If convulsive laughter can cause a heart attack both must have come close.'

Hitchens remembers the 'word games' as having 'their own momentum'. 'Substitutions were extremely popular, that is exchanging a familiar word, usually a noun, for something utterly different, usually obscene, and seeing how unsuitable they were in titles, or routine phrases. "Cunt" for "man" for example. "A Cunt for All Seasons", "This will make a cunt of you", "Cuntkind", "Cunthood", "A Cunt's a Cunt for All That", "Cuntservant", "Cuntslaughter", "Our Cunt in Havana", "The Cunt who Shot Liberty Valance". Then there was the use of two verbs or adverbs with assonantal and alliterative parallels: "Angling for a mangling", "Cruising for a bruising", "Strolling for a rolling" – my favourite "Thirsting for a worsting". Kingsley and Conkers [Conquest] joined in when they were there.'

Hitchens reflects also that these adolescent pursuits could suddenly 'within minutes' be exchanged for discussions of poetry. 'Yes poetry, more so than fiction, and Larkin held our attention more than any other figure. James [Fenton] loved Auden but even he conceded that Larkin was the finest post-war poet in English. *High Windows* (1974) had not long been out and no one questioned its inestimable brilliance. Of course all of this was long before the letters and Motion's biography but we knew, partly from Martin and indeed Kingsley and Conkers that he loathed strikers, the left in general. Immigrants, "abroad" . . . but that seemed completely irrelevant. We all thought him a genius. His combination of an unclassifiably sombre outlook – he seemed weary of everything – with an ability to make such astonishingly beautiful verse appealed to all of us.' Which is an appropriate lead-in to further thoughts on *Dead Babies*. Larkin could distil hopeless, often nihilistic images into beautiful poems. His ability to confound the reader, while demanding their respect for his craftsmanship, invites comparison with Martin's novel. There are, as I have noted, borrowings from his private world but what of its aggregate qualities as a work of fiction? It could be mistaken for a late-twentieth-century version of Waugh's *Vile Bodies*, incorporating an appropriately updated excess of sex, drug taking and alcohol abuse, except that Martin's host, Villiers, murders each of his guests, wife and closest friend included. He derives no particular pleasure from this, but suggests with characteristic hauteur that it is inevitable. He is, he implies, his narrator's and author's avatar; the characters have served their purpose as material for superb stylistic conceits, so they are now dispensable. Try as one might it is impossible to locate a prevailing rationale for the book: it is far too grotesque to be an allegory, even of a society in a terminal dystopian state, yet at the same time the characters are possessed of an energy and unnerving

143

authenticity. Its qualities as a piece of writing are self-evident but it will continue to puzzle, often infuriate those who expect literature to perform a given function. This testifies to its importance both as a work in its own right and as an indicator of Martin's significance as a novelist. *Dead Babies* undermines the polarity between writing that is accessible and vividly evocative – the keystones of traditionalism – and that which poses and leaves unanswerable a catalogue of questions about how exactly we are supposed to deal with this spectacle. When he began as a writer the distinctions between the avant-gardists, the heirs to modernism, and the conservatives of his father's generation were firmly established. Martin was the first to blur them, to create hybridized creations claiming lineage from both camps.

Shortly after Martin was formally appointed literary editor in 1976 he began work on what would be his third novel, *Success*. 'I remember', says Anthony Howard, 'asking him to write a major piece on Peter Porter, one of his first jobs, and he said, yes, of course he would get on with it later in the year. I told him, no, it was for this week's issue. "But I need to conserve my energies . . . I've just started a new novel." Martin, I reminded him, *we* are the ones who pay your salary.' Howard has nothing but praise for him as a colleague and fellow journalist. 'He ran the back end very well indeed, and of course he had valuable contacts. He didn't attempt to dispel the left-wing aura that surrounded the magazine but he succeeded in making it more cosmopolitan, at least in terms of the arts. He commissioned reviews and articles from Larkin, his father, Bob Conquest and others you'd associate more with the *Spectator*. And he was scrupulous with the tedious, practical aspect of the job. In those days we had to go down to our printers in Southend to check largely typed copy against the plates, and Martin did this, every week. Books were his thing of course but he was also in charge of theatre, music, opera, TV. He was very good at his job.'

There seem, then, to have been two versions of Martin Amis, the performer who held court in the Casa Alpino, the Bursa and the Pillars and who might have walked out of *Dead Babies*, and the conscientious, reliable editor. Colin Howard is intriguing on this: 'In company Martin might give the appearance of being rather careless, even dissolute, but it is a false impression, perhaps deliberately contrived. After Oxford he practised exemplary self-discipline. I can only speak of when he was at Lemmons or Flask Walk but he would be at his desk at 8 a.m. at the latest and he'd work for five, six hours without a break. He and Kingsley were very similar in that respect.'

'There was also', reflects Colin, 'something slightly predatory about him – and I don't mean this in a derogatory sense. You felt that he was always collecting material from his surroundings. He was great fun, but one had the sense that he was both taking part and recording.' Colin Howard's observations become particularly telling once we have spent time with Gregory Riding and Terence Service, co-narrators of *Success*.

Gregory and Terence are foster brothers, the latter taken in by the Riding family after his father had murdered his sister Rosie, then aged seven. Improbably Terry and Gregory were born within twenty-four hours of each other and to add further to the catalogue of coincidences Ursula, Gregory's sister – and again his only sister – is seven years of age when Terry is fostered, and shares a birthday with the late Rosie. The obvious question is whether he and Philip and their relationship with Kingsley played any part in the invention of these two figures.

'Kingsley did more than you might think, taking care of us. But – well he was probably having an affair when the two of us were born. He was certainly having an affair with a student and I've a pretty good idea who it was – I won't say. Phil's grouse really was that when I was born my mother had to stay in hospital with me for at least a couple of weeks and he [Phil] was farmed off to some sort of nunnery.' But, I point out, neither of you knew of this at the time, either of Kingsley's extra-marital activities or Phil's temporary placing in what amounted to foster care. 'No of course not, but when told of it later, or when you learn of it, it leeches into your memory of other later things. Certainly for Phil – and he always seemed to have the tough breaks later – those few weeks might have seemed a premonition.' As, no doubt, was the image, for Martin, of his father abandoning fidelity around the time he first drew breath. There are few exact correspondences but the similarities between the gothic foursome of Greg, Terry and their respective fathers and the Amises are striking.

Gregory and Terry describe a twelve-month period, taking turns, month by month, to speak directly to the reader, as if to camera, but it would be wrong to treat their accounts as monologues because the events that animate them are taking place as they speak. Each monthly report involves the blend of puzzlement, bitterness, reflection, self-justification that one would expect if they were addressing each other in dialogue. The fact that their accounts are at once interdependent and isolated, addressed only to an unknown listener creates a special degree of anxiety and candour; they hold nothing back but they can depend on no one but themselves for a response, be it conciliatory or discordant. This device in itself promotes the novel as a small masterpiece. Technically no one had attempted this before and the tense disquiet that accompanies a reading testifies to Martin's achievement. (The technique would later be borrowed by Julian Barnes in *Talking It Over*, 1991, and *Love etc.*, 2000.)

While Gregory's confidence is fed by the 'gloriously wavy hair' and bone structure of an aristocrat, plus his intimidating height, Terry is short, fat, ugly and balding. Sargy Mann: 'Mart and Phil could, facially, have been twins, and they were of largely similar build, except that Phil seemed to be a stretched version of Martin. He wasn't all that tall but the fact that he was much *taller* emphasized the contrast.'

It was not that Martin perceived himself as a version either of Gregory or Terry but the difference between them was symptomatic of his fabric of anxieties. Colin Howard: 'He was preoccupied with the size of his backside along with his concern about his height. And even in his twenties the thought of losing his hair filled him with terror, Christopher Hitchens too. Their obsession with the term "rug" testified to this, as much displaced anxiety as a joke.'

Terry's life with his natural father concludes in Dawkin Street, Cambridge, a place that he finds difficult to describe in detail, except that it 'was full of crappy things' and of course Madingley Road again emerges as a sore that Martin seems unable to leave alone. It is here that Terry's father Ronnie destroys the family for good, leaving him to the benign philanthropic auspices of Mr Riding, apparently scion of minor gentry but of whom we learn little. The dissolute, irresponsible Ronnie Service and the admirably cultivated Riding appear to have little in common, yet they could for some represent aspects of Martin's father before and after his elopement with Jane Howard. Up to the point when Kingsley left Cambridge to join, in Eva's words, his 'fancy woman' he still traded upon his image as a member of the fifties generation: working- or lower-middle-class reprobates, constantly tilting at Establishment mores. In private, he was even worse, seeming determined to test the patience and forbearance even of those similarly inclined. The notorious party in Swansea where he escorted three of the women guests into the garden for sex while the other diners looked askance and sometimes pitiably at Hilly had by the mid-1970s become part of the gruesome family

147

legend. Musing on their respective histories Gregory comments: 'It was conjectured that Service Sr had an intimate say in the death of his wife.'[4] Hilly's apparent attempt at suicide failed, of course, but no one questioned its cause.

To this day Martin professes amazement at how a feckless truant had in little more than four years gained a Starred First at Oxford and completed a prize-winning debut novel. Jane Howard, as he acknowledges, played a significant part in this and in *Success* Mrs Riding, referred to mainly as Mama, is the only character treated with tactful generosity. Kingsley himself, particularly at Lemmons, rejoiced in his role as Country Gentleman yet there was, according to Colin Howard, a hint of self-caricature involved. 'He would sometimes announce, usually from the bathroom, that he was "taking a look around the estate" [archly echoing the title of his 1967 volume of poems]. In truth he was unconcerned with the place's Georgian grandeur and he had no interest in gardens but he enjoyed the contrast between what he'd always been and what he now appeared to be.' A similar contrast fascinates Riding Sr.

> Evidently, too, he was intrigued in a quirky way by certain parallels between our families, parallels at once so fortuitous and insistent that for a while I longingly suspected that some Fieldingesque parentage mystery would one day resolve our destinies. Mr Riding and my father were the same age, and Greg's and my birthdays were only twenty-four hours apart; Ursula, Greg's sister, and mine were both seven at the time, and were alike the survivors of abbreviated twins – and so on . . . As the scandal about my displacement grew, so did Mr Riding's wayward but intense anxiety. He let it obsess him, for all the irritated now-nowing of his wife and the confusion and unease of his children.[5]

Henry Riding's preoccupation makes explicit the troubling animus of the book which Martin himself evokes, while not referring to it directly, in an essay on Vladimir Nabokov written shortly after the novel's publication. The plot of Nabokov's first novel in English, *The Real Life of Sebastian Knight* is almost identical to that of *Success*. It is narrated by Sebastian's half-brother, who is obsessed by their differences and similarities, and by the end of the book he feels that they have become virtually the same person. Martin claims that Nabokov's notion of the sublime involves a perverse exchange of exaltation for an equally compulsive absorption with 'squalor, absurdity and talentlessness'.[6] This catches perfectly the inverted narcissism of Greg and Terry's perceptions of themselves and each other. Each emotive register – predominantly envy on Terry's part and patrician contempt on Greg's – is touched also with a fear of transience, that to maintain a stable sense of who they are, they must fear or resent what they are not. The novel concludes horrifyingly. Terry recollects in detail the killing of his sister by his father and in the subsequent passage we learn that he and Greg had contributed to the suicide of Ursula. They have, finally, acted as one, found space for cooperation and equality.

As a piece of contemporary existential gothic Nabokov's novel outranks *Success*, but Martin was not simply struggling with the presence of his hero. Nabokov's life was as fantastic and unsettling as his fiction and while Martin, then still in his late twenties, could only claim experiences that seemed mundane by comparison he nevertheless found in the former's work grotesque portraits and inclinations that both defied the standard conventions of the novel and seemed profoundly familiar.

When he began the novel Martin's sister Sally was working at a wine bar in the Edgware Road, which seemed to all concerned a guaranteed recipe for disaster. She was at twenty-two already in an advanced stage of alcohol dependency. Sally had suffered worst from the various family upheavals of the 1950s. Unlike Philip and Martin she was far too young to marshal standard teenage responses – notably resentment and nonconformity – as protection against a disintegrating home life. Hilly during that period cared for her already confused, slightly traumatized daughter as well as she could and later she and Kingsley witnessed her decline into alcoholism in her late teens, worsened by occasional bouts of drug abuse. The parallels between the tragic fate of Rosie, Terry's sister, and Ursula, Greg's – both like their respective neo-siblings born on the same day – and the life of Sally Amis are striking. In February 1976 Sally married the owner of the wine bar, twenty years her senior, a wine merchant by trade and minor gentry by lineage. The marriage lasted less than a year. Kingsley, according to Martin, witnessed all of this 'as you might a car crash, stunned, not really involved'. Several days before the ceremony Sally had arrived drunk at Lemmons and collapsed on the staircase landing. Kingsley, on his way to the bathroom, had stepped over her, pausing only to remark, 'You fucking wreck.' His report, three months later to Martin on the register office proceedings and the state of the relationship was similar: 'A complete fucking disaster.' And the name of Sally's husband? Nigel Service.

Sargy Mann's percipient observation on the Martin of the early 1970s is intriguing: that his strenuous command of an intellectual exchange or put-down carried a faint but detectable whiff of anxiety, that signs of mediocrity might begin to expose his previous self. Of his two creations Greg seems the more polished stylist but by around March – the book begins in January – his glissando verbal flourishes become suspect, his self-confidence gradually displaced by self-delusion. He is preoccupied with his class, both as an elevated state into which he was born and as a deserved token of his innate intellectual superiority. Even though Greg must, to preserve his sanity, try to sustain the fantasy we, by the summer of the narrative's progress, are watching its disintegration.

As Greg moves towards the precipice of reality and contemplates failure, Terry uncoils as his deviant and in many ways superior alter ego. Terry is, incontestably, the more distinguished stylist. He was indeed Martin's most accomplished literary creation to date. Unlike Greg he uses language unselfconsciously, never once disclosing an inclination to combine his talents with a career or a project that will lift him above his masochistically resigned condition as a 'yob'. He is drawn with rhapsodic self-disgust to everything that Greg fears – particularly the sweaty, inarticulate, morose corpus of beings who appear to have swamped the city – yet he depicts them and his alternately disgusted and fascinated relationship with them in the manner of Larkin in, say, 'Mr Bleaney'; the foul and unwholesome become the material of brilliant stylistic craftsmanship.

'There was', observes Wheen, 'something compulsive about Martin's preoccupation with "yobbism". He might slip into the idiom, the accent, without warning or purpose. "Snot royt issit. Arlav six more sossige widdat – yer carn't cull dat a fackin brekfist." He was very good but his middle-class drawl was still there.

'The thing is, he didn't really appreciate the unintended absurdity of the contrast. The authentic Amis idiom, accent, was almost, almost, as preposterous as the ones he assumed. He would never have attempted to disguise the voice that was his but at the same time he sought refuge in chameleonesque performances, slipping in and out of roles.' This provides an insight into what caused the seemingly arbitrary battle between Greg and Terry, who at various points in the novel vie for prominence and exchange aspects of their respective personae and rankings in the class system. My mention of this to Wheen prompts an anecdote. 'Yes, one winter I was sent down with him to the Southend printers to deal with the proofs. It was snowing heavily and by the time we'd finished the roads were blocked. So we looked for a B&B. There were all sorts, and our expenses would have been paid in any event, but he spent about an hour toiling up and down until he'd found a place that seemed like part of the set from *Brighton Rock*. It reeked of hopelessness and it was difficult to imagine that anyone other than benefit recipients would use it. But there was a snooker hall next door, with a bar. Equally dreadful in atmosphere. Martin enjoyed himself immensely but every time he opened his mouth everyone else there stared. It must have seemed as if a previously unimaginable alien had arrived.' The peculiar dynamic between Terry and Greg is again evoked.

Wheen and Anthony Howard share a perception of Martin as largely indifferent to the political climate of the late 1970s. Howard recalls a sequence of Friday-lunchtime meetings in the *New Statesman* offices, each attended by a major political figure. 'Callaghan, Ted Heath, even Wilson – though slightly out of the loop by then – they all came, as did Michael Foot and Tony Benn, even some of Thatcher's pre-1979 acolytes, Carrington certainly. Hitch, Fenton, Clive James when he could, they would crowd in as though it was Prime Minister's Question Time, pitching in with energetic queries, and they were by far to the left of any guest.' Martin? 'Well, he had to be "persuaded" to turn up. He viewed the whole thing with a mixture of benign amusement and apathy.'

The seventies was, in Britain, the decade of persistently imminent catastrophe. The extreme left, to which many of Martin's friends belonged, sensed that at last Marx's long-deferred diagnosis would soon be proved: capitalism would bring about its own collapse. In this respect, Hitchens's, Fenton's, even James's and sometimes Craig Raine's attendance at the Friday meetings, could be taken as cases of celebrants anticipating the wake. The politicians who had sustained the rather flimsy post-war consensus between the Conservatives and Labour – which Hitchens calls 'the Weimar Republic without the sex' – seemed about to have their delusions exposed: the economic and political infrastructure was in a state of accelerating terminal decline. Howard continues: 'Martin's novels of the seventies are curious pieces. They evoke the period in a rather skewed, selective manner. I mean, we recognize the characters, their behaviour, mannerisms and so on, and a certain mood is detectable. But if asked to discern the social and political atmosphere of the period in Martin's novels one would come up with . . . nihilism. Or perhaps insouciance.' Again *Success* is brought to mind. It could be perceived as a macabre, minutely observed picture of the mid-1970s, a confection of hedonism, despair, ambition and failure, but at the same time it lacks a specific context: aside from the occasional references to fashion, music, idiomatic traces and so on it could just as easily be 'about' the 1950s. Contemporary society, let alone politics, is present by implication only, brought in by virtue of the reader's recognition of familiar triggers. However, the novel's apparently questionable value as a record of its period should not be taken as a mark of failure. Martin was evolving an unconventional technique of catching the atmosphere of an era through the behaviour of unaffiliated misfits and in robustly fantastic scenarios. Like most novelists he skimmed source material from his own experience, and for Martin this was sometimes richly rewarding.

According to Wheen, Martin's only memorable contribution to the ongoing political debates was 'a peculiar selection of mantras, apocalyptic and cryptic at the same time. "They're taking over, you know." "It's all collapsing, we're close to the end." "The yobs will be in charge soon." In one sense he seemed to be invoking the ill-defined but subnormal state he loved to imitate; he certainly had a fetish for the appurtenances of yobbishness. At the same time he baffled people such as Hitch, who had absorbed every formula for the collapse of capitalism, from left-Hegelianism through post-Trotskyism. He would ask Martin, "*WHO* is taking over?" "What do you mean by yobs? Radical proletarians or converts to the National Front?" It was hilarious really, because Hitch, and others, admired Martin immensely as an intellectual presence and as a consequence they assumed he was addressing the same challenging leftist agenda as they were. He wasn't. He was revelling in the opportunity to slum, a mixture of ghoulish fascination and distaste.'

Wheen captures perfectly the one thing that unites Greg and Terry, their mixture of revulsion for and addiction to the ghastly network of beings who share their urban space. Terry seems unable to avoid the presence of a 'stinking hippy' and an older even more odious figure he calls 'Terry the Tramp' – a wonderful blend of recognition and terror; I also, he implies, might be susceptible to foul decline (and we should note here a resemblance to the GP who lived in the ground floor of Martin's Earl's Court flat). Greg too – at least when he has cast off his pretensions to significance – perceives his environment as horribly polluted with a lesser form of mankind.

It has become a habit of critics to treat *Success* as a diagnosis of British society on the brink of transformation. Graham Fuller described it as a parody of England's class war, with Gregory and Terry symbolizing 'the spiritual decay of the landed gentry and the greedy self-betterment of the "yobs", each appraising the other's position with eloquent disgust or shameless envy'.[7] This insightful Marxian assessment was however made, circa 1987, with the benefit of hindsight, or to be more specific the spectacle of 'greedy self-betterment' offered by Thatcher's Conservatives, who came to power a year after the novel's publication. In truth the strange relationship between Terry and Greg and its slip-stream of sociocultural debris had as much to do with Martin's personal life as with his ambitions as novelist cum political oracle. Consider the following accounts by Anthony Howard and the Rt Hon. Nicholas Soames.

Howard remembers a party at Tina Brown's flat, two years after she had come down from Oxford and was creating currents of envy and star-struck admiration among the London literati. 'She and Martin had stopped seeing each other – nothing acrimonious, simply a mutual agreement that they had other routes to follow. Well, they seemed to have done so, each apparently being with someone else. Anyway, one of the beds had been pushed into the hall to make room for a drinks table in one of the bedrooms. Martin, in mid-conversation, looked down, patted the mattress and said, "Well, hello again, old friend." Everyone smiled, indulgently; no one was surprised or mildly offended. Martin by then [around 1975] was treated as the unpretentious Lothario-in-chief. Women went for him and he was permitted as many self-lionizing remarks as he wished, all fully deserved. But', he adds, 'it was a double-edged sword. He was envied, sometimes vindictively. On another occasion, this time I think at Julie Kavanagh's flat when he lived at least some of the time with her, a man, a writer – I won't name him but he is now reasonably well known – emerged proudly from the bathroom and announced that, heedful of Martin's ill-deserved fame and allure, he'd crapped in the bath.' Nicholas Soames remembers Martin's first visits to Castle Mill House in Hampshire as Brideshead in reverse. He, his brother Jeremy, his father Sir Christopher and mother Mary, were in awe of this star from London. 'Father and Mother loved him. He made them laugh and of course he made Emma happy, after a string of bloody unsuitable boyfriends. He'd stand there on the lawn, croquet mallet swung over his shoulder, rolled fag in mouth and *very* large drink in hand. He was small and ridiculously handsome. The rest of us would be keeling over with laughter at everything he said. God, he held court and everyone relished it.'

Martin's memories of those weekends are similarly rhapsodic. 'Kingsley makes it sound like Blenheim Palace but it was a converted mill house, rambling and beautiful but not a mansion. I'd go trout fishing. I'd never attempted this before but it was as though the fish were trained. Aim a fly at a thread of bubbles and a large brown trout would rise and make the reel whir. It all seemed perfect yet unforced. Kingsley and Jane once came down and I remember a whole afternoon spent over the lunch table, a complete wall of sound, predominantly laughter. I loved Emma's mother. We'd play games, class games. "Mart, are you really from the suburbs? You *sound* like us. Really, dear, are you putting it on?" She'd say things like "That fuckpig of a car is refusing to start again." I'd pretend to be aghast with something like "Mary, how do you know that word? You're a *lady*." "Oh fuck off, Martin dear, the aristocracy are the connoisseurs of obscenity." Jeremy would stare at me with a glass in his hand, mustering his thoughts and then ask, "So, what's it like, being a yob?" and I'd answer, "Fine. What's it like being a pig?" both of us determined not to laugh and going through versions of the same exchange every weekend.'

Nicholas Soames: 'You know, I think Martin in some way provided the energy for those weekends. We weren't a terribly unhappy bunch before he arrived nor too distraught at the end of it all but . . . the Martin period was memorable indeed.' He adds urbanely, 'And he and Emma had a raucously good sex life.'

Greg's fantasy unravels because it has to. His life would not have been countenanced by even the most desperately sex-crazed Walter Mitty. Martin's problem was that he was actually experiencing what in the novel appears as unrealistic wish-fulfilment. It is all very well for a novelist to stretch the credulity of his reader, to toy with the inconceivable; more problematic was to live a fantasy and suffer concomitant doubts about whether it was deserved or appropriate. Nicholas Soames: 'Martin would come down perhaps every other weekend and sometimes he would bring Hitch, who became almost as much part of the family as Martin. After he and Emma broke up I'd bump into the two of them fairly often in London. The fact that they both worked on the *New Statesman* and Hitchens was an ardent Communist seems, now, slightly preposterous but not at the time.' He pauses. 'The sort of parties they attended were very often thrown by the monstrously wealthy. Nothing wrong with being rich, of course, but it was more than evident that this pair of radical bohemians loved being courted by the upper classes, grandees and new money included. They were closely connected with at least two branches of the Rothschild family for example. And then there was Mary Furness, Emma's immediate successor, or at least one of them. *She* was a character.'

Kingsley disapproved of none of Martin's girlfriends, though he often confided observations to his son on their various qualities. Mary Furness was of the same gentrified stock as Emma Soames but while the latter, for Kingsley, called to mind the delicious hypothesis of Jane Howard in her mid-twenties – Jane was nearing her forties when he met her – Mary was a composite of his more disparate memories. More than his first and his present wife, she was as intellectually combative as any of the men with whom she associated. Kingsley referred to her in letters to Conquest as 'Soup Thrower', a reference to an incident in a restaurant that Martin had told him about involving a bowl of the starter.

Martin's previous girlfriends had been indulged by the clubbish, predominantly male gatherings at the Bursa, the Pillars of Hercules and, as Hitchens puts it, similarly 'villainous' establishments. Furness, however, laid claim to full membership. When the Friday-lunch club began she was working as a junior editor at the *TLS* and no one questioned her regular presence at Motherunch's. When Ian Hamilton founded the *New Review* in 1974 she expressed a genuine interest in this disestablished unit, and took a job as Hamilton's assistant in the Greek Street offices, joining the extended editorial meetings next door in the smoking room of the Pillars. Hitchens remembers her well from this period. 'She was forbiddingly clever, and quite unbelievably beautiful. Also, she had a nuclear effect upon men, they were besotted and cowed at the same time, a ferocious drinker – in fact she could drink many of her male associates under the table. And Mary loved arguing, put on a fantastic dramatic display, often ending in terrible scenes. Men wanted her terribly but she frightened them too. I'd known Martin since his time with Gully and then Tina but he was entranced with Mary. No, obsessed would be a better way to put it. The thing was that he couldn't deal with her volatility. He loved it but he tried to overcome it.' She was the first woman to whom he proposed marriage. 'I think 1977. She didn't turn him down. Prevaricated I suppose. I think this ended their relationship. Martin certainly *wanted* her, and I think she loved him. Maybe she was the more astute. It might well have been a disastrous combination.' Clive James: 'Let us say that Mary Furness was the sort of woman that men fall out about. A few years ago they would have done so with swords and pistols, and you'd want to be certain that your rival was dead.' Alan Jenkins, who worked with Mary at the *TLS*, which she joined when the *New Review* closed in 1979, offers a more measured portrait. 'Yes, there was a raffish glamour about her but what was particularly attractive to men like Martin was her intellectual sharpness, and indeed her literary heritage. Certainly her father was minor nobility but he was also a legendary figure in Edwardian culture. He was in the Egyptian Service, a friend of E. M. Forster in Alexandria and was responsible for introducing Forster to Cavafy. Mary's parents were quite old when she was born but she carried a trace of Bloomsbury about her. Her own degree was in Philosophy and she was outstandingly, and often for men unnervingly, discerning . . . sagacious.'

'Martin', according to Hitchens, 'decided that it was all or nothing. Again that was the effect she had. He didn't exactly end their relationship, more that he kept a distance.' Kingsley's comment, in a letter to Robert Conquest that 'soup thrower has been dropped finally, I gather'[8] was a misreading of the situation. Although Martin was candid with his father he could be selective with his confidences and in this instance, at least in Hitchens's view, 'He felt wretched and kept himself largely to himself. He preferred his father to think it was all over rather than admit to hoping that it was not.'

'It would all get much worse,' adds Hitchens. 'We were at lunch, Mart, James [Fenton] and me, and he [Fenton] said, quite innocently, to Martin something like, "Oh, I saw your ex-girlfriend earlier this week, leaving the train at Oxford. Very happy they seemed, obviously spending a few days away." Martin was only slightly taken aback because he assumed James was referring to, I don't know, Gully or even Emma, so he asked, "Who?" "Mary," said James, "and Ian." Even then Martin couldn't quite believe it. He didn't ask "Which Ian?" because he didn't have to.' Aside from his considerable achievements as a writer and editor Ian Hamilton provoked awe as the period's most incautious rake, drinker and financial delinquent. Hitchens: 'He always carried an enormous ring of keys, each to some equally suspect bolthole where he might be entertaining his current inamorata or sequestering himself against solicitors' letters following his most recent divorce. He was the only person I knew who was sued by his *own* solicitor.' Wheen recalls a young ambitious poet, just down from Oxford, who visited Hamilton in the hope of having some of his verses included in the *New Review*. 'Hamilton took him next door [to the Pillars] and ordered two large scotches. The young man looked nervously at his watch and said, "Well, I don't normally like to take spirits before 11.30." Ian turned to him and said in a tone of part rage, part shock, "Good God, man! None of us *likes* it!".' 'Ian', Hitchens adds, 'could drink prodigiously but he never appeared pathetic or dissolute. Slightly mad perhaps. Women absolutely loved him. He was handsome, if reckless, outrageous. In fact he was to women what Mary was to men. They lasted barely a month as far as I recall. But the effect on Martin was deep and enduring. You see, Ian was at this time one of Martin's closest friends. Like Terry Kilmartin he was almost a generation ahead of us – well, fifteen years – but Ian wasn't Martin's mentor, never wanted to be. It was a friendship made up of mutual admiration, cooperative rivalry. They thrived on each other's cleverness. And Martin explained to me that Ian was one of the few to whom he had spoken at length about his feelings for Mary, when their relationship had become attritional. Told him all about her fascinating addictive qualities. So when James reported that he'd seen them at Oxford station his response was more than the standard "Well, if I can't have her I don't want anyone else to." No, he realized that Ian had pumped him for information on the woman who, let us be honest, everyone fancied, and then moved in. Martin didn't speak to him for about two years after that.'

I asked Martin about this and he sighed. 'I'm sure Christopher remembers it all as well as I can. Yes, he deceived me. Much later I was asked to contribute to a Festschrift in honour of Ian and I sat there with a blank page. And it occurred to me that every other male, heterosexual contributor would have thought about the same opening sentence. "He fucked me over with a woman!"' Mary would be resurrected ten years later in *London Fields*.

During Martin's period as literary editor at the *New Statesman* Hitchens was effectively second-in-command of news (comment and political features) at the front end, first under the indulgent Anthony Howard and then, briefly, with the less obliging reformist Bruce Page, who took over in 1978. Howard: 'Christopher was a seamless opportunist. By which I mean that he did his job exceedingly well but made sure he reaped potential benefits. For a while he even had his own PA,' a young lady called Lucretia Stewart who in background and presence merited comparison with Mary Furness, with a hint of the preposterous thrown in. According to Wheen, 'She never held the official title as Hitch's PA but in truth she was his social secretary; well, his and Martin's. Her father had been Ambassador to somewhere, and she was well-connected. She had a private income and she hosted parties regularly. More significantly she knew exactly which to attend and which formal or informal gatherings were the places to be seen. For a while I had an office next door to Hitchens and on a typical morning he would shamble in and Lucretia would be waiting at his desk with a meticulously prepared menu of options, mainly social events: book launches, parties and so on.' She was, according to Wheen, inadvertently responsible for Martin's promotion from literary newcomer to a place in the newly expanding galaxy of media celebrity. 'The events attended by Martin and Hitchens also drew the likes of Peter McKay and Adrian Woodhouse; whoever was in charge of the *Express*'s "William

Hickey" column or the *Evening Standard*'s "Londoner's Diary" would also be around.' All of the photographs of him striking that faintly absurd saturnine facial expression, the Mick Jagger style, came from that time. 'It was all really rather absurd, especially when those two years, pre-Mrs T [Thatcher] are now perceived as the nadir of the post-war political and economic consensus. You know, the Labour minority government, streets filled with uncollected rubbish, power cuts, unburied bodies – even the council cemetery workers went on strike. When Bruce [Page] took over from Tony [Howard] in 1978 Hitchens was disappointed because the only other candidate was James [Fenton], but there was a brief six-month period when he, and Martin, though less volubly, saw Bruce as symbolic of imminent radical change in the broader political landscape. I remember, vividly, one evening in the Casa Alpina, Hitchens was animated, pointing his finger peremptorily. He said, "What Bruce brings is the new order. We, all of us, must realize that Radical Socialism is *urgently* necessary. It is *vital* and its time has *arrived*." Odd, really because a year before that he had taken a job at the *Express*. He came back to the *New Statesman* after about six months, but still.' Did Martin share his views on the forthcoming revolution? 'You know, I think he did ... if Martin bothered at all about politics. Hitchens was his compass which, of course, makes it all the more ridiculous that during this same period the two of them kept company with what was left of the aristocracy.' Perhaps the most amusing example of the latter was Lord James Neidpath who had, famously, been seduced and promptly discarded by Tina Brown almost a decade before at Oxford. He was the same age as Martin, a hereditary peer, heir to the earldom of the enormous Scottish estate of Wemyss and with a property in Mayfair. His county pile was Stanway House – or Strangeway's, as it was known at the time, according to Hitchens – a Jacobean manor in

Gloucestershire. On encountering such a figure as a pal of Wooster, fans of Wodehouse would recoil in disbelief. Eccentric is an understatement. He would, in the 1980s, practise and advocate the benefits of trepanning, which involves the drilling of holes in one's head as a relief for depression and a stimulus for creativity. In the late 1970s he professed himself a sculptor and his attractions for ambitious young ladies were abundant; he was guileless, vulnerable and outstandingly rich. Guy Clinch, of *London Fields*, can claim a little more common sense and pragmatism, but only a little. Hitchens recalls visiting Stanway two or three times. And Martin? 'Perhaps once. Though of course he knew him [Neidpath] . . . everyone did, or of him.' But the two of them found more time for excursions to the Rothschild estate in Suffolk, and, until Martin's break with Emma, the Soameses in Hampshire. Hitchens remembers the Heathcoat-Amory house, Ditchley, in Oxfordshire as the most hospitable, boozy location. 'Bridget was almost our age and a superb hostess, as well as providing us with hilarious gossip, stories, about everyone from the Cabinet downwards. The family was High Tory. We, Martin and I, looked forward most of all to the train – we always took the train to Ditchley for some reason – on Friday evening.' As an avid Trotskyist did he not feel that this was a somewhat curious way to spend their time? He muses, 'Yes, we did a fair amount of country-housing at the time. I'd like to think of us fiddling while Rome burned, witnessing the demise of an epoch. But I won't. We were shameless hedonists.'

'There was', recalls Hitchens, 'a bar called the Zanzibar, in Covent Garden. I think Martin recreates at least aspects of it in *Money*. Anyway, at the time [the late 1970s] it seemed the magnet for . . . well debs, even though that subspecies was supposed to have died out. It hadn't. I'd go with Martin and frequently Mark Boxer would be with us. They were a curious bunch. Probably from the same class as Lucretia and Mary but less concerned with work. The Guinness sisters – we got on particularly well with them. Very sharp, and of course they found Martin very amusing. Sabrina was superb, great fun. She was then being touted for Prince Charles. We called her "Queen Sabreen". Told us hilarious stories of their "arranged" court-ship. Said she would have been bored to death and I suppose her dumping of him was the beginning of the legend of Saint Diana. She and Martin were on good terms, and shared a similar sense of humour.'

The most dreaded part of the year for the *New Statesman* set was the end of summer Party Conference Season. Tedious and entirely predictable speeches would be followed by evenings of excess during which bitterness and sycophancy competed for prominence, but at the time off-camera sessions were largely unreportable. Martin, normally concerned only with the arts, was despatched as chief correspondent for the Blackpool Conservative Conference of 1977. His report[9] is remarkably prescient. His friends on the magazine, Hitchens and Fenton in particular, were implacable in their perceptions of Toryism and its personnel, but Martin, albeit showing little sympathy for their politics, wandered among the Conservatives for a week with an open-mindedness vouchsafed by his true vocation as novelist. His report captures the image of a party in a state of transition, reframing its core principles, but adapting, looking for ways to appeal to those traditionally affiliated to its left-wing antagonists. Martin senses a new energy among mostly younger members of the party but implies that the source for this is the so far untested leader, whom he does not bother to name but who would in eighteen months become the first woman prime minister of the UK.

Before leaving the *New Statesman* Hitchens was sent by his new employers to cover the 1978 Labour Conference in

Blackpool and persuaded Lucretia Stewart to accompany him in some hastily contrived official capacity. Her comments on returning to London became part of the *New Statesman* legend of the 1970s. 'It was', observes Wheen, 'like some bizarre, comic social experiment. Lucretia had never *met* people like this before. She said later, "Those trade union chaps are deliciously charming and amusing. One came up to me, pointed to the 'Press' badge on my lapel and said, 'Aye lass. Ahd luv to.' Another told me that 'last night ah 'ad fifteen red 'ot onion bajees and me bum's on fire'. What on earth did he *mean?*"'

Lucretia was for approximately two years Hitchens's occasional girlfriend. 'It was not that they were unfaithful or undecided,' says Wheen. 'No. Each of them would sleep with anyone and, perhaps for convenience, very often each other. Martin too had a fling with her. A brief one at which Hitchens took no offence of course. Anyway it was shortly after Martin's time with Mary.' The trio would re-emerge in Ian McEwan's screenplay for Richard Eyre's cinematic take on the early years of Thatcherism, *A Ploughman's Lunch* (1983). For research Wheen took McEwan to a couple of party conferences in the early 1980s but the true inspiration for the script came from accounts of the years just before Thatcher by Hitchens, Martin and Lucretia. Wheen: 'Lucretia was most certainly Susan Barrington, the rather snooty journalist played by Charlie Dore, Hitchens was the model for Tim Curry's character [Jeremy Hancock] and I suppose there are slight traces of Martin in James Penfield [played by Jonathan Pryce].'

Lucretia also contributed to a fictional scenario that would surface in *London Fields* almost ten years later. Part of this involves the mildly absurd Jamie Neidpath, with whom Mary Furness had a short affair after her equally brief liaison with Ian Hamilton. Hitchens sees her as fascinated by Neidpath, but certainly not in awe of him. 'I think she treated him as an eccentric, much as an anthropologist might deal with a tribal luminary. Odd really. She was from the squirearchy herself but thought Jamie was thoroughly peculiar.' All of which would be echoed in *London Fields* as Guy Clinch, hopelessly ingenuous aristocrat, tests the patience and credulity of Nicola Six.

Mary Furness was the inspiration for Nicola but there was something of Lucretia there too. Wheen: 'I never had sex with Lucretia but one night I slept over at her flat. She greeted me cheerily next morning and offered me coffee and so on – I was a *bit* groggy – but she was busy at the kitchen table with an enormous elegantly bound diary, had been writing for an hour, she said. You see Lucretia *knew* everyone and, if they were male, slept with many of them. The diary was, she explained, "my pension". It hasn't been published of course but God, it would be gold-dust.' There is an intriguing passage close to the beginning of *London Fields*, the point at which Nicola decides that her fate as murderee is sealed. She has found her assassin:

> When at last she returned to the flat Nicola laid out her diaries on the round table. She made an entry, unusually crisp and detailed: the final entry. The notebooks she used were Italian, their covers embellished with Latin script . . . Now they had served their purpose and she wondered how to dispose of them. The story wasn't over, but the life was. She stacked the books and reached for a ribbon . . . 'I've found him. On the Portobello Road, in a place called the Black Cross, I found him.'[10]

It seems from Wheen's account that Lucretia was not particularly secretive regarding the diaries. 'No, she wasn't,' he says. 'She didn't go on about them but for anyone who stayed at the flat she was honest enough about what she was doing, could hardly be otherwise given the amount of time she gave over to them.' And Martin stayed there as well? 'His fling with her was brief, low-key, but he would have stayed.'

Hitchens adds: 'She was restless and conspiratorial. And to an extent a *femme fatale*. A bit like [Anthony Powell's character] Pamela Widmerpool, beautiful, difficult, moody. You finally find out in *Books Do Furnish a Room* that she is frigid, and frigidity is often a symptom of nymphomania. She wants to do it all the time, but she doesn't enjoy it.' Which brings to mind Nicola Six? 'Yes, it does, but Mary [Furness] supplied Nicola's sublime, captivating dimension.'

In October 1977 Martin attended a party in Holland Park hosted by Tobias Rodgers. Playboys tend to be the products of popular fiction and the media, but Rodgers was the genuine article, an antiquarian bookseller who practised a patrician brand of hedonism. Qualification for his abundant hospitality required either a comparable amount of wealth and good looks, or proven artistic flair. Martin and Hitchens were present, as were Angela Gorgas and her then flatmate, later to become novelist, Candia McWilliam. Both, from Hitchens's recollection, were 'stunningly attractive' but it was Gorgas who found herself the subject of Martin's well-rehearsed charm and wit. 'Although we mixed in similar circles, I'd never actually met Martin before. I'd seen pictures of him in the press so I recognised him and we got chatting pretty quickly. He made me laugh. I mean, I'd known him only a few minutes but I was weeping with laughter. He was funny but he listened too. He seemed totally enthralled by my conversation, which was obviously immensely flattering. It goes without saying that he was very attractive but the photographs I'd seen previously did not do him justice. I knew, as a photographer, that I could do much better. I wanted to photograph him myself and indeed I went on to do just that; I kept a visual diary of our time together. It was just a personal record – at the time I was totally unaware of the importance of those images. I was not to know that over thirty years later those photographs would form a large part of my exhibition, "Martin Amis and Friends" at the National Portrait Gallery.'

Angela shared a spacious house in the fashionable and, even in the 1970s, outrageously expensive Warwick Avenue with Candia McWilliam and its owner Amschel Rothschild. The house had gained a reputation as a salon for those who had either earned some status as incipient stars in the arts and those who, mostly by virtue of inherited wealth, borrowed a layer of bohemian glamour from the former. The assemblies were affected, upmarket and lacked the infectious blend of self-caricature and intellectual point-scoring of the *New Statesman* gatherings. Hitchens, fascinated, went along as did on several occasions Clive James; and one suspects that the mood of pretentiousness that informs his first novel *Brilliant Creatures* (1983) reflected some of his experiences there.

In the first few months of their relationship Martin and Angela would stay over in each other's flats. Martin had recently exchanged the rooms in Earl's Court for a rather more agreeable, though certainly not upmarket, flat in Kensington Garden Square. 'It was', he says, 'arranged by Pat [Kavanagh] and the lease belonged to a friend of hers, Jim Durham. Off Queensway and Westbourne Grove, two rooms, a kitchen and bathroom. Not bad for twelve pounds a week.' Angela remembers it as 'a bachelor pad. It was sparse – there were a few framed silk screen prints on the walls by his artist brother Philip, but Martin had little interest in the visual arts really. The flat was always very neat and tidy, mainly due to his cleaner, Ana, who came twice a week. There was little for her to do as the flat was small with one bedroom and there was never any washing up – Martin never cooked and I rarely did. The fridge was practically empty as we ate out most of the time, often at

Bertorelli's, a popular local restaurant in Westbourne Grove. Martin was very disciplined and would be at his desk working from 8.30 a.m., no matter how late he went to bed the night before. At lunchtime he would break off from writing and relax, either reading or playing his guitar, usually just improvising.' He played the guitar? 'Yes. Very well too, but he rather kept that to himself.' John Walsh has a similar memory of the place from when as a cub reporter he was sent to interview Martin. 'I'd already heard about it, from Craig Raine actually, who had remarked on the empty fridge. "People usually bring their own," said Martin, "I drink mine after opening." He was joking, partly. But what about food? asked Raine. And Martin found this terribly amusing. I thought the place was slightly unnerving. Cell-like. It was as though he was determined to leave no evidence of his presence, let alone his passing. And although he was accommodating enough, the flat made interviewers feel like *they* were in an interrogation cell. Most effective.'

At around the same time that Martin met Angela, Kingsley and Jane moved from Lemmons to Flask Walk, to another impressive Georgian house but one more convenient for Kingsley who now lunched regularly at the Garrick. Hitchens: 'On the surface little had changed. Kingsley was still a brilliant host. "If your glass isn't full it's your own fault." And he would point to a table and cabinet of drinks from which all there were told to help themselves.' But it was clear also that he and Jane were not the same couple they'd been even when he first got to know them, no more than five years earlier. 'Ian [McEwan], Clive [James] and James [Fenton] were still regulars and the banter was as lively as ever but the politics was touched with something a little edgier. The atmosphere in the house reflected a much broader mood. When we all first went to Lemmons, and when Kingsley and Conkers sometimes came out with us, that was 1974 when a minority Labour Government had brought down Edward Heath, and national politics seemed comedic, like musical chairs. But there was, towards the end of the seventies, something far more precipitate . . . change was imminent.'

Anthony Howard, then in his final year as editor of the *New Statesman*, recalls that from 1977 onwards the lunchtime sessions in Theobald's Road were 'comparable to the final gatherings in the first-class dining room of the *Titanic*. We had not quite reached the so-called winter of discontent [1978–9] but there were sufficient warnings of social and economic stagnation. I mean that the unions, particularly the public service unions, held the levers of power; they could effectively bring the country to a halt. They never went so far as to spell out in detail how they would do so but the threat and its consequences were evident to all. Some saw it as the Marxist prophecy about to be fulfilled, capitalism finally brought to its knees by the proletariat, with factors such as the Middle East oil crisis as confirmation that these symptoms reached further than the provincial economy of the UK.' Hitchens? 'Yes, indeed. He took that view, advocating a proactive role for the *New Statesman* as an organ of the revolution. I am not sure who he thought our readers were.' Kingsley provided a caustic commentary on the apparent political crisis, raising such questions as to when it was likely he would be required to hand over Flask Walk as HQ for the Hampstead branch of the Young Communist League. Martin neither apologized for his father – who in any event would have resented this – and nor did he intervene on behalf of his peers. He was, according to Francis Wheen, 'dispassionately amused. But I think, on the whole, he was rather impressed. By Kingsley, that is.' Kingsley commented to Conquest: 'You'll have heard by now that Bruce Page has got the *Statesman*. Everybody there seems too stunned to say anything. Consensus is that he's *either* off his head *or* a colonel in the KGB *or* both *and* that he's a frightful shit . . .'[11]

The contrast between Page and the supposed or professed advocates of the genuine left already at the magazine offers an insight into the unique culture of the *New Statesman* during the 1970s. In Page's view: 'I took over a flaccid middle-ground magazine being dragged towards the territory of what would become the Liberal Democrats. I restored it to its original, traditional readership, those who wanted articles on the pragmatics of politics, from a predominantly Socialist perspective. And it began to make money again.' Irrespective of this closing comment, not many would deny Page's claim to have turned the *New Statesman* into an organ for serious left-wing discourse. But at the same time he brought to an end what had become an unofficial colloquium which had both indulged the joky amorality of the time and more significantly evolved into a group of writers and journalists who would dominate the intellectual establishment for the subsequent twenty years. The Theobald's Road lunches and drinking sessions were certainly not occasions for debate on what each felt about the agonies of the postmodern condition. Triviality, facetious intellectual one-upmanship and sexist wordplay predominated, all of which horrified Page. Howard: 'Obviously, I had "left the building". But I was in regular contact with those still there. By all accounts editorial conferences were like wakes, with everyone, the editor excepted, mourning the death of humour. Page felt that the jokiness of the place was symptomatic of its political impotence.' In fact it was the glue that held together something far less easy to classify.

Martin and Page clashed almost immediately, the latter regarding his literary editor as chief perpetrator of the clubbish bohemian atmosphere that had, in Page's view, infected the most significant part of the journal, the front half. Page's literary tastes were eclectic but governed largely by the mantra that writing of any sort should be accessible to all comers, a British version of Eastern bloc Socialist Realism. 'To show his cultural credentials,' recalls Wheen, 'he would sometimes state at meetings "as . . . observed in . . ."' probably a play by Shaw, or even quote from a piece of verse. I don't remember exactly his favourites but few would have been particularly fashionable after about 1920.'

Craig Raine had tutored Martin at Oxford and occasionally attended sessions with the *New Statesman* set. Although his verse was valued by all at the *New Statesman* in its own right, the decision to award 'A Martian Sends a Postcard Home' the Prudence Farmer Award for best single poem of the year in 1978 was influenced also by the knowledge of all concerned that it would infuriate Page. Fenton, chair of the judges, commented pointedly that 'the Martian . . . insists on presenting the familiar at its most strange', that the governing principle of composition is 'free contemplation, without ulterior motive, eager if anything for the most improbable discoveries'.[12] Hardly the kind of writing suitable for an engagement with the burgeoning winter of discontent. As if to leave Page in no doubt regarding the commitment of the back-end staff to poetry at its most ostentatiously poetic, second prize was awarded to Christopher Reid for his 'Baldanders'. Thus the two most prominent members of what would become known as the Martian school of poetry were given public prominence for the first time thanks, in part, to the new regime of Puritanism at the *New Statesman*.

Martin resigned his post as literary editor two months later and his parting shot was to publish 'Point of View'.[13] McGonagall left an embarrassing stain upon the distinguished legacy of the ballad and E. J. Thribb did something comparable to free verse. It would be unjust to treat Martin's contribution to Martianism as a similar aberration – it is a competent piece – but it none the less invites comparison with both by allowing an apparent duty to precedent to eclipse singularity of purpose.

> Some of us look at the sunset and can
> See only blood in the vampiric sky.
> I've got a clock that turns its back on me.
> In disdain. A watch wouldn't dare do that.
>
> If you don't feel a little mad sometimes
> Then I think you must be out of your mind.
> No one knows what to do. Clichés are true.
> Everything depends on your point of view.

It is worth dwelling upon the immediate consequences of Martin's departure. Page appointed as his replacement David Caute, a figure he judged to be his ideological mirror image, a man who would 'clean up' the shoddy arts sections of the magazine. The appointment was seen by most as a personal snub to Julian Barnes, Martin's deputy, who had applied for the post, and as a general reprimand to those whom Page deemed to have fallen under Martin's cosmopolitan bohemian spell. Fenton left the magazine. An era had ended and it seemed to some as though Martin's exit epitomized its closure. Had he provided its momentum? Anthony Howard: 'I think he did in a way. Now that most of the group and many of its occasional members are established figures we tend to forget that at the time Martin was really the only one who was a "star" both as a writer and someone who featured in William Hickey's gossip column as one of the most eligible bachelors in London.'

While Barnes was working out his notice he and Wheen devised the most potentially obscene Comp. ever, as a memorial to the good times. During the war and later when men were on National Service it was common to include in letters home lurid anagrams alongside signatures. The most famous were 'Norwich' (Nikkers Off Ready When I Come Home) and 'Burma' (Be Upstairs Ready My Angel). Barnes asked readers to bridge the gap between this naughty-postcard tradition and the liberated post-sixties decade. The entries made up the largest 'Comp.' ever, two columns, including 'Nice' (Nine Inches Coiled Expectantly), 'Lyons' (Let Your Organ Naturally Seep), 'Oslo' (Oh, Such Lovely Orifices) and 'Hamburg' (Have A Monstrous Bratwurst Unwrapped, Ready, Gretchen). Did Martin have anything to do with this? I ask Wheen. 'I think he played a part.' It was now Caute's job to deliver the proofs to Southend and he took the opportunity to scrutinize the material only shortly before he left the office. Wheen remembers him addressing Page. 'Filth, disgusting. They've been turning out schoolboy obscenities like this for years. That's it.' The Comp. was not formally closed but it would never again reflect the raucous, dissident aspect of the 1970s era. Wheen: 'After that Page imposed statutory rules and timetables. No more ping-pong in the basement, no extended lunches in the likes of Theobald's Road. Not that it mattered much because the people who had been part of all that had left.'

6

Paris

During 1977 Martin's agent Pat Kavanagh had negotiated a contract for him with Lew Grade's ITC Entertainment to write the screenplay for their forthcoming film to be called *Saturn 3*, a project which combined the enduring appeal of science fiction with a spurious attempt at realism, the latter involving the ongoing Apollo space programme. Martin's script is at once heroic and pitiable, his various attempts at wit, rhetorical bravado, even elegance, being shoe-horned into a directorial enterprise as boorish as *The Vikings*. 'Little of my script', adds Martin, 'was used. The final version was by Frederic Raphael.' Even before he learned of the fate of his contribution he was aware that the whole project would end in catastrophe. The narrative, so called, by John Barry involved scenes of seduction by lonely astronauts and robots, the latter supplementing their incongruous sexuality with a tendency to dismantle themselves. But Martin continued for the simple reason that Kavanagh had settled a fee that went far beyond any advance even the most popular novelist could hope for: £30,000. Alongside this, and as the project at Pinewood became more fractious and unfocused, Martin was offered the job as script consultant, at £1,000 per week. Taking into account the gigantic increase in the cost of that most basic of human aspirations, house ownership, this would today be the equivalent of more than a quarter of a million (in 1978 Kingsley and Jane sold Lemmons, a prestigious Home Counties mansion, for £105,000). Alongside his salary from the *New Statesman*, royalties from other books and occasional payments for journalism elsewhere *Saturn 3* brought Martin's taxable income for the financial year 1978–9 to more than £38,000. This prompted the much-quoted, notorious remark in Kingsley's letter to Larkin in May 1979: 'Did I tell you Martin is spending a year abroad as a TAX EXILE? Last year he earned £38,000. Little shit. 29, he is. Little shit.'[1] Anthony Thwaite, editor of Larkin's letters and friend of both Kingsley and Larkin, commented to me that: 'Of course Kingsley loved masquerade. He was pleased and very proud that Martin was doing so well but he knew that one day the letters would be read by those ignorant of the games he and Philip played [in them]. Performing from the grave I suppose.' Rosie Boycott backs this up. 'More than ten years later, he would still grin at the recollection, the year Martin became richer than him. He joked about it but above all he was proud of him.'

By this point Martin and Angela Gorgas were already in 'exile', in Paris, and seven months earlier, on 28 October 1978, the following notice had appeared in the Court and Social page of *The Times*: 'The engagement is announced between Martin, younger son of Kingsley Amis of Hampstead, London and Lady Kilmarnock of Ronda, Spain and Angela, younger daughter of Mr and Mrs Richard Gorgas of Farnborough, Kent.' Hitchens: 'There wasn't an engagement party, as such, but I remember an informal lunch at Flask Walk about a week after the announcement, six or seven guests. Kingsley was on good form but something had changed. Angela was in raptures, giggling, helping Jane with the food – daughter-in-law-in-waiting I suppose – and Martin seemed quite odd. He was content, apparently, but he appeared to have aged about two decades in as many weeks, sitting in an armchair reading the Sunday papers with a glass of brandy. Looked like he was already married, well, not just married but *middle-aged*. With benefit of hindsight it's probably just as well it was all called off.'

During the six months before the move to Paris Martin and Angela lived as well-heeled bohemians. Gorgas: 'Most weekends were spent in London, going to parties, dinner parties or meeting up with friends in restaurants. We often visited his dad and Jane for Sunday lunch at their home in Hampstead. We occasionally drove in Martin's beaten-up Mini, affectionately known as 'The Ashtray', to spend the weekend at Ammy's [Amschel Rothschild's] estate in Suffolk; Ammy was a charming and generous host and other friends would gather there, Christopher Hitchens and Adam Shand Kydd amongst them. A friend of ours, the artist Anthony Palliser, who had lived and worked in Paris, told us about a flat that had become available to rent. We both thought it would be fun to get away from London . . . and Paris, well, who wouldn't want to live in Paris for a while?'

The flat was in rue Mouffetard which Angela describes as 'ordinary nineteenth-century Paris – the street had a permanent market selling groceries, live rabbits, chickens and so on – which was becoming a trendy area favoured by artists and intellectuals.' 'The flat', says Martin, 'was rented to us from Ugo Tognazzi's ex-wife.' Tognazzi, Italian film director and actor, was at the time they moved in busy completing and then promoting one of the most successful non-US films of all time, *La Cage aux Folles*, in which he starred as the gay owner of a

St Tropez nightclub. 'Externally,' Angela recalls, 'the building was maybe a hundred and fifty years old and shabby-chic, but the flat itself was pure late 1970s. The décor was *incredible*. The wallpaper had a swirling purple and silver pattern – and the carpets were brightly coloured with geometric patterns too, quite a combination! The furniture was leather, aluminium and glass.'

Hitchens, now back at the *New Statesman* and desperately attempting to reconcile his hedonistic Trotskyism with Page's schoolmasterish regime, took over the lease on Martin's 'sock'. His own residence had become not so much downmarket as uninhabitable. Martin might often play the role of feckless reprobate; his friend lived it with enthusiasm.

A few of Martin's relationships had endured but this was his first experience of full-time cohabitation. Domesticity and its attendant mundanities were largely avoided. Despite the fact that it came by arrangement with a friend the flat was, according to Martin, 'expensive' but neither he nor Angela was inclined to change their habit of eating out in cafés and restaurants. 'Workmen's cafés', so-called in Paris, were of course rather different from the greasy spoon joints that Martin and the rest enjoyed in London. There were no proper menus but plenty of bread, cheese, meats, salad and carafes of ordinary wine, and Martin felt a little bereft. It was difficult to 'slum' even in the poorer parts of Paris. Poverty-stricken Parisians still maintained a certain amount of class. 'We quickly found a "favourite bar" which, most importantly, had a Space Invader machine; Martin found this a good way to unwind in the evenings and would sometimes spend hours in front of it.' When not entertaining friends, Martin and Angela settled into an agreed routine: 'As I have already said, he was immensely disciplined. We would usually have breakfast together at a local café but by about nine a.m. at the very latest he was at his desk, writing. He did first drafts in longhand. He would work all day, perhaps with a break at lunchtime – I would buy fresh bread and cheeses from the market and we would eat lunch together if I was around. I worked in a studio nearby, completing commissioned portraits and paintings. I also attended life-drawing classes at a local art school. I don't know if it's the same now but then you didn't have to enrol as a student, you could simply walk in off the street, pay two francs and draw a model. It was fantastic.'

'I came back one afternoon and Martin was sitting in the *salle d'attente* talking and laughing. He and the other man stood up and he said, "Angela, let me introduce Roman. Roman Polanski." They were doing an interview. All very relaxed. I sat down and joined them and Polanski was as funny as Martin.'

The new novel, begun when he resigned from the *New Statesman*, would, he decided, take his literary ambitions and his reputation in a different direction.

His reviews so far had been enthusiastic yet ambivalent. Clearly he was unconventional in that many of his characters challenged established limits of credibility and his dystopian miniatures veered between the arbitrary and the prophetic. At the same time there was the nagging implication that in *Dead Babies* and *Success* the long shadow of his famous father was still just visible. On *Success* Blake Morrison in the *TLS* gives the impression of being sympathetic and slightly apologetic. Clearly he likes the novel but wants desperately to avoid the admission that his enjoyment derives only from Martin's stylistic bravado: it 'contains', he declares, 'elements of social allegory', and is sometimes 'imbued with political significance'.[2] Paul Ableman in the *Spectator* was less charitable. The occasional 'plod through Beckettland [and] meander through Kafka country' is a sop to the avant-garde, somewhat at odds with 'the reader's growing perception that the book is a parable about the old order in England and the new raj of the yobs . . .'[3] No one seemed certain if he was adapting the techniques of the post-war 1950s generation to a more openly degenerate environment or showing signs of incipient radicalism.

The broader literary world – to whose moods Martin was professionally but unapprehensively alert – was at the end of the 1970s entering one of its periodic bouts of discontent with regard to the lack of adventure in British writing.

In 1976 Peter Ackroyd set the tone in his *Notes for a New Culture*.[4] He argued that England – though by implication not necessarily Britain – had 'insulated itself' from the benefits of modernism and maintained the 'false context' and 'false aesthetic' of realism. His ideal was the French *noveau roman*, the kind of fiction writing which constantly uses the genre to re-examine its own precarious fabric. The closing issue of the *New Review* in 1978 comprised a colloquium of writers and critics summoned to pronounce on the state of the novel. The general view was that the British were by varying degrees self-absorbed, unambitious, complacent and reactionary in what they produced, at least compared with American, French and Third World writers. The fact that Martin and the editor of the *New Review*, Ian Hamilton, once close friends, had recently fallen out over Mary Furness had nothing to do with the issue's rather unkind view of the state of fiction, or so one assumes. Weightier academic assessments were equally pessimistic, with John Sutherland in *Fiction and the Fiction Industry*[5] proposing that the relationship between writers and major publishers stifled originality; the latter were concerned only with reliably saleable goods and the former, who needed either to get published or to sustain their income, complied. Bernard Bergonzi updated his 1970 *The Situation of the Novel*[6] in 1979. Both editions, particularly the second, remind one of an angry headmaster's extended report on yet another decade's group of recalcitrant idlers. The English novel was now stultifyingly, almost irrevocably 'parochial' in its range. In Bergonzi's opinion little had changed since the nineteenth century and, lamentably, the crystallization of liberal ideas and actions that made the classic realist novel valuable had now been replaced by a nugatory conservatism; traditional techniques and reactionary values appeared to be working hand in hand. The most famous contribution to this growing caterwaul of disgruntlement came from Bill Buford, who in the third issue of *Granta* in 1980 voiced his concerns in an essay entitled 'The End of the English Novel'. He was prompted to do so, he claimed, by an article in the trade journal the *Bookseller* by Robert McCrum 'a young editor at Faber' (twenty-five years later a major presence in the literary establishment; among other things literary editor of the *Observer*). McCrum had claimed, from first-hand experience, that Sutherland's thesis was valid and, worse, that the publishing houses and established writers were perpetuating bad writing.

Neither Martin, nor for that matter Ian McEwan, were thought worthy of mention in any of these. Instead praise was heaped upon the genuine standard bearers of experiment: Christine Brooke-Rose, Gabriel Josipovici, Ann Quin, Alan Burns and the redoubtable double act of B. S. Johnson and John Berger. The one newcomer cited as a promising heir to Joyce and Beckett was a young man called Salman Rushdie whose single novel then in print, *Grimus*, had appeared in 1975. But at the time Rushdie was on the margins of the circuit patronized by Martin, McEwan, Hitchens, Fenton and Barnes.

D. J. Taylor: 'With hindsight we can find remarkable and original qualities in those early novels [by Martin], but they were treated then as raffish sops to contemporary taste, eccentric, faintly morbid – very funny of course – but still rather orthodox.' In truth, they showed the first traces of a previously

181

inconceivable hybrid involving the purist strain of modernism, the kind of writing that revels in its own strangeness, and a capacity to reduce the most sombre, mirthless readers to guilty laughter. Such a combination had never before even been conjectured upon let alone encountered so it is not entirely surprising that the literary establishment took some time to acknowledge its arrival. However, the delay is one of the reasons why Martin himself decided to renounce the stifling inhibitions of readability and attempt something that might attract the attention of those guardians of high culture, the advocates of experiment. The result, eventually, would be *Other People: A Mystery Story* (1981). Angela was his constant companion during the period of the novel's gestation. He explained to her his persistent interest in the minutiae of a woman's day-to-day life. She recalls that 'he was hunting all the time, picking up evidence, material for his portraits, his pictures in language'. Now, though, he was giving special attention to the ordinary demands of life as a woman, so being there all the time Angela was his main source. 'Why do you choose that kind of make-up, what do you do with your hair and so on? And he was concerned also with things that might seem to have nothing to do with gender – crossing the road, opening a door, pouring from a bottle, acts you don't plan or think about. But all the time he was comparing, looking for differences and contrasts.' The novel was clearly going to focus upon the experiences of a woman, and might even be a story told by a woman? 'Yes, he said so, but he was more guarded about what exactly he intended to do with all this.'

Martin claims only to have a first draft of *Other People: A Mystery Story* and while conceding that he did, as Angela recalls, make copious notes while preparing it they appear to have been lost. 'Actually,' he states, 'I started the novel before I left the *New Statesman*.' Before the appointment of Bruce?

'Around the same time, but the events weren't related. The animus was the question of being someone else and the most obvious difference between my world, my experience and another was sex, gender.'

Other People focuses upon a brief period in the life of Mary Lamb who might, prior to her unexplained state of amnesia, have once been Amy Hide. Parallels between them are inferred, and the principal difference is that Amy exists as a memory, an echo of someone socially privileged, who enjoyed a hedonistic amoral lifestyle, while Mary seems in a state of atrophy with no clearly defined background or prospects.

An attempt to reconstruct the mental territory occupied by the opposite sex might have been the animus for the project but as it developed something else, something far more private and unsettling, began to intrude upon his creative process. Mary Lamb is one of the most elusive figures in fiction. She provides the momentum for the novel, everything that occurs between its opening page and its macabre close is about her, she is the subject of everyone else's attention – pastoral, envious, sexual, malevolent, the list is monumental – yet we have no proper sense of who she is or what she endures. We feel for her, we want to know more of the dreadfulness that seems to attend her permanent state of confusion, but throughout the book she remains as little more than an enigma, a human being shaped by a chiaroscuro of other people's ambitions and failings.

She is, therefore, the perfect vehicle for the adaptation of Raine's and Reid's poetry to the more intricate fabric of fiction. Raine introduced his technique through the whimsical conceit of the Martian, an anomalous figure possessed of all the cultural resources of his inventor yet untutored in the routines of association and recognition that make up our daily lives.

Mary is a credible embodiment of the Martian poems. The mental condition which prefigures the latter – seeing everything

as if for the first time – is a feature of her amnesia. But instead
of having her sound like a shambolic uncorrected version of
Raine's and Reid's drafts, Martin turns her into a mute record
of confusion and rediscovery. We learn of her state of mind not
from what she says but from the narrator, a presence whose
prose equivalent of Martian verse comes close to translation.
Raine famously inverted the standard perception of a car
journey:

> a key is turned to free the world
>
> for movement, so quick there is a film
> to watch for anything missed.

Similarly Mary as a passenger 'watched the . . . warehouses that
marched past slowly on either side and seemed to glance back
over their shoulders at the car' (p. 114). In Raine's universe the
telephone is 'a haunted apparatus' which 'sleeps' and

> snores when you pick it up
>
> If the ghost cries, they carry it
> to their lips and soothe it to sleep
> with sounds.

Mary could easily have walked into the poem, albeit with a little
more confidence on how to unravel these defamiliarized images:

> The bandy, glistening dumb-bell was heavier than she
> had expected.
>   'Yes?' said Mary.
>   A thin voice started talking. Telephones were clearly
> less efficient instruments of communication than people
> let on. For instance, you could hardly hear the other
> person and they could hardly hear you.

'I can't hear. What?' said Mary.
Then she heard, in an angry whine, '*I said turn it the
other way up.*'
Mary blushed, and did as she was told. (p. 106)

Raine's amanuensis wanders along the most unremarkable
vistas, always altering the ordinary and casting curious glances
towards the mundane. The butcher 'duels with himself and
woos his woman customers/offering thin coiled coral necklaces
of mince/heart loaned from the fridge, a leg of pork/like a nasty
bouquet, pound notes printed with blood'. Mary's excursion to
the market involves similarly macabre images.

Mary shopped among the blood-boltered marble, in-
specting murdered chickens. She walked the terraces of
the vegetable stalls, watched by the scarred toothless
louts who swung like lewd monkeys from their wooden
supports. She presided over the icy offal of the fishmon-
gers' slabs, where the bug-eyed prawns all faced the same
direction, as imploring as the Faithful. (pp. 18–20)

Rather than attempting to explain what Martin might have been
up to most of the reviewers sought shelter behind such makeshift
adjectival substitutes for evaluation as 'powerful', 'obsessive',
'dazzling', 'scintillating', 'enthralling' and 'disturbing'. While
one is equally reluctant to treat the novel like a crossword puzzle
several elementary questions trouble even the most indulgent
reader. First, what is the relationship between Mary and Amy?
Second, who is the figure referred to only as 'Prince'?
   In 1977 Martin was contacted by a woman he had known
very briefly almost three years earlier during his first summer as a
literary celebrity. Julie Kavanagh had been with him for a matter
of weeks when they and Hitchens attended an event in a spacious

Mayfair maisonette, their host now lost to the memories of all concerned. Martin began a conversation with Lamorna Seale which would result during the subsequent weeks in a brief but by no means trivial affair. Martin would have continued with the relationship but it was brought to a close largely at Lamorna's behest. She felt reluctant to give up completely on her marriage to Patrick Seale with whom she already had a three-year-old son, Orlando. Seale was almost fifteen years her senior, a journalist specializing in the Middle East who in the 1960s had written several celebrated books on the region and its crises. When Lamorna met Martin at the party she and Patrick were involved in a mutually agreed trial separation, hoping that time apart might give them the opportunity to reflect upon and perhaps later resolve their marital problems. It was for this reason, when they resumed contact approximately three months later, that both were certain that the child she was carrying was not his. They agreed, however, that for the sake of Delilah, as she was to be named, it would be best for Patrick's name to appear on the birth certificate and that the truth about her biological paternity should be kept from her. Lamorna stated truthfully that during their time apart she had had sex with only one person and that Delilah's father was Martin Amis. They also agreed that Martin need not be informed, but two years later Lamorna decided to call him at the *New Statesman* to ask him to meet her for lunch where she showed him a recent photograph of Delilah and announced that she was his daughter. Martin is still unclear about her reason for doing so; she certainly had no wish for him to assume any kind of legal or financial responsibility. He states in *Experience* that when they met she had 'impressed me with her general bearing and burnish – her beauty, her sanity'. Despite this, as he would later learn, she was suffering from severe manic depression. They said they would meet again, though neither broached the delicate question of whether he would be introduced to his infant daughter. Lamorna did state that she had just completed her first novel, to be called *Candida Rising*, which would be published by Michael Joseph the following year, 1978.

Six months after their lunch and shortly after her novel appeared, Lamorna was discovered by her son, Orlando, then five, hanging in the attic of the family home. Orlando shielded his two-year-old sister Delilah from the scene and Patrick soon afterwards hurried his two children down the stairs into the back of the house and lowered his wife's body to the floor.

Martin has not recorded the means by which he heard of her suicide nor his feelings following the disclosure. What is known, however, is that contact with the Seale family then ceased until he was introduced to Delilah in 1996.

Contemporary reviewers had no reason to suspect that anything actual or private informed the various and discordant layers of the writing and were therefore united in their view that the rising star of contemporary fiction was exploring the boundaries between realism and the avant-garde. In truth, however, he was attempting to reconcile his vocation – this was, it should be remembered, his first piece of fiction written after becoming freelance – with events far more traumatic than anything he had either previously experienced or allowed his imaginative faculties to countenance. There are obvious parallels between Mary and Lamorna. The latter's manic depression meant not that she perceived events, experiences and objects differently from everyone else but rather that they acquired associations and qualities that reflected unique aspects of her state of mind. Amnesia, or a separation from a comfortable consensus on how the otherwise harmless mundanities of existence make us feel, is a related though far less distressing condition, and its volitional, creative counterpart is of course Martian writing.

Martin makes it impossible for the reader to discern the nature of the tripartite relationship between Amy Hide, Mary and Prince. He is Mary's guide, the intermediary between her skewed perceptions and the elaborations of the narrator, the Martian prose-poet, and he owns the suburban house in which Amy appears to be the guest. They are not lovers yet they are curiously intimate, sharing routine tasks, discussing his tedious yet undefined work in the city. We know that their relationship is also precipitate, that he will assist her through some kind of alteration.

'I am going away for a while,' he said to her at breakfast the next day.

Amy wasn't alarmed or even surprised. In a way she was pleased. She knew that this was a salute to something in her, and that she wouldn't disappoint him.

'You'll be all right, won't you?'

'Of course I'll be all right,' she said.

They finished breakfast in silence. She walked out with him to the car.

'Something will happen when I've gone,' he said. (p. 196)

'Then something did happen.' Amy goes to the bookcase and takes out Burton's *Anatomy of Melancholy*, which among other things identified the generic symptoms of what psychotherapists would later call clinical depression. Out of the volume falls an ancient photograph, early Victorian, the period when executions still took place in public. On the scaffold stands a group of top-hatted aldermen and city fathers, along with a hooded hangman, holding the noose above the head of the condemned prisoner.

On the back of the photograph Prince has written 'You wait'. She does and in the interim is visited briefly by her sister called

– ridiculously – Baby, who is the only balanced contented individual in the book. She has a young child, a baby girl. She is married, but she informs Amy later that 'It's his', leaving the reader to wonder why a woman might need to state, gratuitously, that the child was fathered by her husband. Unless of course she was not. Soon Amy will walk through a sequence of doors and tunnels, leaving her past behind and find herself in the presence of a man wearing a 'hood or cowl', whom she recalls from the photograph.

> His arms enfolded her. She felt a sensation of speed so intense that her nose caught the tang of smouldering air. She saw a red beach bubbled with sandpools under a furious and unstable sun. She felt she was streaming, she felt she was undoing everywhere. Oh, father, she thought, my mouth is full of *stars*. Please put them out and take me home to bed.
>
> The sensation of speed returned for a moment, then nothing did. (p. 206)

No one has ever offered a record of what hanging feels like but this must come close.

After being told that Delilah was his daughter Martin showed the photograph to his mother. He relates their conversation in *Experience*.[7]

> 'What do you think, Mum?'
> She held the photograph at various distances from her eyes [. . .] Without looking up she said,
> – *Definitely*.
> – What should I do?
> – Nothing. Don't do anything, dear.

Few if any novels have so successfully sustained an environment quite as malevolent as this and a group of characters so impersonally vindictive. All of them, from the yobbish Sharon and Trev to their middle-class bohemian counterparts Augusta and Jamie, bear a remarkable resemblance to the cast of Martin's three previous works of fiction but with a slight but significant difference. Before *Other People* Martin never quite went as far as to exculpate his characters, yet he cleverly deflected attention from their vileness by lending them the cloak of magnificently tailored, very black comedy. Now, however, he allows them to range beyond this protective pall, and aside from their unappealing effects upon the reader, it is Mary/Amy who suffers most from encounters with them. Indeed the atmosphere of the entire text is nightmarish, an enfolding torment for its two principal figures from which they seem to be seeking release. And we know how Amy eventually succeeds in this. Of course, Martin was neither so deluded nor so presumptuous as to assume that he in any way was responsible for the world or conditions that contributed to Lamorna's depression, and there are no direct allegorical parallels between the novel and the tragic private narrative to which he had access. At the same time it must be recognized that a quite remarkable literary document – by turns flawed and ambitious – drew its character from a unique combination of experience and creativity. The Martian poetic sub-genre was unapologetically rootless – it involved writing about writing – and Martin's original objective was to embed its pure literariness in a novel that caught something of a world of endemic disconnectedness. He could not have predicted that an individual afflicted by what he would later call 'the dissociation of sensibility' of the 1970s would become so closely interwoven with the writing of the book.

The bulk of the novel was completed during Martin's

190

nine-month period in Paris. Did he, I ask Angela Gorgas, suggest that there was any connection between the nature of his project and his decision to live for such a long period in a state of alienation from circumstances he knew so well? (And one should note that it was a decision based not upon financial contingency, as alleged facetiously in Kingsley's remark to Larkin: the Inland Revenue had full records of his income for that financial year irrespective of his temporary absence from the UK.) 'Martin is someone who likes to create his own familiar world around him, no matter where he is. At that time, the centre of his world was his writing and everything else fell into place around this – Paris wasn't *so* different from London in that way. We had a small social circle, consisting mainly of Anthony [Pallister's] friends, but friends from London came over too; Hitch, James [Fenton] and Ian [McEwan] were our most frequent visitors.' I asked Angela if he mentioned to her the death of Lamorna or her disclosure that he was the father of Delilah and she stated that she knew nothing of this until more than twenty years later when she read of them in *Experience*. Martin showed the photograph to his mother during a visit to Ronda in 1978 but said nothing to Kingsley, who might otherwise have suspected parallels between invention and actuality – being an adept practitioner of this art – but after he read the book he observed, in a letter to Robert Conquest: 'Tough going I find. You see there's this girl with amnesia shit, you know what I mean, so she's forgotten what a lavatory is and thinks cisterns and pipes are statuary, but then how does she know what statuary is? It's like a novel by Craig Raine, well not quite so fearful as that would be I suppose.'[8] 'You might mention', Martin advised me, 'the odd fact that my name is an anagram of Martianism.'

7

America, Kingsley and Bellow

Martin and Angela returned to London in February 1980. They had discussed moving in together and while neither had reservations about doing so in principle – Paris had worked well and their relationship seemed in no danger of losing its original energy – practicalities meant that they decided to postpone the time-consuming process of finding a suitable leasehold flat in central London, let alone one they could afford to buy. Despite the generous windfall from *Saturn 3* Martin was aware that a future based upon negotiated advances and the fickle mood of the reading public – aka royalties – would be financially precarious. He had decided, therefore, to make use of his experience as reviewer and literary feature writer to become the kind of essayist that the British press had not previously countenanced; in the US a solid tradition had been maintained by the likes of Hemingway, Mailer and Vidal. He discussed his ideas with friends and contacts in the mainstream press, going first to Terence Kilmartin, literary editor of the *Observer*, and to his boss Donald Trelford. He also received enthusiastic responses to his enquiries from the *Sunday Times*, whose editor Harold Evans had recently gone through a divorce in order to marry Tina Brown, now editor of the *Tatler*. Tina and Martin had remained on good terms since their relationship in the early 1970s and she too was intrigued by his suggestion that he could become a roving raconteur and interviewer. Tina had commissioned him to visit the US to interview Truman Capote in 1978, shortly after his departure from the *New Statesman*, and eighteen months later, when he was based in Paris, she sponsored his visit to California where he recorded the baroque self-absorbed lifestyle of Palm Springs residents.

Obviously, newspapers would provide a far more regular and generous income than book publishers. An advance of £4,000 was so far his highest and given that he anticipated producing an average of one novel every two or three years, a life dedicated exclusively to the production of fiction seemed less than feasible. It was agreed, particularly with Trelford and Kilmartin, that his portfolio would comprise two main subjects: other writers, especially US writers; and abroad, predominantly the US. Hence the decision by Martin and Angela to put off permanent cohabitation. He expected to be out of the country so frequently during 1980–2 that it seemed practical for the time being to maintain Westbourne Grove as his stopover and office; Angela moved back into Warwick Road.

His first lengthy visit to the States took place just after he had returned to London at the end of the summer of 1979, paid for partly by the *Tatler* but funded mainly by the *Sunday Telegraph*, for his coverage of Ronald Reagan's presidential campaign. His account of Reagan's arrival and speech at El Paso, Texas, very much sets the standard for his subsequent treatment of America and its citizens. He is never quite awestruck, even in the presence of figures he admires or when avidly recording weird urban landscapes. Instead it is a place that by turns appals and energizes him and the enduring characteristic of his coverage is an implied question: do I wish that I were part of it all or am I relieved that I am not?

This question would prove an abundant source of inspiration for a man whose principal affiliation is to literature. It was as though he had encountered a novel in which the personnel and habits of existence were unnervingly similar to those he was obliged to call his own yet at the same time alien; they spoke and wrote largely in the same language, but not quite, and as far as tradition and identity were concerned, Europe, and for that matter everywhere else, was a shelf of dictionaries to America's open-ended thesaurus. But rather than surrender to this alluring experience Martin requisitioned it, redefined it for the delectation of those similarly intrigued. The US was still, for most people in the UK, the product of television and film but for those who saw themselves as intellectually superior to *Dallas* and *Dynasty*, Martin, in the early 1980s, became the chronicler-in-chief of our cousins across the Atlantic; amusing, outstandingly penetrating and, it must be said, sometimes patronizing.

His description of the Transient Terminal at El Paso Airport as Reagan's personal jet, *Free Enterprise II*, comes in to land is ruthlessly hilarious. He establishes, Woody Allen-style, a feeling of anxious unbelonging.

> I strolled among the Skips and Dexters (all were obliged to wear name tags), the Lavernes and Francines, admiring all the bulging wranglers and stretched stretch-slacks. This felt like Reagan Country all right, where everything is big and fat and fine. This is where you feel slightly homosexual and left-wing if you don't weigh twenty-five stone.[1]

One has no cause to doubt the accuracy of Martin's account –
and given that America is now seen as having fomented a global
epidemic of morbid obesity, how perceptive he was – but at the
same time, the mammoth proportions of the El Paso residents,
their slightly vulgar taste in Christian names and clothing would
not in themselves strike most of us as particularly amusing or
as he indicates symptomatic of the inflexible gigantism of the
US political right were it not for his brilliant and wonderfully
economic verbal choreography. His portrait of the president-to-
be and his wife is fixating.

> The blue-jodhpurred Tijuana band fell silent as Reagan
> climbed up on to the podium. 'Doesn't move like an old
> man,' I thought to myself; and his hair can't be a day over
> forty-five. Pretty Nancy Reagan sat down beside her
> husband. As I was soon to learn, her adoring, damp-eyed
> expression never changes when she is in public. Bathed
> in Ronnie's aura, she always looks like Bambi being
> reunited with her parents. Reagan sat in modest silence
> as a local Republican bigwig presented him with a pair
> of El Paso cowboy spurs to go with his 1976 El Paso
> cowboy boots.[2]

Later in the piece he feeds us details from Reagan's period as
Governor of California and draws attention to inconsistencies
between his record and his promises – his remit was after all
political commentary – but one can sense an air of dutiful
impatience in this, recalling Anthony Howard's stories of him
being obliged to turn up at the *New Statesman* sessions with
eminent figures from Parliament. He really wants to get away
from policy and back to his sketch of Reagan, Nancy and the
surrounding assembly of humorous grotesques. His metier is
not so much writing about America as feeding upon its

abundant wealth of characters and peculiarities. Amis the mischievous novelist is always nudging aside his counterpart the journalist. This slightly unequal division in his affiliations is not of course surprising – he had always been happier with verbal chicanery than transparency – but what is intriguing is the contrast between the novelist manqué of these articles and the figure who actually produced the works of fiction.

For a clearer perception of the former imagine Charles Highway about ten years after graduation or more tellingly a real, older presence, a man always ready to pounce and never willing to allow a banality to remain unmolested or a piece of dialogue or solemn proclamation of intent to get past without first puncturing its pretentiousness. The fact is that Martin's not-quite-literary prose is both outstandingly good and almost identical in temper and manner to his father's fictional style. In the former he has been prolific; aside from uncollected reviews and essays his published volumes of non-fiction amount to around a quarter of his total output. Here, of course, we encounter a tantalizing question. If Martin is so capable of electrifying our standard perceptions of the world, why did he choose to eschew this manner – and to be blunt here, it is called telling stories – in his novels? The obvious answer, already mooted, is that he lived in terror of being classified as Kingsley Amis Mark II.

Martin and Kingsley have much more in common than is first apparent. Pick up a novel by either of them, leaving to one side the most ostentatious stylistic differences, and then compare both with a work chosen at random by any other major post-war writer. What will be immediately evident is a feature in the latter either absent or only modestly executed but which in the Amises is gloriously abundant, and made more noticeable by the comparison. The vast majority of novelists write as if they are either in awe of their material or at least prepared to give the impression that whatever they are writing about – be this another human being, a landscape, or a dinner party – is possessed of some aspect of autonomy or self-sufficiency. Many, of course, create a frisson of apprehension and uncertainty regarding the exact relationship between the controlling presence and their fictional universe but few if any maintain a mood of stylistic tyranny to match that of the Amises.

Both of them, as writers, take possession of their subject matter and even though each might sometimes present himself as daunted by it we know that any sense of trepidation on his part is contrived. Read Martin's encounters with Capote, Vidal, Burgess, Polanski, Asimov, Mailer, Spielberg, Vonnegut, Burroughs, Updike et al. – the cultural first team of the 1980s – and note a singular, persistent feature of his approach. Frequently the overture will combine caustic documentation – pointing up the grandeur or shabby appeal of the location – with a hint of apprehension. One will require no further proof that the latter is fabricated than in what follows: his account of their exchange. We have no reason to believe that the spoken words themselves are anything other than authentic but quite soon we become less interested in what these individuals have to say than in their role as motifs in a skilfully executed spectacle. They certainly come across as beguiling charismatic figures – by degrees unsettling and enviable – but at the same time we begin to suspect that some of these qualities have been conferred upon them by Martin Amis, novelist.

Kingsley's preoccupation with style relates closely to his private spectrum of fears and idiosyncrasies. Behind the legendary mimic and raconteur was essentially a shy individual. Even among those he knew best, and with whom he felt most secure, his manner was that of the performer who would choose deliberately controversial even offensive topics not merely to antagonize others but to sustain the momentum of an argument for its own sake rather than allow the exchange to settle upon matters he would rather keep to himself. He used his consider-able linguistic skills in the club, the bar, or the dining room as a protection mechanism and on the page we encounter a comparable, immensely impressive exercise in control. The fact that he could in his novels distil from this a convincing range of emotional registers and personal dilemmas testifies to his greatness as a writer. Martin's portfolio of anxieties was slim compared with his father's, in all likelihood because through his formative years he had acquainted himself by instinct with various techniques of immunization and avoidance. Even his rapid exchange of fecklessness for scholarly acuity in the late 1960s was not so much a transformation as a remarshalling of innate skills. When I asked Colin Howard for his earliest impression of the teenage brothers, Martin and Philip, he recalled that while both '*appeared* equally reckless and anarchic it gradually became clear that while Philip's behaviour was guileless, perhaps even showing a degree of vulnerability, Martin was shrewd. He knew how people would react to what he said and did and he could almost manipulate them by predicting their responses.' It was not, therefore, too difficult for him to adapt his reading of other people to his writing. Thereafter an enduring feature of Martin's journey through early adulthood and precocious literary success is a tendency to refashion the otherwise unavoidable burdens of existence – emotional or ideological commitment, personal responsibility – as conceits, the most obvious being the exaggerated grotesques that stalk his fiction of the 1970s and early 1980s. In this respect father and son were very much alike; writing for both was a form of displacement. They differed in an equally significant way. Martin took pleasure from the opportunity to reshape the real world while, for his father it offered an escape route from it.

There were other more manifest signs of attachment and compatibility too. Angela Gorgas recalls that for both, the ritual of greeting others was limited to verbal acknowledgement but that the convention was suspended when the two of them met. 'As far as I remember, the two of them would hug, and even kiss each other on the cheek in greeting. When we were in London, nearly every Saturday would be spent at Flask Walk; a long and often very liquid lunch would be followed by *University Challenge* on television with Martin and Kingsley in fierce competition.' Angela reflects on this: 'Let's put it this way – if I or anyone else had been up against either of them it would have been unsettling. You would feel in danger of being humiliated. It's true there was a certain amount of one-upmanship and they enjoyed the verbal jousting but there was no real bitterness or antagonism between them at all.' Even as far back as 1970 when he first met Martin at Oxford Anthony Thwaite was fascinated by the public displays of affection between father and son. He had known Kingsley for fifteen years. 'For Kingsley, body language was generally an appendix to his verbal performances, part of his famous repertoire of imitations. The rest of the time he was physically reserved and it was something of a shock [at a drinks party in John Fuller's rooms in Magdalen College] to see him embracing his young son, particularly in public.'

Their relationship is fascinating, not least because of the apparent anomaly between their sometimes hostile views of each other's lifestyles, opinions and work, but also as a more intimate sense of mutual recognition, something they shared but withheld from others. I raised this question with Rosie Boycott who has known both of them since the 1970s and was Kingsley's regular luncheon companion and confidante in the early 1990s. 'Kingsley was particularly concerned with Sally who by then had a serious drink problem and I suspect he felt something close to guilt about Philip, whom he thought he had neglected. But with Martin, when he spoke of him, and even if he was criticizing him – which was largely bluff and bravado anyway – I felt he was far more at ease. He was certainly proud of him and although he would never have admitted to it in public there was a feeling of rapport, communion between them. I sensed that when he was talking about Martin he became relaxed, his anxieties – and he still had plenty – seemed to lift. I think there was a deep rapprochement, empathy between them.'

Then, in the 1990s when Boycott talked regularly with Kingsley, differences in age and perspective were of slight significance but it was in 1980, shortly after Martin's return from Paris, that events began to accelerate the reversal of traditional roles of father and son. On 1 November Jane left Gardnor House for a ten-day visit to Shrublands, a health farm in Suffolk she had used on several occasions before, mainly as a retreat from the mood of attrition and subdued bitterness that now dominated her relationship with Kingsley. This time, however, the visit was a calculated hoax. Following their return from a cruise in the Mediterranean, a period in the Dordogne and, briefly, the Edinburgh Festival – all of which Kingsley endured with very thinly disguised displeasure – she had visited her solicitor and there deposited a letter with instructions that it should be delivered by hand to Kingsley at the Flask Walk house on the day she was due back from Suffolk.

Apart from her solicitor Jane had informed several others of her intentions: Jonathan Clowes, Kingsley's and her agent; Mrs Uniacke the housekeeper and Colin her brother. Notably she said nothing to Philip, who had been staying with them for the previous nine months following his marriage break-up. The day the letter arrived the only person immediately available to whom Kingsley could break the news was his elder son. Philip telephoned Martin and the three of them spent the night in the otherwise empty house; Colin was at the time working in Huntingdon and lodging there for much of the week.

According to Martin neither he nor his brother spoke to Kingsley on what he might do to rescue the marriage. They were aware that he had replied to Jane, via her solicitor, within days of receiving her letter, but aside from commenting on having done this he said nothing of what he had written. 'It was clear', recalls Martin, 'that an exchange, of sorts, was going on, though they did not actually speak to each other directly, even on the phone. The letters between them have been lost but later Kingsley told Bob [Conquest] and Larkin that Jane would only come back if he agreed to some inflexible conditions, mainly that he should give up alcohol completely. Kingsley was not an alcoholic.'

Martin did not move in to Gardnor House. By then he was already committed to lengthy, regular visits to the US. These would have clashed with what became known as Dad-sitting, but in early December 1980, even as exchanges between Kingsley and Jane continued, he and Philip sat down to discuss the prospect of something neither had previously envisioned. For the time being they would be responsible for the general well-being of their father.

Colin was looking to buy his own property in North London but during his final months at Gardnor House he and Kingsley remained on amiable terms. 'There was no pressure on me to take sides and Kingsley and I got on well enough during those months. Although no one formally took charge it seemed clear that Martin was the gadfly, the inaugurator. Phil was certainly in residence, making sure that Kingsley's repertoire of fears and problems was taken care of – panic attacks, terror of the dark and so on – but Martin was – how can I put it? – he coordinated things, even though he was not always there.'

Martin admits now that he had no realistic expectation of a reconciliation between Kingsley and Jane. 'Everyone close to them knew from around the middle of the 1970s they were simply postponing the inevitable. When Phil phoned me and said "It's happened" I knew what he meant and that any rescue attempts would be pointless.' Until something permanent could be arranged for Kingsley Martin decided that it would be best to maintain those aspects of life at Gardnor House and Lemmons his father had enjoyed most. Consequently, from the end of 1980 until June 1981 the house was the site of an extended low-key wake, commemorating the demise of two minor institutions, Kingsley's reign as the most indulgent host of the London literary scene, and the 1970s culture of the *New Statesman*. James Fenton often visited alone to talk with Kingsley about poetry in general and their particular ongoing endeavours, matters they had previously touched upon cursorily at the Theobald's Road lunches. Barnes, Pat Kanavagh and McEwan would call either on their own or making up a larger group which included probably the most regular visitor, Hitchens, who ensured that the supplies of beer, usually cans of extra-strong lager, wine and spirits – whisky predominantly – never ran low. Kingsley had always enjoyed Hitchens's company. Tony Howard: 'Hitch, even before he gave up on his Trotskyite zealotry, was an endearing parcel of contrasts. He could sound like a humourless advocate of Socialism and within seconds revert to what appeared to be self-caricature or stand-up-comedy cynicism. He was, is, priceless company and I'm certain that he would have reminded Kingsley of himself thirty years earlier.' The elegant walled garden of Gardnor House was most evenings a thoroughfare for 'Dad-sitters' hulking large bags of alcohol and takeaways, to the front door. A decade earlier Kingsley had written that 'the collective social benefits of drinking altogether outweigh the individual disasters it might precipitate. A team of American investigators concluded recently that, without the underpinning provided by alcohol and the relaxation it affords, Western society would have collapsed irretrievably . . . Not only is drink here to stay; the moral seemed to be that when it goes, we go too.'[3]

While Martin has never commented on this period in print Colin portrays him as 'the unseen hand, the choreographer. The *New Statesman* set were all convivial sorts who treated Kingsley with varying degrees of respect and affable caution, but the team spirit behind those months at Gardnor House was not spontaneous. It was effectively organized by Martin.'

Angela Gorgas had been to weekend dinners at Gardnor House on a number of occasions before she and Martin left for Paris and now became one of the regulars, forming a close attachment with Kingsley. He was, she recalls, more relaxed than he had been in 1979 before Jane left. He seemed particularly happy about the prospect of his son's imminent marriage. In a letter to Conquest in March Kingsley responded to his friend's enquiry: 'Martin still sees a lot of Angela. Vile piece in [the *Evening Standard*] getting his age wrong and saying Ang had tried to get him to dedicate new book to her but he had "churlishly" dedicated it to "his mother, Elizabeth Jane Howard".'[4]

The social columnists of the *Standard* and the *Express* in particular had since his return from Paris swarmed like parasites upon the spectacle of Martin and the woman who was officially something other than his latest girlfriend, his fiancée. News that they had lived together in France had soon spread, and speculation on when the wedding would take place supplemented diarists' reports on Angela's presence as his partner at the launch of *Other People* at the beginning of March. The dedication to which Kingsley referred was 'To my mother' and the *Standard* had obviously forgotten that this person was Hilly, now Lady Kilmarnock. Hilly, then living in Buckinghamshire and supplementing Ali's House of Lords allowance with a tiny income from waitressing, was telephoned by Philip some time in spring 1981 with the suggestion that she might secure a more comfortable home and stipend by 'looking after Dad'. Certainly Philip was involved in the negotiations that essentially resulted in a famous domestic trinity of Hilly, Kingsley and Ali. Angela's account, however, suggests that matters were less straightforward. She recalls meeting Hilly in Ronda shortly before she and Ali left Spain for England. 'A really generous and affectionate woman. Interestingly they met once again in England when Martin visited his mother in Winslow near Buckingham.' Angela remembers that it was then that Martin talked with his mother about her looking after Kingsley and moving in with Ali.

After all parties had agreed in principle to the arrangement an exploratory weekend was held at Gardnor House on 24–7 July, attended by Kingsley, Hilly and Ali, Jaime (then aged eight), and Martin and Philip. Once the sale of Gardnor House had been agreed Kingsley, Ali, Hilly and James moved into a rented flat around the corner and six months later in January 1982 Kingsley purchased a small house in Leighton Road, Kentish Town.

Martin's continued role would be dutiful, but with no regular commitments. When they were together they were according to all witnesses closer and more relaxed with each other than ever before. And while Martin could never hope to excuse or defend all of his father's more provocative performances, nor did he reprimand him. Instead he took a position of aloof guardianship.

Hitchens tells of how after the UK publication of *Stanley and the Women* Kingsley's novel was effectively boycotted by US publishers following pressure from those – 'let us be honest – women' he points out – who judged it an outright incitement to misogyny. 'I was outraged. It was an extraordinary case of censorship and I was responsible for placing it with Summit. Anyway Kingsley phoned, thanked me and assured me that he owed me a night out when I was next in London. Well, he kept his word and it was a most bizarre evening, in keeping, I later learned, with what had become his routine. Drinks at Primrose Hill followed by more at the Garrick – predominantly whiskies – then a film before dinner. He insisted that we went to see *Beverly Hills Cop II*, perhaps one of the worst films ever made. Martin and I sat transfixed by its wretchedness but weirdly Kingsley was rocking back and forth with laughter. During the meal he continued, remarking on how this scene or the other had worked so well and again shedding mirthful tears at the recollection. I was confused. Was he genuinely impressed, amused? That seemed preposterous. Or was he involved in some kind of extended act of self-caricature? Was he trying to provoke us? I never properly worked out what was going on, but he was clearly in some sort of decline. What I also recall vividly was Martin's reaction. He did not pretend to share Kingsley's apparent admiration for the film but he showed no impatience or irritation. Undemanding affection is the best way to describe it.'

The poet Dannie Abse recalls a dinner party he held perhaps two years later in the mid-1980s. 'There were about ten of us. We'd invited Kingsley and whomever he wished to bring, and he came with Martin. Everything seemed to be going well enough and the drink flowed. Quite late on, Kingsley began to contribute less to the exchanges, odd because he was generally such an enthusiastic conversationalist, and he knew virtually all of the people there. But it seemed clear to me [and it should be pointed out that Abse is a medical doctor] that he was having a panic attack. I noticed but I doubt that many of the others did – as I said we had all had plenty to drink and were just noisily chatting with each other. Except Martin. He was superb, asked me quietly if he could use the telephone and summoned a taxi. Then by various means he manoeuvred his father into the next room after explaining to others that – well, I forget the excuse, but it was convincing. Polite goodbyes were exchanged and no one seemed to suspect anything other than a need to be up early next morning. As I say, Martin was exemplary. You could see that he was devoted to him.'

No one I have spoken to doubts the sincerity of their enduring mutual affection. Gully Wells: 'As far back as when Martin and I were going out in Oxford, and later through the 1970s, they would argue furiously, mostly about writing – in those days Martin was apolitical, practically apathetic – but the vehemence of the exchanges belied the fact that they simply *loved* talking and that in turn was an extension of something deeper still.' The only time that opinion would become a hedge against affection was when Martin's literary interests began to blend with more obsessive preoccupations, the first of these involving nuclear disarmament. But as we shall see, even then he did not untangle the emotional bond; rather it was joined by new commitments, involving a recently acquired family of his own.

Martin visited the US on three occasions between early 1981 and early 1983. First, he sampled the magnificent farce of Gore Vidal's assault upon the US political establishment. Vidal, when Martin met him, was giving a series of lectures in Lynchburg, Virginia, hometown of Jerry Falwell, a fundamentalist Right Winger so intolerant of the Enlightenment as to embarrass even his fellow Creationist in the White House. Martin liked Vidal, admired his performance as debauched aristocrat and scandalous liberal, but we sense from his articles that he sees him mostly as a curiosity not quite worthy of serious intellectual investment.

Norman Mailer, who during the same visit entertained him in his apartment overlooking New York Harbour, struck Martin almost as Vidal's lost twin, albeit lacking whatever neural mechanisms govern temperance and restraint. Mailer opened all his campaign speeches when standing for Mayor of New York in 1969 with the same noteworthy mantra: 'Fuck you! Fuck you all!', thereafter detailing such manifesto proposals as capital punishment by means of public gladiatorial games, a penalty to be visited upon murderers, burglars and cancer researchers who failed to make progress after two years of toil. By then New York City would be the largely autonomous fifty-first state of the Union with Norman himself as its first leader, Mayor in name but Imperial in propensity.

Martin reports their exchange in the flat sardonic manner perfectly suited to a figure caught in that strange hinterland between the hilarious and the incredible. He does not need to caricature him but he does add a number of observations on the fact that Mailer regards literature as a legitimate vehicle for his advocacy of unrestraint. He does not simply indulge perverse characters but rather functions as their advocate; the history of his fiction parallels his personal record of uncontrite lunacy. Martin: 'He stabbed his second wife several times – following a party at which he had commanded all guests to choose an opponent and beat him/her to a pulp – and then persuaded her not to press charges. Few if any writers would be capable of rendering such a weird scenario as credible fiction, let alone escape prosecution for perpetrating it.'

The Vonneguts, Jill and Kurt, lived on the East Side of town in a residence more spacious and modest than Mailer's – a house – and Martin's attitude shifts from mild dismay and vexation to something close to pity. Kurt Vonnegut, he points out, is still undeniably a pillar of the US literary establishment; all his novels remain in print and feature consistently in university courses on modern American writing. But there is something about his status that invites comparison with Wilde's prosecution, imprisonment and tragic demise. And Martin, cautiously, guides their conversation towards it: without

Slaughterhouse Five he would be at best a minor provincial author, perhaps even unpublished:

> I switched on the tape-recorder and backed myself into the Big Question [. . .] no writer likes to be asked if he has lost his way [. . .]
>
> 'After *Slaughterhouse Five* I'd already done much more than I ever expected to do with my life [. . .] The raid [on Dresden] didn't shorten the war by half a second, didn't weaken a German defence or attack anywhere, didn't free a single person from a death camp. Only one person benefited.'
>
> 'And who was that?'
>
> 'Me. I got several dollars for each person killed. Imagine.'[5]

Back in the city, specifically the oasis of calm that is Columbia University and its environs, Martin pays a respectful call upon Diana Trilling, widow of the critic Lionel and recorder of the incessant contraries of American existence. She had just published a book on the so-called Harris Trial, the murder case involving a WASP millionaire charged with killing her Jewish diet specialist and occasional lover. As Martin puts it: 'It is hard work trying to dream up a home-grown equivalent of the crime – as if, say, the headmistress of Roedean had done away with Jimmy Savile.'

Characteristically he telescopes the particulars of Mrs Trilling's work into some general observations on America:

> The life of the American intellectual is qualitatively different from its British equivalent. In America, intellectuals are public figures (whereas over here they are taken rather less seriously than ordinary citizens – at most, they

are licensed loudmouths). The intellectual life therefore
has a dimension of political responsibility; the crises of
modern liberalism – the race question, McCarthyism,
feminism, Vietnam, Israel – are magnified but also taken
personally, vitally. Spats between writers are transformed, willy-nilly, into unshirkable crusades. The Trill-
ings lived this life together and experienced all its
triumphs and wounds. Lillian Hellman, Martha's Vine-
yard, 1952, 1968, Little Brown, UnAmerican Activities,
the *New York Review* ... it is a ceaseless, swirling
litany.[6]

It is interesting to compare this piece with one he produced six
months earlier, which would become the title chapter of his
1993 volume *Visiting Mrs Nabokov and Other Excursions*. The
Nabokovs had retired to Montreux some twenty years earlier
and Vladimir had died in 1977. His widow and son Dmitri
occupied a large suite in the Montreux Palace hotel, a
monument to the city's prevailing mood of orderly, decaying
grandeur. Martin is deferential to his hosts, living reminders of
the writer he has admired since university, yet throughout the
piece one detects a subcurrent of frustration and puzzlement.
A question lingers in the margins of his account, but unlike
the beautifully choreographed exchanges with Vonnegut he
addresses it during his walk to the meeting – 'Why Montreux
anyway, I wondered ... ?' – without asking Vera herself. It is
as if he has replaced the one-to-one dynamic of his American
interviews – so redolent of the place's energetic incompleteness
– with something more respectful of a quietened, almost
embalmed history. He reflects,

Strolling through the sun and mist of the lakeside, I
thought of the lost and innocuous parklands of an

idealized boyhood. The Swiss children are dapper and immaculate on their skates. The Swiss midges, keeping themselves to themselves, are much too civic-minded to swarm or sting.[7]

Even a cursory knowledge of Nabokov's life will enable us to intuit the subtext of Martin's thoughts: a childhood spent in a pre-Revolutionary Russia not unlike the Switzerland of today, then a journey through the mania of Europe after the First World War, the Weimar Republic followed by Paris and a last-minute escape to the US as the Nazis invaded France. In 'Lolita Reconsidered'[8] Martin contends that Humbert Humbert is unique because he was born out of a sequence of experiences to which few if any writers could make a comparable claim. Nabokov was the ultimate European sophisticate, a minor aristocrat and playboy who wrote poetry in his early teens and watched the edifice, the continent, that had nurtured him destroy itself. In America he found a society begotten by Europe but having long spurned its parentage; a place driven by the excesses and visceral passions that on the other side of the Atlantic had been buried by millennial accretions of Taste and Culture. Thus Humbert came into being, an unapologetic sexual deviant blessed with cosmopolitan sophistication and guile.

Martin was in the early 1980s forming an impression of America as the modern literary Empyrean, capable of dispersing the hidebound incuriosity and predictability of the Old World. *Lolita* was then, and remains, one of his favourite novels but he cannot declare it to be more than that, and certainly not in his view the greatest novel of the twentieth century. Humbert is an incomparably foul individual who beats his first wife regularly, rapes a schoolgirl twice a day and murders his only rival for her enforced affections, the equally gruesome pornography addict Quilty. But he is also the most mellifluously talented narrator ever created. Stylistically the book is exquisite, elegant, yet it is far more successful than any piece of modernist writing in demonstrating the uniqueness and perversity of fiction. Only in the 263-page narrative web spun by Humbert can we permit ourselves to cast aside abhorrence and simply marvel at what can be done with words. *Lolita* is a magnificent piece of work which, paradoxically, will never be allowed to epitomize a grand aesthetic principle. This was a problem for Martin for the simple reason that his own working mantra was indisputably Nabokovian. In each of his first four novels our preoccupation with his ostentatious command of language blurs our attempts to consider what the books actually mean.

Among Nabokov's near contemporaries Martin admires, with profound reservations, Philip Roth and John Updike. Roth is like Nabokov, addictive, a writer with an overabundance of talent who seems determined to waste it. Reading Roth's novels is less a literary experience than a voyeuristic exercise in witnessing mammoth self-destruction. He writes brilliantly but he has only one subject, himself, and the more he delves into this enigma, with its hostages to guilt-ridden Judaism and rapturously specified grim habits, the more he ceases to have any obvious presence or objective as a literary artist. Updike is similarly spavined:

> Updike calls them 'the Angstrom novels', but we know them more familiarly as the Rabbit books. They span thirty years and 1,500 pages. And they tell the story, from youth to death, of a Pennsylvanian car salesman: averagely bigoted and chauvinistic, perhaps exception-ally gluttonous and lewd, but otherwise brutally undis-tinguished. It is as if a double-sized *Ulysses* had been narrated, not by Stephen, Bloom and Molly, but by one of the surlier underbouncers at Kiernan's bar.[9]

211

This morbidly detailed world of anti-hubris, combined with the sort of moral delinquency that puts the self-absorbed Europeans to shame is, according to Martin, unique to the American novel. But it is a uniqueness bought at considerable cost. Roth's Zuckerman and Updike's Angstrom are extensions of their creators and although autobiography is a necessary if oft-denied contingency of all writing, its sprawling US manifestation involves characters without any apparent horizon or purpose. It is almost as though Roth and Updike have spent so long inside their own novels that they have forgotten that fiction should be informed by something that resembles a thematic direction or interest. Again, however, one cannot help but notice the similarities between Martin's reservations regarding Roth and Updike and features of his own early work. Few if any of the characters in the first four novels are straightforward refashionings of Martin Amis but there are without doubt parallels between the man he was during this period and the way he wrote. Examine his non-literary writings and more tellingly listen to the recollections of people who knew him and the following presence emerges: a man who was magnetically entertaining and witty, whose evaluative resources were sharp and intimidating; he was not malicious and nor was he apologetic regarding the favours – emotional, professional, social – bought for him by connections and precocious fame. He succeeded effortlessly with women but few if truth be told would have chosen restraint if offered the same opportunities. Yet at the centre of this chiaroscuro of effects and inclinations is an enigma. He could deal with ideas expertly in print, could even, on occasions, take on the role of advocate or antagonist but behind the performance there was no clear commitment to anything in particular, be this ideological, political or aesthetic. Cynicism, even nihilism, borne with an appropriate degree of accountability, is often to be admired but Martin simply appeared as though he could not find the time for ideas and beliefs. In the novels one encounters a magnificent performance, a man demonstrating his expertise in the manipulation of the reader's emotions and expectations, but once the performance is over we are left with little but a feeling of admiration for someone who can use language so brilliantly. But I write, in part, as devil's advocate, as a reflection of the less than sympathetic commentators on the man and his work. We should wonder: what should a novel do for us? And then we should think again: in asking this question are we not forgetting the uniquely protean status of fiction? Of late a number of historians and political commentators have attempted to isolate the essential character of the 1970s.[10] It is easy enough now to treat the decade as a precipitate time, a period of political apathy that spawned the transformations of Thatcherism, but to do so is to take considerable liberties with the benefits of retrospection: few if any right-wing Conservatives foresaw let alone plotted the events of the early 1980s. And as far as the more elastic notions of culture and the social fabric are concerned, these years could best be described as rudderless, a condition that most people at the time took for granted or more often treated with indifference. Popular culture had arrived in all its popular, tasteless and profitable manifestations; the memory of the horrors and deprivations of the war were being gradually marginalized by a generation for whom the actual experience was vicarious; the two principal political parties seemed to have settled into a game of musical chairs, joined annoyingly by the unions but played according to the principles laid down by the post-war Labour Government. The economy was, it seemed, lurching from one disaster to another but for most this was a distraction from what appeared to be a consensually agreed if rarely acknowledged pursuit of a good time acquired mainly via sex, consumer goods and foreign holidays. Perhaps Martin's novels of this period will come to be recognized as a shrewd index – with some exaggerations – to a society made up of selfishness, atrophy and indifference.

When he first met Saul Bellow in October 1983 in Chicago it was certainly not a moment of revelation. His account in the *Observer* is at once guileless and contrived. Privately he knew what to expect but he provides a flawless performance as someone who does not. He runs through a select recollection of his recent encounters with Capote ('poleaxed by a hangover'), the patronizing Vidal, Mailer the hypocrite – who is laddish and amicable in person but who later goes on to denounce Martin on TV as a 'wimp'; Heller, 'brawny, jovial' and self-absorbed; and Vonnegut, amiably sanguine but 'a natural crackpot'. 'Saul Bellow, I suspected, would speak in the voice I knew from the novels: funny, fluent and profound.'[11] And so he does. From the moment they meet each is aware of an unforced mutual affinity, something that would be maintained in all of their subsequent encounters. Would you, I asked Martin, have been quite so enamoured of the man had you not already modelled your expectations upon his work? (There are some, such as his agent and PA, Harriet Wasserman, who have judged him quixotic, narcissistic and hypocritical.) 'Saul was honest both as an individual and a novelist, or I should say transparent. He never claimed to understand or have solutions to everything and nor did he ever disguise his uncertainties. Back to your question. When I met him my preconceptions were neither confirmed nor overturned. I hardly noticed the change between reading him and talking to him.' Much the same has been said to me by friends of Martin Amis, of Martin Amis.

Bellow's enduring complaint was against an insidious legacy of modernism: the displacement of the autonomous individual – full retinue of failings included – by a recipe for despair and nihilism.

214

His response to this originated in his personal history and became a persistent trope in his fiction. As a child he spoke as much Yiddish as English and by the time he reached his teens, in Chicago, any clear perception of a single community to which he might belong was continually challenged by the fact that his city, indeed his nation, was a random assembly of interests, affiliations and perspectives. But rather than submit to the lazy option of relativism, Bellow bequeathed to his fiction and invested in his fictional heroes nuanced versions of a private credo. None of his most famous figures from Augie March through Moses Herzog and Charlie Citrine to Albert Corde of *The Dean's December* (1982) – a copy of which Martin brought to their first meeting – finds consolation for their various grievances in anything that resembles a doctrine, be this ideological or religious, and in this they reflect Bellow's sceptical humanism. But what he and they also share is a faith in thinking and writing as an impregnable stronghold against despair. Moses Herzog (1964) for example is driven to the brink of a breakdown by his wife's adultery. He writes long letters recording his thoughts on civilization and the plight of the individual, addresses them to living and dead correspondents and never sends them. Bellow's other fictional representatives never quite resort to such a literal investment in writing and the imagination but in various ways each of them restores to their otherwise blighted landscape a sense of humanity, even optimism, simply by their presence as intellectual interlopers, presiding hosts for the messy unforgiving nature of their environment. Martin calls this 'higher autobiography' or HA. 'One of the assumptions behind HA, I think, went as follows: in a world becoming more and more this and more and more that, but above all becoming more and more *mediated*, the direct line to your own experience was the only thing you could trust. So the focus moved inward, with that slow zoom a writer feels when he switches from the third person to the first.'[12] Prior to this sentence he is writing exclusively about Bellow but soon after its conclusion we become aware that he is thinking about how HA became a turning point in his own career. '*Money* [. . .] certainly wasn't the *higher* autobiography. But I see now that the story turned on my own preoccupations: it is about tiring of being single; it is about the fear that childlessness will condemn you to childishness.'[13]

Bellow was present at the conception of Martin's novel, not in person but as an intellectual compass, an example to be followed by a man who had no clear sense of direction. The autobiographical seam running through all of Bellow's novels drew not only upon his private musings; his life was to say the least eventful, involving as a child and teenager daily experiences of poverty and gangsterism in Chicago, wartime military service, periods in Paris and Mexico, three turbulent, and failed, marriages and in the 1970s long periods reporting on the state of Israel, involving an on-the-spot account of the Six Day War. This last had obliged him to come to terms with his Judaic identity and heritage and contemplate the impulses that lay behind two millennia of anti-Semitism, culminating in the Holocaust and the establishment of a Jewish homeland. Martin's experiences of shock and trauma were bought vicariously, mostly from books and film. Notice, then, the lead in to his own explanation of HA: 'In a world becoming more and more this and more and more that, but above all becoming more and more *mediated*.'

Martin was aware that Bellow's ruminations on the nature of existence were corollaries of his harsh acquaintance with life's extremities. The question arose as to how he might distil similar profundity from three decades of cosseting. The only abnormal aspects in his otherwise unexceptional history was the effect of having a famous, unfatherly father and he had already dealt with that on several occasions. So in the absence of tangible promptings Martin considered what else might threaten his emotional and ethical sensibilities and came up with the fact that modern life was comprised largely of representations and falsifications, substitutes for actuality; as he put it, the world is *'mediated'*. It was no accident then that the novel through which he would aspire to a level of gravity and profundity comparable with Bellow involves film-making.

Martin at the kitchen table in 24 The Grove, Swansea, aged six. The ms remains unpublished.
(Getty)

The Amis family outside 24 The Grove, Swansea, 1956. From left: Philip, Hilly holding Sally, Kingsley and Martin.
(Getty)

(*above*) Kingsley, Martin and Philip playing chess in 53 Glanmore Road, Swansea, 1961. Three months later Kingsley would be offered a Fellowship at Peterhouse, Cambridge and the family would move to Cambridge in September 1961. (*Getty*)

(*right*) Martin, 1977, shortly before he completed *Success*. He had two novels in print and was literary editor of the *New Statesman*. (*Getty*)

(*above*) Martin Amis and Angela Gorgas in Ronda, Spain, 1980.

(*below*) Martin Amis and Julian Barnes, 1980.
(both images © Angela Gorgas, www.angelagorgas.co.uk)

(*above*) Martin in the Chesterton Road house he shared with his then wife Antonia Phillips, 1985. '"Unless I specifically inform you otherwise," [John] Self says, "I'm always smoking a cigarette".' (*Money*, 1984). *(Getty)*

(*right*) Martin in 54a Leamington Road Villas, 1985. 'What draws me and many others to the sport [darts] . . . is a liking for human variety, specifically a drastically primitive activity in a drastically modern setting.' *(Getty)*

(*above*) Martin working on *Time's Arrow* in his 'study' in Leamington Road Villas, 1990. *(Getty)*

(*below*) Martin on court at the Paddington Sports Club, 1990. 'I peaked at the age of forty. One legendary summer I performed on the court like a warrior poet ... Chris [Mitas] said "Well played, Mart. You're useless, and if I don't beat you six-love, six-love next time, I'm giving up the game ..." Chris did not give up the game.' *(Getty)*

London's Other Fields. Martin in Highgate Cemetery, 1991. *(Getty)*

(*right*) Kingsley and Martin Amis at a literary event, early 1990s. 'My inner audience consist[ed] chiefly of Larkin and Conquest, especially Larkin. More lately I have added Martin.' (Kingsley Amis, 1993) *(Getty)*

(*below*) The British Book Awards, London, 1995. From left: Isabel Fonseca, Salman Rushdie, Martin Amis. *(Getty)*

Martin Amis and family at the launch of Madonna's book *The English Roses*, London, 2003. From left: Clio, Isabel, Fernanda, Martin. *(Getty)*

8

Self, Marriage, Children

John Self, producer of self-evidently crass TV commercials, is a literary paradox – one of the best ever created. He is definitely not the kind of person with whom most readers of intelligent fiction, indeed any kind of fiction, would wish to spend time. For John Self's life is composed mainly of sordid excess, whether involving sex (pornographically witnessed, purchased or forcibly obtained), cigarettes (a sixty-a-day habit), alcohol consumed by the gallon, drugs selected and self-administered with impressive versatility, or artery-clogging junk food disposed of with fantastic speed. He has a grudging acquaintance with Orwell's *1984*, but this is the totality of his literary, indeed his cultural, experience. The paradox is that the more we learn of this apparently odious individual, and of the equally repellent world he inhabits, the more we become transfixed by him; he even, on some occasions, seems able to procure sympathy. We face this dilemma because as a first-person narrator he is a genius. Like his anonymous predecessor in *Dead Babies* he is able to invest the vile, the grotesque, with something that

218

resembles artistic shape. His account, for example, of his brief excursion to a New York live pornography emporium is admirably polished:

> Finally I devoted twenty-eight tokens' worth of my time to a relatively straight item, in which a slack-jawed cowboy got the lot, everything from soup to nuts, at the expense of the talented Juanita del Pablo. Just before the male's climax the couple separated with jittery haste. Then she knelt in front of him. One thing was clear: the cowboy must have spent at least six chaste months on a yoghurt ranch eating nothing but ice-cream and butter-milk. By the time he was through, Juanita looked like the patsy in the custard-pie joke, which I suppose is what she was. The camera proudly lingered as she spat and blinked and coughed . . . Hard to tell, really, who was the biggest loser in this complicated transaction – her, him, them, me.[1]

Reviewers and subsequent academic commentators have been unsettled by Self, mainly because he is an overreacher. Bad, abhorrent people had of course been written about before – though none of them was quite as unapologetically monstrous as Self – and as a narrator he is more unsettling than Humbert. Self takes charge, and despite his indifference to anything vaguely literary he does so with skill and verve.

Late in the novel he meets Martin Amis and hires the novelist to help him out with the screenplay for a film. Amis gets on reasonably well with Self and often appears concerned with his personal problems, but he never seems able to prevent himself from discoursing on the nature of contemporary fiction and artistic representation per se. For example:

The distance between the author and narrator corresponds to the degree to which the author finds the narrator wicked, deluded, pitiful or ridiculous [. . .] the further down the scale he is, the more liberties you can take with him. You can do what you like with him really. This creates an appetite for punishment. The author is not free of sadistic impulses. I suppose it's the—[2]

At this point he is interrupted by Self (who is bored and more concerned with his toothache), but Amis has made his point, which for the reader is deliberately, mischievously, confusing. Self is obviously well 'down the scale' but Amis's implication that the more uncultivated and unpleasant the narrator the more the author can take 'liberties' should not be regarded as licence for the author to appear superior to his subject. Self, while not sharing his creator's sophisticated frame of reference, can write as well as Martin Amis. What, then, should be made of the strange contrast between Self's proud loutishness, and his stylistic abilities? Self and Amis consider this.

'Do you have this problem with novels, Martin?' I asked him. 'I mean is there a big deal about bad behaviour and everything?'
'No. It's not a problem. You get complaints, of course, but we're pretty much agreed that the twentieth century is an ironic age – downward looking. Even realism, rock bottom realism, is considered a bit grand for the twentieth century.'[3]

As creative manifestoes go this one seems enigmatic, almost self-contradictory, at least until one looks at the novel that contains it. *Money* involves matchless, consummate irony in which repulsive activities and states of mind are made horribly amusing. It outdoes the most transparent realism by causing the reader to feel a kind of complicit involvement with Self and his world.

Shortly after *Money* was published Martin wrote an essay for *Atlantic Monthly* on Bellow's *The Adventures of Augie March* which he ranks as 'the Great American Novel. Search no further. All the trails went cold forty-two years ago.' What he admires most about Bellow's achievement is Augie himself.

> Augie is heading to the point where he will become the author of his own story. He will not necessarily be capable of writing it. He will be capable of thinking it. This is what the convention of the first person amounts to. The narrator expresses his thoughts, and the novelist gives them written shape.[4]

To give an uneducated working man command of a novel without this seeming patronizing, reductive or anomalous was in Martin's view the literary version of the American Dream, and Bellow had made it come true. He would attempt something slightly different with Self.

Martin too 'turns himself inside out'. But he becomes a monstrous exaggeration of all the features of his life during the 1970s – some affected, some innate and feral – when he cultivated the contrast between Amis the artist and intellectual and the laddish sexual predator with louche downmarket tastes. If our credulity is challenged by the presence of someone so bestial and uncouth possessed of such a capacity for brilliant prose we should look no further for reassurance than to the performances of Martin Amis during the first decade of his literary career. Martin did not invent Self any more than Bellow invented March: both were variations upon undesired doppelgängers.

221

Martin offers an account of the parallels between Bellow's career and his own. 'Saul said to me that his first two novels were well-behaved, apprentice novels. [After they came out] he was in Paris on the GI Bill trying to write a novel about two old intellectuals in a hospice having a series of knotty conversations. He said he was hating it, writing that novel and bridling under the recent memory of the war and France's part in it. Eighty thousand Jews deported, most killed, Fascism enthusiastically embraced and not just in Vichy. And this, Paris, was supposed to be the city of light, of the Enlightenment. His landlord hated him, probably, he thought, because he was American and Jewish. Then one day he saw the gutters being sluiced, a brilliant stream of water, and that day he began *The Adventures of Augie March*. What was it like, I asked? He said it was like bringing in the buckets, an incredible sense of release.' He pauses. 'I was at a similar point. I'd written four novels, served my apprenticeship. Then [with *Money*] I really began to enjoy the flow, the loss of inhibition. It was very enjoyable. But when I read it through before handing it to my agent Pat Kavanagh ... It wasn't the indelicacies, no. It was that this was a voice novel. No plot to speak of. Just a voice and the voice sounded ... well, I'd never heard anything like it before. And I spent three terrible days reading it and feeling sick to my stomach. Then I sent it to Pat.'

Another factor influenced the compositional tempo of *Money* and a clue can be found in his emphasis on Paris as the turning point for Bellow. It was there too that Martin completed the last of his 'apprenticeship' novels and where his relationship, engagement, with Angela Gorgas reached an equally precipitate stage. 'As far as I know', says Hitchens, 'nothing happened there to cause either of them to have second thoughts. In fact, it seemed to cement things, the engagement and so on. But I suppose it was as if they had taken a holiday from the real world. In some respects he appeared content but in others . . . I suspect he wanted out.' Remember that during this period he was indeed elsewhere, spending a good deal of his time with his less than respectable creation, Self, a man who, like Augie, first drew breath in Paris.

Explanations differ on the exact cause of the break-up of Amis's relationship with Angela Gorgas at the end of 1981. Most assume that it drew to a sad but inevitable conclusion: his new role as roving cultural correspondent, particular to the US, meant that he spent less time in London and as a consequence the tentative plans they had made for their return from Paris – on a date for the wedding and the purchase of a property in London – seemed to have become permanently provisional and hypothetical. Martin: 'Technically, we were still engaged. We had been for three years. But how exactly do you become "unengaged" – put another announcement in *The Times*? I didn't force the issue but things, well, came to a close.'

The woman he met shortly after this captured his attention for a number of reasons but the fact that he would pursue her so assiduously, almost maniacally for the subsequent two years gives cause to suspect that he hoped that someone so unlike his previous girlfriends would provide an antidote to the manic but ultimately disappointing previous decade.

Antonia Phillips was roughly the same age as him – actually a year older – and good looking. But she also, for someone so young, had a personal history that seemed very much at odds with the confection of transience, trivia and conspicuous hedonism that marked the 1970s and early 1980s. She came from a once-wealthy, East Coast WASP family, but spent most of her childhood in Europe, attending boarding schools in Florence and Paris, going on to read Philosophy at University College, London. Some summers would be spent in America and it was there she met Gareth Evans when he was in the States on a Visiting Scholarship in 1970. Evans had been elected to a Fellowship in University College, Oxford, only a year after he gained his Starred First. He became a tenured don just as Martin was entering his second year as an undergraduate, and the age difference was only two and a half years. He was judged to be a worthy successor to his tutor at University College, Peter Strawson, and during the 1970s his work on the philosophy of language and the mind earned him the reputation as one of the most influential new figures in his discipline. In 1974 Antonia Phillips began postgraduate work in her own field, aesthetics, under the tutelage of Richard Wollheim at UCL. Her MPhil dissertation on Wollheim's groundbreaking concept of the twofold thesis is unpublished but still referred to in academic studies as an important contribution to the field of aesthetics and evaluation. In 1977 when she received her degree she and Evans set out in a hired car from Texas to see the real Mexico, specifically to visit Hugo Margain, now Head of Philosophy in the University of Mexico and previously Evans's student in Oxford. In an attempt to kidnap Margain – whose father was Mexican Ambassador to the US – terrorists shot and fatally injured him. Evans and Phillips were with him in the car and while she survived uninjured he received a gunshot wound to the leg. After their return to England Evans and Phillips became engaged, he was elected to the prestigious Wilde Readership in Mental Philosophy at Oxford in 1979 and six months later diagnosed as suffering from terminal cancer. They married in University College Hospital, London in June 1980 and in early August Evans died there, aged thirty-four.

Phillips had herself considered an academic career and was assured by Wollheim that her Masters thesis was sufficiently original and groundbreaking to become the basis for a doctorate. While considering her options she taught part-time at UCL and took up a post as junior editor on the *TLS*. Her boss was Adolf Wood, who ran an amiable collegiate annex to the main paper comprising Phillips, Blake Morrison, Peter Strawson's son Galen and John Ryle. It had no strict generic focus but reflected an indulgent breadth of recondite interests, mainly in philosophy, the visual arts and literary history.

Martin still did the occasional piece for the *TLS* and he and Antonia first met at a drinks party in late 1981. They began a relationship shortly afterwards at the same time that Martin was pondering the likely consequences of allowing his grotesque alter ego to complete his next novel. The experience of writing *Money* was he recalls like nothing he had previously experienced, nor quite like anything since. 'It would be ridiculous to say I was in a trance. It was not automatic writing, every sentence had to be battered into shape, polished. Yet the book seemed to have acquired a momentum and identity of its own. I was *writing* it, it was extremely hard work, far more demanding than anything I'd done so far, yet I had this feeling of light-headedness, as though I were watching myself at work.' This is beautifully evocative of the phenomenon of John Self, a figure who appropriates and embodies the story. He is more than a narrator. That allocates him a subsidiary role in an intricate design; Self *is* the book but he is obliged to share his demented raucous accounts with two people who unsettle him because he can't properly make sense of who they are and why they are there. The first is the man who created him, in a 'trance' of 'light-headedness', Martin Amis. The second is the woman to whom the book is dedicated and who appears in it as Martina Twain, Antonia Phillips.

Hitchens describes his own introduction to Antonia. 'I was waiting for Martin at JFK and he came through Customs, beaming, wearing an oddly coloured velour hat. He didn't bother with the standard greetings and enquiries and instead nodded back towards a woman who was about to join us in

Arrivals. His first words were, "She's called Antonia Phillips and I'm really in love with her." Smitten is an understatement. I had never seen him like this before. I spoke to her only briefly at that point and she was, of course, charming, beautiful. She set off for the family summer home in Wellfleet on the Cape [Cod] and when Martin and I drove into the city he told me about her. Her tragic recent past, and her family . . . Mother's first husband was one of the most outstanding abstract painters of the mid-century – killed himself – her half-sister, like her mother, was also a painter and had married Matthew Spender, son of the poet, now a sculptor. They lived in a big house somewhere in Tuscany. Pure bohemian aristocracy. He was entranced, and while they were already having some sort of relationship he wanted to take it further, to make commitments. He'd previously made two abortive marriage proposals, one rejected [Furness] and the other atrophied, but now he was determined. You see the attraction of Antonia, aside from the fact that she was good-looking, was that she did not seem in the slightest awed by his reputation or his manner. He'd never come across that before. Well, perhaps with Mary [Furness], but Antonia enthralled him.'

Martina Twain 'is a real boss chick by anyone's standards. Pal she's class, with a terrific education on her, plus one of those jackpot body deals . . . American, but English raised. I've always had a remote and hopeless thing for her.'[5]

Hitchens laughs. 'Yes that's how Martin's pursuit of her often seemed at the time . . . "remote and hopeless". I think she was a little unnerved by his dedication.' Alan Jenkins, Antonia's colleague at the *TLS*, concurs. 'The environment in the office at that time was somewhat raucous and competitive. The place seemed to be crowded with youngish men with ambitions. Antonia was about the same age yet she conveyed a sense of great poise, intellectual ice. Don't get me wrong, she was not aloof, she was amusing, friendly. But at the same time she knew what she was about, was more mature than her, male, peers. Inevitably, everyone was attracted to her and she dealt with this politely, indulgently, but she was clearly not too impressed.' I ask if she could be seen as the model for Martina. 'You know, even twenty-five years ago when I first read *Money*, I saw the parallels. It isn't a *roman-à-clef* but one has a vivid sense of Martina as the character who does not so much attempt to transform John Self but who Self, despite himself, treats as his only route to stability and contentment.'

> The thing about Martina is – the thing about Martina is that I can't find a voice to summon her with ... My tongue moves in search of patterns and grids that simply are not there. Then I shout ...[6]

The 'shout' is the voice of John Self, Martin's alter ego, a distillation and exaggeration of those aspects of Martin's life and career that had defined him during the 1970s and which for Antonia might have seemed by turns fascinating and slightly abominable. Martina treats John Self with kindness, indulgence, even affection. But we know there is something else, something that Self desires, but can hardly marshal the words to articulate, and which she seems reluctant to approve. She has a husband who never actually speaks in the book and is acknowledged only as some nebulous presence to whom she owes at least respect if nothing else, which bears a close resemblance to the effect of the recently departed Gareth Evans upon Martin's pursuit of his widow.

It goes without saying that his ongoing, uncertain relationship with Antonia preoccupied Martin during the writing of *Money*. He and his beloved both feature in the novel but Martin's appearance in it has nothing to do with the solemn pretensions of 'postmodernism' and related formulae cultivated by academia. It is part of a love story. He enters the novel as the detached saturnine witness to his own pursuit of the woman who would soon be his wife. Certainly the exercise in self-scrutiny involved some distortions. Martin was not generally accustomed to consuming a pint of tax-exempt whisky at one go, via his tooth mug, before setting out in pursuit of four Wallies, three Blastfurters and an American Way washed down with a nine-pack of beer. Nor did he routinely purchase handjobs and casual sex from whosoever might provision these services. 'Actually,' Hitchens corrects me, 'he did. Not routinely, no, he didn't need to, but on one occasion he did so, purely for the sake of research of course. He was in New York doing a piece for the *Observer* I think, and working on the novel. He came round to my office at the *Nation* and announced, "I'm going to this handjob parlour and you're coming with me." He insisted that since he'd taken care of dinner two nights earlier the handjobs would be on me, so to speak, and having checked out the most interesting locations he'd decided on our destination. We must leave immediately, he said, for a place called The Tahitia in the lower part of Lexington Avenue. I was hung-over and incapable of challenging him, so we took a cab to a place unlike anything I had previously experienced, indescribably sordid. But when I read the passage in *Money* . . . superbly funny and unnervingly accurate too.'

Although I tarried in the Happy Isles for well over an hour, the actual handjob was the work of a moment – forty-five seconds, I'd say. I had to rack my brains to remember a worse one. 'You must have been really excited,' said She-She quietly, as she started plucking tissues from the box. Yes and no. Between ourselves, it was one of those handjobs where you go straight from

228

limpness to orgasm, skipping the hard-on stage. I think She-She must have activated some secret glandular gimmick, to wrap it up quickly. She then attempted a drowsy recap on the Royal Family but I shouldered my way out of there as soon as I could. The trouble with all this is – it's so *unsatisfactory*. Regular handjobs are unsatisfactory too, but they don't cost five bucks a second. Overheads are generally low. Say what you like about handjobs, they don't cost eighty-five quid.[7]

'You see,' adds Hitchens, 'Martin was going through a period of atonement and candour. I thought, did he really need to go to this handjob parlour? Couldn't he make things up? As soon as we got back to my office he phoned Antonia in England – it would have been mid-morning then – and said, "Hi. I've just been for a handjob with the Hitch." He gave her an outstandingly detailed, deadpan account of the whole thing. There were other episodes, similar to this. He busied himself with the underbelly of US life, far more exaggerated than his taste for slumming in London. Porn arcades, strip clubs, the sort of bars which seem waiting rooms for oblivion. He examined them all, an industrious researcher.' More like 'Lower' than 'Higher Autobiography'. 'Oh yes. He *created* a version of Self and communicated it to Antonia. I think she was amused.' John Self was the hinterland where Martin and Antonia might, often to her amusement, find ground for mutual exchange. Hitchens again: 'Comedy is Martin's ultimate resource and with Antonia, add charm. He was attempting to renegotiate or rather refashion somewhat forbidding gossip, for her, about his past.' That series of negotiations is re-enacted in the novel, with Self taking the lead while Martin in a rather gnomic obtuse manner looks on and Martina/Antonia occasionally steps from the margins to offer wry comments on the whirlwind of absurdity created by Self, from which she alone seems immune. At one point Self comments:

> I was just wondering, *I'm in hell somehow, and yet why is it hell?* Covered by heaven, with its girls and deceptions and mad-acts, what is the meaning of this white tent? I keep looking at the sky and saying, Yeah, I'm like that, so blue, so deeply blue. How come? I've done it before and I'll do it again. There are no police to stop you doing it. I know that people are watching me, and you aren't exempt or innocent, I think, but now someone else is watching me too. Another woman. It's the damnedest thing. Martina Twain. She's in my head. How did she get in there? She's in my head, along with all the crackle and traffic. She is watching me. There is her face, right there, watching. The watcher watched, the watched watcher – and this second pathos, where I am watched by her and yet she watches me unknowingly. Does she like what she is seeing? Dah! Oh, I must fight that, I must resist it, whatever it is. I'm in no kind of shape for the love police.[8]

The notions of the 'watcher watched', the 'watched watcher' and the 'second pathos' are borrowed, by turns respectfully and somewhat light-heartedly, from Richard Wollheim's theory of aesthetics, propounded in his *Art and Its Objects* which was the principal subject of Antonia's Master's thesis. At the heart of Wollheim's model of aesthetic appreciation is his idea of the relationship between the observer and the work of art and he was particularly intrigued by how paintings could almost be made to seem real, to transcend their status as objects, if the perceived could become sufficiently absorbed by their subject. Martin recalls that Wollheim and his wife were the two friends of Antonia he first got to know during what Hitchens refers to as their 'courtship'. 'I remember', says Martin, 'that Wollheim explained to me, very patiently, how he had refined his theories through personal experience, how he would stand for hours in a gallery in front of a painting until he almost became part of it. Fascinating, though I must say rather curious, or so it seemed to me at the time.'

There are two watchers in *Money*, Martin and Martina/Antonia, and the object of their scrutiny is the fantastic, absurd extrapolation of the former who rampages through his own narrative. Hitchens once more: 'When he wrote the novel Martin was making full use of his considerable resources of charm, diplomacy and calculation. He would listen to Antonia and her friends, absorb and pay respectful attention to their interests – he is and always has been a magnificent listener – then he would play versions of himself back to her. A very amusing and, for her, enchanting contrast.' She was particularly amused by his accounts of his involvement with the film of *Saturn 3*, barely three years earlier. This was the point at which the real Martin Amis, his dubious reputation and John Self seemed to coalesce.

'After I'd had time to reflect on that [*Saturn 3*] it seemed hardly believable. The assortment of lunatics and egotists involved was far more fantastic, actually more hilarious, than anything I'd come across in fiction,' says Martin. John Barry had earned a considerable reputation in Hollywood and the UK as a production designer, notably for his work on *A Clockwork Orange*, *Star Wars* and *Superman*. The idea for *Saturn 3* was his and he persuaded Lew Grade to fund it by drawing upon the marketability of his three previous projects: this film, he argued, would be by varying degrees bizarre, escapist and slightly risqué. In the novel his name is shared between Self junior, John, and his father, Barry, but this might well have been to deflect the attention of Barry's friends and relatives (he had died shortly after abandoning *Saturn 3*) from the character he most closely resembles, Fielding Goodney. Goodney is the impresario behind the similarly gaudy and eventually disastrous film, alternately titled *Good Money* and *Bad Money*. The three principal actors in *Saturn 3*, Kirk Douglas, Farah Fawcett and Harvey Keitel, reappear in Goodney's feature as, respectively, Lorne Guyland, Butch Beausoleil and Spunk Davis. Guyland is a late-middle-aged sex-obsessed narcissist who continually announces details of his enduring libidinal prowess and magnificently preserved physique. Martin recalls that Douglas would usurp Barry and address the entire crew on his sex scenes with Farah Fawcett, which he believed should be the thematic centrepiece of the film. As he issued orders he would strike poses emphasizing his muscularity, and on one occasion did press-ups while reflecting upon his achievements as a sexual athlete. 'Once, as if by explanation, he said, "The thing is, John, I'm unbelievably insecure." He was naked at the time.' Keitel was equally outlandish in his routines. Martin dined with him alone one evening in his suite at Claridge's Hotel and found it difficult to concentrate on the actor's elaborate suggestions as to how his character, Benson, should be played: Keitel answered the door, took drinks and sat down for dinner while stripped to the waist and wearing a pair of groin-hugging denims. 'It was a hot evening,' recalls Martin, 'but none the less . . .' Farah Fawcett, the cynosure of male fantasies in the late 1970s – her appearances in *Charlie's Angels* and her famous swimsuit poster amounted to respectable pornography – was by Martin's account 'outstandingly attractive but curiously absent, depersonalized'.

The conflicting demands of these figures, particularly Douglas's attempts to appropriate the film as a vehicle for his raddled ego, eventually caused Barry to abandon the project. He was replaced by Stanley Donen, who exercised a little more control, mainly through his well-rehearsed technique of appearing to indulge the demands of the cast while ignoring them in practice.

Martin had worked closely with Barry on the script and was now obliged by the new regime to do rewrites. 'I was chauffeured to Pinewood, perhaps twice a week to try to rescue the script. Kirk and Harvey appeared to be writing their own lines. My efforts were largely ignored but I was paid a thousand pounds a week.'

The novel offers no examples of Self's efforts as a screenwriter but Martin's sense of being stranded in a circle of hell reserved for Popular Culture is played out when Fielding Goodney is revealed as a charlatan complicit in the financial ruination of John Self, who in turn recruits Martin Amis to rescue a script and screenplay that have taken on a grotesque momentum of their own. By the end of the novel John Self is bankrupt, attempts suicide but survives, at least for several pages of reflective penury: his most impressive, elegiac piece of writing. If one harbours any doubts as to the cause of this mood of rumination, consider Self's suicide note, which is addressed to his cleaning lady; an odd choice given that she features nowhere else in the novel. It begins: 'Dear Antonia . . .'

Kingsley's only recorded comments on Martin's relationship come in a letter to Larkin:

> Don't know whether you saw but young Martin has rung the bell. Put his girl in the pod. Wedding bells to come but no hurry it seems, so it may be in every sense a little bastard that appears around Yuletide. Girl nice but we are not quite grand enough for her.[9]

The pregnancy was not planned but nor did either of them greet the news with apprehension or disquiet; as Kingsley put it, 'no hurry it seems'. During his lunches with Rosie Boycott Kingsley would sometimes reflect upon episodes from his past and in 1993 the imminent break-up of Martin's marriage prompted him to recall a conversation with his son of almost exactly ten years earlier. Boycott: 'He, Kingsley, had been introduced to Antonia. He got on well with all of Martin's girlfriends but he found her both striking and slightly forbidding.' I read out to her the piece from his letter to Larkin, emphasizing, 'Girl nice but we are not quite grand enough for her' and she laughs. 'Well, that sounds like a mixture of self-caricature and involuntary laddishness. I got the feeling that he was as much impressed as intimidated, though she was certainly different from her predecessors. What he remembered most vividly was Martin speaking to him when they were alone. Apparently he had for once lost his rather droll sportive manner, and seemed instead almost "born again". He kept insisting, "She is most certainly the one for me. I'm convinced."'

When they first met Martin was living in the flat. The house owned by Antonia, intended as a London base for herself and Evans, was less than a mile away in Chesterton Road and though both buildings could claim an almost identical legacy – neo-classical with a hint of the baroque favoured by the mid-Victorian bourgeoisie – there the similarities ended. Chesterton Road stood at the border of moneyed, respectable Kensington and Notting Hill, which was then experiencing an infusion of chic glamour thanks to the upwardly mobile chattering classes. Antonia had bought the house at the end of the 1970s, with her family endowment. (In Amis's letter to Larkin, mentioning his soon-to-be daughter-in-law, he adds a note in the margin: 'Also rich.') In autumn 1983 Martin left his (rented) flat and moved in with her but, cautiously, he did not give up the lease. Their pre-marital relationship was not entirely untroubled. As Martin wrote in a letter to Julian Barnes during their much-publicized squabble over his change of agent, 'Twelve years ago you rang me up and said, "Mart, tell me to fuck off and everything if you want – but have you left Antonia?" As it happened I went back to Antonia, that time, twelve years ago.'[10] 'That time' was late 1982–3 and as Hitchens explains, 'It was not as simple as Martin leaving Antonia. To be more accurate, you could say that he sometimes came close to giving up on his arduous pursuit of her. For quite a while after the death of her husband she was reluctant to begin *any* sort of relationship. It was a very long courtship, shall we say. As far as I recall it was almost two years between him introducing me to her at JFK before their relationship became permanent, and in the interim he pursued her incessantly. It would be wrong to say that his previous girlfriends were his intellectual inferiors – they were far too varied to merit such a classification – but it's true that Martin saw in Antonia a unique mixture of sexual attraction – she had an aloof pre-Raphaelite model look about her – and an intellectual challenge. I suspect that she sensed something of the latter in his endearments, and was wary as a consequence. Anyway, it looked for a long time a precarious on-off arrangement, with the breaks usually instigated by Antonia and with Martin charging back again seemingly undeterred. In the end he got more than he'd expected. It must have been like being an undergraduate again, dropping English and electing to do philosophy.' Francis Wheen speculates: 'Well, I hardly knew her well but you have to remember that the group Martin had mixed with since Oxford, journos and literary writers to a large extent, were secure enough in their own company, but even figures such as Hitchens and Fenton, who saw themselves as intellectual virtuosos, felt a little uneasy when up against a trained philosopher. You see the borderlines between serious literary writing, journalism and humour are porous and Martin enjoyed this. It was not quite

235

the same with philosophy.' Anthony Blond, who knew the London literary scene as well as anyone in the early 1980s, adds, 'It [Martin and Antonia] seemed to most like a match made in fiction. I mean that it was difficult to imagine that two individuals so temperamentally ill-suited could put up with each other at a dinner party, let alone settle down together. She was charming and indulgent even but she would not countenance verbal alchemy as a replacement for intellectual weight. Martin was clever yet he was also essentially a performer, as a writer and a man. He flirted with ideas. She, or so the word abroad had it, was the dominatrix, with Mart having to curb his extravagances.'

Marriage and children did not so much change Martin's lifestyle as spring-clean his most enduring habits. Within six months he had finally given up his last token of bachelorhood, his flat, and become husband, householder and father. David Papineau, Professor of Philosophy of Science at King's College London, mixed in the same circles as Antonia in the late 1970s and early 1980s after she and Evans had bought the house. 'Martin', he observes, 'has never had a great deal of time with things like answering letters, paying bills and so on. Add to that rates, grinding banalities such as central heating oil, shopping for *things* – from loo roll to bread – and well, forget it. Antonia took care of everything, uncomplainingly. She knew what she was getting, with Martin I mean.' Martin had not previously cohabited, apart from his time in Paris with Angela when for much of the day she would be out practising her skills as a visual artist. Much as he was enraptured by the presence of Antonia and more noisily, Louis, he was finding it difficult to maintain his routine of almost a decade and a half; social life, meals included, would generally be enjoyed elsewhere and aside from occasional night-time visits from his ongoing girlfriend his home was his office. Chesterton Road was spacious, with five floors. He took one of the first-floor bedrooms as his study and almost immediately found that his custom of compartmentalizing writing from everything else no longer obtained. Antonia had given up her full-time job at the *TLS* after the birth of Louis and even though he claimed that the latter's various quasi-linguistic explosions were comforting he none the less found that his powers of concentration were being eroded, simply because he was no longer operating in a space that was exclusively his own. When Antonia became pregnant again in 1985 they decided that it would be in all their interests if he could find a compromise between his earlier professional habits and married life. He began to visit local estate agents in search of a flat within fifteen minutes' walk of the family home and eventually purchased one that was described by an interviewer as part of 'a solid and gabled Victorian edifice' – accurate and evocative enough yet sufficiently vague to deter literary celebrity hunters. It was in fact a studio in a converted garishly late-Gothic Victorian priory, at the corner of Leamington Road Villas. This was the opposite side of Ladbroke Grove from Chesterton Road. Portobello Market nearby was frequented by the middle-class families who were gradually gentrifying the district but few of them actually lived very close to the network of streets surrounding the market itself. These were the last outposts of Notting Hill shabbiness, many of the terraces unmodernized since the riot-torn Rachmanesque 1950s.

Hitchens recalls Martin's life in Chesterton Road as a blend of contrasts and compromises. 'There was, of course, an enormous sense of joy and fulfilment on his part; after spending so long trying to persuade Antonia that a permanent relationship with him was the right thing for her he had, within two years, marriage and two children. But one sensed that he was also experiencing difficulties within an unfamiliar context. I don't mean domestic chores and so on – he avoided those anyway. No, very often the house seemed like a philosophy symposium; Wollheim and his wife were regular guests, as were [Peter] Strawson and quite a number of others from the UCL philosophy department. Martin got on with them all, he gets on with anyone, but, well, they were not really his sort of people temperamentally. Intellectually he could hold his own but I suspect he didn't particularly enjoy the experience.'

Martin himself remembers Wollheim with respect, some affection and, one cannot help but note, a slight hint of resignation. 'We spent quite a lot of time with the Wollheims, at their house and ours. He was certainly her mentor. A very . . . appealing man. He explained to me his ideas on art and I talked with Antonia about this. Well no, I *tried* to talk with her about it . . . And I once looked at one of Gareth's books. It was rather like attempting to understand quadratic equations, as a nine-year-old.'

Martin would breakfast with his family and be at his 'working flat' by 8.30 a.m. There was a small kitchen where he would make coffee but when he was writing he did not take lunch. He would be back at Chesterton Road by six at the latest, and these nine-hour shifts often included Saturdays.

The only breaks from this schedule would involve either an afternoon playing tennis at the Paddington Sports Club in Castellain Road, less than twenty minutes' walk from the flat and which he joined in 1984, or sessions playing snooker. For the latter he might sometimes visit the Oxford and Cambridge Club but although the place was less ritualistic than Kingsley's Garrick it none the less made him uneasy, as if along with his other sudden shifts towards stability he was stumbling blindfold into middle age. Consequently he became a regular of a far less salubrious snooker hall beneath the Westway, whose other denizens appeared to have income without regular employment, all of which would of course be harvested for the bottom-end milieu of *London Fields*.

He still mixed with members of the *New Statesman* set but most had either married and settled down in London or, like Hitchens, gone abroad. Dinner and drinks parties in their respective houses, including partners and sometimes children, replaced hedonistic meanderings. On some occasions Clive James, Ian McEwan, and the relative newcomer Salman Rushdie would meet for a meal. Most seemed to have more responsibilities now, some professional but mainly domestic.

Paddington Sports Club offered a release from working in isolation in the flat, but certainly not so that he could exchange the pressures of writing for casual conversation and exercise; quite the opposite. He made use of the games and his new group of friends and acquaintances as a laboratory for his competing ideas and inventions. He had developed a passion for tennis when he lived with Colin Howard and Sargy Mann, who effectively introduced him to the game. Neither of his parents had much interest in sport of any kind. Mann: 'He was a very fast learner, quite a natural talent too, but what was most noticeable was his enormous desire to win. I don't think there was anything cut-throat about it, in that he was not concerned with getting the better of a particular opponent. He was playing against himself. He would fly into a rage if his shot was out or in the net, swear and fling the racket down.' Zachary Leader, partner and opponent at the Sports Club, agrees: 'He is not a casual player. A great deal of mental and physical concentration goes into his game. It might sound flippant, maybe, but I sometimes had the impression that games were the gym work and basic training for the intellectual grind. He put a similar amount of effort into chess, even snooker and poker. He writes about them in an ironic self-parodic manner but in actuality he was a very cerebral player, exhausting even to watch.'

His two most regular fellow players at the club were David Papineau and Zachary Leader, shortly to be joined by Andy

239

Hislop who had known Antonia at the *TLS* and was now branching out as a freelance screenwriter. Steve Foster, the club manager, would chat with him in the bar and was responsible for introducing him to Chris Mitas, who features as a humorous presence in *Experience* referred to only by his forename. He owned properties and restaurants, and drove a Bentley. Zachary Leader: 'Of course he knew what Martin did for a living and he glanced at his novels, though certainly not to impress him. I remember once he said, I think of *London Fields*: "Martin, have you ever tried to *read* one of your books?" Martin thought that was very funny. Chris was and is a clever man.'

Violence features in Martin's novels in much the same way that Updike's autobiographical heroes seem restlessly preoccupied with sex. One begins to suspect that in both instances obsession is a mask for perplexity. Aside from being waylaid by two ten-year-olds in Swansea, and rescued by his mother, physical confrontation was something that Martin had never personally experienced and the episodes in *Experience* where verbal combat with Rushdie and Hitchens involves the threat to 'take things outside' are largely grandstanding. In this respect Chris was his education.

'Chris is a fascinating man. He lives in Spain now. He had an exotic past. He was a Judo champion, and represented Britain. We had and still have a very warm relationship. I'd see him four to five times a week. He told me what it was like to be tough, tough. Not villainy or aggression as a state of mind. He was concerned more with the crunch moments, what actually went on in a fight, what you *had to do*. I'd sometimes feel that when I'm writing about bad people – not that Chris is a bad person – *extreme* people . . . there are certain things you can't actually do, describe – because you don't have knowledge, don't have a way into it. Chris did give me a way into it. If I'm to put it into a sentence, when you go into a fight you have to insulate yourself, become a machine. He was outstandingly instructive, through him I was able to stretch myself, to use expressive language that before I couldn't attach to experience.' Chris embodied a world and a way of thinking that his intellectual pals at the Sports Club knew only vicariously.

Martin: 'I can't overstate the influence of Chris on my work. He has given me at least two or three hundred pages. He is charismatic and expressive, but it wasn't Chris's *character* that inspired me. It was the stories he told, the places he took me to, the people he brought me into contact with. I ought to dedicate a book to him.'

'Martin', according to Hislop, 'is eclectic and licentious in the use of people and places for his writing – anything goes – but he does tend towards a preoccupation with things that he cannot fathom, that sadden him personally or that appear frightening, outrageous or grotesque. Chris fell into none of these categories. He is what he is, implacable and transparent. I think Martin viewed him as, well, heroic. Which disqualified him from inclusion, as a character, in the books. Keith [Talent of *London Fields*] was created soon after they met but there is no resemblance whatsoever between them. If anything the presence of Chris as a testament to real London – particularly the parts viewed from the outside by the intelligentsia – guaranteed that Keith would be pure hyperbole.

'You see,' he adds, 'Martin at the time, late eighties, was undergoing a period of transition. He felt quietly ashamed by the absence of a "big idea". He was a wonderful entertainer, great at recycling the more outrageous features of contemporaneity, but he wanted gravity. Two things played some part in his search. In a small degree Chris helped to wean him away from the – let's be honest, slightly prurient – preoccupation with grotesquery; Chris was the real thing. More significant were his children. I lived a few houses away in the same road, with kids of my own, slightly younger, and we'd talk, play football with them sometimes. It was mainly the usual stuff about infant school, their idiosyncrasies and it goes without saying that we worried about their health and so on. But Martin went further. He seemed to feel that having children meant that he was not only responsible for them but entrusted with the destiny of the rest of humanity.'

David Papineau concurs. 'It would be unfair, wrong, to say that he used the boys [his sons] as tropes for a new visionary enterprise, in his writing I mean. No, but one was aware that he had become not just protective of them – we all are – but righteously. They were the future which, in his view, we were treating irresponsibly.' Martin: 'After Ian [McEwan] wrote his Oratorio [*Or Shall We Die?*, on nuclear weapons] I just thought . . . it wasn't for me. I was reminded that I wasn't *that* kind of writer. I was perversely and proudly non-political, especially in my twenties, and I was ridiculed continually by Hitchens at the *New Statesman* for being so quietist. I even refused to join the NUJ, not for specific reasons, I didn't want to be *part* of anything. Politics seemed to me to involve a joining, an encroachment upon individuality . . . and that was inimical to me, then.' It was not that the acquisition of a family suddenly politicized Martin. He continued to treat ideological commitment as an abridgement to truth and experience. But he became alert to something other than the untroubled, even jaunty fatalism he had once shared with his father.

Einstein's Monsters contains five short stories written during the three-year period between Martin's marriage and the book's publication in 1987. While there is no enduring narrative a persistent theme draws the pieces together – apocalypse, anticipated or experienced and caused in all likelihood by nuclear war. It is without doubt one of his most curious works, by turns accomplished and self-righteous.

Before considering the exact nature of its awkward condition let us first examine the cause, evident in the opening paragraph of 'Thinkability', the Introduction:

I was born on 25 August 1949: four days later, the Russians successfully tested their first atom bomb, and *deterrence* was in place. So I had those four carefree days, which is more than my juniors ever had. I didn't really make the most of them. I spent half the time under a bubble. Even as things stood, I was born in a state of acute shock. My mother says I looked like Orson Welles in a black rage. By the fourth day I had recovered, but the world had taken a turn for the worse. It was a nuclear world. To tell you the truth, I didn't feel very well at all. I was terribly sleepy and feverish. I kept throwing up.

Astonishingly no reviewers noticed or felt courageous enough to comment on this act of deferential plagiarism. Read the first page of Salman Rushdie's *Midnight's Children* and you will see what I mean. Martin borrows the prevailing conceit from Rushdie's novel: an ability to transport oneself into a pre-infantile state and reflect sagelike on what was going on at the time. Rushdie's narrator, Saleem Sinai, is born at midnight on the eve of India's day of independence. His chaotic story reflects the unfocused, potentially disastrous condition of India as an emerging nation and every British reviewer and indeed Booker Prize panellist felt suitably chastened by a writer who could play such beguiling games with their own shameful legacy. In 'Thinkability' Martin, like Rushdie, attempts to project himself backwards to the moment of his birth, at which the Cold War began, almost: 'four days later, the Russians successfully tested their first atom bomb'. This seems extraordinarily narcissistic, as if through some solemn ordinance he, born to be a writer, has been elected to declaim on our apocalyptic inheritance thirty-eight years on. His considerable literary skills are then deployed with the conviction of a zealot. He even goes so far as to claim that while his previous work had been random in its approach to less agreeable parts of the prevailing zeitgeist, he was in truth cultivating a private agenda.

> Soon after I realized I was writing about nuclear weapons (and the realization took quite a while: roughly half of what follows in this book was written in innocence of its common theme), I further realized that in a sense I had been writing about them all along. Our time is different. All times are different, but our time is *different*. A new fall, an infinite fall, underlies the usual – indeed traditional – presentiments of decline.

This is not so much *Apocalypse Now* as *Genesis Again*. The Old Testament holds that an endemic flaw in human nature would condemn us to an irrevocable state of misery and loss. In Martin's view the next Fall, the Nuclear Catastrophe, will be even worse.

David Papineau, when he first got to know Martin, was also the father of two infant sons. He recalls that when Martin spoke of Louis and Jacob his manner changed. 'Obviously there was the usual amount of pride, and anxiety; we all felt that, as parents. But once Martin lighted upon the subject of his sons he seemed suffused with a mixture of guilt and responsibility, as if everything that our generation did . . . well, we should be held accountable to the next one for our actions.' This is commendable both in terms of parental duty and a conjugate sense of responsibility for the fate of the rest of the human race. The question remains, however, as to whether the reader of fiction should be subjected to what amounts to sermonizing. The worst example of this is 'Bujak and the Strong Force or God's Dice'. Sam, the narrator, tells us of his acquaintance with Bujak, whose 'life went deep into the century'. He fought in the Polish army against the Germans in 1939 and thereafter as a member of the Resistance. After imprisonment by the Nazis he survived for ten years in the Soviet Union before fleeing to the United States, there to be widowed by a hospital bug. A figure of almost superhuman strength – he lifts a car without the assistance of a jack – who has in the past visited unspeakable reprisals upon Nazi collaborators in Poland and struck fear into a group of North London yobs, one of whom had mistreated his daughter. Now he lives in the same street as Sam in Notting Hill.

The vortex of the story, the reason for Sam's telling of it – he confesses that he has abandoned his writerly ambitions and is offering this account simply because of its compulsive gravity, a clumsy hint on Martin's part that he too is now involved in something more solemn than literary licence – is Bujak's discovery of the bodies of his granddaughter, daughter and mother, raped and murdered by two Glaswegians who are unconscious, drunk, in the next room. 'But, why didn't you kill them?' asks Sam, adding that any jury would have exempted him from guilt.

'I had no wish to add to what I found. I thought of my dead wife Monika. I thought – they're all dead now. I couldn't add to what I saw there. Really the hardest thing was to touch them at all. You know the wet tails of rats? Snakes? Because I saw that they weren't human beings at all. They had no idea what human life was. No idea! Terrible mutations, a disgrace to their human moulding. An eternal disgrace. If I had killed them then I would still be strong. But you must start somewhere. You must make a start.'[11]

This, hardly disguised, is Martin's argument for disarmament. Only those who commend the doctrines of deterrence and retribution – monstrous extrapolations of Bujak's physical potency – have the power to suspend and dismantle them; if only they had the wisdom of Bujak.

Through the story intriguing facts are disclosed. Sam's Jewishness, the fact that many of his family died in the Holocaust, his partner Mishima's past – she lost family in the second atom bomb attack on Nagasaki – all of these improbably assorted and less than plausible details are brought to the surface in response to Bujak's enquiries about Sam's and Mishima's backgrounds. It is almost as though his personal history of suffering the worst that the twentieth century has to offer makes him a magnet for a similar heritage in others. Gradually he evolves as a figure of post-Enlightenment moral authority. Of course he is not perfect – he makes a number of politically incorrect comments on the West Indian residents of Notting Hill – but he has witnessed, perhaps even understands, the most terrible deeds that human beings can visit upon each other and is thus spared from the petty rules of address dreamed up by a liberal intelligentsia who deal exclusively with hypothesis and abstraction.

It is a lamentable piece of work, and not because it is poorly written – Martin's creation of a shrewd but hesitant narrator is a small naturalistic masterpiece – but because it preaches. It is literature suborned to promote a creed, as a means of converting the reader to its author's convictions. Evelyn Waugh was bad enough but his dedication to Roman Catholicism, in fiction and life, was more an exercise in snobbish triumphalism than an attempt to bring others to the Holy See. Martin appears to believe that a story which does not explicitly address nuclear weapons and disarmament might none the less cultivate subliminal parallels for the reader, at least if that reader is as sensitive and intelligent as he is. Irrespective of our opinion on the use of literature as polemic, then, we can certainly add patronizing to the charge sheet. Kingsley wrote to Conquest of his son's evangelical dedication to disarmament:

> Talking of Martin, he has as I said gone all lefty and of the crappiest neutralist kind, challenging me to guess how many times over the world can destroy itself, writing two incredible bits of ban-it bullshit in the Obs (of course), one a 'paperback round up' (of books about the nuclear winter etc.), the other a TV review (of programmes saying Reagan wants to blow up the world), in fact going on like H Pinter does these days I hear. Luckily having now a 2nd baby has given him (M) other things to think about.[12]

Obviously during their exchanges on this matter Martin had been circumspect regarding the cause of his sudden almost neurotic preoccupation with nuclear weapons. The birth of Jacob, little more than a year after Louis, did not give him 'other things to think about'. Instead, it reinforced his vigour and feelings of guilt. Alongside the spectre of a nuclear apocalypse, which plods through the stories in various nuances and cumbersome allegories, the image of childhood, particularly our duty to the coming generation, resurfaces constantly. Pre-empting any speculation on how his father might respond to his stance he offers in 'Thinkability' an indulgent caricature.

> I am reliably ruder to my father on the subject of nuclear weapons than on any other. I usually end by saying something like, 'Well, we'll just have to wait until you old *bastards* die off one by one.' He usually ends by saying something like, 'Think of it. Just by closing down

the Arts Council we could significantly augment our arsenal. The grants to poets could service a nuclear submarine for a year.'[13]

The piece is driven by the kind of hysteria that we associate more with the weird creations of literature than writers themselves. He brands all supporters of nuclear deterrence as 'subhuman', a term previously used with conviction only by the Nazis and the White Supremists of the Southern USA. 'For Jastrow [an advocate of the Strategic Defence Initiative], the unthinkable is thinkable. He is wrong, and in this respect he is also, I contend, subhuman, like all the nuclear-war fighters, like all the "prevailers".' (p. 8) He describes also how he often sits for long periods in the flat/studio where he writes wondering if one of the whines that pierce the London soundscape is signalling an imminent nuclear attack. If he survives the first blast 'then – God willing, if I still have the strength, and, of course, if they are still alive – I must find my wife and children and I must kill them'. Which is not the kind of note on domestic assignments usually found posted to the fridge door.

Will Self: 'Martin has a tendency to project personal paranoia into abstract universals, an ugly miscegenation of instincts with a need for profundity. This need drove his preoccupation with an imminent nuclear apocalypse, AIDs, global warming. Really it is the little guy in a big, nasty, frightening world looking for meaning and purpose. He's still at it, with Islamism. I'm not being patronizing. In fact I think it's rather endearing. The impulse that makes him the finest prose writer of his generation causes him also to be the worst political writer. He is the little man walking down the dark street, a terrific prose poet of fear and anxiety. Also one sees in him the desire of the tragic farceur to be taken seriously. Sometimes, sometimes, he achieves this.'

'Thinkability' was completed in February 1987 when Martin

and Antonia were in Israel. He had been invited to give a paper at a conference on Saul Bellow, held in Haifa. Bellow and his wife Janis were present but neither he nor Martin had much patience for the event itself: academics in 1987 had reached a nadir of jargon-ridden inaccessibility. Their duties completed, the Bellows and the Amises moved on to spend a week in Jerusalem, dining once with Teddy Kollek, mayor of the city, Amschel and Anita Rothschild and Allan Bloom, political philosopher and long-term friend of Bellow. Martin had known Amschel since the 1970s when he ran a 'salon' in the London maisonette he shared with Angela Gorgas and hosted lavish parties at his country house in Sussex.

Martin describes his relationship with Judaism as 'philo-Semitic', an affinity that has deepened over the past fourteen years since the birth of his quarter-Jewish daughters. Hitchens offers an insight into a state of mind, bordering upon an aspiration, that predates this by at least two decades. Hitchens and his brother Peter found out only after the deaths of their parents that they were, via their maternal line, Jewish. Christopher, then in his full-blooded Marxian phase, took this as an inconsequential accident of biology, of no greater significance than hereditary hair colouring. Martin, however, when his friend informed him, 'sat for a moment and then said that he felt envious. It was not that he simply craved some form of tribal identity, rather he was fascinated by Judaism as something that involved a magnificent intellectual legacy and, obviously, a tragic inheritance. It forced its unasked member-ship to confront questions that for others would remain abstractions, sometimes peripheral. Obviously the State of Israel was of significance here.' The Bellow conference marked one of his two visits to Israel during the 1980s, about which his comments now are intriguing if somewhat oblique: 'The place had enormous energy. It was an exciting place to be. There was no small talk.' While Martin does make a cursory reference to the Israeli nuclear programme in 'Thinkability' it is notable that in it there is no reference to the three individuals who were supporters of nuclear deterrence and with whom he had an exchange, uncompromising on both sides, as he composed the piece in Israel in 1987. Kollek did not admit formally that Israel had constructed a nuclear device but he and everyone else were aware that the Bomb existed; Mordechai Vanunu had disclosed details to the *Sunday Times* in 1986. Its purpose, Kollek and others believed, was self-evidently justifiable: it was an essential means of deterrence for a country surrounded by states and organizations dedicated to its annihilation. Bloom had stated in print that the existence of nuclear weapons, and the fear which effectively proscribed their use, was the factor that had preserved an ideologically divided planet from a conventional Third World War. He also believed that the same principle would secure Israel against further invasions such as that which prompted the Six Day War. Bellow, like Bloom, opposed Cold War disarmament and was committed to the necessary survival of Israel, by any means available. Bellow wrote to Leon Wieseltier that 'still more' the 'survival' of Israel 'depends upon a technology which . . . but you know more about this than I do'. There can be little if any doubt that the elided reference is to nuclear weapons. Bellow is worried only that Israel's emergence as a 'mini-superpower' would present the country 'to American leaders, some of them, as a convenient package to be traded for this, that or the other'. He expresses no reservations about the necessity, or the morality, of the nuclear programme.[14]

Martin recalls from their first meeting that Bellow's conversational manner involved shrewd though not malicious trap-laying. 'He treated matters such as politics and the state of the nation with illusionless scepticism.' Obviously they got on well from the beginning but one must notice, even from this brief account, a number of parallels between Bellow and another figure who featured prominently in Martin's life. He too favoured fractious individuality above attendance upon abstract beliefs. Neither suffered fools indulgently nor did they care greatly about the sensibilities of those who might be offended by their views. And despite their self-sufficiency they each countenanced a mischievous sense of belonging, involving, respectively, nonconformist notions of Englishness and Judaism. I speak, of course, of Kingsley.

Martin observes that writers whose experience straddles 'the evolutionary firebreak of 1945' have failed to record in their work this apocalyptic shift in human consciousness.[15] He has already mentioned his father and goes on to include Graham Greene, 'the most prescient writer of our time' as equally negligent. It is, he contends, up to 'younger writers' who have lived on the other side of the firebreak 'to write about nuclear weapons. My impression is that the subject resists frontal assault. For myself, I feel it as a background, a background which insidiously foregrounds itself.'[16] He is, implicitly, if rather clumsily, harnessing his own stylistic signature to a mission. The unaffiliated tenor of his fiction is, it seems, the perfect vehicle for mapping out the perilous state of mankind. How then does he deal with the anomaly that the figure with whom he has most in common, at least as a writer, is, as much as his father, the living antithesis of his convictions? 'There was no anomaly, and that's why. You don't mention things that don't occur to you.'

I have spoken to Martin about this, at length. 'Despite my political apathy I knew, or subconsciously felt, that something *had* been bothering me. It had always been there in my childhood, like a shadow, particularly during the Cuban Missile Crisis. I felt physically sick for a week.

'But when my son was born, *then* the idea of continuation was there. It was the time of the Reagan build-up, but it was as much a subconscious reshuffle ... When we were in Cambridge, West Wratting, we went through the farcical exercise of getting under our school desks after the air-raid siren sounded. Worse, for me, was the TV image of the bullseye of London, surrounded by the ever-spiralling concentric circles of the blast. Eventually I couldn't watch. I used to leave the room. I couldn't stand it.'

Notably, it is not so much the specific recollection of these fears that preoccupies him as a sense of an uncompleted dialogue. 'There is much in the letters between him [Kingsley] and Bob [Conquest] lampooning the idea of nuclear war being imminent. As though it were all as absurd as *Dr Strangelove*.' But, I point out, he didn't see these letters for at least ten years after *Einstein's Monsters* and his 1980s arguments with his father. 'No, but they reminded me of what I'd always felt. Kingsley always pooh-poohed the idea of the end of everything – global catastrophe. He would have been reliably cynical about global warming.'

Despite my abiding contempt for all brands of psychoanalysis I suspect that his father's resolute refusal to fear for the future of humanity is in part the motive for Martin's zealotry. His comments on the period during which Kingsley's opinions, on everything, ossified are particularly revealing. 'Kingsley didn't like the idea of disarmament because he didn't like the people who were for it: the hippy generation, people in sandals.' Unlike his father, Martin did not in late middle-age turn right. In *The Pregnant Widow* (2010) his fears and sense of horror re-emerge in the recollections of his alter-ego Keith Nearing:

Like everyone else alive during the period under review, Keith was a vet of the Nuclear Cold War (1949–91):

the contest of nightmares. In 1970, a twenty-year tour lay behind him. A twenty-year tour lay ahead of him.

He was conscripted – he was *impressed* – on August 29, 1949, when he was ninety-six hours old. This was the date of the birth of the Russian bomb. As he lay sleeping, historical reality stole into the ward at the infirmary, and gave him the rank of private.

Growing up, he didn't feel resentful about military service exactly, because everyone else alive was in the army too. Apart from crouching under his desk at school, when they practised for central thermonuclear exchange, he didn't seem to have any duties. Or no conscious ones. But after the Battle of Cuba, in 1962 (for its duration, its thirteen days, his thirteen-year-old existence became a swamp of nausea), he entered into the spirit of the contest of nightmares. In his mind – oh, the obstacle courses, the sadistic NCOs, the fatigues, the lousy chow, the twirling potato skins of kitchen patrol. In the Nuclear Cold War, you only saw action when you were sound asleep.

During this period, physical violence was somehow consigned to the Third World, where about twenty million died in about a hundred military conflicts. In the First and Second Worlds, the shaping strategy was Mutual Assured Destruction. And everyone lived. There, the violence was all in the mind.

Keith lay in his bed, trying to understand. What was the outcome of the dream war and all that silent combat? Everything could vanish, at any moment. This disseminated an unconscious but pervasive mortal fear. And mortal fear might make you want to have sexual intercourse; but it wouldn't make you want to love. Why love anyone, when everyone could vanish? So maybe it was love that took the wound, in the Passchendaele of mad dreams.[17]

'Thinkability' is a curious document, the most principled produced by Martin at that time. But along with this come lacunae and fallacies. At one point he offers an all-encompassing mantra. 'Besides it could be argued that all writing – all art, in all times – has a bearing on nuclear weapons ... Art celebrates life and not the other thing, not the opposite of life.'[18] Surely 'all writing', by implication literary and non-literary, is not bound by universal obligations to a single agenda? The hyperbole can be understood, if not justified, in terms of the subtext of this passage. A man such as Martin was denied the opportunity to treat the notion of 'all writing' as an impersonal phenomenon for the simple reason that the figure he knew best, probably loved more than any man, and with whom he disagreed virulently, was also a writer.

David Papineau: 'While there was no question about the strength of his personal convictions it sometimes seemed as though it *was* a private undertaking. I don't doubt that he knew about the Cruise Missile protests, Greenham Common and so on, but they seemed peripheral to his own vision of the coming apocalypse. You see, Martin has intellectual enthusiasms that often become obsessions. I think these concerns gelled in the mid-1980s, nuclear deterrence and the transformative experience of fatherhood. Perhaps *London Fields* was cathartic in that respect, in that all the issues are there but they wrestle themselves into a state of torpor and exhaustion.'

9

Dystopian Visions

In 1984 shortly after the birth of his first son, Louis, Martin began work on his most ambitious novel yet, eventually to be called *London Fields*. London Fields is real enough, five minutes by train from Liverpool Street and within the Borough of Hackney. Presently it is undergoing the process of gentrification experienced by Notting Hill around the time that Martin began the book. Then, it was a less than endearing location, its late-nineteenth-century buildings defaced by post-war attempts at renovation and overlooked by 1960s tower blocks, the sort of places in which real-life replicas of Keith Talent might spend time left over from darts, boozing and minor criminality. The blocks could at a stretch be glimpsed from the window of Martin's studio in Leamington Road Villas. I ask him if the place had any specific associations, if he had visited it for any reason. 'No. I used to pass it on my way to the *New Statesman* printers in Southend.' The name stays in the mind, as spectacularly inappropriate. It derives from the sixteenth century when the whole area was largely uninhabited upland pasture used by drovers to keep their cattle just before taking them to market in the City of London, and slaughter. All of the sinuous nuances of the novel are caught in this charmingly incongruous pairing of history and nomenclature: meadows cultivated for the final days of their non-human residents replaced centuries later by the crowded cityscape of concrete, traffic and takeaways.

Martin adds: 'I remember also driving through it on my way north. I was going to Enfield to do an interview for the *Observer* in 1987.' The interviewee was Keith Deller, accompanied by his wife Kim. Keith was the 1983 World Darts Champion or, as Martin puts it, 'for a while the great white hope of darts'. When he met him, Keith 'showed that in darts it is hard to do your ageing one year at a time'.[1] Martin was halfway through *London Fields* and it is no accident that one of its triumvirate of tragicomic characters is called Keith Talent, darts enthusiast, nor that his firstborn is named Kim.

It would have suited my preconceptions if I had found Keith half-drunk in some roadhouse, smothered in tattoos and darts magazines. On the contrary: Keith and his pretty wife, Kim, awaited me over their Perriers in the ante-room of a pleasant businessman's restaurant. There was talk of the gym, and countryside rambles with dog Sheba. No alcohol and no nicotine. It was I who felt like the true darter of the company, with my drink, my roll-ups, my North Circular pallor.

Keith is genial, straightforward, considerate, clear-eyed. He is also charmingly uxorious, constantly deferring to Kim, who, for her part, is fully abreast of Keith's darting hopes and fears.[2]

There is something slightly unctuous in this verbal portrait. I have never met Keith Deller, only witnessed him on TV, and can only take Martin's account on trust, but even figures such as Bellow did not receive such generous patronage as this. On the one hand he did not want his readers to think that he perceived Keith (Talent) as the epitome of a very real underclass of darts-obsessed vulgarians – particularly ones he had actually met on his daring excursions into yob land for the *Observer* – yet at the same time in the *Observer* article there is clear evidence of anthropological prurience – 'The stars *do* look relatively slim, but this is partly because the fans look relatively fat' – which he then feels the need to temper with doses of equitability: 'What draws me and many others to the sport and the spectacle, I think, is a liking for human variety, specifically a drastically primitive activity in a drastically modern setting.'[3] The competition between empathy and horrified fascination seems guileless but in the novel, with the other Keith, Martin does not even attempt to cover up the sense of foul gratification that went into the creation of such a figure. He is similarly shameless in his invention of Nicola Six, the murderee. Because of her presence the novel has frequently been denounced as a condonement of sexism, or more specifically the predatory imperious role of men in society and literature. This was the cause of its failure to reach the shortlist for the 1989 Booker Prize for fiction: two women members of the panel, Maggie Gee and Helen McNeil, insisted on its exclusion for purely ideological reasons, irrespective of its qualities as a piece of writing. The panel chairman, David Lodge, refused to comment at the time but later admitted in a 1992 article that it was to him a 'matter of great regret' that the novel did not reach the shortlist, 'due to the objection of two panel members', which raises the question of why neither he nor anyone else felt sufficiently regretful in 1989 to defend it.

The novel itself is set in 1999, a decade after its completion and several months before the millennium. Sam Young has exchanged flats with the British author Mark Asprey, or 'MA', as he signs himself coquettishly, whose flat is in the same district as Martin's, though, if we believe Sam's account, far more luxuriously appointed. But even the ungenerous would have expected the grottier eastern side of Notting Hill to have improved considerably by the late 1990s, along with the fortunes of one of its most famous literary residents, 'MA'.

Sam's overriding preoccupation is with a sense of dread, and everything he perceives is informed by a sense of imminent apocalyptic terror. On leaving his Jumbo at Heathrow the other aeroplanes strike him as harbingers of something horrifying and ineffable, 'all the sharks with their fins erect, thrashers, baskers, great whites – killers, killers every one'. (p. 2) The absent MA is similar in many ways to the very real Martin Amis, who attends the Paddington Sports Club, helps cook his children's dinner, plays football with them in the park in St Mark's Road, a hundred yards from the family home, yet at the same time Martin elects Samson Young as temperamentally much closer to the real thing – especially their shared feeling of dread. I asked Hitchens if Young bears any resemblance to Martin in the late 1980s and he laughed. 'Very much so, yes. That was of course Martin's first period of obsessive preoccupation. The book Young probably wants to write, aside from the one he's in, is *Einstein's Monsters*. Martin in the mid-1980s was not just convinced that a nuclear apocalypse was imminent, he also treated all of the ethical shortcomings of humanity at that point as symptoms of mass condonement of nuclear weapons. So, yes, Young's sense of everything being in rapid terminal decline mirrored Martin's thing with nuclear weapons. The question is, of course, is Young a didactic instrument or an exercise in self-criticism?'

He is certainly a curious portrait of the artist in sagacious middle age. His author is not dying but as Zachary Leader puts it: 'When I got to know him he was obsessively concerned with staying in good condition, no doubt as a hedge against his habits, smoking in particular.' In his mid- to late thirties, he was intent on closing the door against physical decay. Martin was plagued by the spectacle of his father, whose avoidance of exercise was a matter of principle. At that time Kingsley was in a poor state, weighing in at about sixteen stone, but even back in the sixties, when he was Martin's age, he had become, prematurely, portly. 'Martin in the 1980s became noticeably more competitive as a tennis player, not because now he wanted to win – he had *always* wanted to win – he was simply driving himself that much harder. He became extremely fit.' Sam Young concertinas the myriad anxieties of ageing, uncertainty and declining ambition into a horribly simple predicament: he is attempting to write something significant, his first for twenty years, while suffering from a terminal disease that leaves him no more than two months to complete his task. This causes us to question the origins of Young's moments of private introspection, when he is not living vicariously through the stories of his creations but experiencing London first-hand. Is his sense of everything as informed by impending doom an accurate account of the world in 1989, seemingly hurrying towards the brink of catastrophe, or a reflection of his own melancholic state? The mood of morbid resignation obtains throughout the novel and secures an axis of uncertainty for everything else, most significantly the nature of the three other characters, all the inventions of Young. Each of them is sufficiently odd, variously prepossessing, pitiable and grotesque, to guarantee our fascination, but constantly we have to check our musings against how we feel about them. Are we supposed to respond to them as literary characters in their own right or as perverse indices to Young's state of mind? This is why it is a gross misinterpretation of a complex book to treat Nicola Six as an endorsement of sexist attitudes and fetishes. She exists, vividly, on the page but before jumping to conclusions about the preconceptions she reflects, consider instead a far more perplexing model. For Young she is indeed a fantasy and he alone is responsible for the scenarios in which she reduces both Guy Clinch and Keith to lustful delirium by her sheer presence. He has created her, yet he is aware that she will have far more volition and autonomy than any previous act of authorial patronage.

Even before they meet, Young sees her from the window of Asprey's flat, a figure dressed in black, despatching a parcel to a rubbish bin on the other side of the road. I ask Martin: did characters in his fiction begin life in that way, as figures seen from a distance, maybe never to be encountered again, but provoking speculations on what kind of personal history lay behind their observed habits and actions? 'Some, yes. This kind of speculation is not just the preserve of the novelist. When we see people on the tube, sitting opposite us, or alone at the other side of a bar we inevitably speculate on what they've been doing minutes, hours, days, decades, before this moment, and where they will go afterwards.' Young has a special advantage. He retrieves the package from the bin and discovers the memoirs of Nicola Six, the springboard for a mixture of detective work – he believes what she writes – and reverie: he wants to know even more.

Hitchens provides an invaluable insight. 'Very little that has happened to him is wasted, in his fiction. He does not borrow exchanges word for word or transplant idiosyncrasies, without adjustment, but if you've shared some of the same experiences and then encounter them in the novels the effect is very unnerving. You *recognize* things – in the same way that you recognize a familiar face or tone of voice – but at the same time you marvel at how he has transformed them. Not simply disguised them, no, Martin is an artist. He *improves* on the original, even if his creation is far, far worse as an individual.

'Nicola Six is a classic example. For anyone who knew Mary [Furness] in the 1970s and then during her relationship with [James, 13th Earl] Waldegrave, the resemblances were electrifying. Her parents were not killed in an air crash but that passage where Nicola goes to the airport, ask anyone and they'll know who he had in mind. "In the midst of life . . ." Her version would be, "In the midst of death we are in sex."' Nicola drives to the airport VIP lounge in which relatives are provided with free drinks and live television coverage of the crash site, scattered wreckage and body bags included. 'Coldly Nicola drank more brandy, wondering how death could take people so unprepared. That night she had acrobatic sex with some unforgivable pilot'. (p. 16)

Zachary Leader and David Papineau both noted that when Martin was planning or in the middle of a work of fiction his conversation was often a release from the preoccupations of his hours alone in the Leamington Road Villas flat. 'He never attempted to take over a conversation,' says Leader. 'Instead he would ensure that his particular concerns were appetizing. Whoever he was talking to would want to join in.' He told David Papineau how he had experienced an emergency landing, when flying to Spain to join Antonia and the boys for a holiday. No one was hurt but he was plagued for months afterwards by vivid moments of recollection which appeared to follow no obvious sequence. He explained to Papineau that what puzzled him most was the part played by time in the fabric of occurrences and emotions. 'He asked me about philosophical theses on time, not to build some model for a fictional experiment;' recalls Papineau, 'that would come later with *Time's Arrow*. No, what concerned him were the ways in which the mind – memory, cognition, perception, ratiocination and so

261

on – operates in relation to time. Specifically are our mental activities subject to the independent progression of time or is the latter conditioned in part by perception? He was fascinated most of all by the so-called "causation solution", which involves the distinction between the past and the future. The present is an illusion, or rather a trick of language. Basically we can affect the future by acts which will determine events yet to occur – though the exact cause might not be predictable – but the past is immutable, nothing about it can be altered.' Nicola Six does not have the power to alter the future – as Papineau explains it is impossible to change what has yet to take place – but she has an anarchic effect upon anything that falls within her orbit of desires and emotions. Clive James remembers Mary Furness as 'a woman who made men behave immoderately. The usual assembly of caution, reason and restraint went straight out of the window. Yes, Martin captures that well in the book [*London Fields*] with Nicola driving everyone completely mad. Like Mary she procured a blend of raging desire and trepidation. She didn't intend to dominate – she was too impetuous and good-natured for that – but she certainly caused them to lose control.' All except Young who acts as witness to this sexual frenzy rather than victim or participant. He it was who had watched Nicola disposing of her diaries outside the flat. He rescues them from the bin and has unique access to her past, her life of provocation and usurpation. Martin, through Young, was revisiting his past. Mary was the only woman who had caused him a feeling of heedless dereliction. He could remember this just as he could recall Lucretia Stewart's obsessive concern with her diary, her record of a London lifestyle that could, if published, make the eighteenth-century city seem virtuous by comparison and cast shadows upon the spotless profiles of many of its now eminent figures. Wheen called the diary her 'pension plan' and one wonders if a sense of caution, allied to fear, caused her to decide against cashing it in with a publisher or tabloid newspaper.

In Nicola's diary, she announces herself to Young as a murderee, a woman who can predict the time and nature of her own death. She has chosen to bring about her own demise through her almost magical powers of enchantment and at the end of the novel it is Young who commits the act, an outcome that in turn appears to have been devised by Mark Asprey who will then publish the novel as his own. Young takes a lethal dose of pills and lies down on the bed in Asprey's flat, leaving the manuscript in the next room. Martin: '*London Fields* is a kind of postmodernist joke, in that Sam, the narrator, is transcribing something that appears to be happening. His record as a writer confirms that he is incapable of making things up but at the same time Nicola, Keith and Guy are fantasies.' What about Mark Asprey? 'He is an anti-writer.' You mean the sort of writer who, unlike Sam, is entirely undeserving of pity? 'Yes, he is a deflected parody of what at the time was my public image, which was wholly the creation of the press. He is despicable, arrogant, calculating, undeservedly successful. If the press were to be believed then "MA" would suit both Martin Amis and Mark Asprey very well.' So if Mark is your media-generated alter ego is Sam a little closer to the real thing? 'To an extent. Though of course the division is never as simple as that.'

At the time the novel was published Louis and Jacob were respectively five and three years old, not far from the ages of the two characters in the novel whose role seems somewhat gratuitous, Kim Talent and Marmaduke Clinch. Kim is a baby of cherubic mien, to whom Sam addresses the final passage of the novel in the form of a letter. Marmaduke, meanwhile, is a hulking toddler capable of visiting destruction upon anything within range and reducing his parents to a state of terrified despair. The effect is hilarious, as if a keenly accurate portrait of upper-middle-class London family life has been infiltrated by a version of Damien from *The Omen*. 'Babies, toddlers,' muses Martin 'can be angels and demons in the same package, every parent knows that.' Young's letter to Kim Talent is untouched by the dark irony, grotesque images or hyperbole that battle for prominence in the rest of the book. He is about to die and his final thoughts are fixed upon the future prospects for the one individual who transcends the grisly narrative that will close with his death. 'With fingers all oily from being rubbed together, in ingratiation, vigil, glee, fear, nerves, I cling to certain hopes in hopes of you. I hope that you are with your mother and that you two are provided for'. (p. 469) That last sentence is tinged with a slight ambiguity – is 'you two' mother and child or has Martin's attention slipped momentarily from the fictional to the personal? 'You two' could easily be Louis and Jacob, just as 'Antonia' slips ghostlike into the closing passage of *Money*. This blurring of the difference between the private and the imaginary brings us back to Martin's comment on Young. He 'is transcribing something that appears to be happening . . . he is incapable of making things up but at the same time [his fellow characters] are fantasies.' I disagree with his dismissal of the novel as a 'postmodernist joke'. It is more like a balancing act between invention and private uncertainty.

After the birth of Jacob it was agreed that Antonia would also take charge of the children's schooling. She it was who enrolled both at the nearby Montessori infants' school, having already placed them on the waiting list for the prestigious Lyndhurst House Preparatory School in Hampstead. Lyndhurst House was, despite the left-leaning inclinations of many of its shrewd media-connected parents, the epitome of Thatcherism: meritocracy at a price. Martin now left Chesterton Road by eight at the latest, and the flat was coming more and more to resemble the places where he had lived before his marriage. When he moved in it had a cool Spartan quality, his only concession to the past being a 1970s pinball machine purchased from a café off the Fulham Road at the end of that decade. Rob bought him a dartboard shortly after his visit to Keith Deller. Martin hung it on the kitchen door and practised with Talent-like concentration in an attempt to organize aberrant ideas before returning to his desk. On school holidays that overlapped with his work schedule or sometimes on Saturdays the two boys would be driven, by the live-in nanny, to what became known as 'Dad's other house'. Antonia's tastes were a little more conventional than Martin's. Martin would get home by 6 p.m. at the latest, either to ensure that both parents were present for a family meal, or occasionally fill in for the nanny. 'I was earning points, as everyone does. I enjoyed being with the boys but marriage involves credit and debit. Antonia was, is, a strong character. The fact that I was a writer did not mean that I was granted special privileges, quite correctly.' His nights in would buy him nights out with the likes of McEwan, Papineau, Leader, Mitas, and Rushdie, a game of snooker followed by a meal in a carefully selected low-life restaurant – usually Greek, Italian, Chinese or Indian – and, very rarely, poker.

The idea for Asprey as absent owner of the flat and cynosure of media gossip and fantasy came partly from the arrangement insisted upon by Antonia after the birth of Louis. Chesterton Road was open to mutual friends only, and even then casual or unprompted visits were discouraged. Anyone connected with Martin's work who wanted a rushed meeting would have to go to the flat, and this included journalists. As a consequence all of the interviews with him during this period not conducted in studios or hotels give the impression of his as a curious bipolar existence. By the end of the 1980s the flat had acquired an air of scruffy permanence. He did not eat there but he had a TV, video, stereo, small fridge and kettle. Glasses, bottles of wine and spirits stood on a rustic sideboard. Martin did not drink when he was at work – the stock was to provision thirsty interviewers – but the place appeared lived-in, an impression substantiated by an array of jackets hung near the door. The small stack of children's toys in the corner and photographs of Louis and Jacob on the desk were mildly disconcerting and journalists who had done the most scrupulous research on Martin had to remind themselves that he was still a family man with a wife and two children. Antonia was hardly ever mentioned in the interviews, the result of her ordinance that she and the children must be excluded from his media profile.

John Walsh remembers interviewing Martin at the Cheltenham Literature Festival. 'It was some time before *London Fields* was published but obviously Mart was promoting the book. I think he'd just sent it to the publisher. We were in the quiet lounge of a hotel and he was with Antonia and Louis and Jacob. I'd met them as a couple before but there was most certainly an air of detachment about them then. Nothing specific – I mean, I wasn't interviewing Antonia; it was about Martin – but there was an uncomfortable, tangible sense of discomfort abroad, something that is evident beneath the surface in brief movements, positionings, body language, routine exchanges on ordering drink and so on. They communicated, as of necessity, but they did not actually *look* at each other.'

Martin now found himself divided between the life he had eschewed for a permanent relationship with Antonia and an uncertain atrophied version of the latter. 'Yes,' adds Hitchens, 'and from what I heard it went a little further than that. He had promised himself and her a new regime of monogamy and to an extent he kept his word but after Jacob, well, I know of only a few transgressions but their marriage became a little fraught.'

In the light of this the absence of 'MA' can be taken as the fictional counterpart to a very real sense of personal dislocation. At this potentially transitional point in his life and marriage

Martin is unsure of where to place his allegiance. Will he soon be returned to his past? (We know that the aloof hedonist MA will arrive after the final page to reclaim both the novel and his life in London.) Or will the problems recently visited on his marriage repair themselves? Hitchens: 'Martin certainly did not wish to end things. The intensity of feeling that drew him to Antonia was still present, and the boys . . . well I don't need to say any more about his feelings for them. He *wanted* things to return to the way they were but seemed powerless to do anything other than hope that they would.' All of this accounts for the dreadful fate of those for whom Sam Young seems, at least in part, responsible. 'Maybe Young was Martin's expedient conscience,' observes Hitchens, 'the opportunity to kill off a past – ghosts of Mary Furness, alias Nicola Six, included. But keeping the option open for it to be returned to – "MA".' Perhaps, but aside from its origins in Martin's personal life the result was a remarkable novel. It is not, however, one that should be treated as even a remotely accurate index to the state of London, and by implication, Britain, in the late 1980s.

One of the most revealing interviews with Martin was conducted for the *New York Times* by Mira Stout shortly before the launch of *London Fields* in the US.

> 'London is a pub,' he declares [. . .] 'Not the pub with the jolly butcher and the smiling grannies; it's the pub of eight or nine alcoholics, a handful of hustlers and nutcases and a few token regular people. It's a stew [. . .] the whole idea of the pub as a place for the working man has vanished. Who's working? Now the pub is where you go all day. We're in a gentle, deep decline.'

Stout, an American writer who evidently viewed London with a somewhat less jaundiced eye, contrasted Martin's observations with her own impressions of the city. Burlington Arcade is crammed with shoppers, the queue for tickets to the latest Andrew Lloyd-Webber musical tails down the street, the roads are gridlocked with shining BMWs, Mercedes and Porsches, the average Brit looks to her 'Richer than they did a decade ago' and Thatcher's government, much cited as the cause of an ongoing catastrophe, is now in its tenth year, with a very healthy majority. 'On the surface, all looks well indeed,' she observes. Rather than state outright that Martin's vision of London is slightly warped she opts very effectively for irony. 'London's malaise is subtle, and class-inflected . . . [the novel] floodlights the sagging underbelly of Thatcherite consumerism'. It is interesting to compare Martin's portrait of the pub as epitomizing our decline with David Papineau's description of the curious assembly of individuals who could be found in the bar of the Paddington Sports Club, the snooker club under the Westway and the Green Star. 'On average we would be in the company of a couple of minicab drivers, off shift, a croupier or [card] dealer, perhaps a bouncer or two. People who worked at night but wanted to relax in the afternoon, either with a couple of drinks or playing games. The "we" includes musicians, at least one composer, academics and of course the odd writer. Various aspects of the "other" London, night workers, self-employed bohemians and whoever else was on flexitime.' It hardly seems necessary to point out the differences between Papineau's account and Martin's but as to the reason why they differ, let us say that Martin was toying fashionably with the zeitgeist. Few if any writers of the late 1980s would dare to admit that Thatcher's London was a bearable let alone agreeable place to live. So Martin adjusts the dystopian lens and instead of Papineau's image of the gainfully employed undertaking relaxation we find Keith, Guy, Wayne, Deane, Duane, Norvis, Curly, Boden, Chick et al., shuffling through the sinister, noisome spaces of the Black Cross, the Shakespeare, the Butcher's Arms and the Blind Pig, towards feckless oblivion. Martin informs Stout: 'I think Thatcher has done a lot of harm. The money age we're living through now is a short-term, futureless kind of prosperity [. . .] Money is a more democratic medium than blood, but money as a cultural banner – you can feel the whole of society deteriorating around you because of that. Civility, civilization is falling apart.' Leaving aside for a moment the fact that Cape's small contribution to the 'money age' had been a considerable advance for *London Fields*, this could easily have come from Sam Young, as indeed could Martin's comment on the environment. 'It's as if the planet had aged four billion years in the last two centuries. If this had happened to a human being, you'd say, "Jesus, what's he been up to? He looked like Apollo yesterday, now he looks like Methuselah!"' Stout, without comment, tapers Martin's declaration into a description of the close of their meeting.

> I accompanied Martin to a book party for environmental causes. He picked me up in a taxi around 6 p.m., clutching a furled copy of *Tennis* magazine. His hair neatly combed, he was dressed almost as smartly in a Prince of Wales plaid suit and dark coat [. . .] It was a rare, beautiful evening, and Amis was in a relaxed mood. South Kensington's facades flowed regally past the taxi window, transformed by sunlight. Kensington Gardens were overflowing with fresh summer foliage. London looked startlingly clean.[4]

The droll subtext is clear enough: your London does not seem terribly dire and apocalyptic to me. Stout's presentation of West London, or at least its more ostentatious residents, enjoying the benefits of affluence is accurate enough but we should treat with caution her suggestion that Martin has buried his head in the luxurious sand. The novel with which *London Fields* invites comparison is Justin Cartwright's *Look At It This Way* (1990), a wry treatment of the allegedly endemic contemporary mood of greed and narcissism. Cartwright's is a morality tale shot through with touches of the surreal and would even today be treated, particularly by those who loathe Thatcher, as an example of Flaubertian social realism. But truth is a multi-faceted thing and I would contend that in years to come Martin's novel will be recognized as an equally challenging engagement with its era. Nicola, Keith, Guy, even Young himself are weird presences, not the kind of people we routinely encounter in the real world, yet like Dickens's more unusual creations they also seize our attention, ignite fears, fantasies and delusions. Their state is untraceable to a particular cause but each carries a trace of panic and flux.

Within months of the publication of *London Fields* intemperate reality would trample across this reverie of nuances. Salman Rushdie's *The Satanic Verses* (1988) has much in common with Martin's novel. The two figures, Gibreel and Saladin, come to London by an unusual though symbolically resonant route; they plummet into the city from an airliner blown up by terrorists. Certainly the arrival of Sam Young is rather more conventional – his plane does manage to land – but all three act as witnesses to the absence of anything remotely reassuring in the fragmented, poisonous landscape of late-1980s Britain. Section V of Rushdie's novel offers a harrowing portrait of urban London, a place where greed and exploitative nihilism have replaced anything resembling compassion or integrity. This rampant disdain for principle is embodied in a figure referred to as 'Mrs Torture' (pronounce it rapidly and connect with 'Margaret'). Saladin is sombre witness to all this while at the same time he is visited in dreams by a spectral presence called Mahound, a derogatory version of the name of the prophet Mohammed. Mahound is a troubled figure, uncertain of his own faith and distracted, lubriciously, by three female goddesses, Hal, Uzza and Manat.

Critics have, with learned solemnity, treated the work as a late-twentieth-century revival of the true ideology of modernism, as a dynamic leviathan that both bemoans and magnificently represents the state of humanity – a dream of lost faith mired in heartless consumerism. This postmodern rite of self-congratulation was, however, accompanied by a formidably literalist sequence of interpretations of the book, with consequences. It was banned in India, South Africa, Bangladesh, Sudan, Sri Lanka and Pakistan and on 14 February 1989 the Ayatollah Khomeini of Iran issued a fatwa sentencing Rushdie to death under Islamic law. Rushdie became a state-protected fugitive, accompanied by members of Special Branch, and moved between MI5-approved safe houses for the subsequent ten years.

Rushdie's second marriage was ruined by the bizarre regime of attempting to maintain a public profile – he continued to produce fiction, do interviews and write for the press – while remaining invisible. His friends from the literary world publicly condemned the fatwa while in private offered Rushdie a version of the social life he had enjoyed before 1989. They too were advised by the security services that any disclosure that they had offered more than private support might invite acts of maniacal zealotry similar to the murder of the book's Danish translator but despite this they continued to speak publicly on his behalf. Martin appeared on TV to express his abhorrence of the fatwa and interviewed Rushdie for *Vanity Fair* as a token of solidarity (see *VMN*). It was not until February 2009, almost two decades after the issuing of the fatwa, that Ian McEwan felt confident enough to tell of how he and his friend had shared a feeling of shock and disbelief as Rushdie spent one of his first nights in hiding at McEwan's house in Oxford. Fenton too had a house outside Oxford where Rushdie would stay over as a relief from the stifling environment of London. Martin's contributions to a precarious state of normality in the city were many, including small parties – close, trusted acquaintances only – and male poker nights in Chesterton Road. Antonia's insistence that the media profiles of Martin must not include the location of the family home – usually no more than a vague reference to the sprawling ill-defined district of Notting Hill – was fortunate in this regard. Even if a determined maniac or cell had attempted to trace Rushdie's contacts with his friends they would have no idea where this one lived. Still to this day Papineau recalls the poker nights with a residue of anxiety. 'Five years ago, maybe even two, I wouldn't have admitted this, on record, to anyone. "This" being the fact that I spent evenings playing poker with Martin, Salman and others.' He means of course that fundamentalist Muslims tend to treat association as condonement, and each as a justification for punitive action in the name of Allah. 'The evenings', Papineau recalls, 'were a mixture of the routine and the mildly surreal. Once when I arrived before Salman I witnessed the full ritual. The doorbell would be rung by a plain-clothes policeman and two of them would come in first, not to search the place, just to make sure that other parties had not arrived earlier and taken control. Martin would offer them a beer or wine which they would politely decline and instead have tea or coffee in one of the adjoining rooms and watch TV. It must have been a dreadful job, tedious I mean. But they seemed cheerful enough. I come from South Africa, but well, playing poker in a comfortable middle-class part of London with two men next door, Heckler and Koch automatics at the ready, did seem odd to say the least.' How did Rushdie seem? I ask. What was his demeanour?

'I didn't really know him before the fatwa, but he didn't appear anxious. Convivial and up-beat would describe him best I suppose, yet with knowledge of what was happening I suppose you could say he was positive, resigned.' Who were the other regular attenders? 'Ian McEwan once or twice, me. Hitchens when he was in London. Hitchens was one of the first to go into print with an unhesitating defence of Rushdie and the novel.' According to Papineau, 'Martin provided the conversational sparkle, the animus.' No subject was allowed a seminar-like predominance and an undercurrent of humour endured. Did they talk about Rushdie's predicament? 'Oh yes. That was the cause of a good deal of black repartee.' Once things wound down the two policemen would go out first to check the street, having summoned the driver by radio, and Rushdie would leave before the others. Andy Hislop recalls an evening that was even more surreal. 'The sitting room was at street level, as was a study next door and for some reason no one thought of closing the curtains. One evening I arrived late and the spectacle was that of the instantly recognizable profile of the world's most wanted man – most wanted by fanatics anyway – faced across the card table by that of probably Britain's best-known novelist [Amis]. There was a bottle of whisky, half-empty wine bottles, glasses, thick clouds of smoke. The next window, equally well lit, showed two bulky plain-clothes policemen watching TV, also smoking, drinking mugs of tea. But they were also nursing sub-machine guns. I suppose they might have deterred passing Islamist terrorists, but what struck me was the contrast, boozy conviviality, defended by the realm.'

Given Rushdie's oft-expressed contempt for Mrs Thatcher and her regime, connoisseurs of black comedy would indeed – if this were a piece of fiction – be suitably amused. I asked Papineau and Martin if anyone present was caused to feel slightly uncomfortable with the fact that the Thatcher government was now Rushdie's protector and, by implication, exemplary guarantor of free speech. Neither of them recalls a particular exchange on this matter, though they both concede that, especially with hindsight, it was a subject for reflection. 'Implicitly acknowledged, yes,' says Papineau. The one exception to this was the running commentary offered to Martin by Chris Mitas. Mitas knew that Martin and Rushdie were friends and when news broke of the fatwa, the riots in the subcontinent and orchestrated street protests in the Middle East, he began to raise questions, to which Martin alludes in *Experience* in a cryptic and misleading story about a dinner at the Caprice restaurant in London attended by himself, Hitchens and Rushdie. The subject of Martin's anecdote is not, however, Rushdie's status as a fugitive, but rather their divergent opinions on the qualities of Samuel Beckett's prose. The evening ended with Martin caricaturing a short passage by Beckett and Rushdie asking, 'Do you want to come outside?' Next afternoon Martin was at the Sports Club amusing Chris and his friend Steve Michel with his account of the night before. 'Steve said, "*Did* he? Well I hope you took him outside and gave him a fucking good hiding." Now, now, I began, resuming the usual debate . . .' The 'usual debate' was usually addressed by Martin and Chris who on this occasion postponed his contribution, sitting in 'silence [. . .] tensely hunkered forward, giving me his shocked stare'. In due course he ventured, 'Offered you out? I wish he'd fucking offered *me* out.'[5] Needless to say the subject was no longer Beckettian syntax.

Chris Mitas never liked Salman Rushdie, principally because he never publicly expressed any gratitude to the government. This was the 'usual debate' to which Martin refers. Mitas offered Martin a counterbalance to the left-liberal consensus beneath which a great number of uncomfortable inconsistencies were concealed.

The birth of Martin's sons occasioned his sudden preoccupation with the nuclear apocalypse, but despite the zealous mood of 'Thinkability' the stories of *Einstein's Monsters* fall somewhere between his previous state of detachment from moral absolutes and a sense of precipitate concern. By the time the boys had reached nursery-school age, that intermediary period between pure innocence and early adulthood, Martin had decided to immerse himself further in the more shameful aspects of supposedly civilized humanity in the twentieth century. According to Hitchens, 'He was clear enough about his anti-nuclear stance but he talked much more in this period about the ways in which evil had deepened incrementally with political, ideological advances of various sorts. He was still politically uncommitted, and his interests were not morbidly self-absorbed. It was clear that he was, well, concerned with the relationship between the fairly recent past and the imminent future. The latter, of course, meant his concern for Louis and Jacob. It was as though he had now suddenly discovered something frightful, a rationale for acts of mass murder. Nazism. What lay behind this, still, was his terrified image of a world into which he would eventually have to release Louis and Jacob. We, Martin, the rest of us, had been born within a few years of the end of the war. So while we knew it only vicariously, there was a stench of something quite terrible that stayed with us, the children of the 1940s. It is still there.'

Time's Arrow is a novel not merely about the Holocaust but the only one so far that obliges us for its entirety to share the mind and perceptions of a Nazi war criminal. The book's origins belie its gruesome content. Wellfleet is arguably the most languid, agreeable and expensive town in Cape Cod. There the Phillipses kept a house, which Hitchens describes. 'There was the town itself, which incorporated a fair number of classy colonial-style places, the best backing on to the beach. But further inland the landscape was wooded, and while driving down already narrow lanes you'd come across a sign nailed to a tree calling you to the gravelled drive of somewhere hidden behind the trees. The names would often have mythopoeic resonance – "Mrs Roosevelt The Elder's Residence" – that sort of thing. Well, the Phillipses' place was against type. It originated as a group of farm buildings, a low-slung barn and some sties, none habitable, never in fact having been inhabited by human beings at all. But Antonia's father either inherited them, plus the land, or bought them from a distant relative for practically nothing. Anyway he converted them into an extremely quirky dwelling, unostentatious and rustic to say the least. But they were wonderfully homely too and eventually of course, given the locality, probably worth a great deal of money.'

Martin, Antonia and the boys would spend on average three to four weeks there each year, usually in late July or August. Hitchens: 'I sometimes visited, and the place, not only Antonia's house but the whole town, seemed like the summer retreat of the crowned heads of US intelligentsia. Chomsky was a neighbour and regular visitor, likewise Tom Wolfe and the major-domos from the Ivy League faculties and political think-tanks in DC were scattered around. A close family friend was the historian and psychologist Robert Jay Lifton who also lived close by. He and Martin got on very well.' During the 1960s Lifton had presided over radical, groundbreaking seminars, based mostly at his house in Wellfleet town and conducted during the summer, outside the conventions and restrictions of the academic schedule; at the time he taught at Columbia University. The prevailing topics were war and violence and his book *The Nazi Doctors* (1986), which Martin acknowledges as the most significant influence on his novel, reflects his preoccupation with the extent to which those involved in crimes against humanity experienced or avoided contrition and guilt. Lifton was at the end of the 1980s almost sixty and nearly twenty years older than Martin, 'but', recalls the latter, 'he was exceptionally fit. He was addicted to tennis. The summer I got to know him properly we played every other day. And we talked a lot, mostly about the Holocaust and people he had met who had actually been involved in its implementation. Killers as brutal and repulsive as any in recorded history but who seemed to have drawn down a curtain between what they had done – few if any denied involvement – and what anyone might have expected them to *feel*. His accounts were compulsive. And as an individual – not merely an extraordinary intellectual; that goes without saying – but as a man, he was astonishing. You see *he* was Jewish. He did not attempt to deny his feelings. But to remain composed, to deal with these things and these people took a lot of courage and self-control.' A good deal of the thematic momentum for the novel comes from Lifton but Martin omits to mention a less tangible but equally significant tributary of influence. In *Experience* he writes of his shock at Bellow's reluctance, despite his goadings, to condemn outright the US preoccupation with the death penalty. While avoiding comment on its implementation in his home country Bellow states, 'Well. Look at . . . Eichmann. What are you supposed to *do* with a son of a bitch like that?'[6] Lifton's work was of enormous practical assistance, as was Martin Gilbert's mammoth study of *The Holocaust*, but it was Bellow's comment which provided a visceral counterbalance to both, a touch of what Martin calls 'thinking with the blood'.

In the concluding chapter of *Time's Arrow*, Unverdorben appears to enter a state of reflective resignation, perhaps because he has reached the point at which his birth and beyond that oblivion is imminent (the novel goes backwards in time). We learn from him that he was born and brought up in the town of Solingen, 'famous for its knives, its scissors and its surgical instruments'.

In addition, modest Solingen harbours a proud secret. I'm the only one who happens to know what that secret is. It's this: Solingen is the birthplace of Adolf Eichmann. Schh . . . Hush now. I'll never tell. And if I did, who would believe me?[7]

No one, because as he writes this Eichmann is ten years old and Nazism does not yet exist. The allusion seems at first gratuitous, until we begin to consider the parallels between the very real mass murderer and Martin's invented version. Eichmann, like Unverdorben, would systematically erase his past, by almost identical means; both for example made use of sympathetic members of the Roman Catholic hierarchy in Italy to obtain false documents. Eichmann, however, was kidnapped in Argentina by agents of the Israeli Secret Service Mossad, tried in Jerusalem and obliged by a variety of witnesses to revisit his acts of gross inhumanity. Israel is the only country with no history of capital punishment: it was not abolished, but rather prohibited at the foundation of the state in 1948. For Eichmann, however, the irrevocable prohibition was suspended. The reason for his execution was not righteous vengeance, but something far more elemental. Martin: 'During his trial he rarely if ever disputed the validity of the evidence against him – particularly his executive role in the deportation to the extermination camps of vast numbers of Jews – yet he seemed genuinely puzzled by why his acts should be deemed criminal; in his view he was no more than a bureaucrat.' To allow him to exist would be to indulge an implicit legitimization of the Holocaust: that, at least in Bellow's opinion, justified Israel's single use of a constitutionally forbidden act.

For *The Nazi Doctors* Lifton interviewed a large number of medical practitioners who had either escaped with light sentences or gone unpunished for their activities in the extermination camps. Eichmann features only marginally but Martin was engrossed by the link between him and a figure who dominates Lifton's book, despite his absence as an interviewee, Josef Mengele. Mengele was by far the most influential doctor to have worked in Auschwitz, and he appears in *Time's Arrow* as 'Uncle Pepi', a figure of authority held in awe by every other doctor at the camp but whose presence in the narrative is evanescent, ghostlike. Mengele also disappeared into the shadows. Like Eichmann he found his way to Argentina, but Mossad failed to track him down and he died in his bed. Martin kidnaps Unverdorben at the point where his equally agreeable post-Holocaust existence is about to close peacefully and, like Mossad with Eichmann, obliges him to relive his past.

Lifton's book revealed the part played by medical practitioners in the Holocaust but its genuine claim to originality was the identification of an endemic feature, which he calls doubling, exhibited by all those who took part in the mass exterminations, and which was evident also in Eichmann's behaviour at his trial.

[N]one of them – not a single Nazi doctor I spoke to – arrived at a clear ethical evaluation of what he had done, and what he had been part of. They could examine events in considerable detail, even look at feelings and speak generally with surprising candour, but almost in the manner of a third person. The narrator, morally speaking, was not quite present.[8]

Despite his lifetime of experience as a psychologist – he was sixty when the book was published – Lifton admits to there being no formulaic explanation for doubling. It is not a straightforward case of denial or psychological self-protection – none of them disputed what they had done. Nor had they numbed themselves to the moral and ethical values of more civilized societies. (One, suspecting Lifton's Jewishness, referred to their shared 'tragic inheritance'.) The only conclusion was terribly simple: they had consciously, enthusiastically committed evil acts and now preferred not to reflect upon their nature. This was the inspiration for Martin's daring experiment with the reversal of narrative time. All of those involved in the Holocaust recalled what had happened but neither they nor anyone else could alter the past. Martin: 'The book [*The Nazi Doctors*] was riveting, forbidding, but I think it was Lifton's private account of how he still felt incapable of fully grasping the mechanisms of denial of these men that engrossed me most of all.' Lifton's interviewees no longer feared retribution and those who had gone into exile with false identities felt equally exempt from responsibility for irrevocable occurrences.

Technically it would have been possible to create a contrast between two points in the narrative, one involving Unverdorben's activities in the camps and another his existence closer to the present as Dr Tod Friendly, but this would have demanded solutions to issues that were, as Lifton showed, inexplicable. As Martin argued, cause-and-effect rationalism would have been imposed upon 'a figure who was too evil to be permitted the indulgence of an explanation'. Unverdorben witnesses, in reverse sequence, all of the events that precede his imminent death in suburban USA. When he explains how he removes the gas canisters from the chambers so that the prisoners can be allowed to return to the point of selection on the ramps and then board the train we know that he is neither denying nor seeking some form of exculpation for what really happened. The effect, however, is almost identical to Lifton's description of his interviewees.

Some part of these men wished to be heard: they had things to say that most of them had never said before, least of all to people around them – but the narrator morally speaking was not quite present.[9]

The other figure who influenced Martin considerably in the planning of the novel was David Papineau, with whom he had discussed, when writing *London Fields*, the distinction between our experience of time and our attempts in language to represent its passage. 'There are standard models in the teaching of philosophy for illustrating the multifaceted problem of time. One, used most frequently and which interested Martin, is the film played backwards. The exercise involves a selection of events on the film that might, plausibly, occur in real life, walking backwards, cars always apparently in reverse gear, the contents of our stomachs seemingly vomited into glasses and on to plates. Even recorded conversations played backwards to sound like an unfamiliar linguistic exchange. Many of these occur at the beginning of *Time's Arrow*. They were padding mainly, very effectively deployed to prepare the reader for far more difficult tasks.' In the opening pages Tod Unverdorben asks, 'Why am I walking *backwards* into the house?' and wonders why the woman in the pharmacy says 'Dug. Dug', instead of 'Good. Good', in reply to his casual enquiry on her health. (p. 14) He is conscious of the difference between progressive and regressive time. However, in Auschwitz he either ignores or forgets the distinction. To remain conscious of it would also involve an acceptance of volition, not of time as a sequence that contains us but as a series of causally related acts and events – such as the placing, rather than the removal of the gas canisters. Papineau: 'What would happen in a film if a vase of flowers were to be deliberately pushed from a table? If the glass smashes on the floor the fragments, water, flowers disperse and *none* of this is reversible. We could of course play it back on film, but this has nothing to do with the reversal of time.' We witness something that is entirely implausible, literally impossible beyond the artifice of film. It is the manufacturing of an impression.

> In this new lab of his [Uncle Pepi] he can knock together a human being out of the unlikeliest odds and ends. On his desk he had a box full of eyes. It was not uncommon to see him slipping out of his darkroom carrying a head partly wrapped in old newspaper. The next thing you knew, there'd be, oh I don't know, a fifteen-year-old Pole sliding off the table and rubbing his eyes and sauntering back to work, accompanied by an orderly and his understanding smile.[10]

Unverdorben is fully aware that this too is a manufactured illusion, that just as it is impossible for a vase to be reassembled, its contents returned to it and the whole assembly replaced on the table, without even the assistance of an outside agency, so too the mutilated, murdered fifteen-year-old Pole can never be restored to life and led back to work. He knows this but he will not concede that he is witnessing events in which he participated, played backwards. Like Lifton's interlocutors he becomes 'not quite present'. Martin's considerable achievement exists not in the ostentatious use of narrative experiment but in the gradual mutation and development of a character never previously represented in fiction. In Part 1, set in the US, Unverdorben refers to Tod in the third person while implicitly acknowledging he is fully aware of a shared legacy.

> Tod and I can feel the dream just waiting to happen, gathering its energies from somewhere on the other side.

We're fatalistic. We lie there with the lamp burning, while dawn fades. Tepid sweats form, and shine, and instantly evaporate. Then our heart rate climbs, steadily, until our ears are gulping on the new blood. Now we don't know who we are. I have to be ready for when Tod makes his lunge for the lightswitch. And then the darkness with a shout that gives a fierce twist to his jaw – we're in it. The enormous figure in the white coat, his black boots straddling many acres. Somewhere down there, between his legs, the queue of souls. I wish I had power, just power enough to avert my eyes.[11]

He, they, know what awaits them as they stumble towards their collective past. They cannot 'avert their eyes' because they and their experiences are coterminous. In Part 2, however, Unverdorben goes against Lifton's report on his interviewees and opts for a first-person account. But he does so not in acceptance of responsibility – and here Martin interweaves his borrowings from Lifton and Papineau – but by becoming part of the film in reverse, with his hand receiving the magically reassembled vase, or guiding the living prisoners from the gas chamber back to the train. He becomes even less 'quite present' than Lifton's interlocutors. He does not deny participation but he exempts himself from the standard rules of intent, cause and, ultimately, culpability.

The novel was shortlisted for the 1991 Booker Prize, but was beaten by Ben Okri's *Famished Road*. This time, no doubt heeding the publicity generated by *London Fields*, the committee remained tight-lipped on the nature of their decision. In his *TLS* 'Books of the Year' entry the conservative philosopher and commentator Roger Scruton – not one of Martin's natural allies nor a personal friend – wrote that 'we have witnessed the slovenly butchery of Martin Amis' to the benefit of 'the fey and pseudo-sensitive Ben Okri'.[12] In Scruton's opinion the decision was made 'on the grounds of immorality, despite (or maybe because of) the fact that *Time's Arrow* is the first Martin Amis novel to contain the faintest hint of a moral idea. It is also, in my view, brilliant.' With that closing sentiment most other reviewers agreed, but a notably loud and tiny minority would, one suspects, have influenced the Booker Committee. In the US Rhoda Koenig in 'Holocaust Chic', argued that Martin's display of technical genius was an affront to the memory of the six million Holocaust dead[13] while in London James Buchan in the *Spectator* stated outright that he had made use of Auschwitz 'for profit'.[14] It is extremely unlikely that a contributor to the *Spectator* had knowledge of, let alone respect for, the opinions of the Marxist academic Theodor Adorno. Nevertheless Adorno's comment on literature and the Holocaust exposes and explains an endemic feeling of unease among writers. He said, in 1951, in *Cultural Criticism and Society*, that 'after Auschwitz no more poetry can be written'. The claim is hyperbolical but Adorno's essential thesis is that poetry and all literature is a trivial, frivolous mode of representation unsuited by its nature to deal with a post-Holocaust state of mind.

In the light of this one can detect another reason for Martin's failure to take the Booker Prize. Nine years earlier in 1982 Thomas Keneally won with *Schindler's Ark*, undoubtedly the most popular, serious fictional treatment of Auschwitz, subsequently filmed by Steven Spielberg as *Schindler's List* (the title change being an outrageous example of dumbing down, made on the assumption that many filmgoers would be puzzled by the Old Testament resonance). There is no rule, written or unwritten, which forbids repetitions of subject in the awarding of major literary prizes but one will search in vain for two novels in the Booker or Pulitzer list in which the same overarching theme appears within a four- to five-year period.

Given the controversial tendentious nature of writing fiction on the Holocaust, the Booker judges would have been glancing anxiously over their shoulders and what they saw, with Keneally, was an inspired but essentially cautious work. *Schindler's Ark* is a documentary account reassembled as a novel. Every significant fact and character is drawn from verifiable sources and Keneally intervenes only to provide perspective, narrative pacing and dialogue, and even then he does his best to mould the principal characters according to reports of the manner and speech habits of their real counterparts. Again there is no evidence that Keneally was responding consciously to Adorno's dictum but he was certainly attending to it in spirit, in that the vulgarizing presence of literature is reduced to an absolute minimum. While Keneally sidelines the figures who were directly responsible for the atrocities, concentrating instead on the quixotic, humane Schindler and the victims, Martin for the first time in fiction focuses directly upon the personal history, albeit in reverse, and mental condition of one of the perpetrators of the Holocaust. The only serious writer to have previously attempted anything comparable was George Steiner in *The Portage to San Cristobal of A.H.* (1979). The novel, which Martin discussed with Steiner when the latter was Visiting Professor at Oxford in the mid-1980s, offers us the thoughts and reflections of Adolf Hitler, thirty years after his survival of the bombing of his Berlin bunker. The hypothesis is daring but what we actually experience is Steiner's complex historical explanation for the Holocaust (that the Jews, via intellectual assimilation with and sometimes dominance over prevailing Christian post-Enlightenment thought, provoked their own destruction) voiced by a suspiciously erudite 'A.H.'. No writer had attempted a naturalistic, psychologically transparent portrait of a Nazi mass murderer and the reason for their reluctance is self-evident. Once a character becomes the centrepiece of a literary work, irrespective of their foul proclivities (cf. Humbert Humbert), they are possessed of a charismatic vibrancy. Three decades before *Time's Arrow* was published Hannah Arendt produced an account of Eichmann at his trial.[15] Like Lifton's interviewers Eichmann in person was disarmingly commonplace: only the proven fact that he was responsible for one of the most atrocious acts in history overturned the impression of banality. Thus Martin faced an outstandingly difficult task: could he use the uniquely untransparent devices of fiction to create a bridge between the impression of the commonplace – displayed by all of the post-war Nazis – and their unimaginable capacities for evil? He has often been accused of lacking the talent or inclination for endurance, relying instead on a chiaroscuro of brief performances. In *Time's Arrow* he turns this criticism on its head, sustaining an immensely complex, original conceit for 180 pages, and in doing so he achieves far more than a display of skill. He shows, contra Adorno, that literature is uniquely capable of making us face the actuality of the Holocaust and the irredeemable vileness of its perpetrators.

10

The Break-Up and
The Information

Depicting Martin Amis as a feckless replica of his father is a reproachful enterprise, and as I write this sentence I feel the presence of a qualifier. During the period following the publication of *Time's Arrow* the parallels between father and son are so abundant that one is reminded of the film *Groundhog Day* where every morning Bill Murray's character awakes in full knowledge of what fate has in store for him for the next twenty-four hours. The events will be exactly the same as those of the previous day, beyond his control; except in Martin's case he is being handed this premonitory menu by Kingsley, and for hours substitute years.

Kingsley was forty when he was introduced to Jane Howard at the Cheltenham Literature Festival, and Martin exactly the same age when he first met Isabel Fonseca. Both men were at roughly the same stage in their careers with five and six novels, respectively, in print and each procuring a reputation as having altered the literary mood and temper of their time. Their

287

ongoing marriages had begun after pregnancies, with another son for each born shortly afterwards. For both of them, life was becoming more settled and routine, until Kingsley's affair with Jane became something more than a secret.

Christopher Hitchens: 'Isabel [Fonseca] was in some ways a composite of Martin's previous most glamorous girlfriends. I think they [Martin and Isabel] met through the *TLS*. They mixed in the same circles but it was at one of the dinners for Salman that Isabel had helped organize that they really got to know each other, in 1989 or thereabouts. He had just despatched Nicola Six to the reading public and then he meets a version that outdoes his creation. She was being hotly pursued by Salman, among others, but Martin . . . well let's say he moved quite rapidly to the head of a long queue.

'I remember, it was 1992. Five of us had gone from Nigella Lawson and John Diamond's wedding reception at the Groucho to dinner in the West End. There was Martin, Antonia, myself, Isabel, and . . . I can't recall the others. Anyway we were walking towards the restaurant, I was talking to Antonia, and Martin and Isabel were alongside us and . . . I don't know if you've ever experienced this but I sensed a frisson. Nothing in particular but he and Antonia seemed oddly detached from each other. I don't think Isabel was the cause, at that point anyway.'

Will Self got to know Martin at this time. 'He is exceptionally good at what he does, as a writer, but sometimes his desire to be taken seriously as a commentator on immutable ethical and philosophic issues is at odds with his talent. He treats intellectualism as an observance, a necessary ritual, I mean as a writer. And this has also had an effect on his private life. I know he has been, still is, presented in the press as egotist, hedonist, even dilettante, but actually he worries immensely about the *consequences* of what he does and says. In print, particularly as a critic, he can be pretty frightening, yet the individual is quietly taking stock, worrying about causing distress, trying to improve things and so on. For his work this was problematic, but at least . . . Well, Scott Fitzgerald said only writers can hold two intrinsically opposed views simultaneously, or something like that . . . But his personal life suffered as a consequence. Those close to him suffered, though this was certainly not due to a nefarious or malicious element of his character. When his marriage broke up he was trying to be honest without causing distress. Unfortunately, this had the opposite effect.'

Hitchens clarifies: 'He left Antonia in May 1993. That is to say he moved to the flat. He didn't have much to take with him. I can't testify to exactly what was said but I gathered from conversations with him shortly afterwards that he'd been selectively honest. He informed Antonia that it would be better for both of them if he went, but left her to surmise that their marriage, troubled anyway, ought to be brought to something like a conclusion.'

'In spring 1992,' Andy Hislop remembers, 'Martin called and asked if I was free, short notice, and would I like to spend a few weeks in Tuscany. Tuscany? Anyway, Antonia's half-sister was married to Matthew Spender and they had a house there. It sounded superb, agreeable weather two months before the miserable English summer and so on. But, God, it was a dire experience. I sometimes felt I was there as protection for Martin. He wanted to play chess continually and the weather was the worst on record in that part of Italy, freezing. The atmosphere in the house was colder by far. Martin and Antonia went through the motions. He was introverted, she . . . she seemed unsettled, sad.'

Zachary Leader offers an intriguing picture of Martin in the period after he had left Chesterton Road, and shortly before the story appeared in the press. 'I had just returned to London after about six months on a Huntington Library Fellowship in California and when we met at the club for a game it was clear that there was something odd about him. He was affable, yes, but it was an effort. He was not withdrawn or evasive. Displaced would be a better way to put it. Hilly, his mother, described it well when she said that there is in father and son an "Amis passivity", a tendency to retreat from the less agreeable windfalls of fate or consequences of your own actions. But she qualified this. For Kingsley it involved retreat and obfuscation. Martin's version was a lot more penitential. He was willing to take full responsibility for everything he did and said. In this case though he appeared to be suffering the physical effects.' Did he tell you what was troubling him? 'Yes, he did, eventually. And again that was before the press got their hands on it. It was his life and not my business to pry but he was straight about what was happening. He did not attempt to excuse himself or play down the effects of what had happened to those closest to him.'

Virtually all the gossip columnists who ran the story in summer 1993 went immediately for parallels between father and son. Kingsley's career as a serial adulterer would not become public knowledge until the publication of his letters, but there were few in the literary world who had not heard the stories. Therefore to avoid libel actions editors listed Martin's lovers from the 1970s – or to be more accurate those who had already featured in contemporaneous reports and whose links with him were incontestable, notably Mary Furness, Angela Gorgas, Victoria Rothschild, Emma Soames and Claire Tomalin; Tina Brown was conspicuous by her absence – and pointed up the uneasy parallels between two men who had grown impatient with marriage and family life at almost exactly the same age. The *Evening Standard* went for a gimcrack version of the Oedipus Complex. 'Martin betrayed his two children, just as Kingsley betrayed him, and just as Kingsley was betrayed when his father left everything to Kingsley's step-mother, so that he did not even have a photograph of his mother.'[1] The author's name, Rohan Daft, brings to mind one of Martin's creations, now turned nemesis. Anne Barrowclough and Tim Walker in the *Daily Mail* decided to spread their bets. 'Regardless of what he did to whom, Amis's friends agree that his treatment of women left something to be desired. Some say this was because he was trying to emulate his father, Kingsley, who left Martin's mother, Hilly, for novelist Elizabeth Jane Howard when Martin was just twelve. Others say that the divorce left him deeply insecure and he was just trying to find lasting love and security. Others, more cruelly, say that because Martin is short, he has had to prove he is at least as attractive as the tall guys. But many say that Martin's behaviour occasionally gave the impression of deep misogyny.'[2] It was even suggested in the *Mail* and the *Daily Express* that for him lust was concurrent with social climbing. Emma Soames, 'Churchill's granddaughter', was enlisted as the obvious example and the beautiful 'heiress' Antonia's thoroughbred widowhood – her late husband being a brilliant Oxford don – treated as morbidly irresistible bait to Martin's ambitions. The allegation that Martin's ravenous libido is a compensation for his shortness is an enduring motif in all of these pieces and all of the more salacious revelations and psychological profiles come from unnamed 'friends'. The articles fed mainly upon unsubstantiated gossip and were designed to sate an appetite of vindictive prurience among the general public – though whether this was real or a reflection of something endemic to the media and literati is debatable. Peter McKay in the *Sunday Times* suspected the latter, while also taking a swing at vituperative feminism: 'This kind of rubbish is driven by sexual jealousy. Amis is seen as a man who has slept with prominent women and is punished accordingly by women writers who fear their own little tyros may follow his example.'[3]

One reason why the alleged sources were routinely anonymous, more likely invented, was that the people who knew Martin best were disinclined to say anything at all to the press. Equally significant was the fact that even if someone could have been persuaded to speak they would have had very little to say, at least about Martin. Zachary Leader's image of him as withdrawn, in a state of resigned passivity is confirmed by David Papineau. 'I gather that he spoke to his father about the break-up, but I had the impression he thought it wrong to burden friends with his own problems.' The exception here was Hitchens, in whom Martin did indeed confide and who would later serve as best man at Martin and Isabel's wedding. The article which caused more pain than the gossip column pieces was by Toby Young, a writer and journalist who had been a friend of Isabel's at Oxford. Young accuses Martin of outright hypocrisy, pointing out that not only was he guilty of exactly the same offence of which he had publicly accused his father but that he had made use of his undying love for his children as a conceit in his anti-nuclear diatribes of the 1980s.[4] Sixteen years later when I spoke to Young he expressed a degree of regret, if not exactly contrition. 'Martin, especially during the 1970s, had earned himself the reputation as a shit, and not only because of his roll-call of disappointed girlfriends. But still, I regret writing that piece for the *Sunday Times*. My real concern at the time was that his work was taking on a somewhat pious tone and he seemed to endorse the notion that novelists are particularly sensitive souls who can detect underlying moral failures the rest of us aren't aware of – a kind of secular priesthood, if you will. Complete balls, obviously, but I should have focused on that and not his divorce. In *Einstein's Monsters* he had gone on gallingly about how his commitment to nuclear disarmament was fed by his devotion to the future of his children. Then he dumps them in exchange for a younger, prettier version of his wife. Those were the facts but in bringing them together I committed the fallacy of *ad hominem*. I learned subsequently that he was seriously harrowed by what happened, that he took full responsibility and so on. Anyway I have nothing but goodwill towards Martin – how could I not towards someone who has brought me so much pleasure over the years?'

Isabel Fonseca was thirty-one in 1993. J. M. Kaplan, her maternal grandfather, had once owned Welch's Grape Juice and was a multi-millionaire. Her mother Elizabeth was a painter and her father Gonzalo, a Uruguayan and internationally acclaimed sculptor. Her brothers Caio and Bruno – the latter dying tragically early, aged thirty-six – also became painters and her sister Quina is a costume designer. Isabel grew up in a townhouse of bohemian aspect in West 11th Street, Greenwich Village and summers were spent at her grandparents' house in East Hampton. Aged eighteen she spent her gap year in Paris mixing with artist friends of her parents and attempting distractedly to begin a novel. After taking a degree in Comparative Religion at Barnard College she was accepted by Oxford to read Politics, Philosophy and Economics at Wadham in 1984. To be a Fresher at twenty-two was not that unusual but if you came with a cosmopolitan heritage, an Ivy League degree and a wardrobe that bespoke chic maturity, the response by post-sixth-form female peers was easily predictable: envy.

She did not make too many close friends at Oxford, at least not female ones, but within a year she had become a magnet for men who expected their intellectual reputation to guarantee other attractions. She commuted regularly between London and Oxford and would eventually rent a flat just off Ladbroke Grove. She was several times photographed in London restaurants with the American film star John Malkovich but the only

293

serious relationship she had during this period was with a man of roughly her own age, the late poet and critic Mick Imlah.

After Oxford she worked briefly at the *Independent*, then, for a year, at Bloomsbury Publishing and finally settled, for five years, at the *TLS*. She first 'met' Martin on the telephone, having been asked by her editor to persuade him to do a feature article. She knew who he was, of course, but was intrigued by the sound of his voice.

Peter McKay, in the *Sunday Times*, stated shortly after news broke of her relationship with Martin that she 'is described as a literary groupie'.[5] While working at the *TLS* she invested a great deal of time in a research project which had fascinated her since her undergraduate years, and which she discussed with her brother Bruno, who shared her interest. The gypsies of central and eastern Europe had been persecuted for centuries, more recently large numbers were murdered by the Nazis, and little was known of their fate following the descent of the Iron Curtain. Isabel scrutinized all available sources in print and on record but after the Soviet bloc disintegrated after 1989 she began to make tentative enquiries about visiting countries thought to have retained a considerable population of gypsies. From this she prepared a synopsis and sample chapter and approached Random House. The advance offered was sufficient for her to give up the *TLS* job and to fund the large number of visits she undertook between 1991 and 1995 to Germany, Albania, Czechoslovakia, Moldova, Poland, Bulgaria and Romania.

The book *Bury Me Standing*, published in 1995, was well reviewed and eventually translated into twenty-two languages. Much of the research was done prior to the beginning of her relationship with Martin and her life during that period belies the term 'literary groupie'. She spent roughly half of the four years it took to research and write the book outside London in areas of eastern Europe about which little then was known. Beyond the urban centres of some of these countries – particularly Romania and Albania – not much had changed since the nineteenth century and strangers were treated with a mixture of curiosity and outright hostility. Isabel did not court attention as an attractive extra at literary soirées. She was invited, and talked to, because she was engaged in a daring and original project.

Alan Jenkins, who has known Isabel since the mid-1980s when she began to review for the *TLS* and he was deputy editor, is particularly aggrieved by the 'literary groupie' slur. 'When she was doing research for the book [*Bury Me Standing*] she faced very real dangers. Many writers, many male writers, would not have gone near those regions. But it is a token of her human gifts that she did not glamorize, even mention the terrifying risks she took, either in the book itself or as part of the publicity campaign. We are bombarded with authors who advertise their bravery and recklessness in newspaper profiles on their books about remote, dangerous regions. Virtually every week on *Start the Week* or *Midweek* a vainglorious adventurer will turn up. But Isabel kept quiet about what her research involved, very often grave physical threats. She cared greatly about the book's subject but would not allow her ego to have any part of this. She is very unassuming.'

The parallels between European gypsies, a wilfully dispossessed 'tribe' with a legacy and language of their own, and the much larger, more integrated Jewish population are engrossing – Isabel herself, through her mother's line, is Jewish – and this became the subject of conversations between her and Martin at parties and dinners after the publication of *Time's Arrow*, the same year she began her research.

All who met him during the period between the summer of 1993 and autumn 1994, when in the US he made final agreements with Antonia on their separation and forthcoming divorce, corroborate the picture of withdrawal and introspection offered by Zachary Leader. By October 1993 he had moved out of Chesterton Road and lived permanently in his flat in Leamington Road Villas. The occasional visits by Louis and Jacob prior to this, indulging their concern about where their father was during the day, became more formalized. He would pick them up on Friday evenings and drive them back mid-afternoon on Sunday. He was not barred from the house but it was agreed that random visits would add further to the boys' ongoing sense of confusion and disquiet. He still went to the tennis club, but less frequently, and, according to Chris, played with a noticeably reduced amount of tenacity. He held conversations but through a combination of nuanced hints and body language made clear that he was for the time being treading water and that some things would not be discussed.

The Information was begun in 1990 but its gestation can be sourced to this period. Martin was obliged to privately scrutinize his state of mind and his ability to act upon circumstances caused by himself. Irrespective of what this entailed in life – divorce and most painfully separation from his sons – he encountered also a peculiarly fruitful idea for a novel.

London Fields is his most ambitious novel, *Time's Arrow* his most daringly significant and *The Information* by far his most enthralling. In it we encounter two versions of the author, a split that occurred in life after he left Antonia for Isabel and retreated into a state of almost masochistic self-contemplation. The first time that he mentioned the book in public was during an interview in 1990 shortly after *Time's Arrow* had gone to press. He had not as yet written anything but he was preoccupied with an idea: 'It feels at the moment like a light novel about literary envy'. 'At the moment' it did but within the next three years the envious, mutually hostile relationship

296

between two novelists – Richard Tull and Gwyn Barry – would mutate into a far more singular, personal and irresolvable antipathy.

The former has published two novels. Of the first, *Aforethought*, we are informed that 'nobody understood it, or even finished it, but, equally, nobody was sure it was shit. Richard flourished'. (p. 40) He was feted as a challenging radical new presence. His second novel, *Dreams Don't Mean Anything*, was published in Britain, but not in the US. His third, fourth, fifth and sixth remain unpublished; his current, most ambitious piece, is unfinished and he supports himself and his family, just, by working for a vanity publisher, editing an obscure literary journal and reviewing for those newspapers still prepared to pay him. Richard's friend from their university days, Gwyn Barry, succeeds magnificently with his first novel *Summertown* and is about to do even better with his second, *Amelior*. Richard treats both with the special kind of disdain that those with claims to cultural hauteur reserve for the merely competent and, even worse, the popular 'purest trex: fantastically pedestrian. It tried to be "touching"; but the only touching thing about *Summertown* was that it *thought* it was a novel'. (p. 43)

The Information is one of the best novels about writing novels of recent years. It does not address this subject by turning in upon itself, by employing self-referring, metafictional devices; it is at once more accessible and compelling than that. The third-person narrator – in truth Amis himself – allows us into the emotional landscapes of a number of its characters but none is so intimately scrutinized as Richard's. We are told that

> He was an artist when he saw society: it never crossed his mind that society had to be like this, had any right, had any business being like this. A car in the street. Why?

297

Why *cars*? This is what an artist has to be: harassed to
the point of insanity or stupefaction by first principles.
The difficulty began when he sat down to write. (p. 11)

Richard's problem is that the 'first principles' which underpin
his idealistic, ambitious conception of what a novel should do
– a combination of an epiphany and a thoroughgoing analysis
of the state of everything – are what ensure his failure to realize
these ambitions. Barry, however, has opted for the kind of
writing that improves upon reality, makes it far more agreeable
for the reader. And what of Amis, one is inevitably prompted
to ask? The 'information' of the title is something never
properly disclosed. It is capable of causing terrible dreams,
animating unease, distress and destroying relationships, but we
only learn of its effects, not its nature. We never learn precisely
what it is, but we know that had Richard been in charge of the
book he would have attempted to disclose its essence, and the
novel would never have been written.

Martin projects aspects of himself into each of his creations.
He shares with Richard a preoccupation with the transformative power of language. Even permanently hung-over narrators
such as John Self cannot in Martin's hands be content with the
routine lexicon of things and movement. Cars 'tunnel' through
the 'grooves and traps' of a street, their posture is supinely 'low
slung' as they 'shark' through New York. Martin abhors the
lazy predictability of language but he does not, like Richard and
other adherents of the avant-garde, subject the reader to the
grievous agony of high modernism; he prefers the tricks of the
literary conjurer. Martin has popularized literary nonconfor-
mism, created a hybrid in which anti-establishment originality
is blended with something that the purist experimenters had
failed to achieve, books that are compulsively entertaining and
often make us laugh out loud. In this respect he begins to bear

a superficial resemblance to Gwyn. True, he has certainly not produced fiction which flatters the reader's intellectual self-regard while pandering to their fantasies and delusions. He does not write like Gwyn but in terms of their public image they have much in common, that rare combination of media-promoted celebrity and high-cultural ranking.

In 1992, eight years after its publication, *Money* had sold 270,000 copies and *London Fields*, over three years, 210,000. Compared with mass market novelists such as Jeffrey Archer, John Grisham and Barbara Taylor Bradford, these are modest figures but even when well-publicized prizes such as the Booker push 'serious' writers into the realm of the bestseller a quarter of a million would be treated as a successful total. Martin frequently matched his more popular compatriots in the serious literature compound, and his public profile, albeit unsolicited but ever present, left his peers in the shadows. Few writers whose mid-career work had been allocated chapters in books called *Exploring Postmodernism* (1987) or *Doubles: Studies in Literary History* (1985) had also been pursued by scandal-hungry tabloid hacks and joined by royalty, rock stars and disgraced politicians in the gossip columns of the *Daily Mail* and the *Evening Standard*.

There is something of Martin in both Gwyn and Richard and the most amusing performance from this double act occurs in Part 3 where they take a jet-hop tour around seven US cities to promote the sequel to Gwyn's most recent success, *Amelior Regained*. Richard is there as a result of his friend's patrician generosity; he will write the publicity and profile material – skills he has painfully acquired working for the vanity publisher – while Gwyn enjoys apparently limitless quantities of fawning approbation. On the way out Richard embarks on 'a journey within a journey', progressing from his own seat in coach-class where the reading matter is 'pluralistic, liberal and humane:

Daniel Deronda, trigonometry, the Lebanon, First World War, Homer, Diderot, *Anna Karenina*' (p. 288) to business world. Here he expects to find 'lightweight middlemen like A. L. Rowse or Lord David Cecil' suffused with 'teacup-storm philosophers, exploded revisionist historians, stubbornly Steady State cosmologists or pallid poets over whom the finger of sentimentality continued to waver'. (p. 289) But no, the middle-ranking executives are absorbed by 'outright junk. Fat financial thrillers, chunky chillers and tub-like tinglers.' In first class it is even worse; there the 'drugged tycoons' read nothing at all, or at least cannot be bothered with the unregarded books 'jacketed with hunting scenes or ripe young couples in mid swirl or swoon' that lie face down on the passengers' 'softly swelling stomachs'. Gwyn, comfortably supine in first class, is reading something: his schedule of promotional stopovers.

I asked Martin where he was most often seated during his many cross-Atlantic odysseys of the 1980s, generously sponsored by the *New Yorker*, the *Observer*, the *Sunday Times*, *Atlantic* et al. 'Well, it would depend on the nature of the assignment, and who'd commissioned it.' But, I persevere, you surely never ended up like Richard in 'coach'? 'Usually it was coach. On book tours, business.'

The cities visited, not accidentally, are those in which Martin established affinities and found inspiration for his portraits of deranged excess and expedient grandeur. New York, Miami, Boston, Chicago and Washington feature prominently. Our perspective throughout involves a combination of Richard and the narrator. Gwyn is ever present, content in his role as feted best-selling author, but always viewed from the outside. The underbelly of America from which he is spared is sampled by Richard, who shambles daily to his friend's luxuriously appointed suites after vacating his drab motel room.

Obviously the America experienced by Gwyn comes closer to

Martin's own rather pampered journeys around the country. He did occasionally indulge his taste for slumming, but these were excursions from the norm. Richard is the embodiment of the fears and anxieties that accompanied his creator's sudden rise to fame during the mid-1970s, when it all seemed rather too good to be true. One of the reasons why Martin stayed on at the *New Statesman* during the 1970s was that *The Rachel Papers*, *Dead Babies* and *Success* sold so few copies. His advances after *The Rachel Papers* were relatively generous but none of his first three novels sold a sufficient number of hardbacks for him to draw anything more than small royalty payments. Martin became successful not because his early work sold well but through his attainment of what became known in the trade as mediagenic status. His early books were the subject of fierce critical debate and his lifestyle and journalism combined, of course, with his parentage guaranteed him a profile that was ready-made for the marketing and promotions departments of publishing houses. Bizarrely Cape invested far more in promoting *Other People*, his least reader-friendly novel at that point, than in all of his three previous works combined. It too sold relatively few copies but the tide of publicity enabled Pat Kavanagh, his agent, to negotiate the sale of his paperback rights to Penguin, who pooled their considerable resources with Cape to ensure that *Money* (1984) was spectacularly well advertised, including an American marketing tour not unlike Gwyn's. It went into paperback six months after the hardback issue.

Richard follows Gwyn around and accompanies Martin through the novel as a memory of what this author might have been. Gwyn's Mephistophelian agent Gal Aplanalp is persuaded by him to have Richard's most recent, shamelessly impenetrable contribution to postmodernism, *Untitled*, taken on by the self-consciously radical American publisher Bold

Agenda. As Gwyn alights upon his scenes of promotional aggrandizement Richard has to take care of his own publicity. In New York he has been given a sack containing eighteen copies of the book with which, space and Gwyn permitting, he will attempt to attract the attention of those booksellers and agents who can spare time from the enchantments of *Amelior Regained*. By accident or design – we never learn if it is an act of disdainful neglect or malice on Gwyn's and Gal's part – the eighteen books in the sack make up the entire print run. Experimentalists, it seems, will be indulged with an ISBN and little more. The episode, darkly comic in its own right, is rooted in fact.

Chris Mitas tells of how in 1990 a surprise birthday party had been arranged for him at a dining room in the Queen's Park Rangers Stadium. He had supported the club since his childhood and was now on good terms with its owners and directors. Present were Martin, Charles Saatchi, Emma Freud, several QPR players and other figures from Chris's complex social and professional life. Among them was Suzy Hammond, a US TV presenter and producer. Martin asked her about her work and chatted with interest until she enquired about his. He was, he replied, a writer and she insisted that if he needed any help with agents or publishers in the US she would be happy to put him in touch with influential figures. They exchanged cards and during the journey back to West London with her husband and Chris she told of how she had met this charming amusing man who was working on a bizarre novel about time travel. She thought it was a long shot but she was confident that one of the wackier specialist publishers in New York – not unlike Bold Agenda – might show some interest. They roared with laughter. Martin was amused but has confessed that a twinge of horror accompanied their conversation. 'I thought, well yes, but what if I *were* the person she thought she was talking to, with the same name, the same mannerisms and a complete failure. I shivered.' The incident occurred as the figure of Richard was forming in Martin's imagination, shortly before he began his affair with Isabel, and sometimes one has cause to suspect that they were linked by an implied subheading: *mea culpa*.

It is of course impossible to disentangle *The Information* from the media frenzy which preceded its publication. The first hint that Martin might have somehow acquired an improbable source of wealth – his broken marriage was already well publicized – came in a short anonymous piece in the *Evening Standard*[6] reporting that he had recently returned from the US 'during which he allegedly spent $20,000 having all his molars removed and new ones pegged'. The article slyly infers that the dental work was prompted as much by vanity as distress. By December press speculation, fuelled by unattributable sources in the publishing industry, began to focus upon Martin's alleged demand to his publisher Cape, who had put out all of his previous books, for an advance of £480,000. Cape insisted that £300,000 would be their limit. It was also stated that Martin had 'dumped' Pat Kavanagh, his lifelong agent, and wife of his friend Julian Barnes, for Andrew Wylie, which is only partially true. Wylie had negotiated Salman Rushdie's contract for *The Satanic Verses* and secured an advance payment from Viking of £500,000 for the American rights, and he was often present at the morale-boosting drinks parties for Rushdie at Martin's house and other locations long before his name became associated with Martin's in the gossip columns. In Hitchens's view Martin was impressed less by Wylie's much-vaunted skills as a high-stakes negotiator than his conscientiousness, 'even his daring. I would say that Martin's decision to change to Wylie was made during a weekend at the latter's house in Watermill, Long Island. I was there too, and during the evening Martin learned of how Wylie had been solely responsible for getting

Salman's *Satanic Verses* into paperback. Agents and publishers were running scared but Andrew was determined, and he was not motivated by financial reward, no, he was infuriated by the cowardice of the Western publishing industry. His role went largely unrecorded, and not because he too feared reprisals. He was surprisingly modest. You see Salman was there too, at Long Island that weekend. He insisted on telling us about what our host had done. Martin, for all his flaws, values courage and integrity greatly. That, I'm certain, was the decisive moment in the Wylie affair, that was why Martin chose to move to him.'

Hitchens adds that it was he who had urged Martin to consider another agent. 'Yes I actually suggested Andrew to him. He was my agent at the time and I knew how well he worked.' Originally, according to Hitchens, Martin had 'misgivings' because of Wylie's reputation as a ruthless advocate and negotiator; he was known in the trade as the 'Jackal'. 'Martin is not particularly avaricious, and he never wishes to cause distress. It took a long time for him to be persuaded to even consider Andrew. As I say, the weekend at Long Island was the turning point but that is only part of the story. The notorious dumping of Pat [Kavanagh] and the bust-up with Julian as reported by the press was a half-truth, which Martin to his enormous credit did not overturn in *Experience*.' So what really happened? 'First of all, even when he had accepted that Andrew could do a good job on his behalf he couldn't bear the thought of having to tell Pat, and of course Julian, that he was moving to Wylie. In a way it was rather like the break-up of his marriage. He could not forgive himself for being part of something that had to happen. So he even attempted to take them *both* on as his co-agents, with Pat dealing mainly with the UK and Wylie with the States, simply because he was distressed by the prospect of upsetting her, and Julian. But it was absurdly impractical, it could not work. As I said to him, if Pat is genuinely your friend then she will accept that your business decisions – because writing is your *sole* means of support – must override nostalgic attachment. He had to be shown the facts before he accepted that his two-agent idea was impossible.'

Then there was the notorious letter from Barnes to Martin written shortly after the latter had informed Pat of his decision. The document is in Martin's possession but copyright means that it is not quotable verbatim without Barnes's permission. Nevertheless, Martin's friends commend him unreservedly for abstaining from at least an indication of its content. Hitchens: 'It affected him greatly and one detects his mortification in *Experience* but to his credit he didn't indicate what his erstwhile friend actually wrote.' According to Hitchens, Martin was left stunned by two passages in particular. In one he stated that Salman, through his association with Wylie, would be killed, but appeared to feel no anguish at the thought. Next he offered Martin hearty congratulations on the break-up of his marriage and the distress caused to Antonia. 'It was beautifully, evilly, crafted, especially the last comment on Martin's marriage. He didn't of course compare this explicitly with Martin's decision to leave Pat but he didn't need to. Julian is an excellent, compelling stylist. Without actually saying so he made Martin feel like he had sold his soul to the devil. I mean, it was hardly as though Pat had gone bust, she was still one of the most prestigious, prosperous agents in London. But let's be blunt, she wasn't as *good* as Andrew. Business is business and Julian's response was made up of pure malice. I'd never seen a letter like that. Martin eventually got back with him, to an extent. But I have not.'

Martin had discussed the financial prospects for *The Information* with both Kavanagh and Wylie as early as 1993 and it was only when Cape refused outright to move beyond their £300,000 that Martin elected to follow Wylie's advice and, in effect, put the novel up for auction. HarperCollins took it, along with a volume of stories, for £505,000, following intense negotiations with Wylie. Harper, unlike Cape or the other mainstream London houses, was a multinational conglomerate with New York and San Francisco offices of their own rather than alliances with US counterparts, and in this respect Wylie was fully within his professional remit to conduct these exchanges. Rather than taking over from Pat Kavanagh, he was doing a better job as Martin's other agent. It was not, therefore, all that surprising that he was thereafter retained as his sole representative on both sides of the Atlantic.

Patricia Parkin was at that time a senior editor for Harper and while she was not directly involved with *The Information* she provides an interesting perspective on the deal. 'You have to understand that Harper had become less a literary publisher than a branch of a gigantic media organization. It was already an amalgam of a number of once independent houses but with the takeover by [Rupert] Murdoch the atmosphere changed noticeably. There was talk of "Loss Leaders" and as much attention was paid to the publicity potential and saleability of the author as to the quality of the book. At the popular end of the list we had recently advanced twenty million pounds to Jeffrey Archer for *three* books. Twenty million! I mean, compared with that, Amis's half a million was peanuts.' Did the new regime at Harper, I ask her, influence the offer for *The Information*? 'Oh of course it did. Even among what one might call the "serious" literary authors there was a feeling that the new publicity culture would guarantee sales. Obviously there was the famous horserace of the Booker Prize. Until *Waterland*, for instance, Graham Swift was a respected but largely unknown presence but once that reached the Booker shortlist in 1983 his advance for his next [*Out of This World*] was, I think, 125,000 pounds. That was almost a decade before *The*

Information so take into account inflation and it is not too far off. Ian McEwan got 250,000 pounds for *The Innocent* [1990], mainly because of his adaptations for film. Amis had not won the Booker of course but he had, aside from Rushdie, attracted far more press attention than any other writer at the time.' Did this play a part in Harper's bid? 'It did, yes.'

The ascent of Gwyn is based on a combination of experience and hard-headed prescience. Martin knew, halfway through the novel, that like his creation he too would soon enter the egregious cultural marketplace but he could only guess at the outcome. His speculations were offered compass by a some-what unlikely source. Martin ranks Milton's *Paradise Lost* the greatest non-dramatic poem in English; and David Papineau, Zachary Leader and Will Self all agree that during the period of the novel's composition, particularly as the draft went through a number of major revisions in 1994, conversations with Martin would turn with unerring frequency to Milton. Leader: 'He seemed preoccupied with the fact that both poems [*Paradise Lost* and *Paradise Regained*] rely upon dialogue as the engine for decision and indeed fate.' In *Paradise Lost* the exchanges between Satan and the fallen angels, between Gabriel and Adam, Eve and Satan, Michael and Adam and in *Paradise Regained* between Satan and Christ are more than turning points in the narrative. For the first time figures who had previously been immune from such questions as motive took on the temperamental complexities of Shakespeare's characters. It was in this groundbreaking moment in literary history that Martin found his cue for the relationship between Richard and Gwyn. Their 'dialogue' is uneven, weighted predominantly towards the perspective and dilemmas of Richard, yet like Milton's figures they seem more like contrasting versions of the same presence than irreconcilable opposites.

The Information is important because it pre-empts and

sometimes outranks *Experience* as a story about Martin Amis. In the latter he takes cautious steps back, edits, magnifies and diminishes emotional registers, slices up his chronology into digressions, anecdotes, sometimes epiphanies. The novel, however, is a far more painfully transparent account of his most troubling memories and his ongoing state of mind. It is a Miltonic dialogue, shot through with precedents set by Freud, Proust, Joyce; a conversation with himself.

Open the novel almost at random and tortured, sometimes repentant fragments of his life will burst into sharp relief. Consider the matter of sex. Despite his radical portraits of the contemporary world – a touch of arch modernism shot through with the baroque – Martin has frequently been judged reactionary verging upon misogynist in his representation of women (see, famously, Laura Doan on *Money*).[7] The opening passage of William Boyd's *Brazzaville Beach* would no doubt be treated by feminist critics as an exemplary representation by a male novelist of gender difference. The narrator, one Hope Clearwater, having already disclosed her gender in the prologue, begins her story by reflecting upon two acquaintances, both male (p. 3). Hauser is not present, but she comments on his 'cynical gossip, all silky insinuation and covert bitchery'. Clovis, however, is sitting close by. He is, apparently, a curious figure, prone to shifts between 'raffish arrogance' and 'total and single-minded self-absorption' and given to 'instinctively and unconsciously cup[ping] his genitals whenever he was alarmed or nervous'. Hope then describes how an ant seems to have trapped itself under her shirt and how 'Clovis impassively watched me remove my shirt and then my bra'. Clovis's indifference to what some men would treat as a sexually provocative gesture is eventually explained when we are told of how soon afterwards he clambers into a nearby mulemba tree, swings with 'powerful easy movements' through the branches and is 'lost to sight, heading north east towards the hills of the escarpment'. (p. 4) Clovis is an ape. Boyd provokes in the reader a composite network of assumptions on maleness and follows up with an implicit glance towards the way that some women deal with these same issues. In Hope's case the blurring of the distinction between a subhuman and the general condition of maleness is in part a reflection of her enlightened post-feminist singularity and in equal degree her sense of affinity, as a human, with the apes which she and her colleagues are studying in Africa.

Boyd was not the only member of the post-1960s generation of male writers who showed signs of ablative contrition on behalf of their gender. McEwan's first two collections of short stories *First Love, Last Rites* (1975) and *In Between the Sheets* (1978) contain, arguably, the most repulsive team of sadists, rapists, paedophiles and pornographers ever assembled by a single author. The question of whether McEwan is pandering to some prurient super-gothic taste among his readers or apologizing for being a man is surely answered in the only story where the mood lightens, almost triumphantly. Called 'Pornography' it involves two nurses who take revenge upon a practitioner of that trade by promising him a perverse treat. Then they strap him to a bed and cut off his penis. He had it coming to him, as of course do all males who indulge such tastes and practices, it seems to suggest.

Martin's most famous public pronouncement on how men should deal with feminism came much later in a 1991 review article which he reworked as a lecture for several US universities delivered when he was completing *The Information*. He takes the secure middle ground, presenting the post-1970 New Man as a well-meaning rather bathetic figure: 'There he stands in the kitchen, a nappy in one hand, a pack of Tarot cards in the other, with his sympathetic pregnancies, his hot flushes and contact premenstrual tensions.'[8] Martin reserves an equal amount of ridicule for his reactionary successor, promoted by the likes of Robert Bly: the Wild Man, the 'deep male' embodying 'Zeus energy', 'masculine grandeur' and 'sun-like integrity' capable of bestowing upon long-suppressed women their just rewards, in the bedroom.

One could perceive this as a commendably even-handed puncturing of two equally absurd extremes, but where does Martin really stand on the matter? Let us return to *The Information* and to what is an undisguised caricature of Boyd's opening passage. At a meeting attended by the two competing novelists, two newspaper columnists and an 'Arts Minister', Gwyn offers his writerly manifesto:

> 'I find I never think in terms of men. In terms of women. I find I always think in terms of . . . *People.*'
> There was an immediate burble of appreciation: Gwyn, it seemed had douched the entire company in common sense and plain humanity. (p. 30)

All apart from Richard, who offers an inventive hypothesis:

> It must make you feel nice and young to say that being a man means nothing and being a woman means nothing and what matters is being a . . . person. How about being a *spider* Gwyn? Let's imagine you're a *spider*. You're a spider and you've just had your first serious date. You're limping away from that now, and you're looking over your shoulder, and there's your girlfriend, eating one of your legs like it was a chicken drumstick. What would you say? I know. You'd say: I find I never think in terms of male spiders. Or in terms of female spiders. I find I always think in terms of . . . *spiders*. (p. 31)

As the novel proceeds Gwyn's felicitous concern for equality of representation becomes part of a game played between them with Gwyn as languid tormentor and Richard as hapless victim, whose only palliatives are his own acid comments. When Gwyn informs him: 'Guess what. We had an intruder last night,' Richard, almost instinctively, replies,

> 'Really? Did she take anything?'
> 'We're not really sure.'
> 'How did she get in? Was she armed, do you know?'
> Gwyn closed his eyes and inclined his head, acknowledging the satire. He had a habit, in his prose, of following a neuter antecedent with a feminine pronoun. From *Amelior:* 'While pruning roses, any gardener knows that if she . . .' Or, from the days when he still wrote book reviews: 'No reader could finish this haunting scene without feeling the hairs on the back of her . . .' Richard clucked away to himself, but these days he often opted for an impersonal construction, or simply used the plural, seeking safety in numbers.
> 'Through the front door.'
> 'She didn't turn violent, did she?'
> 'Come on, don't be a tit. It's very upsetting actually.'
> (pp. 238–9)

It is not that Martin is satirizing Boyd or any other enlightened new-manish writer. Indeed, we are never certain of whether Gwyn's political correctness or Richard's bitterness is the more irritating. It is one example of how, throughout the book, he picks over various aspects of his life, work and reputation. He neither attempts to justify nor apologise for anything; rather he seems to take some perverse pleasure in being unable to make sense of it. There are many other instances of this.

Shortly after their exchange on the 'intruder' Gwyn accompanies Richard to a pub, his refuge from his work at Tantalus Press and indeed from his cramped flat, the latter bearing a close resemblance to Martin's in Leamington Road Villas. The Warlock is recognizable to everyone who used the Paddington Sports Club as its slightly grotesque facsimile. Among such invented regulars as Hal, Mal, Del, Pel, Bal, Gel and Lol, Martin distributes very real figures from his time there in the early 1990s, notably Dave [Papineau], Steve [Michel] and Chris [Mitas]. (p. 240) When not on court or discussing matters variously abstruse or ephemeral Martin and friends would divert themselves with the so-called quiz machine, a cross between pinball – given that the subject of the question would be randomly selected – and the multiple-choice formula of *University Challenge*. Richard is perceived by the regulars with a combination of grudging respect and pity. Not only can he be relied upon to answer every question, he even offers unprompted reflections on their context, which earns him the nickname 'Cedric' after the affected old slob who presents an afternoon quiz show about words. 'Well,' observes Chris Mitas, 'Mart didn't have a nickname but he was seen by a few members as an eccentric. It was not that he was the only writer in the club but he was the only one who treated the quiz machine as if his life depended on answering every question.'

In the novel the real Chris and Steve exchange first names, with the former featuring as Steve Cousins. Like Chris Mitas, Cousins is an enigma. Papineau describes Mitas as 'a thoughtful yet a rather forbidding, presence. The club was a peculiar place, drawing in figures from all professions and backgrounds but "our set", academics, media people, artists, writers and so on, were fascinated by Chris. He was easy tempered – but it was more than that. We feared that he could outrank us, us the careerist thinkers. His mind was uncluttered and efficient.' And so it is with Steve. At one point he describes to Richard how to kill someone, the preparation involving a gradual depletion of the victim's resistance to fear so that when the final act occurs they accept it almost with gratitude.

'It's like the world has—'
'Turned against them.'
'Like the world hates them.'
'Go on,' said Richard limply.
'So that by the time it happened, by then, they just – they just hang their heads. They're ready. It's the end of the story. They've felt it coming. They're ready. They just hang their heads.'
'This is magical. This is poetry.' (p. 252)

It is also a near exact transcription of Chris Mitas's account to Martin of how, in judo, he had evolved a method of reducing his opponent to an acceptance of defeat.

The Information seems at first to nod towards the post-modern trend of choosing titles capriciously irrelevant to the content of the book, but the opposite is the case. When he wrote it Martin was experiencing the most troubling, problematic period of his life, a condition made all the more implacable by his knowledge that the entire sequence of events had been caused by him. He had no one to blame but himself. He had made his choice without external pressure, was determined that it was the right one and found himself having to deal with the consequences – most notably the effect upon his sons – by engaging in lengthy tortured exercises in self-scrutiny – evidenced by the uncharacteristic air of quietness noted by his friends. He is searching for the information, some predictable trait in his character or personal history, perhaps a persistent behavioural handicap that might at least serve to placate his

313

dilemma with an explanation. His search is fruitless but out of it are born Richard Tull and Gwyn Barry, or to be more accurate the uncomfortable relationship between each of them and everything else, especially the people who surround them.

Richard accompanies Demi to her family's ancestral pile, ostensibly to conduct an interview with the celebrity wife of the famous novelist (pp. 261–9) and the episode is nightmarish, far more so than the scenes of murder and mayhem enacted in a similar location in *Dead Babies*, with which it invites comparison. Byland Court is rather like Brideshead but this branch of the aristocracy is not destined for tragic self-lacerating decline; no, they are, mid-1990s, still comfortably installed and obviously insane. Demi's sisters Lady Amaryllis, Lady Callisto, Lady Urania and Lady Persephone sit breast-feeding babies and behaving as if extraneous matter – from dog faeces in the library to their cognizance of other human beings – is superfluous and unwarranted. Her brothers shoot ducks with visceral abandon and seem equally immune from what might heedlessly be termed the real world. The inhabitants of this privileged demesne are content and it is Richard who feels as though he has been despatched to a lunatic asylum – an impression assisted by an overdose of cocaine and his night-time raid upon the wardrobe-sized drinks cabinet.

Twenty years earlier Martin had been the regular guest at the Soameses' residence in Hampshire, Castle Mill House. 'He was', recalls Nicholas Soames, 'marvellously entertaining and to his credit he indulged the banter regarding his height and leftish associations. They were amusing weekends and I think he enjoyed his role as misfit. Sundays would begin with the pantomime of church. First Martin politely excused himself but we played on this, pretending that he was offending family lore, as our guest.'

I can't believe they're doing this to me, he said to himself, in the van with Urania and Callisto and Persephone. He felt he was pleading – with whom? With the Labrador's puppies, blind, burrowing, and wet with their new-born varnish. Oh, Christ, how can they do this? To me, me, so lost, so reduced, and snivelling for sustenance. A soul so sick of sin, so weary of the world's shadows and figments. Jesus, they're not really going to do this, are they? They are. They're taking me to fucking *church*.

In the village square the van opened up, and let him out. (p. 294)

There is no particular psychological condition which demands horror-struck revisitations of otherwise innocuous episodes from our past, at least as far as I am aware. 'Oh yes,' adds Soames, 'his trousers were frequently the subject of fascinated attention, particularly by my father who was intrigued by the various bright shades of velvet sported by Mart. Never quite seen anything like them before.'

After introducing himself to the Earl of Rievaulx – with a suitably unctuous 'How do you do' – Richard is subjected to an interrogation that could have come from Pinter. 'What are you?' begins the Earl, and, before Richard can properly explain the nature of his profession, indeed his vocation, follows up with: 'So! You grace us with a *second* visit. We thank you for your condescension. Tell me – what keeps you away? Is it that you are happier in the town? Is it the lack of "hygienic facilities"? Is it all the children and babies, is it the *progeny* you abhor?' As the exchange reaches its apogee Pinter seems to have been exchanged for a *Carry On* scriptwriter.

'Get them *off*.'
Richard stopped breathing . . .

'Get them *off*,' he said, one rising scale, with that final *whoof* of dogged rage. 'Get them *off*. Get them *off*.'
Did he want them, did he covet them? . . .
Demeter re-entered the room . . .
'I'm afraid your father', said Richard, 'has been bearding me about these trousers.' (pp. 278–9)

The novel is sewn from fragments of Martin's previous and contemporaneous existence but is not in a purist sense autobiographical. Martin invokes his affair with Emma Soames and his weekends at Castle Mill House neither as a caricature of himself, or them, nor as some contritional revisitation of social climbing. His only guiding principle is arbitrary distortion, which also begets the recasting of the Paddington Sports Club as the Warlock and his ransacking of his and his friends' attitudes towards feminism in Richard's taunting of Gwyn. The novel is about its author but this is Martin Amis dismantled and chaotically reassembled, the constituent parts all recognizable but no longer quite where they used to be or working as they should.

'The literary world', comments Andy Hislop, 'is made up of people with adhesive memories and those with no retentive care for the past at all. Martin is the supreme example of the former, but for him memory is like an allergy. Moments from which others might be immune become for Martin the cause of irrational neurosis or complaint. You see he *lives* by observation, always retaining and remaking the stuff of his world and frequently the past becomes disease-ridden, malignant.' Richard, on Martin's behalf, becomes preoccupied with The Information, the possibility that something immutable can protect him from what seems to be a torrent of delusions and misrepresentations – from the desperate clients of the Tantalus Press to the world of Gal Aplanalp and Gwyn in which authenticity has long since given way to image-making. We, the readers, accompany him through this apparently hopeless spiral of despair, until we encounter the one element of the novel where unalloyed pain and fear steady his progress, though with little consolation. Richard's children are the only people, indeed the only features of his existence, who inspire in him untainted emotion.

The two most poignant passages of *The Information* and *Experience* are, if not exactly accounts of the same event – one is ostensibly fictional – then certainly provoked by a single cause. In *Experience* Martin recalls an episode in 1993 when he drove away from Antonia's house in Wellfleet where the two of them and their sons had holidayed every summer for the previous nine years. He would return, he knew, but nothing would be quite the same again; he would still be their father, biologically – legally – but a change had taken place. Towards the close of the novel following Richard's break-up with Gina he sees his eldest son in the street and something is wrong, peculiar and inexplicable.

Richard saw his son Marco – Marco a long way away, and on the far side of the street, but with Marco's unmistakably brittle and defeatist stride. There was something terribly wrong with Marco: there was nobody at his side. And yet the child's solitude, his isolation, unlike the father's, was due to an unforgivable error not his own. There was always somebody at Marco's side. In all his seven years there had always been somebody at his side . . .

Father and son started hurrying towards each other. Marco wasn't crying but Richard had never seen him looking so unhappy: the unhappiness that was always made for Marco; the unhappiness that was all his own. Richard knelt, like a knight, and held him. (p. 492)

On the first morning Jacob pushed my coffee cup an inch nearer my right hand and said, 'Enjoying your stay so far?' . . . Five days later, as I prepared to leave, the pond outside the house was obediently reflecting the mass of doom stacked up in the sky. My sons were constructing a miniature zoo on a patch of grass; Louis showed me the little stunt where you dropped a coin down a complicated tunnel and were then issued with your ticket of admission. But I wasn't staying, and they knew it. They knew I was leaving. They knew the thing had failed – the whole thing had failed. I said goodbye and climbed into the rented car.

– I just can't stop thinking about it. I just can't get it out of my mind.

– There's nothing you can do with things like that [said Kingsley]. You can only hope to coexist with them. They never go away. They're always with you. They're just – *there . . .*[9]

'[*The Information*],' says Martin, 'was one of the few novels I nearly abandoned. And that was to do with feeling terrible because I was getting divorced. Divorce is as bad as dying. You suffer not just psychologically but physically. It's that violent. It's like physical pain for months, even years. The pain will come out at the time or percolate and come out much later but it's absolutely ineradicable. When I wrote it I was feeling ragged and infested with the failure . . . of my marriage.' The second of hesitation in that last sentence discloses the uncomfortably intimate relationship between his private state of mind and the book he often wished to abandon but never could. Compare his comments with his general reflections on morality and the novel. 'I never judge my characters. They have lives of their own. Whatever I inherit from my father, I inherit from my mother a deep reluctance to judge. If I said to my mother, "I'm a junky, kleptomaniac . . . pornographer," she'd say, "Yes, dear." And so it is with me and my characters. I am very interested in where my characters stand morally. But at the same time I don't feel the urge to convert them, or punish them, because that doesn't square with how I write fiction.' In this he is the complete antithesis of his father. Kingsley was certainly not a moralist, yet he cautiously manipulated the balance between our perspectives and those of his characters. Even if the latter managed to blind themselves to the consequences of their actions or hid from anything resembling contrition he made sure that we would experience both on their behalf. His reasons for doing so were complicated but his wish to displace private unease into his writing certainly came into it. Martin, in *The Information*, is far less calculating. He does not, as he stated, attempt to 'convert' or 'judge' his characters and here he faced a dilemma because nor could he allow them absolute autonomy. He is the kind of writer to whom cold objectivity is anathema and the imprint of the physical and psychological 'pain' he experienced during the novel's composition is detectable in his characters and their spectrum of weird experiences, ranging from the surreal to the distressingly moving. The result might not have been what he intended at the beginning but despite that it is a novel of extraordinary complexity.

11

A Gallery of Traumas

The Information was the fictional preamble to *Experience*, but
while the former drew its momentum primarily from Martin's
marriage break-up, the two-year period prior to and following
the publication of the novel involved equally traumatic and less
fathomable occurrences. Consider the weekend of 8 (Friday) to
10 (Sunday) July 1994. He had picked up his sons from school
on the Friday and driven them to a village just north of Oxford
to stay as guests of Ian McEwan in the same house that had
been one of Rushdie's first refuges following the issue of the
fatwa six years earlier. That night the 'toothache' that had
troubled him persistently for the previous twelve months
returned with a vengeance. His right-side wisdom teeth, already
in a precarious state, had acquired an infection, causing his face
overnight to resemble that of someone auditioning for the part
of the elephant man. His right cheek and jaw became swollen
to the extent that his nose, lips and eye sockets were pushed into
garishly asymmetrical shapes. When he saw Isabel again on the
Tuesday she took charge and contacted a dental surgeon in

New York regarded by her family as peerless, an event that three months later was seized upon by the press as evidence of his egotistical vainglorious squandering of advances.

With regard to the Saturday, his arrangement was to take the boys back to London, but not to stay overnight in his flat. He would collect Hilly and Philip from Primrose Hill and drive them with Louis and Jacob back to Oxford where the boys were to be deposited with Antonia, who was spending the weekend with acquaintances of her first, late husband. Within twenty-four hours Martin had spent an evening with one of his oldest friends, retired to the same bedroom in which another had spent his first days in flight from any number of figures with a religious sanction to kill him, accompanied by the two individuals about whom he cared more than anyone else, but only by a narrow margin. He had also said hello and goodbye to his father and was now heading back to McEwan's house with his mother and elder brother. All of this was accompanied by an unremitting painful deformity of his cheek and jaw. It was as though sequences of his life were being lifted from the private vault of recollection and played forwards and backwards, recklessly, and by Sunday the experience would become even more troubling.

His mother and Philip had joined him so that the three of them could attend the memorial service held in Cheltenham on Sunday for his cousin, his mother's sister's daughter, Lucy Katherine Partington. Lucy Partington had been a missing person since 1972, the year Martin returned to Lemmons from Oxford. Posters carrying her photograph were displayed throughout the West Country and pleas for help by her mother and brother broadcast on national TV and radio during the subsequent twelve months, when Martin was completing the novel that would transform him from bright undergraduate to literary newcomer. He knew of these events, partly through media coverage, and on occasion via telephone exchanges with Hilly, then in Spain. But as he later confessed, he was at the time too preoccupied with his work to give much conscious attention to his cousin's disappearance. They had met on numerous occasions, as children. He did not know her as an adult and assumed she had 'disappeared' of her own volition. She was in fact one of the many victims of the mass murderer Fred West, her fate disclosed only when the police began analyses of remains in the cellar of West's Gloucester house in 1994.

Lucy Partington features in *Experience* as a figure whom Martin feels that he knows well – she has, for example, five more entries in the index than his sister Sally. He comments: 'I spent several summers with them, throughout my childhood. David was my closest confidant for many years. I spent months in their house, and went on holidays with them. David came often to Swansea and Cambridge. Much later, he came to stay with us in Uruguay.' The following passage is engrossing and goes some way to explain why Lucy played such a part in the coalescence of more tangible feelings of grief and confusion. He is at the memorial.

> Very soon it was clear to me that something extraordinary was happening. As I wept I glanced at my weeping brother and thought: how badly we need this. How very badly my body needs this, as it needs food and sleep and air. Thoughts and feelings that had been trapped for twenty years were now being released [. . .] Formulaically, perhaps, but without mysticism, I can assert that I felt bathed in her presence (and felt unrecognizably the better for it). This is where we really go when we die: into the hearts of those who remember us. And all our hearts were bursting with her.[1]

This, for many, is the most disquieting moment of *Experience*, in that there is a sense that he is intruding upon the private grief of others, and at the end, in the letter he writes to his cousin's mother, Miggy, he appears to acknowledge that some sort of explanation is due. But the impression he sometimes gives in *Experience* of being an emotional interloper is contrary to the truth. His cousins, David and Lucy, and his aunt Miggy were almost as important to him during his childhood as Kingsley and Hilly and his siblings. He tells us in his memoir of what, genuinely, he feels about their tragedy but as individuals he lends them a respectful distance. Only on a few occasions does he allow us to see how close they were. 'David was one of the requited loves of my childhood ... My brother is, of course, irreplaceable, and so is my half-brother, Jaime. But for much of my childhood I earnestly wanted David to be my brother, and he wanted it too, and the affinity is still there.' (p. 61)

There were other events he preferred to exclude from his public accounts of this period but which undoubtedly had a considerable impact upon everything else. Hitchens: 'Martin was obliged to play diplomat and choreographer, difficult with confused children, both under ten years old, and apart from the practical problems he was divided emotionally. I've no idea what he actually said to the boys, about the break-up, but what troubled him privately was the fact that *he* was the cause of this.' Isabel Fonseca: 'They [his sons] were very small. Martin and I agreed that it would be better for the boys if we didn't cohabit – give everyone time. We didn't for two years after he left.' Less than nine months after the events of 1994 something equally shocking occurred.

In May 1995 Martin returned to London after a three-week tour of the US, promoting *The Information*. Among his mail he found a letter from Patrick Seale, legal father of his daughter Delilah, whose mother had committed suicide twenty years earlier. Seale put it to Martin that since Delilah was now twenty-one, it would be best that she become acquainted with her natural father and proposed that they meet to discuss an introduction. Martin had, much earlier, told Isabel that he had a daughter little more than fifteen years younger than her. She accepted the news of their forthcoming meeting, which she would attend, with mature sensitivity. Next he told Louis and Jacob. They were spending Saturday in his flat and two days earlier rumours about the 'lost child' of the celebrity novelist – the ink was hardly dry on the most recent comments regarding his avarice and alleged resort to cosmetic surgery – had reached the *Daily Express*. The question of when it would be best to disclose to his boys that they had a much older sister was, Martin admitted, one that had troubled him only briefly. The group of journalists constantly ringing the bell of the house they had recently moved into in Regents Park Road throughout Saturday afternoon saw to that, despite his repeated suggestions through the intercom that they should 'go away'. The boys, he proudly recalls, were as guilelessly solicitous as Isabel – they sympathized with Delilah's tragic loss of her mother at such an age – and showed no reservations about getting to know the adult half-sister suddenly conjured into existence. Two days after learning of his new sibling Louis answered the doorbell and admitted Delilah to the house where Jacob was waiting. None, according to Martin, seemed to feel even the slightest sense of unease.

'That year, 1995,' recalls Martin, 'was extraordinary. While lives altered around me I seemed ... in a vacuum. Lucy and Delilah ... David. Without me there *was* no connection, except in the equally profound sense of *effect*.'

I ask again about David Partington and Isabel states, 'They spent almost every summer together in Gloucestershire. Martin was very close with Marian and David, and his aunt Miggy.'

Martin continues: 'He seemed like a kind of *rural* version of someone not unlike me. They'd lived a very rural life, in Gloucestershire, and I sometimes wondered how growing up outside the city would have changed me. Life there was innocent . . . If there is a single value that stands in your mind and your work . . . For Kingsley it was decency . . . but in me, what I value is innocence. And he [David] and his family were that.' Though cynics have accused him of appropriating another family's tragedy there is a great deal of sincerity in this disclosure, albeit artlessly deflected. I asked him what he meant by 'innocence'. 'The Bardwells [the maternal grandparents he shared with the Partingtons] were innocent. Leonard Bardwell, "Daddy B" and his wife Margery were benign eccentrics. Quite rich, but altruistic. They gave enormous amounts to charity. And I think that the Partingtons inherited more of those genes than we did. My childhood was idyllic, theirs was . . . arcadian, unsullied. Innocence can never really coexist with its opposite, experience, which was why Kingsley was so contemptuous of the Bardwells. Their enthusiasm for morris dancing, folk culture . . . all endearing, harmless, but Kingsley loathed it and got his revenge [with the Welches in *Lucky Jim*]. And innocence attracts its other opposite, guilt.' I wonder still about what he means by guilt. The obvious interpretation would be the specifics of culpability, the committing of an injustice, specifically that of West who ruined the Partingtons' arcadia. But I wonder if he also had in mind something closer to his own sense of experience, the painful burden of conscience. Referring to Kingsley's resentment towards the Bardwells, 'He was irritated in particular by Daddy B, his innocence. But more than that he was irritated by innocence in general . . . My mother inherited their innocence.' And you? 'Maybe not so much.' He admits by implication to be heir to Kingsley's rogue gene, a hybrid of experience and guilt. Louis and Jacob, Antonia, Delilah, David, the departed Lucy and Lamorna made up a fabric in which a sense of loss, if not of innocence then at least of a hoped-for idyll, was a unifying feature. Martin himself felt, with a misplaced notion of guilt, as though he had moved between them like a virus. One of the most beautiful passages in *Experience* is in the letter to his Aunt Miggy recalling the day he had visited her to talk about his treatment of the murder of Lucy in his memoir. In the end they did not mention it, and later Miggy wrote to tell him that her doubts had been replaced by feelings of peace. From the letter one senses in Martin the need for a comparable sense of release. 'The village, the lane, the circular drive with its millstone, your lawn, your ponds, your Michaelmas daisies. I recalled covering this garden in a series of desperately ardent sprints, moving from clue to clue (those were your rhymes, I think) in a hunt for Easter eggs, nearly forty years ago. The village seems sanitised now . . . Yet the place still transports me, and I am back in an unfallen world'. (p. 384) But such moments, as he knew, are transient.

Later that same year Kingsley would re-enter Martin's emotional vortex, accompanied by Eric Jacobs.

Jacobs was a talented journalist and ghost writer who had become friends with Kingsley at the Garrick in the early 1990s. They got on well, being of similar temperament and sharing opinions on such essential matters as politics and drink. No written record exists of who suggested an authorized biography but when I interviewed Jacobs for my own literary biography of Kingsley he stated that they began discussing the project, at Kingsley's instigation, soon after the publication of the latter's *Memoirs* in 1991. He also stated that from the start he felt a palpable antipathy from certain members of the family and its broader circle. 'Hilly I got on with rather well, not Ali (Kilmarnock). Martin clearly disliked me.' After Kingsley's death and the quarrel over Jacobs's deal with the *Sunday Times* to publish his private diary of meetings with Kingsley, including confidences, as a supplement to the biography, Martin did indeed feel aggrieved, though to his credit he ranked him more as misguided than contemptible. Martin's description of his dealings with Jacobs, in an appendix to *Experience*, is by equal degrees candid and tolerant yet it is also incomplete. It involves only the moment when their relationship, such as it was, effectively ended. Martin had known him, though not well, for three years prior to that. Jacobs's biography is much like Boswell's life of Johnson, with the subject if not quite dictating the book to his faithful amanuensis then certainly presiding over its shape and temper. The most obvious instance of this was Kingsley's insistence, which Jacobs did not have the tenacity to doubt let alone question, that none of his fiction is even remotely based on actual events and individuals. Kingsley also specified which of his friends and relatives Jacobs could approach for interview, and was equally implacable on those who must be excluded. Most of the Amis family, with the notable exception of Hilly, were in the latter category. As a result we are offered an account of Kingsley's life that appears unhindered by censorship – he was selectively honest to Jacobs about his infidelities before the break-up with Hilly for example – but sufficiently skewed and provocative to raise questions. When he agreed to take on Jacobs and throughout their three years of lengthy alcohol-fuelled exchanges, Kingsley had no forewarning of his own imminent death. His health was troublesome, but aside from his various stomach complaints there was no evidence that his distinctly incautious lifestyle – he was at least three stone overweight and he consumed inordinate amounts of beer, wine and, his preference, malt whisky – was doing serious damage to his heart. There is then at least circumstantial evidence that he acted as ghost writer in all but name in order to effect a promotional relaunch of Kingsley

Amis, the testily resourceful thinker, writer and seducer, very much worth reading about and, more importantly, worth reading.

Martin witnessed this with a mixture of concern and unease. The biography would tell a story he assumed he knew as well as anyone, yet he had been neither consulted nor interviewed. Moreover he was becoming aware of the fact that Jacobs had unique access to material that disclosed aspects of his father's life that he knew only sketchily, notably the correspondence between Kingsley and Larkin. The letters were part of Larkin's archive in the Bodleian Library, Oxford and had been sold to the library on condition that access would be closed until all correspondents were dead. Kingsley intervened on Jacobs's behalf, stating that while still alive he was happy for any potentially embarrassing disclosures to enter the public realm.

The biography was published barely three months before Kingsley's death and Hilly, previously happy to cooperate with Jacobs, found herself obliged to deal with yet another aspect of her ex-husband's chameleon-like personality. The affairs had been consigned to the past but she was shocked by the use of her father, mother and brothers as a cunning joke in Kingsley's letters to Larkin. The caricature of the Bardwells was the inspiration for the hideous Welch family in *Lucky Jim*, a literary curiosity which certainly did not amuse Hilly.

She did not read the biography until the parts of it involving her family were pointed out to her and by that time Kingsley was dead. Martin, however, witnessed its subsequent effect on his mother. This, plus Jacobs's decision to publish his diary so soon after the death, caused him to invoke his prerogative as executor to his father's literary estate and exclude Jacobs from any further access to manuscripts or correspondence. Jacobs paused during his exchange with me to reflect on what had happened. 'I probably should not have taken the diaries to the

Sunday Times. But I am freelance, I make money by selling what I write and my adviser in all this was Gillon Aitken [partner at the time in the same firm as Martin's new agent Andrew Wylie]. Martin was, I suppose, justified in his anger but there was another agenda. You see, Kingsley and I were part of the same set. Drinkers, generally conservative – though I far less so than him – and sceptical about the world we were asked to put up with. I think Martin resented the fact that his father had chosen one of his own as his biographer and then as the editor of his letters. But of course he made sure I was not allowed to do that – better an academic, the sort who would display clinical detachment.'

Martin had known Zachary Leader since the 1980s and it was at the Paddington Sports Club in 1996 that he raised the possibility of him replacing Jacobs as editor of his father's collected *Letters*. Leader was a respected scholar and critic whose reputation was grounded in his previous work on worthy if somewhat recondite aspects of Romanticism. The letters, as both he and Martin were rapidly discovering, would involve far more newsworthy issues. Anthony Thwaite's edition of Larkin's *Selected Letters*, followed shortly afterwards by Motion's authorized biography of the poet,[2] were still, barely three years later, causing arguments and prompting accusations among academics and members of the literary intelligentsia and the reading public. Larkin was, it turned out, far more insular and misanthropic than his official profile had indicated. Even worse, he had indulged a life-long taste for pornography which, allied with his misogynistic brand of lechery for the real thing, placed him beyond the pale in that period of post-feminist male contrition. Finally, and indefensibly, he had, in at least three letters, used the term 'Paki' and 'nigger' in reference to British-based individuals of Asian or African-Caribbean origin. The following, by Tom Paulin, typified the response to the letters: 'a distressing and in many ways revolting compilation which imperfectly reveals and conceals the sewer under the national monument Larkin became.'[3]

Martin's response to what seemed to many a literary witch-hunt appeared in the *New Yorker* in July 1993. It is not so much a defence of his father's friend as an impatient critique of what Motion had done. Thwaite to his credit had not left out any letters that were notably more controversial than those he included; as an editor he had provided a dry unprovocative commentary on places, times and people. But Motion, at least in Martin's view, had assumed the role of sanctimonious bystander, treating many of the finest poems as symptomatic of the poor man's pitiable state of mind.

In 1996 Martin and Leader were becoming increasingly aware of the other half of Larkin's story, the part involving the ebullient presence of Kingsley Amis. It was clear that Larkin's letters to Kingsley were not simply disclosures of his state of mind but one element of a partnership, that for much of their respective lives they had shared a world exclusive to the two of them.

As we have seen, the period between 1994 and 1996 involved for Martin continuous and confounding reminders of his past and his relationship with those closest to him; some like Delilah emergent and others, particularly his father, soon to depart. Leader: 'Editing the *Letters* was in itself fascinating and demanding of course, but Martin and I were in regular contact. We would arrange meetings and tennis matches at the club, sometimes he came here [to Leader's house in north-west London], less frequently I might go to his house. When he and Isabel bought their house in Primrose Hill we [he and his wife] would go to dinner. We talked about a lot of things but in the end we would be drawn towards Kingsley. I'd ask about people and events in the correspondence, which were not documented elsewhere, and Martin would sometimes rely on his memory or advise me on who to contact for details. Conversely, Martin would use the letters as landmarks for his own memories, not just of the family. Something that Kingsley had mentioned in a letter to Larkin or Conquest would serve as a trigger for recollections of seemingly unrelated moments in his own life.' This would provide much of the raw material for *Experience*.

He was divorced from Antonia in July 1996, a legal procedure demanding the presence of neither party and uncontested by both, but which earned coverage in the *Evening Standard* and the *Daily Mail*. Isabel was five months pregnant at the time and their first child, a daughter (Fernanda), would be born in November 1996. In January 1995 they had purchased, jointly, the house in Primrose Hill. The divorce had cost him a great deal, including his entire inheritance from his late father, his flat in Leamington Road Villas and almost all of his bank savings. After splitting the cost of the new house with Isabel he was broke.

When I interviewed Andy Hislop he asked me a curious, and I assumed rhetorical, question. 'Why do you think that Martin married Antonia and then left her for Isabel?' Having worked with both women at the *TLS* and known each as Martin's partners surely he would be better able to explain this. 'Yes,' he replied, 'I suppose I should. But, you see, I have at least to pretend that I and everyone else are puzzled by his choices and decisions, when in fact all who know the three are fully aware of what prompted him to act as he did. But no one actually speaks of it. They are both [Antonia and Isabel] very attractive, yet in different ways. Antonia one can imagine as a figure who would stir the attentions of a portraitist or professional photographer. Hers is the kind of presence we generally associate with art – appropriate enough given her preoccupation with aesthetics – and I don't wish to give the wrong

331

impression of her because she is an amusing, energetic person, but, well, she exhibits an abundance of rationalism. I'm sure others have said the same but she was strikingly different from any of the rather brash impulsive women Martin seemed to prefer during the seventies. In practical terms this suited him perfectly, because he hated having to deal with *jobs*. Everything from the electricity bill to the school fees for Jacob and Louis were Antonia's province.

'Well, Martin certainly did not fall out of love with her. More that he grew up, by which I mean that he became aware, more aware, of the kind of individual he is. I think the contrast between them contributed to that. You know, often he does not conceive of a novel at all. He might simply begin with writing no more than a paragraph, prompted by an enduring question or an image. It could turn into a short story or 500 pages later a book like *The Information*. He is an enormously careful, inventive writer but he hates making plans that might inhibit what could be seen as the natural evolution of the story. And that really is an extrapolation of his personality. There is the old cliché that opposites attract and maybe that was the case with Mart and Antonia. Perhaps the contrast in their personalities could have been dealt with if he had not met Isabel.

'Isabel, as I've said, is more or less the equal of Antonia in terms of their attractiveness but in other respects they could not be more different. Isabel exudes sexuality. You could marvel at Antonia's grace but Isabel encourages in others an openness and spontaneity. Why? Because she is a weird combination, clever but completely uninhibited and transparent. Martin was always caught between his anxieties and the public image of the literary celebrity. Antonia enabled him to sideline this tension but Isabel caused him to release and face it. When he met Isabel he simultaneously gave in to irrational impulse and found himself, if that makes sense.'

Hislop's account is perceptive. At the same time his remarks on Martin's assignment of the practicalities of life to Antonia, echoed by other friends, would benefit from some clarification. While Antonia may have written the cheques, Martin paid all school fees before and, after the break-up, underwrote the building costs for the fifth floor added to the house. Following the divorce settlement he maintained generous child support and later still funded his sons through university.

The circumstances which prompted him to buy his private workplace in Leamington Road Villas in the 1980s were almost identical to the ones of his first years with Isabel; Antonia had just given birth to their first child and the house in which they all lived as a family was, he found, unsuitable to his other vocation as a writer. Now, however, he, Isabel and Fernanda existed in a house of roughly the same proportions and age as Chesterton Road but where he felt able to work, according to his strict daily routine, in an attic converted to a study. It was not that Fernanda, followed two-and-a-half years later by Clio, was less noisy or demanding than his sons or that Isabel was in some way less ubiquitous than Antonia – in fact quite the opposite – but he had suddenly found a means of reconciling two aspects of his life that had previously demanded separation.

The first full-length novel to emerge from this new regime was a heroic failure, but no less intriguing for that. *Night Train* (1997) is Martin's only attempt at what is known condescendingly as 'genre' fiction, in this case the crime novel. Genre fiction is perceived by its nature as inferior to mainstream literature. It relies more upon formulae and undisguised escapism than upon pure aesthetic principle, at least in the view of the literary establishment. Nevertheless, many mainstream novelists like to test their versatility against such enterprises. Kingsley in *The Riverside Villas Murder* (1973) fashioned a gripping murder mystery from personal recollections of 1930s suburbia, and

Julian Barnes during his early career as a fiction writer adopted the nom de plume Dan Kavanagh whose creation, the bisexual private eye Duffy, endured for four profitable novels.

Martin's downmarket excursion began, like many of his full-length pieces, as a short story and he completed it with uncommon speed in just over twelve months. Its flaws, however, derive from the fact that it matured rapidly, ad lib, alongside his early drafts for *Experience* in 1995. Martin's favourite crime novelist, indeed the only one he has ever rated as a serious writer, is Elmore Leonard (and it is no coincidence that he did a lengthy review of Leonard's *Riding the Rap* for the *New York Times* in May 1995). Leonard has a talent for superbly authentic dialogue which is also the engine for his stories. His narrators often appear superfluous, with each character becoming a convincing embodiment of their words and the novel's uniquely American context. Only in the US can a novel draw upon such a combination of idiomatic languor and menace. Martin's creation, the police detective Mike Hoolihan, is an honourable though unsatisfactory attempt to borrow from and refashion Leonard's technique. The idea of a woman cop who not only carries a male first name but also sounds like a man when she speaks and narrates her novel was doomed from the start. It bore an uncomfortable resemblance to the contritionally correct strategies ridiculed in *The Information*, and derided by Martin in essays on maleness and masculinity. I asked him why, when this was self-evidently a blind alley, he had persevered with the novel about Mike. 'She was I think the least *connected* person I had ever invented.'

Mike Hoolihan is involved almost exclusively with the inexplicable suicide of the scientist Jennifer Rockwell, a woman of supreme intelligence with no obvious reason for killing herself. Rockwell's counterparts in Martin's life were numerous and included the mother of Delilah, Lamorna Seale. Already in

Other People he had made use of fiction as a means of exploring her mindset. Now, however, the act of suicide seemed to have followed him into his private, contemplative zone where the present blended with the past. Amschel Rothschild presided over the house party in Holland Park where almost twenty years earlier Martin met Angela Gorgas. Gorgas had been part of the dreamily privileged Rothschild set, and she and Martin would spend long weekends at Amschel's family estate in Suffolk. The estate was large, included enough game birds and stags for the licensing of both shotguns and rifles, and Martin at another party in 1996, this time in Primrose Hill, quizzed Amschel on the technicalities of firearms as part of his research for *Night Train*. Three months later Amschel hanged himself in a Paris hotel room, having displayed no previous signs of depression or distress. Amschel at the party was, according to Martin, as energized and animated as the figure he remembered from the 1970s and this curious blend of time travel and termination reminded him of another equally horrible, inexplicable event from those years. His affair with Claire Tomalin did not affect his continued and platonic friendship with her daughter Susannah, whose suicide, again by hanging, caused him especial distress. Anthony Howard remembers him at the funeral 'weeping uncontrollably'.

Paradoxically he began to see parallels between what he called his 'personal trinity' of suicides and the death of Lucy Partington. The discovery of her body provided something of a solution to the terrible twenty-year-long sense of anxiety that followed her disappearance, but beyond the fact that she was murdered her death was still enveloped by questions, some grotesque but unavoidable – how? when? – and others broaching such issues as the nature of Fred West. Martin, like the rest of the country, awaited the trial of West with impatience and anxiety. At some point West would have to confront his condition as a human being, someone who shared essentially the same characteristics as the rest of us. If this apparently rational, albeit abhorrent, individual was capable of such unmotivated brutality, what did such acts say about humanity per se? The question was never addressed because West killed himself in prison while on remand, awaiting trial. I ask Martin now, what did he feel? Relief? Even frustration? 'I suppose contempt would be the most accurate description of my feelings. Not because he had denied us an explanation for the death of Lucy and others, more for the way he took his life. He was calculating and ingenious, gradually secreting threads and cotton tapes from the work room which he bound together with otherwise insubstantial strips of fabric from his bedding and mattress. He even planned the date with care, a bank holiday when cell monitoring was at a minimum, and he made certain that the laundry basket he kicked away was the one object in his cell – unlike the chair or table – that made no sound as it overturned.' There is a bizarre and stark contrast between his self-inflicted demise and the horrors he visited upon his victims. His motive for committing suicide was self-interest – he wanted to spare himself the consequences of his crimes – but the question of why he killed so many others remained unanswered.

Mike Hoolihan has to deal with only one suicide, but the ferment of potential solutions prompted by the death of Jennifer Rockwell mirrors Martin's own confrontation with events united by an enduring feature: they were incomprehensible. He admits now that this feeling of mystification, of being unable to move forward to a point of coherence in his perceptions of the world or back to a memory of stability or solace, is what caused him to abandon chronology as the structural principle for *Experience*. As a consequence the memoir reads rather like Proust without the boredom, a jagged momentous tour of the most amusing and troubling episodes of Martin's life. It is assembled apparently at random but, looked at more closely, a symphonic arrangement surfaces in which hilarity is always waiting to assuage despair, and loss is ever in pursuit of elation. Just to ensure that we do not suspect him of grandiloquence the shifts in tone are persistently accompanied by vast, digressive footnotes, often more intimate or engrossing than the main text and, appropriately, more transient.

Experience works beautifully because of its refusal to impose shape upon events variously terrible, nebulous or intimately profound; it is one of the best literary autobiographies ever produced. *Night Train*, which grew out of the same nexus of trauma and loss, fails for the same reason. 'I was', recalls Martin, 'working in a house again, for the first time in more than a decade. I had a study upstairs and the experience of being so close to my place of work emphasized the curious transformative undertaking of *being* Mike Hoolihan. I would shave, have coffee and I was at the same time preparing myself for an exchange that was about to take place. I had to become a woman, start thinking and sounding like a woman, who was a police [Hoolihan refuses to use a gendered noun to describe her job], plus a recovering alcoholic.' But this territory had already been explored before, in Paris in the late 1970s, with the assistance of his then fiancée Angela Gorgas. Why was he doing it again? 'Hoolihan was my least affiliated character. I wanted a novel with no author-surrogate, but at the same time I was frequently moved by her plight, which is why the ending felt so terrible. She writes the last paragraph *drunk*.'

David Papineau recalls that when he was writing the book Martin became inordinately preoccupied with 'overarching explanations for cause and existence, everything from Chaos Theory to the clash between inherent significance and moral relativism', and Chris Mitas fixes upon a particular evening when their excursion from a snooker club to a bar and restaurant was attended by an exchange, prompted by Martin, on the limits or otherwise of the known universe. 'He seemed to have done a great deal of reading.' On what? 'Everything . . . Were we on our own . . . in the universe? It was a question that bothered him. This was his bad period . . . everything, including the death of his father, came so soon after the break-up of his marriage.'

The death of Kingsley features prominently in the index to *Experience* yet Martin says little about how he felt. He tells of how he phoned Saul Bellow and simply told him that his father was dead, and of how soon after his death Kingsley appeared to him in a dream – silent, benign, seemingly content – and he returns compulsively, movingly, to events in the hospital that seem like a terribly slow countdown to Kingsley's last moments. But the recollection that stays most poignantly in the mind is: 'I hated it, in the Phoenix Ward, when he turned away from me – when he turned away.'[4] The words are vividly resonant for me too because much later in 2010, three months after the death of his mother, he used almost the same phrase, 'she turned away'. And he spoke for the first time about his state of mind during the weeks and months after Kingsley's death. 'I felt a sense of . . . release' and he goes on to insist that this had nothing to do with palliation or ease. 'I couldn't stop writing, obsessively. The opposite of my usual routine. I couldn't stop.' He does not comment on the quality of his output, simply that he and it would not stop. *Night Train* preserves that directionless compulsion and its quality as a novel suffers proportionately.

By the time *Night Train* was published, Martin seemed again to have reached a plateau of stability. He and Isabel were married in June 1998 and Clio would be born on 10 June 1999. The marriage ceremony took place in Westminster Register Office, with Christopher Hitchens and his and Isabel's close friend, the writer Kate Bucknell, as witnesses. 'Then', says Hitchens, 'we went to a Greek restaurant in Primrose Hill, to be joined by at least a dozen others.' Martin knew that the gossip-hungry tabloids – especially the middle-brow papers such as the *Daily Mail* and the *Evening Standard* – employed researchers to monitor the posting of civil marriage banns so even if hacks or cameramen were despatched all that could be recorded was the confirmation of what was already known; Martin and Isabel were married in the presence of his oldest friend, with no other celebrity guests. The event would hardly be worth reporting, reasoned Martin, and he was almost correct. The *Mail on Sunday*, in desperation, asked at the registrar's reception for the standard price of a ceremony and triumphantly compared the assumed £87 spent on the wedding with the half-million-pound advance of three years earlier.

In August *Heavy Water* was published, dedicated to Delilah and Fernanda. It is a curious collection, with three of the nine short stories dating from the 1970s, one from 1981, and the rest written in the tumultuous years between 1992 and 1997. One might view the selection sympathetically as a reflection of Martin's ongoing preoccupation with his life history, or an honest invitation to compare the wary apprentice – one piece, 'Denton's Death', was written shortly after *The Rachel Papers* – with the literary elder statesman. Some reviewers, however, took a more cynical view, as indicated by the title of Elspeth Barker's piece in the *Independent* of 27 September, 'Barrel. Bottom. Scraping. Innit?' In her opinion this 'dismal volume' displayed a contempt for the intelligence of the reader, being simply an assembly of anything previously unpublished in a single volume, irrespective of its quality. There is evidence to substantiate Barker's accusation, given that one wonders why none of the material which predates *Einstein's Monsters* was at the time deemed worthy of inclusion in it. 'Denton's Death' was first published in 1976 in *Encounter*. The editor was Anthony Thwaite, whom Martin had known well since Oxford. When the story arrived, did Thwaite suspect that Martin was invoking the unacknowledged but ever present culture of favouritism that had guaranteed the publication of his first novel? 'Oh certainly, of course.' Did it affect his decision to publish? 'Yes and no. It was not a substandard piece but at the same time it carried an air of overwrought ambition, the sort of thing produced by a brilliant recent graduate still relying upon the protection of grand exemplars.' In this case the old master is probably Kafka, with extra flourishes of nihilism and horror. We do not learn anything of Denton beyond his being subjected to a prolonged overture to his death by three unnamed persons and a machine.

The title story 'Heavy Water' is appended with an interesting and rather misleading note, '*New Statesman*, 1978; rewritten 1997'. Martin did indeed do a story for the *New Statesman* in 1978 very similar to the one which appears in the 1998 collection, but he fails to mention that both draw upon a third, non-fictional piece, an account of his own experience on the cruise ship Oriana. He had been commissioned by the *Sunday Telegraph* to do an account of the new fashion for cruise holidays. Cruises had hitherto been enjoyed mainly by mature or retired members of the middle classes, but like various parts of the Mediterranean they were of late becoming affordable to the proletariat. This was Martin's dispensation from the *Telegraph*, a newspaper with a solidly bourgeois-class Tory readership: tease out the incongruities between a pursuit designed for educated, tasteful customers and the activities of these counter-jumping newcomers. In the article 'Action at Sea'[5] he offers a characteristically dry account of how individuals who for most of the year spend their leisure time in working men's clubs or in front of the TV adapt themselves to the delights of the Mediterranean. The short story appeared less than a month earlier in the *New Statesman* (22 and 29 December 1978). Obviously there are differences, with the fictionalized version involving a woman called 'Mother', her mentally retarded son John and an odious heavy-drinking trades union leader taking time off from his work on behalf of the oppressed. His name 'Mr Brine' carries a dissonant echo of the Labour Party cabinet minister George Brown, an authentic member of the proletariat more notable for his drunken performances in the House of Commons than for his ideological zeal. Brine is of course the Home Counties, high-Tory pronunciation of Brown and by that measure we might also catch a fleeting reference to another working-class hero who seemed to have disowned his past, John Braine the novelist, whom Martin interviewed and presented, contemptuously, for the *New Statesman* in 1975.

One can see why Martin rewrote it eighteen years later. In the interim Britain had been transformed completely by Thatcherite consumerism. The economic benefits and debits of the period are still open to question but what is beyond dispute is the fact that Mrs Thatcher, albeit without premeditation, transformed the public image of the Labour Party. Tony Blair's New Labour, which took power the year Martin revised the story, unshackled itself from the nomenclature of Socialist principles, especially the embarrassing collateral notions of class distinction and conflict. Thatcher's governments did severe damage to areas which relied on coal and steel as their principal employers but they also alienated the standard voter from such prescriptive classifications as 'working-class'. As a consequence the new version of the story plays down the loud vulgarity of Mr Brine, or at least his seaside-postcard chubby, cloth-capped dimension, and focuses more upon the tragic relationship between Mother and John. The original would have seemed to the reader during that first year of the Blairite new dawn as at best a dated, improvident curiosity. But this is my assessment. Martin is more succinct: 'I rewrote it. It wasn't good enough. That's all.'

For a story which could be expected to strike a more sympathetic chord, especially among those who had become accustomed to perceive Thatcherism and John Major's shambolic coda as a baleful inheritance, go to 'State of England' and be introduced to Big Mal and Fat Lol. They, along with their various girlfriends, wives and sons, Jet and Clint, could easily be close relatives of John Self and Keith Talent, except that John and Keith are never allowed to move too far beyond their creator's caustic domain. True, they are monstrous but our potential for disgust or opprobrium is smothered by admiration for the craftsmanship that has made them quite so compelling. Mal and Lol, however, acquire an unprecedented degree of autonomy. The narrator never fully retires from the scene and their yobbishness is often lent a certain laughable dignity by Martin's wry asides. But never before had Martin allowed his more horrible creations such command of the stage. The reason for this is that he did not so much invent as encounter them. It was as though his track-suited gargoyles of the 1980s had foreshadowed with commendable accuracy a very real change in the social fabric.

'I was', states David Papineau, 'with Martin when "State of England" began in effect to write itself. We were at the sports day. You see, our children went to the same school in Hampstead, and parents were invited to attend and indeed participate in an afternoon of races, football matches and other games.'

The story begins with Big Mal standing 'on the running track in his crinkly linen suit, with a cigarette in one mitt and a mobile phone in the other'. (p. 35) His wife Sheilagh, 'She', is fifty yards away on the clubhouse steps also holding a cigarette and mobile. They are talking earnestly, to each other, and continue their exchange via their mobiles despite having moved close enough for an ordinary conversation. Martin executes this beautifully, with a collateral joke involving 'She's' weary enquiry about the wound on the side of Mal's face, acquired she assumes during the previous night's drunken 'rucking' session with Fat Lol; eventually she is almost able to touch it. One could imagine how well this might have worked on film, the sketch carrying a rueful subtext regarding the ongoing, circa 1991, obsession with electronic gadgetry, particularly among the uncultured, moneyed classes: astute, amusing but a little implausible.

'That's the point,' adds Papineau. 'That part of the story actually happened. We watched it. Well, the man didn't have a wound and we couldn't hear what they were talking about, but this absurd performance with mobiles – and in those days they were the size of bricks – happened in front of us. It was an excellent school and the place had come with flawless recommendations, official and informal. It was I suppose a sign of the times that old-fashioned notions of class and status had been sidelined by competitive meritocracy. A fair number of the parents were rather like Big Mal. The school paid no attention to their background, what they did for a living or the fact that they might have broad East End or North London accents. So long as their children were intelligent and well motivated and the fees could be met, that was all that mattered.'

Jet's school, St Anthony's, was a smart one, or at least an expensive one. Mal it was who somehow met the startling fees. And showed up on days like today, as you had to do. He also wanted and expected his boy to perform well.

During his earliest visits to the parent–teacher

interface, Mal had been largely speechless with peer-group hypochondrias: he kept thinking there was something terribly wrong with him. He wanted out of that peer group and into a different peer group with weaker opposition. Mal made She do the talking . . . (p. 38)

The one other part based on fact and observation occurs at the conclusion of the dads' race. 'Martin actually saw that,' recalls Papineau. 'Many of the fathers looked a little out of sorts, the Mal types.' Mal, in a heroic attempt to impress Jet, propels his lumpy graceless body towards the finishing line. His performance is hindered also by the wounds sustained the night before, their cause disclosed in the penultimate section. Mal and Lol had been out attending to one of their many enterprises, in this case clamping the cars in a National Car Park.

Big Mal heard it first . . . A concentrated body of purposeful human conversation was moving towards them, the sopranos and contraltos of the women, the sterling trebles and barrelly baritones of the men, coming up round the corner now, like a ballroom, like civilization, uniforms of tuxedo and then streaks and plumes of turquoise, emerald, taffeta, dimity. [They turn out to be opera-goers]

'Lol mate,' said Mal.

Fat Lol was a couple of cars further in, doing a Range Rover and tightly swearing to himself.

'Lol!'

You know what it was like? A revolution in reverse – that's what it was like. Two bum-crack cowboys scragged and cudgelled by the quality. Jesus: strung up by the upper classes. (p. 69)

This part, of course, is pure invention but it is difficult to discern from the story where exactly Martin's sympathies lie. He imparts to Mal and his fellow low-lifes an endearing energy, in a fastidious Dickensian manner. These figures are acceptable company only as bizarre exaggerations, not as they really are. 'Well that's true,' concedes Papineau. 'Martin – we – knew the Mals only superficially. They provided him [Martin] with superb source material but the rest was speculation. The part involving Asian babes, with Mal's mistress, became a running joke. He would amuse us by speculating on the lives they led beyond the sports days and parents' evenings.' Mal's particular Asian babe is Linzi, whose real name is Shinsala, who has adopted an East End accent far more impenetrable than Sheilagh's 'with the one little exoticism, in the way she handled her pronouns. Linzi said *he* where an English person would say *him* or *his*.' This is particularly distressing for Mal, given that 'she' crops up so frequently in conversations with Linzi, 'like "the way she wears she skirts". Or "I hate she". It sometimes gave Mal a fright because he thought she was talking about She. Sheilagh'. (p. 42)

Martin's fellow parents certainly appeared symptomatic of social transition and mutation, but questions must be asked about what he chose to do with these promptings. Mal, Lol, She, Jet are endearing, vividly realized presences, but they tell us as much about the 'State of England' in the early 1990s as Wodehouse's characters do of the 1920s and 1930s.

'What Happened to Me on My Holiday' treads an extremely fine line between elegiac candour and disingenuousness. It is narrated by Louis Amis, and Martin's re-creation of the mindset of his eleven-year-old son is flawlessly convincing, as is the impression that he is telling his own story in an American accent. Its subject is indicated by the bracketed dedication beneath the title, '(for Elias Fawcett, 1978–1996)'. Elias

Fawcett was the young son of Natalia Jimenez and Edmund Fawcett, political writer and journalist. The Fawcetts were close friends of Antonia and Martin and although six years older than Louis, Elias was a regular visitor to the house, his promise as a rock guitarist engaging the attention of the Amis boys. In August 1996 he overdosed on a heroin-based drug following a concert and never regained consciousness.

The story is far more meticulously autobiographical than anything that would be found in *Experience*. Martin and Isabel did not have a permanent residence in the US. Sometimes, during summer visits, they would stay in the guest house at Isabel's mother's property in East Hampton. 'But,' adds Martin, 'there wasn't always room for us. We rented a couple of houses over the years.' The events recorded by Louis did occur during one of these years, when they rented a house barely half a mile from Isabel's mother's.

Louis's cousin Pablo ('Bablo') is Isabel's elder sister's son.

Clearly Bablo does nad yed underzdand whad death is.
Bud who does?
Death was muj on my mind in the zummer – muj on my mind. Begaz of Eliaz. Eliaz died, in London Down. And zo death has been muj on my mind.
My dad zed thad early in the zummer Eliaz game round do his vlad. He game round do big ub a jagged – bud the jagged was in my dad's gar, and the gar was elzewhere, having ids baddery vigsed, edzedera, edzedera. Dybigal Eliaz – jazing a jagged agrazz down. Zo he hung around vor the whole avdernoon, blaying the binball machine and, of gorze, the elegdrig guidar. And my dad zed thad his memory of him was really vresh: his memory of Eliaz, or Vabian, whij was his nigname, remained really vresh. Isabel also ran indo him during

the early zummer, in a doob drain, on the Zendral Line,
under London and ids zdreeds. Dybigal Eliaz, with all his
bags and bundles, his jaggeds nad hads, gayadig, vezdive,
brezzed vor dime I- and zdill darrying vor a halve-hour
jad. Zo the memory is vresh. And my memory is vresh.
Bud is id zo vresh zimbly begaz Eliaz was zo young – zo
vresh himzelve? (pp. 227–8)

The random and seemingly insignificant incidents – Elias calling
at Martin's flat to collect a jacket ('jagged'), staying over to play
pinball and his guitar, and chatting with Isabel on the Central
Line tube – are authentic, as was Martin's brief intimation of a
ghostly presence in his room. (He assured me that he had not
made this up.) Not all readers of the story would be alert to
every aspect of Martin's well-publicized life during the previous
five years, yet it is difficult to imagine that any would be
completely ignorant of it. It is thus puzzling that Martin's
author-substitute, his son, should open his account by giving so
much attention to how he and 'Jagob', 'zbend the early bard of
the zummer in Gabe Gad, with my mum, and the lader bard in
Eazd Hambdo, with my dad'. (p. 223) They tell how 'Ungle
Desmond', Antonia's brother-in-law, drives them to meet
Martin in New York and after 'lunj' they travel with their father
on a 'big goach' – innocently praising its 'zbadlighds to read by
and a lavadory in the bag' – to 'my dad's rended house in the
woods. Nothing fanzy: in vagd, id good have been in Og-
lahoma, with a big ub drug in the driveway, an old gar zeed on
the barj, and the neighbours alays guarrelling'. (p. 223)

The re-creation in an appropriately guileless manner of an
eleven-year-old's perception of death is a considerable achievement but one that begs a question. Was it intended as a
memorial to a young man barely six years older than the
narrator, or is a more intricate intention detectable? The

absence of any unease or rancour in Louis regarding Martin's twin affiliation to 'Mum' and 'Isabel' is notable, as is the general mood of an idyllic equilibrium between the young narrator's account of his period in Wellfleet, the Phillipses' house, and the weeks with Isabel and her family. Indeed, one begins to wonder about the amount of detail which Louis brings to his description of the grimly ordinary rented property.

The attention to authenticity is extraordinary – given that only Martin and two or three others could attest to the accuracy of such minutiae – and one suspects that Martin is seeking out the consolations of intimate fact as a contrast to emotional turmoil because, according to Hitchens, Martin's son did not become entirely comfortable with his relationship with Isabel until their mid- to late teens, sometime after the summer in which the story is set. In this respect it can be seen as a rehearsal for *Experience*, a book that would involve the same blend of confessional transparency and discretion. Martin: 'I felt [with *Experience*] the burden of chronology immediately but the idea of typing out "I was born on August 25, 1949" made me feel bored almost beyond description. I knew straight away that I would have to do it thematically. In a sense it was similar to writing a novel, except, of course, that you're constrained by the truth.' He also states that among the competing impulses behind the book's genesis was the overriding 'pro bono obligation. I am the writer son of a writer father. No one else is or ever has been. I wanted to say what that was like.'

During the period when Martin was preparing *Experience* the most enduring influence upon the tempo of the book was his encounter with Kingsley's letters, regular batches of which were supplied to him by Leader between 1996 and 2000. Much has been written on how Kingsley altered during the fifty years between his going up to Oxford and sclerotic old age. But dip into his letters at random and one has the unnerving impression that each might have been written within months of the others, despite an actual separation of perhaps three or four decades. Outlooks change, of course, but it is as though we are sampling variations upon a theme: the love affair between the man and his language endures and never fails to fascinate. Martin, in *Experience*, achieves a remarkably similar effect. Each chapter opens, perhaps with a piece of dialogue, or an event, a relationship, a conundrum – often one touched upon tangentially elsewhere in the book – and like some creature released from captivity it is allowed to chase through another ten to twenty pages, sometimes disappearing from sight, leaving behind engrossing digressions, and then take us forward again without reaching a specific destination. An impression remains, but never a conclusion and so we carry a feeling of fascinated irresolution into the next chapter, waiting for something of what first intrigued us to resurface.

Martin was taking a lesson from his father in an art that seemed to him and most of his generation redundant in the late twentieth century, the mischievous and demanding skills of letter writing. He knew that the more controversial aspects of his life had already fallen prey to the scandal-hungry media and he could, of course, have answered the charges and insinuations with verifiable facts, but to do so would have involved a form of surrender. He would have been playing the media at their own game, supplying them with what they had previously been denied, and even though the truth was far more mundane than they hoped, it would amount to a victory of sorts; he had bowed to their incessant pressure to disclose. Instead, he replaced grubby detail with elegantly deflected emotion. Hunt through the book and you will find that most of Martin's evocative moments, be they pensive, tragic or climactic, will correspond to a report in the press coverage of his life during the previous thirty years. He tells us often no more than we already know, but he intercuts this with an equally convincing sense of uncertainty: it is not that he is trying to hide facts, more that he is telling the truth about his own confused private responses to them. When you read his father's letters you will be convinced that you know Kingsley Amis, and then you rationalize your empathy: you never knew him but the smoke and mirrors effect of the writing lulls you into the delusion that you did. And so it is with *Experience*.

In 1996, shortly after Kingsley's memorial service, Hilly and the Amis children – Martin, Philip and Sally – put his Primrose Hill house on the market, sold it in 1997 and bought a flat in Mornington Crescent where the Kilmarnocks lived for a few years before moving back to Spain. Philip, with his new wife, followed them a year later but these acknowledgements of Kingsley's passing were belied by the behaviour of Sally. She kept a flat in Kentish Town, five minutes' walk from where her father and the Kilmarnocks had lived and little more than fifteen minutes north of Martin's studio flat in Notting Hill. It became her shrine to her late father, the walls covered in memorabilia advertising talks and book launches, shelves bulging with editions of his works. Kingsley had never been the perfect father but she had always treated the open invitations to dinner and overnight stays in Primrose Hill as a redoubt against her otherwise chaotic personal life. Now, all that had disappeared. Martin would welcome her to his house when he and the family were in London, and he visited her when he could. She died in November 2000, four months after the publication of *Experience*.

Hitchens: 'Sally could be unintentionally hilarious. She was guileless, innocent, but that was the tragedy. She grew up in a world of unlicensed misbehaviour but, unlike us, she couldn't protect herself from collateral damage.' And she is recreated, with tender consideration, as Violet in *The Pregnant Widow*.

12

Novelist and Commentator

The reasons for their decision to move to Uruguay were numerous and varied and, as Isabel states, 'had nothing to do with the media or book reviews' as some newspaper columnists would later allege. 'It was just the fact that we realized soon our girls would be too old to be out of "proper" school. I always wanted them to learn Spanish – which they did. Martin agreed. He loved the place.'

Every year around two months would be spent in New York or East Hampton, and Isabel would fly over to see her mother in the city four times a year on average. 'My mother's place in East Hampton, which she bought from my grandfather's estate, is a series of [converted] farm outbuildings. The main house, which was my grandparents', was left by them to The Nature Conservancy. It [her mother's place] is very unfancy, an old slate barn converted for summer use. Not for winter.' Uruguay would enable them to have a place of their own outside London and, being in the southern hemisphere, offer an escape from British and US winters. Isabel is, on her father's side, half

Uruguayan but had visited the country only twice, on both occasions when she was still in her teens. Her relatives had suffered greatly during the military dictatorship with several of her cousins imprisoned, one for eleven years.

In the weeks after Sally's death Martin and Isabel checked flights to Montevideo from Heathrow. 'In 2000', Martin recalls, 'we went there [Uruguay] for three weeks over the Christmas holidays, summertime in the the southern hemisphere. We didn't want to be in a hot city, Montevideo, and heard about José Ignacio, not then the slightest bit *chic*, from a cousin of Isabel's who runs a restaurant in the village.' Isabel continues: 'We rented a small house there and the following Christmas we rented the same house. But instead of three weeks we stayed three months, January to March. We decided it would be nice to skip the London winter and get the girls to start learning Spanish. Martin wrote much of *Koba* in the ramshackle garage of that house.

'At the end of that year we bought a plot of land in the village. I have eighteen first cousins in Uruguay. Rodolfo, one of these, is an architect and he oversaw the project, though I designed the house myself. Martin wanted it but was not involved in the house at all.' Rodolfo's expertise and experience proved invaluable when Isabel was dealing with the strict Uruguyan planning regulations. The house would be brick and stucco with large windows facing to the sea and exposed beams made from giant, ancient salvaged timbers from the old dockyards of Montevideo.

It was, they agreed, perfect in the sense that the region had a magnificent quietness and beauty about it. Isabel: 'Very flat, large Atlantic waves. Something like Long Island might have been a century earlier.' In Maldonado, a forty-minute drive away, there was a nursery and infant school which Clio and Fernanda would attend.

Alongside this Martin went twice a year to Ronda, usually staying for four to five days. He, Isabel and the girls took rooms at a hotel in the town and spent their days with his mother and Ali Kilmarnock in the Casa almost eight miles away in what was left of the wilderness of Andalusia. The ramshackle farmhouse was barely big enough for the Kilmarnocks themselves, but according to Martin his mother seemed more contented during that period than at any time since his childhood. From when she had worked at an animal sanctuary, before she first met Kingsley, Hilly had nurtured an affection for animals as part of her household. What the Casa lacked in space and facilities as a building was amply compensated for by five acres of land, complete with a few olive and fruit trees. Goats, sheep and chickens roamed the stone-walled campos, while a couple of affable mongrels and an ever-expanding tribe of cats slouched about the house. Clio and Fernanda were particularly enamoured of their grandmother's carefree existence among the treasured non-humans – only the eggs were ever eaten – and Martin began to feel that *Experience* was less an act of completion than an opening to a new tempo of sensations. He did not become overly elated or exultant; quite the opposite. He had gone through a similar stage with *Einstein's Monsters*, published when his boys were roughly the same age as Fernanda and Clio. 'I believed in it [nuclear disarmament], and I still do irrespective of 1989 [the disintegration of the Soviet bloc] and I concede that my ideas were . . . impassioned.' His later work on politics would also involve passion, but passion informed by a measured scrutiny of our recent history as a species.

Koba the Dread (2002) was set in train by *Experience* and matured during the two years in which London changed status from Martin's adult base to a precarious staging post for elsewhere. When Martin had pored over the copies of his father's letters one aspect of his reintroduction to Kingsley had registered, but he had not thought it worthy of more than cursory mention in his own memoir: politics. Jacobs and Kingsley himself had been transparent and outspoken about his rightward drift during the 1960s. The weekly meetings at Bertorelli's of similarly disposed writers and journalists – notably Robert Conquest, John Braine, Tibor Szamuely, Bernard Levin and Anthony Powell – were the stuff of legend and to an extent self-caricature. There was no 'dialectic', since all of those present were convinced of and agreed on their beliefs – good food, drink and conviviality topped the agenda. Martin had observed this as a wry spectator, occasionally playing a stand-in role as the voice of leftish youth, which neither he, nor his father nor the likes of Conquest took too seriously. Almost three decades later, however, he began to wonder if the mood of frivolity had blinded him to something much more significant. He admits that in 1968 just before going up to Oxford he had treated Robert Conquest's recently published *The Great Terror* with a mixture of respect and indifference. 'I read a page or two. I knew its thesis and its context from the controversy it stirred up but at that time its effect upon me was slight.' What brought the book to mind once more was a trip he made in 1995 to Poland. He refers to this in a brief postscript to *Experience* without mentioning the effect of his visit to Auschwitz. He describes being obliged to confront something that should not have been conceived and executed by sentient, rational human beings, and of how as a fellow member of this species he feels 'a sense of *lousiness*, like an infestation'. (p. 370) He takes it for granted that any other person would experience if not an identical sensation then at least a comparable blend of outrage and self-disgust. But just as important was what struck him soon afterwards: that while there was a collective feeling of revulsion at what the Nazis had done, the fact that Stalin's reign of terror had claimed more lives than Hitler's was treated more as a historical statistic than a shame upon humanity. It was not so much what Conquest's book disclosed that horrified him, but his remembrance of how it had been received in 1968. Few, even among the most resolute leftists, disputed its accuracy as a historical document but equally no one seemed willing to fully accept the moral repercussions of these facts. He considered a morbid hypothesis: what if, say, Martin Gilbert's magisterial *The Holocaust* had in the mid-1960s been the first thorough documentation of how the Nazis had planned and almost succeeded in implementing the complete extermination of European Jewry? The scenario was bizarre but not entirely implausible. True, the defeat of Nazi Germany meant that its vast programmatized crime had been disclosed to the world within a few years of 1945. Much of what actually went on behind the Iron Curtain and before that during Stalin's most profligate period of mass murder was still a state secret, but vast numbers of defectors and escapees had testified to the horrors of an authoritarian regime. Martin's friends and colleagues at the *New Statesman* during the 1970s had not regarded the Soviet Union as a workers' paradise but it was for them a flawed yet heroic prototype for their ideal. He respected Hitchens as his most ruthlessly intelligent peer, and he was, and would remain, his closest friend. To what extent, wondered Martin, had he deliberately blinded himself to what the regimes of Eastern Europe had done?

In October 1999 Martin and Isabel accompanied Robert and Liddie Conquest to a public debate in Conway Hall, Red Lion Square. Its subject – as Martin later put it 'very boring indeed' – was Britain's membership of the European Union. The attraction lay in the principal participants themselves: Christopher Hitchens (pro-membership) versus his brother Peter (anti-). The former had since the 1970s reformed his inflexible

Trotskyist stance – reality, in the virtual disappearance of Communism from the world stage in 1989, had contributed to that – but the Hitchens brothers remained at opposing ends of the political spectrum, Peter contributing articles to the *Daily Mail* that made Thatcherism seem spinelessly irresolute by comparison. Despite their differences they were well matched as ferocious rhetoricians and entertainment was guaranteed. What lingered in Martin's memory of the event, however, was an apparently innocuous aside from Christopher who reminisced about the building as one in which he had spent numerous evenings debating the future of humanity with 'my old comrades'. His well-rehearsed self-deprecating manner – the joke being that such idealists, like their opinions, were now a trifle antique, even redundant – raised a laugh; even Conquest joined in. Martin offers his reflections on the event as a coda to *Koba the Dread* and wonders,

> If Christopher had referred to his many evenings with many 'an old blackshirt', the audience would have . . . Well, with such an affiliation in his past Christopher would not be Christopher – or anyone else of the slightest distinction whatsoever. (p. 256)

The intellectual and political establishment is able to indulge Communists, practising and retired, for various reasons – there was the war, of course, in which the suicidal heroism of ordinary Soviet troops inflicted the first and decisive blows upon Nazi Germany. In this regard affiliation involved a degree of exculpation-by-gratitude. Just as significant was the perception of Communists and radical Socialists as essentially humane and unselfish individuals, even when the pragmatics of their vision involved a fair amount of catastrophic self-delusion. Combined, these two allowances served to protect Stalin, even after the extent of his murderous authoritarianism became known, from the same demonic status as Hitler. In *Koba* Martin successfully, and for many discomfortingly, dismantles this gradation of evil.

He conducted far more research for the book than he had previously undertaken for any project, reading almost eighty volumes covering everything from the memoirs of ex-political prisoners to studies in pre- and post-Glasnost Soviet history. One night in 2001 after he had spent the best part of a week pursuing further evidence on the horrors perpetrated in five prisons mentioned in Solzhenitsyn's *Gulag Archipelago* he experienced a horrifying, shameful moment of self-revelation. He had followed Solzhenitsyn's darkly comic prompt to construct an accurate league table for the most notorious prisons in central, non-Siberian, Russia: the Butyrki, the Lubyanka, the Lefortovo, Sukhanovka and the Taganka. The process of evaluation was pared down to the most imaginative and effective methods of torture and subjection employed in each and the consequent level of terror that their name struck in prisoners awaiting news of their first custodial destination. This might have seemed a rather ghoulish endeavour but Martin was attempting to immerse himself in what Solzhenitsyn and others had described as a mythology of terror, the condemned fearing the future in much the same way that the fallen would contemplate the various horrors offered by the circles of hell. One night – he thinks it was a Friday – he felt that Butyrki had emerged as the most horrible of the five. On the one hand it was run with brisk efficiency and carried the elitist badge as the detention centre for the most distinguished intellectuals. Equally, it seemed designed specifically to break the spirit of such figures.

As part of his divorce settlement Martin had sold his flat in 1997, but as with Chesterton Road he had found it difficult to work full-time in Primrose Hill, especially after the birth of Clio. Fortunately the new house came with a one-room self-contained studio physically separated from the main building, but little more than five yards from the door to the basement kitchen. He was here, poring over accounts of Butyrki and comparable places, when from across the small garden began a screaming of the hopeless, endless, wall-penetrating kind practised particularly well by infants. It was Clio. Next morning she had acquired a nickname, 'Butyrki'. At the moment the wailing began Martin was imagining how hundreds of prisoners had dealt with one of the most effective methods of suppression, indeed murder, employed at Butyrki; the gradual, calculatedly gradual, crowding of cells each day with more and more inmates so that those who were already there knew, and communicated to newcomers, that they were in effect being crushed to death. Martin was sure that some must have screamed, but it would not have been a scream prompted by the immediate infliction of pain; no, it would be a release of despair following a lengthy period of contemplation and dreadful resignation. A scream from nowhere; and his daughter reminded him of this. Her cries fractured the rumblings of a North London night; she became Butyrki and within days he became ashamed of what he had done.

> Nearly always, when I use it, I imagine a wall-eyed skinhead in a German high-rise (and I'm sure such a person exists) with a daughter called Treblinka. Treblinka was one of the five ad hoc death camps, with no other function (unlike Auschwitz). I am not as bad as the wall-eyed skinhead. But the Butyrki was a place of inexpressible distress. In 1937 it held 30,000 prisoners crushed together. And it isn't right. Because my daughter's name is Clio: muse of history. (pp. 260–1)

Although he makes only a nuanced reference to this moment in an appendix to *Koba* it was in truth the book's driving force. It laid open an implicit almost conspiratorial consensus on the Western world's view of itself and the horrible century just closed: Stalinism was evil but not as evil as Hitler's Nazism. In the frivolous meshing of his daughter's crying with the name of a prison, he had connived in it. The implicit question, pursued ruthlessly through the book is, why has this happened? Eventually he reaches something of a conclusion: in their work many political theorists and historians, while certainly not apologists for Stalin, provide a rationale for moral relativism. Ian Kershaw and Moshe Lewin in *Stalinism and Nazism: Dictatorships in Comparison*[1] contend that while the Holocaust 'is the only example which history offers to date of a deliberate policy aimed at the physical destruction of every member of an ethnic group, under Stalin no ethnic group was singled out for annihilation'. Martin concedes that this is true but only partially. Lenin and Stalin had indeed not been obsessed with a single ethnic group but they had practised an egalitarian form of genocide, targeting geographical and nationalist centres, such as Georgia and the Cossacks, which they deemed a potential threat to the political predominance of the Party. Indeed, had Stalin lived a year longer, his own well-planned anti-Semitic pogrom would have been well under way. Martin concludes: 'the distinction may be that Nazi terror strove for precision, while Stalinist terror was deliberately random. Everyone was terrorized, all the way up: everyone except Stalin'. (p. 85)

There was also, contends Martin, a long tradition of intellectual snobbishness which, without exculpating Stalin – he had clearly presided over a disaster – at least set him apart from the uncouth ideology of Hitler. Marx, drawing upon Kant and a magnificent tradition of philosophic insurrection going back to the Enlightenment, was undeniably a great thinker, while Fascism was state-sanctioned mob rule, cultivating the base prejudices of the ill-educated with its programmes of racial purity through eugenics. Here, Martin again quotes Solzhenitsyn, who contended that both Communism and Fascism were forms of ideological enforcement. The former might have appeared more just and righteous than the latter but neither allowed for dissent; the individual was denied the opportunity to opt out of what others deemed an improvement upon his condition.

This, he knew, would be his most contentious work yet, not because it would divide critics – he was used to that – but through its more private register for those who had remained his friends since the 1970s, particularly Christopher Hitchens. 'I remember,' says Hitchens, 'we were at a Huntington Library Symposium, "British Comic Writing Since the War" I think it was called. Anyway, Martin altered the flamboyant mood and confided in those who wished to know that he was embarking on a completely new project, disclosing the truth about the Soviet Union and its evils. I confess that my heart sank. Not because we were likely to disagree on the matter; no, because I suspected he would make a hash of it. Up until then Martin wouldn't have known the difference between Bukharin and Bakunin.

'But he did that thing. You could always tell the symptoms. He became absorbed, completely, exclusively. About a year later I went with him from London to the Hay-on-Wye event. We were very well served; someone had sent a car for us. During the whole three-hour journey along the M4 he sat there completely absorbed in memoirs of survivors of the gulags. He hardly spoke. Believe me, this was not Martin being rude. I'd known him for thirty years and we were content with each other's mannerisms. There was nothing particularly odd about it, except that he seemed even more compulsively absorbed than he had been with any previous project.

'I admired his commitment but you have to remember why he needed to dedicate himself in this way. He was trying, in little more than a year, to absorb accounts, material, that he had previously treated mostly with indifference. He was entering a contest with historians and political theorists who had spent thirty to forty years dealing with this. His determination was commendable but, to put it bluntly, he would always be behind, an amateur. I don't think he did enough work. In fact it was impossible for him to do enough work.' In Hitchens's view Martin's polemic is undermined by his unfamiliarity with the topic, despite his Herculean efforts. 'Yes, I feel he prejudged the project. His reading was thorough but not impartial in that he was looking for material to buttress his prejudices.' Again and again Martin compares the levels of murderous brutality practised by the Nazis and Stalin's Communist Party and finds them equally abominable and irredeemable. And then he examines how each is graded implicitly and routinely within the post-war cultural fabric of the West, detecting indulgences for Stalinism in everything from acceptable jokes to the enlightened ideologies of the left-wing intelligentsia. His conclusions, or more accurately his findings, are that the latter cultivate and promote an intellectually respectable apologia for mass murder.

Martin gives sceptical attention to the image of Trotsky as the, relatively, blameless hero of the post-war left, the romantic dissenter, keeping the purist flame of the revolution alight until he was assassinated by Stalin's thugs. This, too, he argues is part of the ghastly myth, that until his flight from the Soviet Union Trotsky was as politically inflexible and dismissive of human life as Stalin, though far less competent in his pursuit of ultimate power.

Trotsky was a murdering bastard and a fucking liar. And he did it with gusto. He was a nun-killer – they all were [. . .] 'We must rid ourselves once and for all', said Trotsky, 'of the Quaker-Papist babble about the sanctity of human life' [. . .] Trotsky's *other* theory of permanent revolution (we should call it Permrev) consisted of the vain hope for a series of revolutions in foreign lands, the process concluding with global socialism. Some prominent comrade further remarked that only then, when Communism ruled the earth, would the *really* warm work of class struggle be ready to begin [. . .] And I instantly pictured a scorpion stinging itself to death.[2]

This is a supplement to points made more laboriously in the body of the book. It is in an open letter at the conclusion, open but entitled 'Letter to a Friend' and addressed with wry premeditation to 'Comrade Hitchens!'

The two of them had discussed the nature and direction of Martin's book on several occasions during 2000–01, both over dinner when Hitchens was in London and in their regular transatlantic phone calls. Perhaps Hitchens had not quite grasped the extent and vigour of Martin's argument because Martin's letter is by no means an apology, more a reminder that their friendship would not cause him to pull his punches. After Hitchens received his review copy he sounded, says Martin, 'slightly hurt and perplexed, as though I had turned something I didn't properly understand into a personal accusation'.

The address to Comrade Hitchens was in truth prompted not by Hitchens himself but by a letter written to Martin on his behalf and without his prompting or knowledge by James Fenton, who was also well-informed of the nature of the book before its publication. Hitchens learned of it only later from Martin. 'What you have to realize', states Hitchens, 'is that

James is an extremely *moral* person, perhaps it is in his genes, son of the cloth and so on. Anything surreptitious or dishonest he cannot stand and that was how he perceived Martin's presentation of me in particular, and the left-wing activists of the 1970s as a whole. He certainly did not dispute Martin's right to disagree with, even deride, our beliefs and outlook, but he saw Martin's portrayal of us as individuals as a betrayal of friendship, malicious misrepresentation disguised as patrician artistic licence. I have never seen the letter but I know that it upset Martin, very, very much, even more than his well-published quarrel with Julian [Barnes]. My fall-out with Martin was short-lived but he and James did not speak for quite a while.'

In his review[3] Hitchens cites works and sources that raise questions about Martin's thesis, but far more effective is his implicit and persistent querying of his suitability as a political writer. It is unlikely that most readers would be familiar with all the works referred to either in Martin's book or the review, but the latter leaves us with a single overarching impression. As Hitchens puts it at one point: 'Amis [is] exhibiting a tendency to flail.' That is, the combination of rhetoric and intuition that serves him so well as a novelist is a poor substitute for a thorough grounding in twentieth-century political history.

The other letter at the end of *Koba the Dread* is 'to my father's Ghost', in which Martin is far more candid than at any point in *Experience*, stating for the first time that they saw in each other versions of themselves: 'If our birth dates had been transposed, then I might have written your novels and you might have written mine. Remember the rule (truer in our case than in most): you are your dad and your dad is you'. (p. 272) He qualifies this by pointing out that Kingsley had in his twenties courted Communism. 'You were ideological and I am not.' There were, he concedes, excuses for his father's dalliance with authoritarianism – middle-class guilt or more fervently a desire to enrage his parents and many of his peers. In the end, at least as Martin sees it, Kingsley exchanged pro-Communism for anti-Communism as a creed while he, Martin, has remained constitutionally immune from it for all his adult life. A sceptic might treat this as Martin air-brushing out feckless indifference in favour of something more honourable and considered, but earlier in the book he does at least present his father as one of the few who thirty years earlier resisted the predominantly leftist consensus on recent history. 'Even in 1975 [when Martin became full-time literary editor of the *New Statesman*] it was considered tasteless or mean-spirited to be too hard on the Soviet Union. No one wanted to be seen as a "red-baiter" – or no one except my father.' (p. 47) Martin might not have been a 'red-baiter' but during that period he recoiled from the enthusiasms of his two Trotskyist friends, Hitchens and Fenton. 'It was', points out Hitchens, 'passages such as that which distressed James. Martin was buying a position of moral superiority from a history of [his] narcissistic apathy.'

Martin is indeed rewriting his past, but he is doing so while casting respectful glances towards a man whose views he had previously indulged as eccentricities. Hitchens in the closing paragraph of his article presents the 'old Kingsley ... as he declined into a sort of choleric, empurpled Blimpishness, culminating in his denunciation of Nelson Mandela as a practitioner of Red Terror. The lessons here ought to have been plain: Be very choosy about what kind of anti-communist you are, and be careful not to confuse the state of the world with that of your family ...'

Colin Howard and Sargy Mann testify that during the period when Kingsley held court at Lemmons, 'the *New Statesman* crowd treated him with a mixture of affection and respect. There was a good deal of role-playing on both sides, they amused each other with exaggerated caricatures, foam-flecked lefties versus the embattled Tory. It was largely a game' (Colin Howard). Hitchens, in his anger at Martin, seems to have conveniently forgotten this aspect of Kingsley's 'Blimpishness'. The Old Devil would no doubt have been greatly amused.

By a bizarre coincidence *Koba* was sent to its publishers, Cape, the week after two hijacked passenger planes destroyed the Twin Towers of the World Trade Center, on 11 September 2001. For the subsequent five years Martin rarely left that curious hinterland between creative writing and serious journalism which Hitchens had urged him to vacate. His first article on the massacre 'The Second Plane' appeared exactly a week afterwards in the *Guardian*. Like most others he had witnessed it on television but his article has a personal slant. Isabel's sister had just taken her children to school and was on Fifth Avenue when the 'glistening underbelly' of a Boeing 767 passed seemingly 'only yards' above her head before smashing into the first tower. In this piece Martin reaches no particular conclusions – it appears composed in a state of shock – aside from the assumption that the planners and perpetrators were beyond the realm of civilized conjecture in terms of their state of mind and motivation. But the opening sentence is memorable: 'It was the advent of the second plane, sharking in low over the Statue of Liberty: that was the defining moment.' Connoisseurs of his work might have been reminded of the first sentence of *Money*:

As my cab pulled off FDR Drive, somewhere in the early Hundreds, a low-slung Tomahawk full of black guys came sharking out of lane and sloped in fast right across our bows. We banked, and hit a deep welt or grapple-ridge in the road: to the sound of a rifle-shot the cab roof ducked down and smacked me on the core of my head.

The transgressive idiom he and John Self had invented in 1980 as a threat to the reader's sense of normality now seems to have become his comfort zone, somewhere to which he can retreat from a world horribly threatened and unsettled.

A lengthy, measured assessment of what 9/11 meant appeared more than six months later, again in the *Guardian*, in an article entitled 'The Voice of the Lonely Crowd'. Trenchantly, he accepts the role in which the sneering Hitchens cast him, as the literary writer viewing the world through the prism of his technique and vocation, and begins by claiming that students of literature have over the past forty years been systematically misled. The Leavisites, still in the ascendancy when he was at Oxford, treated literature as moral palliative for the decay of religion; provided, of course, that one read books that were suitably energizing, such as the novels of D. H. Lawrence. More recently, and at the other end of the spectrum, matters such as evaluative judgement had been sidelined in favour of a model of 'culture' as all-inclusive and immune from such divisive concepts as merit. This, he concedes, might seem rather tangential to the matter of a terrorist atrocity witnessed live by millions, but his point is that the politically correct 'dumbing-down' of literary criticism is symptomatic of a pernicious state of atrophy among Western intellectuals (see also Foreword to *TWAC*). Everyone, it seems, agreed that this was an atrocious act but few if any were willing to examine the system of beliefs that had prompted it. Suitably galvanized, he takes up the challenge.

> The champions of militant Islam are, of course, misogynists, woman haters; they are also misologists – haters of reason. Their armed doctrine is little more than a chaotic penal code underscored by impotent dreams of genocide. And like all religions, it is a massive agglutination of

stock response, of clichés, of inherited and unexamined formulations.[4]

The article is significant in its own right but it also triggered a series of murmurs which within the subsequent five years would become a crescendo of accusations, issuing mainly from the constituency of middle to leftist writers and journalists who had previously treated Martin as an acceptably capricious fellow traveller. The first response came from John Pilger – begun one assumes as soon as he read Martin's *Guardian* article and published in the *New Statesman* exactly a week later. Pilger invokes, as a contrast to Martin's embodiment of an angry Western writer, the Palestinian poet Mahmoud Darwish:

I love life
On earth, among the pines and fig trees
But I can't reach it, so I took aim
With the last thing that belonged to me

This 'last thing' is his body; the lines are spoken by a putative suicide bomber. Without explicitly stating that the oppression of the Palestinians was, justifiably, the cause of 9/11 Pilger makes use of Darwish's poem as a subtext for his list of injustices and acts of mass murder visited upon the people of Gaza and Afghanistan by the alliance of the US – aka George Bush – and Israel.[5]

Martin's political essays of 2001–7 are reprinted in *The Second Plane* (2008) and in each he ratchets up his conviction expressed in 'The Voice of the Lonely Crowd' that religious extremism – particularly but not exclusively Islamism – should be treated as an inflexible ideology, comparable with Nazism and Communism. He was, he knew, challenging the mantras of the intelligentsia, particularly those fuelled by post-colonial guilt. Not since Orwell has a literary writer made his presence felt so forcefully in the adjacent realms of politics, history and serious journalism, and Orwell was in truth a political writer by instinct and novelist by default. To properly appreciate Martin's sense of commitment we should look at aspects of his life, pre-9/11, which after that found greater coherence and momentum.

Martin's long-term relationship with Judaism can best be described as cordial and distracted. He reflects, 'As long as I can recall having had opinions about anything I have been a philo-Semite. It goes back to the year before Oxford, 1967, when I was doing A-levels, in London, which I would largely fail. My first real girlfriend was Jewish. I refer to her in *Experience* as the model for Rachel, but her real name was Cynthia. She lost her virginity to me and two weeks later she was donating blood for the wounded from the Six Day War. I remember her mother's house in Golders Green. Her grandmother offered me Maxwell House kosher blend. The coffee was indeed kosher; I've never come across it since.' It was the evening at the Bellows' house in 1988 which crystallized his sense of affiliation. It receives more attention in *Experience* than any other event yet Martin is curiously evasive about the true cause of the dispute between his closest friend and his adopted literary father. 'It began', he tells me, 'with Edward Said, whom Hitchens idolized and of course, soon, the real subject surfaced, all of us knew it would, Israel.' Bellow and Hitchens were almost indistinguishable in their perception of Judaism more as a legacy than a faith or ideology. 'This', Martin explains, 'was a matter for intellectual discernment and reason, but it was only, what, a year earlier, that Hitchens had discovered he was Jewish. Christopher was determined that ethnicity should play no part in his commitment to the pure secularism of political discourse. As I put it in *Experience* he would not "think with his blood".' This phrase, which resonates through *Experience*, recalls a moment from his teenage relationship with Cynthia. 'In a sense. To be crude, she gave me her blood and almost immediately afterwards she gave it for Israel.'

Hitchens's recollection of the evening, the day, differs significantly from Martin's account to me and the version in *Experience*. On the latter, 'Martin is quite brilliantly misleading. Nothing he states is wrong, but he remoulds the events superbly. A testament to his immense skill as a novelist. My so-called "cerebral stampede", the image of me "compacting the little gold box of Benson and Hedges" as my peroration reaches its crescendo and finally my apologia "Edward is a friend of mine. And if I hadn't defended him – I would have felt bad." Followed by Bellow's "How do you feel *now*?" Well, he did not make up the dialogue, but let's say he selected parts of it that suited his version from a much broader fabric. There was a great deal he left out that would provide a more truthful portrait of what occurred. For example, after we'd finished dinner and moved to a coffee table there was, in front of us, a copy of *Commentary* magazine, carrying the headline "Said, the Professor of Terror". It sat there like the revolver in the Chekhov play. I hadn't met Bellow before but from reputation, and from immediate evidence, he was not the sort who regarded an argument as a personal slight. We knew Edward Said – with whom later by the way I lost patience – would have to be talked about and talk we did, energetically. Martin's presentation of himself as embarrassed moderator trying to hold me in check is nonsense. Well, it is a version of the truth. He was appalled that his hero and his friend came from different camps on the Middle East but the image he presents of a night ruined by my inflexible belligerence is actually a picture of his own sense of unease, panic. He was out of his depth so he dramatises an exchange that was conducted in a civilised manner. Those final two lines, when he gives Bellow the punchline "How do you feel *now*?",

a form of moral victory against an ideological bully, me . . .
Wonderfully contrived, but a lie. Both lines were spoken, but
convivially, self-mockingly. We'd *stopped* arguing. For some
reason Janis [Bellow's wife] always spoke ill of me after that,
but I didn't like her. Bellow himself was amused, not offended.
Next day, when we got back to Wellfleet, to Antonia's place,
she was there and Martin must have bottled it up on the journey
because he tore into me. Antonia seemed stunned. It was our
worst argument.'

Bellow's own account of the evening appeared in a 1989
letter to Cynthia Ozick. It is worth quoting at length not least
because of Bellow's shrewd and coolly detached reading of the
events, especially his remark, 'Hitchens appeals to Amis. This
is a temptation I understand.' Despite the mood of weariness in
Bellow's description he and Hitchens later went on to become
friends.

And now, as a preface to business, I have something to
relate to you: My young friend Martin Amis, whom I
love and admire, came to see me last week. He was
brought here from Cape Cod by a chum whom I had
never met, not even heard of. They stayed overnight.
When we sat down to dinner the friend identified himself
as a journalist and a regular contributor to the *Nation*. I
last looked into the *Nation* when Gore Vidal wrote his
piece about the disloyalty of Jews to the USA and their
blood-preference for Israel. During the long years of our
acquaintance, a dune of salt has grown up to season the
preposterous things Gore says. He has a score to settle
with the USA. Anywhere else, he might have been both a
homosexual *and* a patrician. Here he had to mix with
rough trade and also with Negros and Jews; democracy
has made it impossible to be a gentleman invert and wit.

Also the very source of his grief has made him famous and rich. But never mind Gore, we can skip him. Let's go on to our dinner guest, Martin's companion. His name is Christopher Hitchens. During dinner he mentioned that he was a great friend of Edward Said. Leon Wieseltier and Noam Chomsky were also great buddies of his. At the mention of Said's name, Janis grumbled. I doubt that this was unexpected, for Hitchens almost certainly thinks of me as a terrible reactionary – the Jewish Right. Brought up to respect and to reject politeness at the same time, the guest wrestled briefly and silently with the *louche* journalist and finally [the latter] spoke up. He said that Said was a great friend and that he must apologize for differing with Janis but loyalty to a friend demanded that he set the record straight. Everybody remained polite. For Amis's sake I didn't want a scene. Fortunately (or not) I had within reach several excerpts from Said's *Critical Inquiry* piece, which I offered in evidence. Jews were (more or less) Nazis. But of course, said Hitchens, it was well known that [Yitzhak] Shamir had approached Hitler during the war to make deals. I objected that Shamir was Shamir, he wasn't the Jews. Besides I didn't trust the evidence. The argument seesawed. Amis took the Said selections to read for himself. He could find nothing to say at the moment but next morning he tried to bring the matter up, and to avoid further embarrassment I said it had all been much ado about nothing. Hitchens appeals to Amis. This is a temptation I understand. But the sort of people you like to write about aren't always fit company, especially at the dinner table.

Well, these Hitchenses are just Fourth-Estate playboys thriving on agitation, and Jews are so easy to agitate. Sometimes (if only I knew enough to do it right!) I think

371

I'd like to write about the fate of the Jews in the decline of the West – or the long crisis of the West, if decline doesn't suit you. The movement to assimilate coincided with the arrival of nihilism. This nihilism reached its climax with Hitler. The Jewish answer to the Holocaust was the creation of a state. After the camps came politics and these politics are nihilistic. Your Hitchenses, the political press in its silliest dishevelled left-wing form, are (if nihilism has a hierarchy) the gnomes. Gnomes don't have to know anything, they are imperious, they appear when your fairy-tale heroine is in big trouble, offer a deal and come to collect her baby later. If you can bear to get to know them you learn about these *Nation*-type gnomes that they drink, drug, lie, cheat, chase, seduce, gossip, libel, borrow money, never pay child support, etc. They're the bohemians who made Marx foam with rage in *The Eighteenth Brumaire*. Well, that's nihilism for you, one of its very minor branches, anyway. Yet to vast numbers of people they are very attractive somehow. That's because those vast numbers are the rank and file of nihilism, and they want to hear from Hitchens and Said, etc., and consume falsehoods as they do fast food. And it's so easy to make trouble for the Jews. Nothing easier. The networks love it, the big papers let it be made, there's a receptive university population for which Arafat is Good and Israel is Bad, even genocidal.[6]

Irrespective of Bellow's comments on Judaism, it would be difficult to find a shrewder account than this of the political affiliations and private alliances that grew out of the 1970s, particularly at the *New Statesman*.

Martin has always eschewed beliefs and abstractions of all kinds but Judaism, because of its paradoxes, its often infuriating refusal to conform to an easy classification, invites his admiration, even his empathy. 'Fernanda and Clio are Jewish, but like their mother [Isabel] what they are entails no acquiescence to doctrine.' Judaism in its manifest diversity provides him with a counterpoint to a fundamentalist creed, Islam, that outdoes even Communism and Nazism in its suffocation of reason. Between 2002 and 2007 Martin produced twelve lengthy articles in which his preoccupation with Islam incessantly breaks the surface despite the nominal concerns of these pieces. In October 2006 for example he was commissioned by the *Sunday Times* to cover the Poker World Series. Vegas in 2006 provides an abundance of raw material for his well-tuned caricaturist's antennae, from main players with names that could have come from his fiction (Chris Moneymaker and Joe Hachem for starters) through strip clubs, lap-dance parlours, all-nude cocktail bars, twenty-four-hour hotel room hard-core porn and endlessly available prostitution. He has been here before many times and to his credit Martin invigorates the familiar with a refreshed tempo of fascination and disgust. But there is something else too, as ubiquitous as the prostitution yet brought with him by the author. 'The Taliban ... stamped out sports and used the stadiums for public floggings and executions. The Taliban would have warm work to do in Las Vegas.'[7] The Western world even at its most inexcusably dissolute is preferable to governance by inflexible doctrine. Clive James: 'Martin is the finest literary critic of his generation and literary criticism is the most testing of all combative forms. It demands, equally, intuition, evaluative logic and a stylistic elegance that matches its subject. Normally, these qualities would be incompatible and to practise each with ease and make them cooperate is the sign of a master. Martin can do this but in his maturity [with *The Second Plane*] he brought it also to his political writing. He does not expect ideas to connect as an all-embracing world view and nor does he attempt to force them into abstract presuppositions. He *thinks* with the mind of a poet, but not recklessly or self-indulgently.' We are talking of a now notorious passage in his essay 'Terror and Boredom: The Dependent Mind' where he describes how, checking in for the flight from Montevideo to New York, his six-year-old daughter Clio is subjected to a methodical search with close attention given to the contents of her rucksack including story tape, crayon and fluffy duck. He confesses: 'I wanted to say something like, "Even Islamists have not yet started to blow up their own families on aeroplanes. So please desist until they do. Oh yeah: and stick, for now, to young men who look like they're from the Middle East".'[8] James: 'If that had been part of a novel Martin would have been spared the ire of the sanctimonious left. I believe that the barriers between fiction and non-fiction, literature and everything else inhibit the expressive potential of language, basically free speech. Martin transcends these distinctions. This is pure realism, he is giving expression to what virtually all of us felt at the time, but not without comment. Soon afterwards he goes on to make the point that in *repressing* our feelings, according to the ordinances of political correctness if you like, we have subjected ourselves to a regime of "boredom" similar to that of the Caliphate in which enjoyment – art, games, sex – is forbidden.' In Britain he would not face the full backlash until after 2006, but in the interim he would endure the most pitiless and malevolent sequence of reviews of his career so far, prompted by the novel he began while completing *Koba*.

In *Yellow Dog* (Cape, 2003) Martin appears also to have been drawn towards a collective fascination with provoking readers' credulity while holding their attention. The book involves several interlinked stories. Principally, we spend time with Xan Meo (who despite his name is a white Anglo-Saxon;

Xan is short for Alexander), a middle-ranking actor turned over-ambitious writer whose gangland background revisits him, literally, with a duffing-up in a Camden Town bar. As a consequence Xan sheds his liberal new-mannish persona and regresses to what we are caused to suspect is his genuine state, combining misogyny, aggressive lust and disturbing thoughts about what he might like to do with his four-year-old daughter.

Next we encounter Clint Smoker, repulsive flatulent columnist of the *Morning Lark*, a downmarket version – if such could be envisaged – of the *Daily Sport*. Clint is humiliatingly poorly endowed and conducts a virtual relationship with a quiescent woman on the Internet. Alongside Clint we come upon the memorable presence of Henry IX, monarch of this crackpot kingdom who bears a close resemblance to the Prince of Wales with shades of Wodehousian absurdity and *Private Eye*-style satirical hyperbole thrown in. Simultaneously we learn that flight CigAir 101 from London to Houston is, probably, about to go into a nosedive due to the weird machinations of its most unusual passenger Royce Traynor, who happens to be dead and coffined in the airliner's hold. Also it is likely that an apocalypse-sized comet will fly by close to the earth. In case one is not already too distracted by the menu of narrative oddities so far, Martin then takes us, for no obvious reason, on a tour of the California pornography industry.

Of the reviews in the mainstream press on both sides of the Atlantic more than 60 per cent found the work irredeemable and among those who praised it one detects a hint of sentimental indulgence, as if they too know that Martin has done something dreadful but cannot bring themselves to condemn him for it. The detractors seem united in their unease with the book's resolute contempt for continuity, its parts seemingly being drawn from four separate novellas and dumped ad hoc in the same volume.

A dud piece of work so militantly chaotic, sprawling, and garbled that I had to read it one and a half times in order to fathom what in the name of Crikey was going on. And even now I am not sure . . . Overwritten overcrowded and underpowered . . .[9]

Given that we have reached a point, idly referred to as the postmodern, where coherence is almost *de trop*, one might have thought such excesses would be excusable, even celebrated, but what really exercised the patience of the disparagers was that this monument to the avant-garde was built upon an apparent preoccupation with filth.

It reads [not] as a fully fashioned novel but as a bunch of unsavoury outtakes from an abandoned project: nasty bits and pieces best left on the cutting room floor.[10]

Much . . . of the novel reads as if it was cobbled together from the sort of dirty jokes you might find on an internet porn site.[11]

Big ideas intrude on what might have been a collage of poisonous cameos sustained by nothing but their own weird energy . . . Amis's intellectualism . . . sticks out like a parson at an orgy and shrinks and shrivels whatever it goes near.[12]

It isn't even abnormally bad. It isn't special; it's just kind of crummy.[13]

For thirty years Martin Amis has been pointing out that pornography is boring, and now . . . he has conclusively demonstrated the truth of that proposition.[14]

[A] dispiriting performance . . . The novel reads like a midlife crisis, a writer's equivalent of buying a sportscar and running off with a woman half his age.[15]

376

It reads like the work of a less talented, less funny Martin Amis imitator . . . Redundancy and embarrassment win, hands down.[16]

Its plot randomly lurches and heaves like a person suffering from seasickness . . . the satire [is] feeble . . . It's a very flawed book.[17]

You get the picture. The book is not flawless or unimprovable – nothing is – yet it is none the less ambitious and original. The revilers and those who reluctantly indulged it were united in one respect: none could locate a precedent for what he had done. Hence we find an overwhelming majority who mask their own sense of insecurity with unreserved condemnation. It is certainly the case that the links between the four strands of the novel are tenuous at best but it cannot be denied that the predominant presence, the figure who forms an alliance with the narrator in the classic third-person manner, is Xan Meo. Irrespective of the fact that the particulars of the book are variously implausible and repulsive in their nature and appear randomly discontinuous we are aware of a controlling presence; we know that the portrait of Clint the irredeemable grotesque comes from the same hand as the moment when Xan and his daughter see a fox on the roof of a garden shed and share the experience of its 'entreating frown with its depths of anxiety'. The effect is comparable to viewing, in sequence, a set of paintings each with a different synoptic content and mood by an artist whose technique is inextinguishably unique. Xan's closest literary relative is Humbert Humbert, but Nabokov's creation is made almost acceptable by the fact that we listen only to him; his creepily delicious prose style seems to both testify to his foulness and protect him from the world of decent ordinary people. But Xan is far more infectious, leaving an imprint on everyone else

377

in the novel, from the most repulsive to the innocent. And he reaches out via his narrator, to us. One detects the Nabokovian legacy in Martin's essay of ten years before. 'Haven't we been conditioned to feel that *Lolita* is *sui generis*, a black sheep ... that Nabokov himself somehow got "carried away"?'[18] How prescient he was, given that this is exactly what many of the reviewers said of *Yellow Dog*. Xan is, so the opening chapter wryly informs us, a 'Renaissance Man', an actor for whom celebrity means the crossing of borders between popular and high culture. We are introduced to him as he leaves the family home in North London. The cartography is rather skewed but each junction, road and building unpicks a memory from Martin's recent life. Xan 'passed the garden flat, opposite, which he now seldom used. Were there any secrets there? he wondered. An old letter, maybe; an old photograph, vestiges of vanished women ...' (pp. 5–6) This flat is very much like Martin's, now exchanged for a studio in the backyard of his house. Did he, I ask him, sometimes pass it, and experience that inevitable sprinkling of recollections, fragments of an irretrievable past, that cling to a place where we have spent so much time? 'Inevitably.' After the flat he comes to a crossroads. 'If he turned right he would be heading for pram-torn Primrose Hill – itself pramlike, stately, Vicwardian, arching itself upwards in a posture of mild indignation'. (p. 6) Primrose Hill, Kingsley's final retreat following his own turn right and where he would drift from a state of antiquated grandiloquence to his pitiable, almost childlike condition in those last days. Xan has time to check out the high street bookshop where his debut collection of short stories *Lucozade* is still piled invitingly under the notice, 'Our Staff Recommends'. Martin has now inured himself to the repetitive, reflexive media presentations of him as a playboy who writes novels in his spare time. 'Curiously,' he observes, 'it is always one-way traffic. Martin Amis the Mick

Jagger of contemporary fiction. Why isn't Mick Jagger ever referred to as the Martin Amis of contemporary rock?' He is joking, to an extent. In *Yellow Dog* Xan Meo achieves just such a reversal, becoming a respected *littérateur* while maintaining his customary status as a media-generated image, a face that people will recognize from newspapers irrespective of their knowledge of what he actually does: 'He was a conspicuous man, and knew it, and liked it, on the whole [. . .] His face held a glow to it – a talented glow, certainly, but what kind of talent? [. . .] he was famous, and therefore in himself there was something specious and inflammatory, something bigged-up'. (p. 8) Martin himself, when walking around the familiar parts of north Kensington, Notting Hill, Portobello, Regent's Park, the area of London where he had lived since the 1970s, felt similarly 'conspicuous'.

Xan is walking northward, a long way still from Notting Hill, but were he to continue he might, like Martin, mistake silhouettes of strangers for people he knew intimately. 'Up ahead he picked out a figure that reminded him, or reminded his body, of his first wife – his first wife as she was ten years ago'. (p. 9) Xan's destination is a bar, called Hollywood, an establishment which has attempted with negligible success to exchange its origins as a rough-house pub situated on the Regent's Canal near Camden Lock for Beverly Hills-style ambience. It exists, standing close to the canal bridge that separates the upmarket Regent's Park area from the less salubrious Camden Town. It is significant that 'Hollywood' should be the site for Xan's encounter with the nastiest element of a subculture his creator had long cultivated as a mainstay of his fiction. The spokesman for the three hard cases who send him to hospital is Mal Bale, last come upon in 'State of England', Martin's caricature of the dodgy types whose children attended the same school as Louis and Jacob. This is an act of contrition and prurient masochism. From it emerges a version of Xan whose conditioned resources – predominantly rationalism and self-control – begin to give way, following his head injury, to far more visceral inclinations, instincts that few would allow themselves even to privately contemplate, let alone indulge. No character like him had previously appeared in fiction. Humbert is virtuous by comparison.

Paedophilia, even as an inclination, has been written about openly only since the 1980s, but not in fiction. To have a principal character, whom we are otherwise invited to treat with amusement, fascination, even sympathy, confide in us his sexual attraction to his infant daughter was a very dangerous strategy; some reviewers saw it as condonement. But despite those who might suspect Martin of having dispensed with a sense of proportion or, even worse, flagged up autobiographical signals, his method was ruthlessly single-minded. He had dealt in his writings with several embodiments of vileness, notably Unverborden of *Time's Arrow* and more recently the Islamist suicide bomber in *The Second Plane*, but now he was bringing the hypothesis home, almost literally to a household and a family that mirrored his own.

The other prompter was Kingsley. 'During the last few weeks of his life my father slipped in and out of focus as the man I had known since my childhood. In those last weeks he lost control.'

Yellow Dog is about losing control but as a work of art it is as cleverly orchestrated as anything Martin has produced. Had Xan and his world been its exclusive focus – as was Humbert's for *Lolita* – the charges of its myopic reviewers would be justified, but the rest of the book, the weird assembly of Henry XI, Clint Smoker and the dead Royce Traynor, is an extrapolation of Xan's disturbed and disturbing condition. They are refashionings of characters from Martin's earlier work, now horribly unfettered, but the novel is far more than an exercise in self-absorbed freakishness. There are just enough parallels between the world of the novel and the one we are in to make us pause and consider uneasily: are we that far from the former?

The Booker panel mirrored the reviewers in its dealings with the novel, which reached the long list but went no further. The chair that year was John Carey, who judges it 'an immensely complex, disturbing book. I am not a great fan of experiment for its own sake but this was outstanding because it made you question the routines of detachment and aloofness that are generally taken for granted. It is difficult to find a proper compass for a response. I thought it superb but the rest of the panel were unanimous in their disdain.' D. J. Taylor included? 'Yes, he too would not countenance it as a potential winner.' Did he get the impression that the inclination to moralize was inhibiting critical scrutiny? 'To an extent, yes.'

Rumours about Martin and Isabel's plans for Uruguay were circulating between tabloid hacks six months before *Yellow Dog* went into print. As early as February 2002 the *Mail on Sunday* stated that they had 'tracked down Martin Amis who has moved to the remote Uruguayan village of José Ignacio to overcome writers' block'. The following day, Monday, the literary editor of the *Independent*, anxious to secure Martin for a forthcoming review, had his assistant call the house to see if the phone rang out. Isabel, who had not seen the *Mail*'s article, was puzzled though not entirely surprised. No, Amis did not have writers' block; no, their life in Uruguay had nothing to do with post-9/11 trauma; no, they were not completely abandoning life in Britain, she stated to an *Independent* junior reporter despatched to see what exactly was going on.[19] 'I told the reporter all this,' repeated Isabel, 'but I could see from her eyes she wasn't listening.' And so it continued until late March 2004 'when we finally moved into the house, which was not ready when we arrived'. Isabel and a friend spent a week furnishing the Uruguayan house from antique and junk shops and reclamation yards in Buenos Aires, and then rented a van to deliver by ferry the eclectic mixture of items. 'There is', she points out, 'no Ikea in Uruguay. There is almost nothing to buy – you have furniture made or you get stuff from auctions. Buenos Aires was cheaper – it had just crashed – and there was more stuff to buy.' Was it purely coincidental that their move in autumn 2003 came almost immediately after the reviews of *Yellow Dog*? 'Yes,' answers Martin. 'We had arranged for the girls to start at a very easy-going primary school and they had to be there by mid-March. That's all.'

During the period between their first visit to Uruguay in 2000 and their arrival four years later, the media had now encroached upon the modest exclusivity of the country. Earlier that same summer Naomi Campbell and Giuseppe Cipriani had rented properties there, much to the excitement of the London and US press. Nevertheless, the region chosen by Martin and Isabel remained immune from the attention of celebrities and the press. 'It was', says Martin, 'fashionable for about two to three weeks per year, and mainly for Latinos. We lived there all year round. It could be very cold and windy.' He continues: 'When the girls arrived at school their teachers would welcome them with a kiss, and kiss them goodbye when they left for home. It was perfectly natural, but of course in a London school such physical contact would seem scandalous.' His study overlooked the beach and Atlantic. He had never before worked in such an environment and felt the difference immediately. 'The sound of the sea is good for the soul.' Which made writing difficult. 'I had read Anne Applebaum's *Gulag: A History*, and the novel would eventually take its title from the three pages in which she described the House of Meetings, where inmates would be allowed conjugal visits. The contrast between this magical location and the one that I was forcing on to the page caused difficulties. How could I write about victims of the Gulag when I was here? It was too stressless a place. I kept thinking: this piece of work is begging me to abandon it.' He did not, of course, and *House of Meetings* was published shortly after the Amis family returned to London in August 2006.

'I had written a novel about the Holocaust, but from the point of view of the perpetrator. I don't think I could have envisioned the experience of a victim. But this one *was* about a victim, and told by a victim. Lev and [the unnamed narrator] were freezing to death on the Arctic circle and I was here with my daughters and wife, in a society that seemed flawless; everyone looked happy and fit, the routines of manners and civility could have come from a 1950s film, and their attitude to children was wonderful, a combination of affection and benign authority. Very few cars, so you could park anywhere. Isabel and the girls spoke Spanish but I didn't. Many people were bilingual and indulgent but often I would spend days alone with my own thoughts, in English, and that helped with the novel.' The narrator addresses his black stepdaughter, who edits the text, with a few footnotes, but in a way he is talking to himself.

House of Meetings counters the charge, perennial since the 1970s, that Martin is a magnificent stylist but nothing more. The narrator on several occasions (notably p. 57) mentions Conrad and Dostoevsky as the West's favourite Slavic writers. They were, he contends, united in their difference, with 'old Dusty's' characters 'fucked up *on purpose*' while Conrad exposes his to a more authentic, unwanted experience of pain. There is a much deeper implication here in that both writers, at least for Westerners, were dislocated from their linguistic roots; Conrad because he adopted a foreign language for his profession, Dostoevsky as a figure who fascinates many outside Russia, very few of whom have read his work in its original form. In this respect, they influenced Martin. He was writing a novel based upon stories gleaned from works such as Applebaum's while alienating himself from his own stylistic homeland. He was doing a translation of Martin Amis. Translators are confronted by two often divergent forces: re-create mood and tone or move towards the undeviating subject. Martin chose the latter while leaving traces of the former in his wake.

Sometimes the narrator seems to be a withdrawn etiolated version of his creator, with fragments from the heyday of *Money* still scattered through the prose. But such flourishes are rare. The novel rests upon an attendance to fact, experiences far too dreadful for linguistic ostentation, even of the ghoulish Dostoevskian kind.

It would of course be absurd to suggest there were creative parallels between Martin's new life and the subject of his novel: as he stated, the former was seamlessly benign, wholesome, often luxurious. Nevertheless, the fact that he felt, in his own words, 'marginalized', albeit voluntarily, from 'the city, and modernity, always my environment and my subject' is intriguing. The newly fashionable Atlantic coast of Uruguay might have had little in common with Siberia yet alienation from his routines provided some impetus for the gargantuan task of writing prose completely incompatible with his literary temperament.

'My allocated daily task was watering and tending the garden which separated the house from the unpaved dirt road.' This was the Martin Amis who previously had treated making tea as the summit of his practical achievements. 'I learned the names and requirements of plants and eventually felt familiar with the personality of the garden.' He sometimes moved from his ground-floor study and worked at a table on a terrace in the garden. Isabel: 'The house was not on the beach. It was in the village but you could see the sea from upstairs, which is why I put the living rooms there and the sleeping below.'

Martin was able to sustain his long-established addiction to tennis. In East Hampton the Fonsecas had a court where he would play with family members and friends during the summer, and in José Ignacio he made use of the excellent clay courts. There was no club and the courts were available to anyone in the vicinity who could find an opponent.

The lack of regular poker games also caused some withdrawal symptoms, mediated slightly by his setting up of a game, initially about once a month, in the restaurant that was run, though not owned, by Isabel's cousin Martin Pittaluga and Guzman Antagaveytia, who became Martin's good friends. Soon, a number of local residents became enthusiastic participants, despite the fact that many had never played before. Martin taught them.

London Fields, *Time's Arrow* and *Yellow Dog* are exceptional partly because of their intransigent refusal to conform to the predominant tenor of his own fiction or to discernible precedents elsewhere. *House of Meetings* is similarly out of key, and even more demanding.

First-person narrators present difficulties for writers because the better they are at telling their story, the more the edifice that sustains their credibility is likely to crumble. Martin, convincingly, overcomes this with a simple device: the novel is a 200-page email written by the narrator to his stepdaughter during the days before his prearranged assisted suicide. He can therefore be excused the occasional digression, or prophetic reflection on a life about to close. More significantly, given that this is a private exchange we, as interlopers, will always be attempting to resolve ambiguities, make sense of omissions or nuances. There are some things that Venus, the recipient, might intuit that will always be lost to us and aspects of her stepfather's temperament and personal history that will always beguile us: does he take it for granted that she will be able to fill

385

in the gaps or is he practising a strategy of evasion with her too? The effect is by turns infuriating and addictive. In his unnamed narrator Martin creates a perfect vehicle for his exploration of several interwoven themes. Predominantly the novel is about life in the gulag in the 1940s and 1950s, but it also begs questions about the extent to which inmates can be trusted as witnesses to their own suffering and that of others. Notably, do they (and by implication would we) protect ourselves from a combination of guilt and a pain too horrible for full recollection by refashioning the truth?

The speaker is honest about the less appealing aspects of his past. He did during 1944–5 'rape [his] way across what became East Germany', like most of his Red Army comrades, and later in the camp he commits acts that the 'pigs' [guards] reward with privileges such as food. He kills three informers. He does not apologize for his record and we respect him all the more for this because although he never states this explicitly we detect that for him contrition, even explanation, would be strategies of avoidance. Yet his honesty is itself perplexing. The two other individuals caught in his narrative thread are his brother, Lev, sent to the same camp, and Zoya, a Jewish beauty who entrances them both. While the speaker tells of his brutal deals with unhesitating candour his account of this triangle of love and rejection is mischievously costive. He infers persistently but begrudges transparency. What, we wonder, actually occurred in the House of Meetings when Lev was allowed access to his wife, Zoya? It affects the lives thereafter of all three but the speaker never explains what we suspect he knows. Similarly, his own relationship with Zoya is presented tangentially, as though only brief moments can be recalled, not their resonance. He dwells, for example, on how she seemed to dislike the taste of his kiss, and does not explain why their relationship was apparently so catastrophic. The contours and exigencies of a private world are obscured, deleted, while brutality is offered without caution. He is being selectively honest, telling of matters that most would wish to forget or suppress while protecting emotional intimacies. The resultant work is the closest that anyone has come to a fictional version of Browning's dramatic monologues, in which the speakers are horribly enchanting but not fully present – figures who cause us to ask questions about the events that made them what they are.

The reviews were on the whole excellent but while each found something to praise none appeared able to decide on what exactly Martin was attempting to do. Typically, in the *Guardian*, M. John Harrison wondered if it was 'the history of a love-triangle relationship' since it was, he felt, 'too novelized to be quite the history of a state', and went on to ask 'what is it?'[20] His perplexity is an unwitting testament to Martin's achievement in walking a very narrow tightrope. On the one hand his research was based on impartial non-fiction, with only Solzhenitsyn allowing his experiences to seep into novels and even then with pathological detachment. At the same time Martin was fascinated by the verbatim testimonies of survivors in books such as Applebaum's. Each was by parts horrifying, gripping yet curiously incomplete. Ex-inmates offered accounts of the terrorizing minutiae of camp life and routines for survival but, Martin admits, 'I wanted to follow them out of the book, to where they live now – if they lived at all – learn more about what had happened to them after their release.' Thus his storyteller weaves an authentic account of tyranny into private portraits, his involuntary memories of love and his unfixed relationship with his brother.

His background reading, based on his work for *Koba*, was thorough but coldly vicarious. He had never visited Russia and had met only one individual with personal experience of the Stalinist purges: his father's friend Tibor Szamuely, and that had been more than twenty years earlier when his interest in politics was peripheral at best. As a consequence he searched elsewhere for filaments of the storyteller's personality, whose manner is that of an erudite autodidact – he has spent the last twenty years in the US – switching between reflection, self-directed irony and caustic aphorisms. Resignation, cynicism and a hint of despair wrestle for attention and throughout we detect an echo of Martin's recently deceased hero. Bellow died in 2005 and Martin tells of how during his last days, in bed at his home, he was visited by his friend Gene, who asked wryly, 'Well, what have you got to say for yourself, Bellow?' 'Saul answered,' reports Martin, '"I've been thinking. Now, which is it? Is it, there goes a man? Or is it, there goes a jerk?" Gene replied, unemphatically, "There goes a man," and Saul said, "I'll take your word for it."' Laconic, self-deprecating, boisterous, this was Bellow's style even on his deathbed. Open *House of Meetings* at any page and you will encounter its facsimile.

For the relationship between the brothers he went again to his personal history, and Philip. 'When Sally was young we were competitively protective of her. We used to say: "If anyone fucks her we'll kill them." Well, gradually, I moved aside. Philip was the elder brother and at the end he was there far more than I was. During the worst times he was trying constantly to protect her. And when she died Philip and Hilly went a little crazy for a few months. I didn't, but I suffered for that. Not at the time, several years later.' There is no sister in the novel, but the storyteller recalls his brother, falteringly, as a man he admires, and for whose fate he feels contrite responsibility. Martin's own inclination to revisit points in his past was augmented by his life in Uruguay. 'I felt unencumbered by the usual demands of the present, able to move freely through my earlier experiences. Women – mistakes, admissions, things that didn't work – became weirdly omnipresent, more important than anything else – children excepted – and I would ask, "Did I have a good time with women?" and answer, "Yes, I did." It all went well. And I would compare this with a conversation I'd had with an old friend. "It wasn't like that for me," he said. "I suffered, was heartbroken and knew that I'd caused pain to others."' The friend was Rob Henderson who had died of cancer in 2001. The conversation had taken place a few months before his death but a version of it resurfaces at the end of the storyteller's account.

> *Women can die gently, as your mother did, as my mother did. Men always die in torment. Why? Towards the end, men break the habit of a lifetime, and start blaming themselves, with full male severity. Women break a habit too, and start blaming themselves no longer. They forgive. We don't do that. And I mean all men, not just old violators like me – great thinkers, greater souls, even they have to do it. The work of who did what, and to whom.*
>
> *What was the matter with me and women?*[21]

Martin and Isabel knew that Uruguay would be temporary, but as Martin states it was an undertaking they chose without coercion. They were certainly not influenced, as some gossip columnists claimed, by media pressure. 'You have to believe that the media don't much bother me. I care, some, about what they say about my work, but not about my character.'

House of Meetings was planned for publication in late 2006 and they decided that they would leave Uruguay that same year. But if they left for good in the autumn where would they go? Primrose Hill was rented out until 2007 but even if they elected to stay for a further twelve months they had then to decide on where Clio and Fernanda would grow up, and most significantly receive their education. For a while the US seemed the more attractive option. New York was expensive but if they sold the London house they could find something, perhaps a brownstone in Brooklyn. New York appealed to Isabel because her mother, brother and sister lived there. 'But,' she says, 'we could never afford a house in the West Village – properties there now go for ten- to fourteen-million dollars, and my mother has lived there since 1956.'

Martin had since the early 1980s come to regard the States as his second home, but could he deal with it as his first? The matter was still undecided when in March 2006 he received a letter from Manchester University. He had been offered a job, on very attractive terms, including a generous salary, the rank of Professor, and very little hindrance to his commitments as a full-time writer. The prospect was tempting but was not the decisive factor in their choice to stay in London. 'We chose London', insists Martin, 'because my three other children lived there.' They would, they agreed, remain in Primrose Hill at least until the girls were into their teens and through the crucial years between primary school and precipitate examinations. And it was not until 2011 that they made the move to Brooklyn. There was still a year to run on the Primrose Hill rental agreement and they decided to buy a flat in Westbourne Gardens for the interim.

The practicalities of their return were but trifles compared with the storm of collective condemnation, verging upon loathing, that awaited Martin in response to his recent writings on contemporary politics, in particular 9/11 and Islam.

Terry Eagleton, in the Introduction to his reissued *Ideology*, proffered what he claimed as a verbatim quote from an article in which Martin allegedly observed that 'The Muslim community will have to suffer until it gets its house in order' and suggested that we should strip-search people who look like they're 'from the Middle East or Pakistan'. Eagleton goes on to comment that these are 'not the ramblings of a British National Party thug ... but the reflections of Martin Amis, leading luminary of the English metropolitan literary world'. Having dealt with the son he lines up Amis senior as his next target, describing Kingsley as 'a racist, anti-Semitic boor, a drink-sodden, self-hating reviler of women, gays and liberals', adding triumphantly that 'Amis fils has clearly learnt more from him than how to turn a shapely phrase'.[22]

'For one thing,' says Martin, 'he was slovenly in his use of quotations. Those quotes were in any event misrepresentations of what I'd said, by interviewers. They did not come from an essay – in fact he cited, incorrectly, the "Age of Horrorism" as their source in his later *Guardian* piece.[23] He had cobbled together phrases from interviews I'd given on the consequences of the tube bombings in 2005,[24] probably from the Internet. I said in one interview that I felt a definite *urge to say* that the Muslim community should get its house in order. I made it clear on every occasion that I did not *advocate* such measures, but that most people felt this visceral response. Which would very quickly be tempered by reason. Eagleton botched the context of what were impromptu responses to the bombings – for which I make no apology, it was how I felt at the time – or he failed to check his sources.'

Eagleton's accusations prompted a melee of earnest dudgeon lasting through October and early November. Several well-practised advocates of post-colonial repentance came out against Martin (notably Ronan Bennett, in the *Guardian*, 19 November and Yasmin Alibhai Brown, in the *Independent*, 8 October) while a greater number spoke in defence of him and his father. John Sutherland (*Guardian*, 4 October) played the safe, sardonic card by keeping clear of the particulars of the case and presenting Eagleton as a throwback to days when intellectuals took Marxism seriously. Philip Hensher (*Independent*, 9 October) focused mainly upon Eagleton's accusation that Kingsley was homophobic, which he found bizarre and entirely groundless. Geoffrey Levy (*Daily Mail*, 11 October) dismantled the rumour of Kingsley as anti-Semitic, and Michael Henderson (*Daily Telegraph*, 6 October) mounted an assault on Eagleton's coercive populism, his implicit assumption that since Thatcher everything even moderately conservative, be it aesthetic or political, must be open to unshackled abuse. Jane Howard and her brother Colin wrote to the *Telegraph* on the same day (9 October) with rebuttals, from personal experience, of every charge that Eagleton made against Kingsley. Colin wrote of how Kingsley had helped him feel more confident about his homosexuality and added that 'calling him anti-Semitic would be actionable were it not so absurd'. However, as Sutherland had sagely observed, the dead cannot pursue libel actions; hence the virulence of Eagleton's attack on Kingsley. Eagleton himself re-entered the debate on 10 October in the *Guardian*. The article occludes any opinion based upon observation or intelligence and favours ideology. Typically: 'There is something rather stomach-churning at the sight of those such as Amis and his political allies, champions of a civilization that for centuries has wreaked untold carnage throughout the world, shrieking for illegal measures . . .' By an astonishing act of teleology Martin is transformed into the spokesman for a creed, a military-political grouping and he finds this sleight of hand by parts hilarious and unsettling. 'I am unaffiliated, whereas Eagleton can't get out of bed in the morning without the dual guidance of God and Karl Marx.'

A late contribution to the exchange was made by Christopher Hitchens (*Guardian*, 21 November 2007). 'You don't have to know him [Martin], or for that matter be an expert on Jonathan Swift to see that the harshness Amis was canvassing was not in the least a recommendation, but rather an experiment in the limits of permissible thought.' By 'permissible' Hitchens does not refer to thoughts which merely allow for justifiable outrage or disgust. He means that a consensus now governs public debate, and that one of its implicit regulations forbids pronouncements based upon moral or ethical absolutes. Hence, Martin's attack upon Islamic extremism as an evil doctrine based upon fanaticism and theocratic inflexibility is presented by Eagleton and Ronan Bennett as a purblind fixation, allowing for no recognition of the allegedly morally superior democracies as perpetrators of genocide and injustice in Iraq, Afghanistan and, according to Bennett, Ireland. In the same issue as this article the *Guardian*'s letters page contained a letter from Ian McEwan, summed up by his statement: 'I've known [Martin] for almost thirty-five years, and he's no racist.' However, four other correspondents on the same page found him beyond redemption or rehabilitation.

Hitchens, to his credit, does not offer unqualified support for Martin's declared positions on these matters. Instead, he endorses his courage as someone willing to think and write beyond the stifling confines of moral relativism. With this in mind we should consult a lengthy article published on 11 September shortly before the news broke of Eagleton's assault on the Amises. Obviously, Eagleton had not read it when he prepared the preface to *Ideology*, and Martin when he wrote it had no intimation of the imminent furore to be caused by Eagleton's book. A prize for prescience should, however, go to Martin given that he foreshadows, pre-empts and provokes virtually every accusation soon to be laid against him. Memorably he tells of how shortly after his return from Uruguay, he was invited on to the panel of BBC's *Question Time* and asked about 'our progress in what was now being called the Long War'. His answer was, he claims, 'almost tediously centrist', arguing that the West had got its priorities wrong, that instead of first attacking Iraq it should have spent the preceding five years constructing a pluralistic, democratic society in the then still tractable Afghanistan while containing Iraq through tough sanctions and if necessary military blockades. Instead of provoking the standard motley chorus of responses Martin was treated by the audience as though he had advertised the benefits of legalised child prostitution. One woman 'in a voice near-tearful with passionate self-righteousness' stated that since the Americans had incited the widespread hostility in Muslim countries which contributed to 9/11 they should in atonement 'be dropping bombs on themselves'! His attempts to visualize this faintly deranged hypothesis were, he recalls, 'scattered by the sound of unanimous *applause*'. He reflects, 'We are drowsily accustomed, by now, to the fetishization of "balance", the ground rule of "moral equivalence" in all conflicts between West and East, the 100-per-cent and 360-degree inability to pass judgement on any ethnicity other than our own (except in the case of Israel). And yet the handclappers of *Question Time* had moved beyond the old formula of pious paralysis. This was not equivalence; this was hemispherical abjection.'

Certain facts testify to the astuteness of Martin's assessment, most significantly the startling similarity between the response of the audience to his reply and Eagleton's rampage through a digest of questionably sourced quotations. Both resemble, paradoxically, the reflexive intolerance of fundamentalist Islam, recalling eerily the Rushdie affair in which transgression of doctrine was greeted with inflexible condemnation. Bizarrely, as Martin points out, the doctrine he had transgressed involved a degree of bitter self-loathing that would have stretched the credulity of even the most resolute nihilist of a century earlier.

I have dwelt upon this issue because from it Martin has emerged as the only figure since the mid-twentieth century to have proved equally controversial in his literary and political writings. 'I took a great deal of flak after *Koba* from political writers and historians. They are intensely territorial. You know. "Listen, stick to novels and a bit of journalism, leave the heavy-duty stuff to us".' Thankfully he chose to ignore their advice.

His post-1990s political essays, along with two short stories on related themes, were collected as *The Second Plane* (2008) and by far the most engrossing is 'Terror and Boredom: The Dependent Mind', which draws together material from several pieces published in the *Observer* and at almost fifty pages in length constitutes a short polemical monograph. It also deposes the belief that literary writers are inherently impaired as serious commentators on the world, reversing the tenet on which the myth is based: in this piece Martin's experience as a novelist provides him with a special perspective on the so-called 'Age of Terror'. He tells of how recently he had completely abandoned a 'thriving' short novel. This had happened before but previously the cause had been the routine problems of apathy leading to creative disaffiliation. Now it was different:

> [The] reasons were wholly extraneous . . . And I had discovered something. Writing *is* freedom; and as soon as that freedom is in shadow, the writer can no longer proceed. The shadow was not a fear of repercussion. It was as if, most reluctantly, I was receiving a new vibration or frequency from the planetary shimmer.[25]

The novel centred upon Ayed, an Islamic terrorist, or more accurately a contemporary manifestation of Sayyid Qutb whose book *Milestones* is widely known as 'the *Mein Kampf* of modern Islamism'. Ayed, operating in Afghanistan, is astute enough to realize that paradigm shifts such as 9/11 demand further assaults on the previously insuperable, so he formulates a plan to scour all of the prisons and madhouses in Afghanistan for compulsive murderous rapists and unleash them on Greeley, Colorado. It was there, in 1949, that Qutb became convinced that the US, and by implication all non-Islamic states, was populated entirely by idolatrous, wanton, depraved individuals – women in particular – who in the Qur'an are described as embodiments of Satan, intent upon drawing every Muslim away from his strict doctrinal path. Greeley, in 1949, was a relatively innocent location. The dance, which Qutb records in *Milestones* as exemplifying the US as a pullulating hell house of debauchery, was sponsored by the local Presbyterian Church and at that time, throughout Greeley, alcohol was forbidden. This had, Martin concedes, all the makings of a very black comedy, except that Qutb became celebrated as an 'awakener', with the barbarous heathens of pre-Islamic Arabia now exchanged for the promiscuous infidels of the West, by parts Satanic and subhuman. Thus it was but a short step from his researches into the life, works and influence of Qutb to the creation of Ayed, planning to visit upon small-town Greeley an appropriately hellish brand of vengeance. The same logic, involving a theology-based concept of proportionate vengeance, had inspired the attacks on the Twin Towers. It was at this point, Martin confesses, that he found he could no longer proceed with the novel. It was not that it had become an absurdist exercise in hyperbole; rather, he abandoned the book because its horrifically implausible scenario was so closely allied to the recorded recent history of Islamism. He had, of course, written before in fiction about hideous occurrences and their perpetrators, notably in *Time's Arrow*, but then he felt that few if any of his readers would dispute the verifiable nature of the events or the state of moral turpitude they invoked. But not now. 'The opening argument we reach for now, in explaining any conflict, is the argument of moral equivalence. No value can be allowed to stand in stone, so we begin to question our ability to identify even what is *malum per se*.'[26] Or, evil in itself. He felt he was writing about something very real yet almost too terrible to comprehend and which most of his readers would be conditioned to misinterpret as hyperbole.

The Eagleton controversy rumbled on in websites and the margins of letters pages until the end of the year. Then a mischievous caller informed the *Manchester Evening News* that contractual details of staff at the city's university could be made available if a sufficiently assiduous enquirer invoked the Freedom of Information Act. On 25 January 2008, the *Evening News* ran a front-page article announcing that the recent celebrity appointment at Manchester University was being paid £3,000 per hour, 'the same as a professional footballer', which for local readers would evoke such presences as Ronaldo and Wayne Rooney. They reached this figure by dividing his £60,000 salary by the minimum number of hours he would teach per academic year – based on their inaccurate surmise – and assumed, correctly, that his contract exempted him from such drab activities as devising questions and marking exams and written assignments.

Technically, the information published was correct, but the impression of Martin as a spoilt opportunist was misleading, especially for readers unfamiliar with the Machiavellian world of contemporary higher education. What the newspaper did not explain – and its story was soon recycled in the London dailies – were the circumstances of Martin's appointment. The university created the job and approached Martin in early 2006 when he was still in Uruguay. They already employed eminences such as Will Self and John Banville on a part-time pro-rata basis as so-called Visiting Professors, mainly to add kudos to their postgraduate programme in creative writing. Ostensibly, Martin's appointment as a full-time Professor was designed to substantiate their claim to have the most significant contemporary authors on hand to instruct those who wished to further their own literary ambitions, fees paid. In truth, however, the university's motives and priorities lay elsewhere. The Research Assessment Exercise occurs on average every seven years and each university department in the UK is evaluated and graded according to its research performance, pre-eminently its publications over a specified period. The deadline for submission for the 2007–8 exercise was 31 December 2007 when publications by all permanently employed staff would be forwarded for scrutiny. The rewards for achieving a score within the top 5 per cent of a given discipline went far beyond recognition and eminence. Only the very highest-scoring departments would receive major boosts in government funding. As a consequence during the two-year period prior to the 2007 deadline a procedure which did indeed resemble the activities of Premier League football clubs was undertaken by universities powerful and rich enough to do so: head-hunting. Eminent academics would be poached from other institutions to beef up the research profile of their new employers. For English, novels could be submitted alongside groundbreaking critical monographs, so Martin – arguably the most controversial and influential novelist of his generation – was bought.

He and his proactive agent Andrew Wylie had been successful over the previous ten years in securing lucrative deals with publishers and the most recent had been in 1999, involving the newly formed Miramax organization, a multi-media enterprise committed as much to film production as it was to the printed word. The contract which Wylie negotiated with Miramax's chief executive involved generous advances for his subsequent three books – US rights only – a number of articles for *Talk* magazine, edited by Tina Brown, and a film screenplay, his first since the disastrous *Saturn 3*. The film was an adaptation of

Northanger Abbey and he wrote two pieces for *Talk*. Martin needed the money because he had generously committed himself to paying for many of the day-to-day costs of his sons' permanent home in Chesterton Road, and their private education. When he signed the deal with Miramax Louis was about to enter the sixth form, having gained spectacular grades at GCSE. Encouraged by Antonia and Martin, Louis and Jacob aimed to go to university, which would be far more costly than school. Fees had now been brought in by the Labour Government and if his sons were to be spared the burden of debt after graduation a substantial amount would have to be invested for the next few years. Martin had, moreover, underwritten a mortgage of several hundred thousand pounds to cover the purchase of land and building costs for the Uruguay house. So although the Miramax contract was generous it involved payment only on production of material and in 2006, little more than two years before his sixtieth birthday and with his daughters about to begin the same expensive journey through the financially demanding education system, the regular salary offered by Manchester appeared an attractive prospect. He recalls that after agreeing to take up the university post he was reminded of a conversation with Philip Larkin. The latter had taken him to dinner in All Souls, Oxford where he was Visiting Fellow, editing the *Oxford Book of Modern Verse*. Martin was in the second year of his degree. 'He glanced towards the collection of eminences and commented that academia had always reminded him of the Church in the eighteenth century, comfortable undemanding sinecures to be filled by bright second sons from the minor gentry, now of course the middle-classes.' There was, he thinks, a hint of bitterness and envy in these observations. While Manchester was a top-of-the-range redbrick, it had come up with a contractual package very similar to an All Souls Fellowship (which involves very little, if any, teaching) and he was at first, he admits, both flattered and a little puzzled. It was not until 2007, when he was asked for copies of his publications since 2001, that Larkin's analogy of the eighteenth-century Church of England began to make way for a less charming business-oriented image. In one sense he had been bought to bring in prestigious publications, which would ensure a generous government grant for the next six years, while his designation as Professor of Creative Writing, allegedly a forcing house for undiscovered literary talent, carried something of an air of pedlar of religious indulgences and miracle cures. His mere presence as a great writer promised inspiration for those willing to cough up the fees for a postgraduate course, or so the website and promotional material implied. Martin put as much effort into teaching as he previously reserved for literary criticism but he was realistic enough to accept that Creative Writing cannot be taught in a way that is remotely comparable to academic criticism. His approach was tangential. He encouraged students to accept that a precondition for writing good literature is an ability to recognize quality in the writing of others.

He commuted between London and Manchester during term-time and prepared rigorously for each seminar, teaching two classes per fortnight in the autumn term. As for the accusation that he was an overpaid celebrity it should be noted that the contract was devised and proposed by Manchester and that its seemingly disproportionate generosity regarding minimum hours on campus is the routine formula for the employment of high-profile academics. Sutherland, in his wry piece on the dispute with Eagleton presented the amusing scenario of two distinguished *littérateurs* exchanging blows in the Senior Common Room, Eagleton too being a Professor in the Manchester English Department. Eagleton replied, in stern Marxian manner, that a serious debate on racism was being trivialized, adding 'not that we have anything as posh as a senior common room at Manchester' (*Guardian*, 10 October 2007). Actually, they do. Which brings us to a wonderful irony unwittingly disclosed by Sutherland in his portrait of brawling intellectuals. They were indeed unlikely to meet in the admittedly modest SCR given that Eagleton was employed on the same basis as Martin, head-hunted from Oxford to boost the Manchester RAE rating and on minimum teaching hours. He retired in 2009 but before that he had visited Manchester far less frequently than Martin, 'commuting' from his home in Ireland.

'What Happened to Me on My Holiday' was a purist exercise in autobiographical fiction; not even the names were changed. *The Pregnant Widow* is a far more complex, troubling piece of work. Martin did indeed spend much of the summer after his second year at Oxford in a castle near the Mediterranean, near Rome. In the novel, the grand residence belongs to an acquaintance of Lily, Keith Nearing's girlfriend, and in the real world the holidaymakers were Martin himself and Gully Wells.

Kenrik is reminiscent of Rob Henderson, Martin's anarchic, self-destructive best friend from the late 1960s and early 1970s. Nicholas, Keith's brother, carries traces of Philip but more closely resembles Hitchens, and Violet, their sister, is a tragically undisguised portrait of the late Sally Amis. The poet and editor Neil Darlington, frequently referred to but never actually encountered, stands in for the famously elusive Ian Hamilton. According to the author, Tina Brown rescued him from a period of sexual self-abasement, which he terms his 'Larkinland', and Gloria Beautyman performs a similar service for Keith, but beyond that there is no resemblance between Tina and Gloria.

And who, we wonder, is the beguiling Sheherazade, whose presence distracts Keith from everything, and whose memory haunts him throughout the book? In all probability she is Serena North who was there throughout the summer and was according to Hitchens 'superbly built'.

A question arises. Does Martin's decision to write what he has admitted as a 'blindingly autobiographical' novel diminish its quality as a literary work? The short answer is no; quite the contrary.

His father once paid him the backhanded compliment of finding a 'terrible compulsive vividness in his style', the subtext being that performance had replaced substance or plot and the extent to which he has overindulged his abundant talent will remain a matter for debate.

In *The Pregnant Widow* he retains his stylistic signature, which many have attempted to replicate, none with any success, yet by turns modulates and remodels it. Its closest counterpart is his most significant non-fictional work, *Experience*, a beautiful book which had frightful consequences: it spawned a decade of misery memoirs by the intelligentsia. But it did something else too. It prompted a hypothesis. What would a novel by Martin be like if written in the manner of his memoirs? Now we have it.

For the first time in his writing career he treats all of his creations with a combination of respect, altruism and kindness. We forget that they are inventions, and wonder about the causes of their variously endearing, troubled, despondent states. Perhaps, then, we can detect a rationale for his otherwise gratuitous display of autobiographical links. It is his mantra. The linking of each of his creations to individuals for whom he personally feels a degree of attachment, even affection, guarantees in the novel a concomitant demand for care and responsibility. Perhaps he has even invented a new sub-genre: beneficent autofiction.

Despite the absence of much resembling a plot, it is an

addictive read. We live with the characters, follow them in and out of focus, and wonder continually about Keith, our companion in this experience. There are some shrewd digressions, on the much-debated sexual revolution, and more intriguingly on the contrast between those parts of Europe that have 'just come staggering out of the Middle Ages' and their young, hedonistic invaders. All these reflections are amusing and insightful enough, but we return continually to the enigma of Keith.

The name itself evinces the wound-scratching, sometimes contrite, temper of the book: Keith, or more frequently Little Keith, was one of Martin's many pseudonyms for contributions to the *New Statesman*'s literary competitions of the 1970s, the nickname used by friends and family during the same period and the forewarning of many of his most pitiable inventions. The narrative, such as it is, never releases us from his presence, and he is a curious figure – shy, self-conscious, perplexed – and via him we apprehend a summer which will stalk the future lives of all with whom he shared it.

Later, in a 'Coda' in which we follow him through his subsequent life, and leave him aged sixty, we also encounter an accumulation of great sadness and regret. In 2003 we join him in a pub near his home. He hates the place, but has neither the energy to leave it nor any inclination to explain why he is wasting his day there, alone. It is, however, an appropriate location for the mood of despair and weary resignation that accompanies his reflections on friends and family.

By 2009, he has still not detached himself from the night, ten years previously, when he witnessed his sister's death. Amis can reduce even his most sombre, mirthless readers to guilty laughter, but he has not hitherto shown a capacity to provoke tears:

Yes, Violet looked forceful. For the first time in her life, she seemed to be someone it would be foolish to treat lightly or underestimate, ridge-faced, totemic, like a squaw queen with orange hair.

'She's gone,' said the doctor and pointed with her hand. The wavering line had levelled out. 'She's still breathing,' said Keith. But of course it was the machine that was still breathing. He stood over a breathless corpse, the chest filling, heaving, and he thought of her running and running, flying over the fields.[27]

In these closing sequences Keith is the most grievous, heart-breaking individual so far created by his author. If, as is implied, he speaks for him, then one can only feel something akin to heedful pity. But it is only a novel, is it not? Near the end the narrator raises a similar question: 'Yes, we're close again, he and I . . . I? Well, I'm the voice of conscience . . .'

This book is a unique, sometimes exquisite experience that begs to be returned to after a first encounter. If there is an enduring theme it is age. Despite the fact that virtually 70 per cent of the narrative is an account of Keith's youth, his twenties and thirties, there is within this a troubling, persistent sense of impatience. The unanswered, perhaps unanswerable questions that attend the 1970s generation are less moral and existential conundrums as prerequisites to a point at which they will simply be redundant; not forgotten but despatched to an irrecoverable past. There is a quite outstanding passage at the conclusion of the novel, like nothing he has written before and in that regard a testament to his range and versatility. Keith is alone in his shed preparing to return to the house for a quiet dinner party with family and close friends. It will mark his sixtieth birthday. It was completed shortly before Martin's sixtieth in 2009 when the final draft of the novel was sent to

Cape. Keith's mood is difficult to ascertain; he is by parts distracted and uneasy but the prevailing temper of the piece is that of eloquent resignation. The prose absorbs the edgy bafflement of its subject and confers upon him and the scene – a scene that we too are about to leave – a sense of contentment. It is a beautiful moment, an ending that we would be more accustomed to expect from the masters of nineteenth-century fiction than a writer of the twenty-first.

Sixty is for some a landmark and the most enduring record of Kingsley's thoughts on this are in his letter to Larkin, congratulating his friend on his and reflecting on his own, just passed. The two men were born in the same year. As usual the mood is deadpan, mordant, self-lacerating: 'All over bar the shiting [. . .] Well of course a lot of things make sense now that didn't at the time. Hurtful things. Sad things, lonely things look quite different from INSIDE THE LAVATORY PAN.'[28] This brings to mind Martin's comments on how their respective attitude to the nuclear apocalypse highlighted to him, for the first time, intrinsic constitutional differences between them: nihilism with hilarious commentary (Kingsley) versus solicitous contemplation (Martin).

Outside *The Pregnant Widow* Martin contemplated sixty in a way that was a little more Kingsleyesque. Andy Hislop recalls in 2009 a tennis match involving him, Martin, David Papineau and Zachary Leader – all little more than a year apart in age – as a combination of black comedy and ill-repressed frustration. All appeared to be suffering from strains, chest complaints and problems with posture. 'Probably, merely a coincidence. Four men in their forties might well have turned up with a similar recipe of ailments, but since we had arranged this as a kind of wry tribute to our past it all seemed like a miserable joke played by someone else, as we slouched and shuffled round the court.' Martin was, apparently, amused. Tennis was beginning to feature much less frequently in his weekly routine. Strains were becoming abundant and he had since 2002 been an occasional member of a fashionable West London Pilates club. His associates were mainly ballet dancers.

Thereafter, every time he appeared in public, ageing and its effects appeared to exercise a prurient fascination. At his interview with Robert McCrum at the Writers' Centre, Norwich, on 11 May 2009, he returned continually to the 'tremendous humiliation' of physical decay. He and Clive James, at Manchester University on 7 December 2009, combined their droll improvisational skills to create a double act far more depressing and hilarious than Beckett's Estragon and Vladimir in a session called 'Literature and Ageing'. He and Craig Raine were equally deadpan but less amusing at the Oxford Literary Festival on 30 March 2010. At the Hay Literary Festival on 6 June 2010 he paused during a general excursus on his sense of dread to comment that 'being a grandfather is like getting a telegram from the mortuary'. His daughter Delilah reported that when she informed him by phone shortly afterwards that she was pregnant (with Isaac, now three) and commented, 'That obviously means you're old, now, Grandpops,' he had been amused.[29]

All of this was mere froth compared with the *Sunday Times* (24 January 2010) interview which preceded the serialization of *The Pregnant Widow*. In this he foresaw a 'population of demented old people, like an invasion of terrible immigrants, stinking up the cafés, restaurants and shops. I can imagine a sort of civil war between old and young in ten or fifteen years' time.' His solution was to have 'Euthanasia booths on street corners where they can end their lives with a martini and a medal'. Predictably, outrage and disgust came forth from everyone: religious bodies opposed to assisted deaths, pensioners' groups and even supporters of voluntary euthanasia who felt that his rather lurid image, including martinis, cheapened their cause. Since the end of the 1990s Martin has become so attuned to a cultural ideology of ill-considered reflex that his own rhetoric is now often gratuitously provocative. Beneath the play, however, was a more thoughtful, candid observation. 'Medical science has again over-vaulted itself so most of us have to live through the death of our talent. Novelists tend to go off at seventy, and I'm in a funk about it, I've got myself into a real paranoid funk about it, how the talent dies before the body.' This might sound a little elitist, even narcissistic. What about people who don't write novels, one might ask; surely they don't resent the 'over-vaulting' achievements of medical science in allowing them to live longer?

There is a certain amount of self-abnegating deception in Martin's performance as an artist in fear of losing his dynamism. Behind this is a man quietly content with one of the endowments of age. His family is expanding, and throughout his life the enduring feature of his personality is his love and commitment to those closest to him. He has become a benign patriarch.

Before sending this book to the publisher my last meeting with Martin was in autumn 2010. He was, as usual, obliging and cryptic in equal parts. Tuesday or Wednesday would be fine, but which or when was left open for speculation. I arrived at the time that had become almost our routine; he'd have finished work and it would be an hour or two before he joined his family. Six o'clock, and I stood outside the Amis residence, disconcerted. The house was unlit, the shutters – usually closed to ensure privacy – open. It looked empty and an estate agent's sign seemed to confirm my impression. Tales of subjects holding their biographers in contempt, particularly close to the end of things, were rife but moving house seemed a little extreme. Eventually the cleaner answered the bell and ushered me to

Martin's shed at the back of the house. A photograph of Hilly – stunning and happy – was prominent on his desk. She had died only three months before. Yes, he replied, they were moving, in summer 2011. To the US. Schools had been arranged for the girls but he is not quite ready to cut his ties with the country where he grew up and made his name as a writer. His two sons remain in London, as do Delilah and his grandchildren. The flat he and Isabel bought in Westbourne Gardens is still theirs. It is presently let but after the move they will keep it as their, occasional, London base. Attention has shifted to Isabel's relatives in New York, some of them ailing and ageing and the place that was Martin's experiment with elsewhere, his existential surrogate, will now be his home.

13

Significance: Is He a Great Writer?

It depends on what one means by 'great', but if being primarily responsible for changing the direction of British fiction is accepted as a criterion for greatness then the case for Martin Amis must be at least considered.

The history of the novel, at least prior to the 1980s, involved to a great extent a struggle between those authors who could not help but incorporate into a story a self-conscious reminder of how peculiar and unusual it is to write stories – a founding principle of modernism – and those who treated the re-creation of the world in a book as a straightforward act of craftsmanship. Numerically and in terms of mid-to-low cultural popularity the latter were by far the more predominant, and while extreme embodiments of both still exist, the sense of there being a polarized conflict between them has largely ceased. Competition for aesthetic and intellectual pre-eminence has segued into a middle ground where techniques that once secured difference are now part of a shared taxonomy of devices, all infinitely adaptable and acceptable. In short, the history of the novel, in so far as it was sustained by a bifurcation of radical versus conservative, postmodern versus counter-modernist, is over. Ali Smith, Jeanette Winterson, David Mitchell, Nicola Barker, Iain Sinclair et al. are still heirs to the likes of Joyce, Woolf, Beckett and B. S. Johnson but their techniques have become as domesticated as that cosy monument to modernism, affectionately termed 'the Gherkin', that is now as agreeably familiar a part of the London skyline as the dome of St Paul's. The author-in-the-text, that gesture which was once the badge of avant-gardism and warned of serious questions regarding the nature of representation, is now a hoary routine, a version of which occurs even in the diaries of Bridget Jones. Martin blunts its groundbreaking edge and uses it instead as a foil for his stylistic versatility and addiction to black comedy – radicalism has been suborned to populist exigency. When Ali Smith has her swimming champion describe her final suicidal dive into oblivion in the lift shaft in *Hotel World* we are back again with that old reliable, the interior monologue, the linguistic record of that which never would, never could, be spoken, patented by Joyce. In the hands of Smith, however, it is a little more polished and reader-friendly. As the character's chest collapses and its contents plunge into her throat, she reflects: 'For the first time (too late) I knew how my heart tasted'. (p. 6) Joyce, radical purist as he was, would never have allowed Molly Bloom such a wonderfully grotesque, well-crafted conceit, but Smith has one eye on the market, on the reader who wants to be impressed and entertained rather than merely confounded.

And then there is the more extravagant version of the author-in-the-text conceit, the book that toys with our registers and expectations and continually raises the question: am I or am I not a novel? Andrew O'Hagan, Nicola Barker and Iain Sinclair are all practitioners but while the method still evinces an echo of fearless unorthodoxy – once again returning us to the apparently vexed issue of whether fiction and truth may be interchangeable – its cultivated clubbability makes it as shocking as the maze in the country-house garden is frightening. Magic realism returns faithfully and comfortably in the fiction of Salman Rushdie in much the same way that Kingsley Amis's penchant for droll bitterness was always a signatory feature of his; in each case it is not so much a sense of surprise that accompanies its discovery in the novel as that of familiar reassurance. The battle between counter-modernists and post-modernists is over, the former have become more flexible and the latter more market-orientated.

It would of course be absurd to claim that Martin Amis is solely and exclusively responsible for this enormous and so far rarely acknowledged shift in the literary landscape. But the more closely one scrutinizes the nature of the change the more evident it becomes that precedents for this hybridization of experimental and conventional fiction can be traced principally to his writing.

Consider a random selection of novels published over the past twenty-five years and see if there is anything easily identifiable as a common feature.

John Lanchester's *The Debt to Pleasure* (1996) presents a fascinating, quirky spectacle and refuses to submit to anything resembling thematic interpretation. Tarquin Winot, the narrator, is plausible enough – his mannered prose style is both enviable and irritating – but beyond that it is impossible to assess him. He kills people and appears to enjoy it; there is no more to be said.

In Nicola Barker's *Behindlings* (2002) we encounter Wesley, a man who steals ponds, feeds his fingers to an owl and spends a night asleep in the carcass of a horse. He attracts a band of disciples and enthusiasts who are beguiled by his unfathomable, apparently motiveless activities. He seems to stand for nothing in particular and does not even understand why he behaves as he does.

Cherry (2004) by Matt Thorne involves Steve Ellis, a thirty-three-year-old teacher, a bachelor whose lifestyle and circumstances are rendered in meticulous detail: he is a disappointed man with no aspirations beyond maintaining his routine of drinks in the local pub, occasional dinners with friends and TV at home. Soon, however, peculiar things begin to happen. Steve meets an old man in the pub, buys him a drink and invites him to his flat to watch a video he has made of a woman walking down the street. A few days later Steve is visited by an Indian man who asks him to fill out a questionnaire on his 'Perfect Woman'. His fantasy – demure, intelligent, beautiful and with an hourglass figure – is made real and they have a relationship. She, Cherry, eventually leaves him – after his bedroom ceiling collapses and her toenails fall off – and Steve is again contacted by the old man from the pub who informs him that if he wants Cherry back he must assassinate a person called Tom who is actually a force for evil, known to some as the Fox. Does he? The ending is bizarre and unspecific, and the entire book seems designed continuously to incite and extinguish the desire to discern cause and continuity.

Toby Litt's *Ghost Story* (2004) appears to be focused upon a particularly distressing event, a couple's experience of a stillborn child, but grief is by no means straightforwardly dealt with. Agatha, the child's mother, experiences weird sounds and movements in their new house and adopts a complicated and potentially dangerous attitude to their other child. Sometimes we perceive events via Agatha's troubled mind and then without reason the perspective will shift elsewhere, in one instance to a manic chapter-long description of the builders renovating the house, written in a single bravura sentence. Also the main narrative is prefaced by two brief stories, one about someone who turns into a hare, another about a man whose wife gives birth to fox cubs and, perhaps most disturbingly, an autobiographical memoir in which Litt writes in harrowing detail of his girlfriend's three miscarriages. One could surmise that these discontinuities are purposive, perhaps even an avant-garde form of mimesis with the reader's undoubted experience of confusion and disquiet meant in some way to correspond with similar emotions attendant upon the characters. At the same time, however, one senses that Litt is deliberately attempting to curb the reader's conventional inclination to interpret the text according to any rational notion of internal coherence or correspondence with the non-fictional world.

In Ali Smith's *The Accidental* (2005) Amber, a woman of thirty or so years and indeterminate origin, simply arrives without explanation and becomes the *deus ex machina* for an entire English family. They do not know how to respond to this uninvited guest – being decent middle-class sorts they can hardly just throw her out – and in a bizarre variety of ways she takes each of them over. Michael, for example, no longer seems in control of his seductive, learned sophistry – Amber has him babbling in Byronic *octava rima*. Again the narrative is both implausible and made horrifyingly believable by Smith's neo-realistic manner. We recognize the figures but do not understand why they behave in such a bizarre way.

Hilary Mantel's *Beyond Black* (2005) is resolutely conservative in style. Its two principal characters, Alison and Colette, are rendered with unforgiving clarity as are the dismal London landscapes, mostly the suburbs, in which they are obliged to exist. Alison has had a foul, battered childhood, her mother is a prostitute and she has to put up with being a size 22; Colette, her conniving leechlike companion, is an equally dispiriting figure. Alison's profession? She's a medium, a communicator

413

with the spirit world, but before expectations of this as symptomatic of dim credulous desperation are realized, Mantel begins to populate the novel with dead people, or more specifically their non-physical yet vividly realized presences. Mantel's visitors from the other side are in varying degrees as seedy, ugly, boring and downright uninteresting as their living counterparts; mostly they are thoroughly unpleasant and possessed of a malicious animus that, disclosed as a common element of the afterlife, would be equally surprising to agnostics, atheists and believers.

One should not of course overlook Will Self, a self-confessed fan of Martin's work, who announced his presence with a volume of short stories called *The Quantity Theory of Insanity* (1991), of which Doris Lessing wrote: 'absurdity unfurls logically from absurdity, but always as a mirror of what we are living in – and wish we didn't'. Cunningly Lessing does not explain whether our unease is generated by the world created by Self or its reflection of the one we are in, because Self's trademark is to constantly invite us into an act of recognition while almost simultaneously dispersing it. In *Cock and Bull* (1992) a submissive wife grows a penis and rapes her husband who, helpfully, has been provided with a vagina at the back of his knee. He, being a stereotypically macho individual, plays rugby and enjoys the aggressive male-orientated culture of the game. During a tour with his team he finds himself pregnant and is overcome with unforeseen emotion. It seems to be a novel designed for readers with a particular taste for the grotesque but like all of Self's fiction it defies such straightforward categorization. At the beginning of the novel and before their anatomical transformations occur Dan and Carol are presented very effectively as normal individuals, average to the point of cliché. They are outstandingly credible and they, like the reader, are confounded by the intrusion of the unimaginable into their

414

routine existences. The novel is addictive not because of its ghoulish characteristics but because Self visits upon people whom the reader recognizes events that are utterly implausible.

So to return to the question. What, if anything, do these writers, their works and their characters have in common? For one thing they are most certainly not heirs to modernism. It is true that Ali Smith, and David Mitchell in his acclaimed *Cloud Atlas* (2004), play games with chronology and narrative space that are self-consciously unusual but at the same time their style is elegantly conservative and the figures who drift between different periods and states of mind are comfortably familiar. Of the rest the repertoire of imposture appears limitless and unclassifiable, except that all these works have opted out of any obligation to explain or justify their excursions from credulity and mimesis. These books are very readable but at the same time they are made up of scenarios that do not make sense and individuals that seem unaccountable to standard notions of the way we behave and think. Authenticity, in terms of the elementary devices of description and dialogue, is rigorously maintained yet by a variety of acts and means, believable characters defy any rational consensus on the nature of reality. And one other thing unites them: Martin Amis inaugurated the subgenre to which they belong. He has been instrumental in changing the face of British fiction, but does this make him a 'great' writer? This question raises another: has the change been beneficial for the state of the novel?

The factor which, more than any other, divides advocates of modernism from supporters of conventional fiction involves something other than writing; essentially it concerns the nature of the world outside the book. Adherents of modernism argue that a narrative as a sequence of events possessed of a coherent logic is not only a literary fallacy but a reflection of a collective delusion: we deceive ourselves by pretending that the random, inexplicable, even unbearable features of our lives make sense, rather in the way that a traditional novel makes sense of the world. Even if there is no happy ending we have the (false) comfort of something close to an explanation. The realists contend that while the traditional novel should not be treated as a panacea for fear or doubt it does at least imitate the innumerable permutations of behaviour and understanding that make up what most of us accept as reality.

These two positions might seem irreconcilable, but consider the work of Martin Amis. He incessantly provokes the reader's desire for familiarity and reassurance, for something or someone that seems to have walked into the novel from the world we know. Yet equally our sense of empathy, of entertainment by mimesis, is undermined: suddenly the invitation to suspend disbelief is withheld and we are confronted with the inexplicable, the fantastic, the abhorrent. But is Martin simply playing games, indulging some pseudo-intellectual taste for the horribly incomprehensible? Or is he reminding us that fiction, for writer and reader, is a unique, morally and intellectually challenging experience? He makes us think, by juxtaposing the routine and the familiar with challenges to both; some of the latter are grotesque, many unnerving and pitiable, a few unaccountably vile. Self, Unverdorben, Meo, Keith Nearing, the frightful Johnny; all are terrifyingly believable, sometimes addictively so. Must we perceive them only as brilliant inventions – which would enable us to keep a distance from them – or do they carry into their fictional world something of what we know is part of ours, even though we might desperately attempt to blind ourselves to this. In short he lays down an intellectual challenge, but does he do any more than that?

It would be simplistic and an insult to the literary integrity of all involved to apply the rule of direct 'influence' to any set of writers. A more accurate model is close to the theory popularized by Richard Dawkins in *The Selfish Gene*, originally propounded in George S. Williams's *Adaptation and Animal Selection* (1966). We are, argues Williams, blindly programmed to preserve those genetic features most likely to ensure our survival: Darwinism with a ruthless edge. Literary writers do not operate by blind instinct but nevertheless their choice of how and what to write is influenced, to some degree subconsciously, by an instinctive drive towards survival by being noticed. From the 1970s onwards the bipolar opposites of purist realism and modernism were respectable paths to eminence, but the former was well trodden and highly competitive and the latter by equal parts noble and financially unrewarding. Far more attractive, therefore, was territory largely unmapped by the literary establishment and academia, a form of writing that existed but which was unclassified. Its vague unspecified nature guaranteed a cache of originality and nonconformity, sometimes bought with a supplement of skill. Practitioners could not be treated as allied to a particular trend or sub-genre because their activity did not have a name. It did, however, exist – let us for the sake of convenience call it conservative postmodernism – and it had an originator, Martin Amis. It could be argued that over the last thirty years, society, and our sense of accountability that is partly dependent upon society, has generally become more amorphous, superficial, even brutal in its exchange of collective responsibility for selfish individualism, and many would blame the so-called Thatcher Decade for this. It might further be argued that an oblique, morally irresponsible brand of fiction is an appropriate response to those transitions. But appropriate in what way? The conservative postmodernists, Martin's legacy, can hardly be seen as offering some kind of mimetic reproach to our world. Their novels show us terrible things and horrible people but they do so to fascinate us, not to encourage judgement. In this respect they might be seen to be complicit with the cultural fabric which many, including many of them, hold to be contemptible. Their radicalism is attuned to the demands of the marketplace. Most readers of 'literary fiction', post-1980s, are graduates, alert to the chic attractions of being at once clever and unconventional. But in both instances this is a sham sustained by commissioning editors and market analysts in the mainstream publishing houses. It could therefore be argued that the hybridized novel, inaugurated by Martin Amis, is a profitable intellectual fashion statement which dumbs-down and vulgarizes the spirit of true modernism while neglecting to say anything significant about the real world.

Martin's novels of the 1970s were subtly groundbreaking, invoking Burgess and Ballard in treading a fine line between reflections of the non-fictional world of the time and exaggerations of its more perverse characteristics. They captured perfectly the idioms and behavioural undercurrents of the era – and in this respect the genetic imprint of Kingsley is detectable – while at the same time raising questions on motives and states of mind that could not be addressed in terms of orthodox perceptions of the human condition. He was, in truth, uncertain of which direction to take, shifting between orthodox social satire (*The Rachel Papers*), prophetic black comedy (*Dead Babies*) and poorly executed experiment (*Other People*). All show some small signs of the manner that would be adopted by Barker, Litt, Thorne, Smith, Self et al., but it was with *Money* that he found a technique that owed nothing to precedent.

With *Ulysses*, James Joyce showed his contemporaries the world as they had never previously conceived it, at least in language, and as a moment of precipitation in literary history his achievement is immense. We should not, however, overlook the fact that Joyce's rationale for the project, his objective, was misguided and came to nothing. He wanted to liberate the novel from its hidebound bourgeois conventions; assemble it from all of the different forms and registers that make up our encounters with language. He hoped to democratize fiction, to make it part of the lived experience of everyone, including the culturally bereft lower classes. He failed momentously. Were it not for the aesthetic elitism of the academy, *Ulysses* would long be out of print or at best turned out in limited editions by clubs dedicated to the memory of its creator. Purist modernism has since this original moment suffered a similar fate: jealously preserved on the margins of the real literary world by advocates of experiment for its own sake. John Self turned modernism on its head. *Money* is equal to anything written since 1922 in its ability to shock and confound the expectations of the reader. Self presents us with several problems. If we are sane we would not voluntarily seek his company but from the first page of the novel we cannot avoid it. He is an addictive, manically talented, superbly flawed performer. A man like this should not be able to command our attention, indeed our guilty amusement, in such a way. The entire novel should self-destruct as an exercise in glaring discontinuity and anomaly. But it does not, and Martin outranks Joyce in his achievement of bridging the gap between the 'literary' novel and the world that has nothing to do with high culture. Nevertheless a question endures. We can admire Self and his story as a superb literary undertaking, but are he and it anything more than exhibitionism? Perhaps we would not, in the real world, seek his company because his existence outside the book is inconceivable. Surely, one might contend, novels must to some degree mirror the world we live in. Self opened a door for later novelists that had previously been both locked and concealed. Through it, later, would march numerous creations of Will Self, beginning with Ian Wharton in *My Idea of Fun* (1993), A. L. Kennedy's Hannah Luckraft of *Paradise* (2004), Ali Smith's Amber from *The*

Accidental (2005), Matt Thorne's Steve Ellis in *Cherry* (2004), David Mitchell's Jason Taylor of *Black Swan Green* (2006) and many more. Self's successors are not replicas of him. They differ from him and each other in myriad ways, yet they also preserve a key feature of Martin's original. Each of them is let loose across a text that bears an oblique resemblance to the world we know and each, like Self, raises the same question: do they oblige us to look again at what we take for granted, or do they indulge our desire for whimsy at the expense of truth?

London Fields and *The Information* could easily be mistaken for the other parts of a trilogy inaugurated by *Money* – there are some similarities – but such a classification would obscure their importance as individual works. There are a considerable number of novels which attempt to capture the essence of the so-called 'Thatcher Decade' – some with the benefit of hindsight – and virtually all of them adopt a solidly realistic manner which seems appropriate to so traumatic a period. (See Justin Cartwright's *Look At It This Way*, 1990; Ian McEwan's *The Child in Time*, 1987; Julian Rathbone's *Nasty, Very*, 1984; Jonathan Coe's *What a Carve Up!*, 1994, *The Rotters' Club*, 2001 and *The Closed Circle*, 2004; David Caute's *Veronica, or The Two Nations*, 1989; Tim Parks's *Goodness*, 1991; Maggie Gee's *Grace*, 1988.) Martin's two novels do not seize upon the most obvious tokens of the mood of avarice that allegedly transformed the entire UK, at least for those in the country who could afford to be greedy. All of this was in any event becoming the principal preoccupation of newspapers and other media; fiction was left to prey upon the leftovers, as indeed did most of the novels bracketed above. Instead in *London Fields* and *The Information* he incorporates something far more elemental yet difficult to describe: a sense of individuals no longer quite sure of who they are or even who they want to be; characters who are neither quite themselves nor satisfied with their projected image. Dislocation or fragmentation had of course been dealt with in literature before but never previously had they been accompanied by such a network of disconcerting, ultimately unanswerable questions as to their cause, nature and solution. What Martin calls the 'background', the circuitry of transactions, emotions, activities, even places that seem so familiar, is vividly realized yet often surreally distorted. Are Talent, Young, Nicola, Tull, Barry formed, often wrecked, by a society out of control or are they authors of a selfish individualist zeitgeist, their surroundings a projection of their own fears and fetishes? The dynamic between these two interpretations is incessant, with the books continually provoking us, obliging us to question our given assumptions about those years, yet never allowing us to reach an easy conclusion. At the same time one must compare this effect with what happens in Julian Rathbone's *Nasty, Very* (1984) and in Justin Cartwright's *Look At It This Way* (1990), Charlie Bosham, the central character of Rathbone's novel, is a thoroughly unpleasant individual, a ruthless businessman without the veneer of charm to compensate for his feral selfishness. He becomes an MP in Mrs Thatcher's new Conservative Party of the 1980s and it is difficult to imagine a more controversial attempt to capture the state of the nation in fiction.

In *Look At It This Way* Tim Curtiz, a US journalist, begs comparison with Samson Young of *London Fields* in that each is an outsider offering us a picture of London at the close of the decade. Curtiz, one has to admit, is astute:

> Sometimes in London you get great glimpses of enormous wealth, great piles of money [. . .] money which has grown by leaps and bounds in the last ten years as everything, the very fabric of the country, has reached the point of critical mass. This wealth appears to have no

physical limits. Low temperature nuclear fission of wealth has taken place, on a scale which is a surprise even to the beneficiaries [. . .] How has it happened? Nobody really knows. It is necromancy, it is alchemy. The philosopher's stone has been found. (p. 59)

We have to ask yet again: does the type of writing evolved by Martin provide a more subtle and challenging perspective on our world than Rathbone's or Cartwright's, or does it offer a form of intellectually respectable escapism?

The question also arises of what part, if any, Martin's near contemporaries, and friends, played in the subtle alteration in the fabric of fiction writing since the close of the 1970s, the creation of a previously unenvisaged hinterland involving the best of conventionalism and the avant-garde. And here I have in mind primarily Barnes, McEwan and Rushdie. Compared with Martin their influence has been negligible.

McEwan is the best of the three. Open one of his works at random and encounter a narrative presence disclosing events with urbane transparency and choreographing compellingly authentic dialogue. At the same time we feel that something, often something macabre and inexplicable, is lying in wait to rip through this portrait of the ordinary. This is his signature, a sense of two strata or planes of existence coming together, perhaps through an accident, with consequences that are numinous, sometimes inexplicable. McEwan's weak spot is his reliance upon this as an all-things-to-all-men framing device, equally adaptable to his stern treatment of Thatcherism (*A Child in Time*), the Cold War (*The Innocent*) and the Iraq conflict (*Saturday*). It is dependable but its durability weakens its effect. McEwan shocks us without causing an inordinate degree of confusion and he certainly does not provoke rage, which is why he has won the Booker and Martin has not.

At the other end of the spectrum we find Rushdie. *Midnight's Children* is a literary landmark, but his career overall is Magic Realism by rote: endlessly proclaiming his rejection of the standard menus of representation and, as a consequence, endlessly predictable. He has been writing versions of the same book for almost four decades. Imagine that Joyce decided against despatching experiment to the oblivion of impenetrability that is *Finnegans Wake* and instead recycled versions of *Ulysses* until the 1950s (while avoiding his own untimely demise): thus you have an account of something similar to Rushdie's career. In Martin's oeuvre the differences between, say, *Dead Babies, Money, Time's Arrow, Yellow Dog* and *House of Meetings* are so striking that one might think they had been written by different men. If there is a consistent feature in his work it is to be found in his almost maniacal preoccupation with different levels of perception and representation: the dreadful inequitability between what we know, or admit, and say.

It could be argued that Barnes comes closest to him in terms of eclecticism and versatility. Perhaps, but he is an author who buys his deserved admiration with meticulous caution. *A History of the World in 10½ Chapters* is a very British bow to the architecture of modernist writing. *England, England* is dystopian allegory so beautifully executed that it politely spares us feelings of unease let alone fear, and the monologists of *Talking It Over* marshal their distress so excellently that we admire more than pity them. Barnes is outstandingly talented, and by equal degrees reserved and thoughtful. Unlike Martin he does not deliver unexpected punches: he does not force us, despite ourselves, to confront our conflicting impulses when we read the novel. He asks us to *think*, certainly, but the request is rather polite and circumspect.

Each of these figures has played a part in the momentum for

change in British fiction of the past three decades, but Martin Amis has been more influential than any of them.

In 1971, David Lodge invented the now famous image of the novelist at the crossroads. Until the 1920s only one road existed, the one taken by the realists, but modernism created an alternative route. In 1971, Martin was working on his first novel and throughout the following decade he returned again and again to the junction and took hesitant, uncertain steps in both directions, never fully committing himself to either. *Money* was groundbreaking because with it Martin demonstrated that the one-or-the-other option was not as straightforward as Lodge claimed. The hybrid novel was born and its imprint would endure both in Martin's work and in the writing of ambitious newcomers, alert to market trends. Lodge, in 1992, conceded that by then the situation of the novelist bore less resemblance to a figure standing at a junction than a person in 'an aesthetic supermarket' facing an unprecedented abundance of styles, techniques and scenarios; the novelist/customer could now select and combine these in any way they wished.[1]

One could therefore applaud Martin for having jolted the British novel out of its atrophied state at the crossroads, but in doing so one would also have to accept that change for change's sake is always advantageous. The expansion of the 'aesthetic supermarket', the hybrid novel, did not bring about the extinction of realist fiction, which continued to thrive in bestseller lists, but it reinforced a mantra that had obtained among the most influential members of the literary establishment since modernism: that if writing does not at least question precedent it will be in some way handicapped. The realists continued to produce novels but they remained on the margins of the cultural centreground. This occurred during the period that British society underwent dramatic changes comparable only with the 1930s and the Second World War. The

Conservative governments of the 1980s dismantled the legacies of 1945 and we are still dealing with the aftermath. Opinions will continue to differ on whether naturalistic or experimental techniques provide the best vehicle for an engagement with the world outside the novel, but I suspect that in thirty years' time when academics come to examine how fiction recorded the history of late twentieth- and early twenty-first-century Britain, figures such as Justin Cartwright, Julian Rathbone, Jonathan Coe and Tim Parks will feature more prominently than the aesthetic supermarket shoppers or indeed their mentor, Martin Amis.

No one would argue that novelists should be burdened with an obligation to offer what George Eliot in *Adam Bede* praised as 'a faithful account of men and things' rather than what she called 'an arbitrary picture' of them, yet one cannot help wondering what might have happened if Martin had taken his fiction in a slightly different direction after *Money*. Specifically, what sort of novels would he have produced if the manner and techniques he perfected as a journalist and political writer had become the mainstay of at least some of his fiction? His decision to shun this option had nothing to do with aesthetic idealism. He was influenced primarily by the fear of being seen as a replica of his father, yet his anxiety was misplaced. Realism allows for a far greater degree of individuality and stylistic versatility than fashionable opinion would have us believe. Evident in Martin's journalism and criticism of the 1980s and 90s and his more recent, controversial political writing is a man who compels our attention, and demands our support or fervid disagreement. It is this same range of skills that informs and energizes the kind of novel that we cannot put down, involving characters and problems so crisply realised that we continually ask ourselves why this happened, what this character is really like and how it will all end. In short, Martin might have produced novels that involved what Larkin called, with approval, 'a beginning, a middle and an end' but which bore the distinctive imprint of Martin Amis, superb stylist and polemicist. He could have demonstrated his independence from Kingsley without giving up on realism – each has a literary voice that transcends the confines of technique – but he took a different route. As a consequence he also deprived the realist novel of the presence of an unsurpassable satirist and analyst of human motives. The power of the genre as the most unforgiving commentary on our times has been weakened by his spurning of it.

Martin Amis is by virtue of his effect on fiction as a whole an immensely important writer, but I feel that we should reserve judgement on 'greatness'. He is still writing and literary history is slow in reaching a consensus. We will see.

Notes

Chapter 1: Before He Left

1. Zachary Leader (ed.), *The Letters of Kingsley Amis* (London: HarperCollins, 2001), 7 March 1950, p. 228.
2. Ibid., 22 October 1956, p. 487.
3. Ibid., 24 May 1958, p. 535.
4. *Experience*, p. 165.
5. Review of translation of *The Enchanter*, TWAC, pp. 261–3.
6. Zachary Leader, *The Life of Kingsley Amis* (London: Cape, 2007), p. 464.
7. *Experience*, p. 102.
8. *Dead Babies*, p. 319.
9. Leader, *Life*, pp. 511–15.
10. *Experience*, p. 101.
11. *Dead Babies*, pp. 223–4.
12. *Experience*, p. 106.

Chapter 2: Wild Times

1. *The Rachel Papers*, pp. 49–50.
2. Leader, *Life*, p. 546.
3. Leader, *Letters*, 4 August 1950, p. 242.
4. Ibid., 12 June 1950, pp. 232–3.
5. Ibid., 27 November 1950, p. 247.
6. Ibid., 30 July 1950, p. 238.
7. *Experience*, p. 9.
8. Ibid., pp. 86–7.
9. Leader, *Letters*, 19 June 1946, p. 73.
10. Ibid., 18 April 1946, p. 56.
11. *Experience*, pp. 19–20.

Chapter 3: Oxford

1. *The Rachel Papers*, p. 210.
2. Ibid.
3. *Experience*, p. 41.
4. Ibid., p. 44.
5. *My Oxford* (ed. Ann Thwaite) (London: Robson Books, 1977), p. 209.
6. *The Rachel Papers*, p. 211.
7. *My Oxford*, p. 207.
8. *The Rachel Papers*, p. 66.
9. *My Oxford*, p. 207.
10. *Experience*, pp. 270–2.

Chapter 4: The Novelist

1. Leader, *Letters*, 19 April 1969, p. 714.
2. *Experience*, p. 214.

3. *Dead Babies*, p. 107.
4. *Experience*, p. 49.
5. *Dead Babies*, p. 78.
6. Ibid., pp. 79–80.

Chapter 5: The Seventies

1. *TWAC*, pp. 3–9.
2. Julie Kavanagh, 'My Life with Martin Amis', *Daily Telegraph*, 2 June 2009; Emma Soames, 'How Churchill's Granddaughter Was Seduced and Then Breezily Betrayed by "Scribbling Dwarf" Martin Amis', *Daily Mail*, 6 June 2009; Tamasin Day-Lewis, 'Am I the "Leggy Temptress" in Martin Amis's New Novel?', *Daily Telegraph*, 17 February 2010.
3. 'The Coming Thing', review of *The Best of Forum*, *New Statesman*, 28 September 1973.
4. *Success*, p. 49.
5. Ibid., pp. 26–7.
6. 'The Sublime and the Ridiculous: Nabokov's Black Farces', in Peter Quennell (ed.), *Vladimir Nabokov: His Life, His Work, His World* (London: Weidenfeld & Nicolson, 1980), p. 76.
7. Graham Fuller, 'Yob Action', *Village Voice*, 1 December 1987.
8. Leader, *Letters*, 13 December 1977, p. 842.
9. 'Blackpool Diary', *New Statesman*, 14 October 1977.
10. *London Fields*, p. 22.
11. Leader, *Letters*, 18 March 1978, p. 845.
12. James Fenton, 'Of the Martian School', *New Statesman*, 20 October 1978.
13. 'Point of View', *New Statesman*, 14 December 1979.

Chapter 6: Paris

1. Leader, *Letters*, 10 May 1979, p. 871.
2. Blake Morrison, review of *Success*, *TLS*, 14 April 1978.
3. Paul Ableman, review of *Success*, *Spectator*, 15 April 1978.
4. Peter Ackroyd, *Notes for a New Culture: An Essay on Modernism* (London: Vision Press, 1976).
5. John Sutherland, *Fiction and the Fiction Industry* (London: Athlone Press, 1976).
6. Bernard Bergonzi, *The Situation of the Novel* (London: Macmillan, 1970, 1979).
7. *Experience*, pp. 51–2.
8. Leader, *Letters*, 9 March 1981, pp. 915–16.

Chapter 7: America, Kingsley and Bellow

1. *TMI*, p. 89.
2. Ibid.
3. Kingsley Amis, *On Drink* (London: Cape, 1972), p. 11.
4. Leader, *Letters*, 9 March 1981, p. 917.
5. *TMI*, p. 137.
6. Ibid., p. 55.
7. *VMN*, p. 114.
8. 'Lolita Reconsidered', *The Atlantic* 270, September 1992, pp. 115ff.
9. *TWAC*, p. 379.
10. Francis Wheen, *Strange Days Indeed: The Golden Age of Paranoia* (London: Fourth Estate, 2010); Andy Beckett, *When the Lights Went Out: Britain in the Seventies* (London: Faber, 2009); Dominic Sandbrook, *State of Emergency: The Way We Were: Britain 1970–1974* (London: Allen Lane, 2010).
11. *TMI*, p. 199.

12. *Experience*, pp. 176–7.
13. Ibid., p. 177.

Chapter 8: Self, Marriage, Children

1. *Money* (Penguin edn), p. 47.
2. Ibid., pp. 246–7.
3. Ibid., p. 248.
4. *TWAC*, pp. 451–2.
5. *Money*, p. 39.
6. Ibid., p. 119.
7. Ibid., p. 104.
8. Ibid., p. 222.
9. Leader, *Letters*, 18 June 1984, p. 976.
10. *Experience*, p. 249.
11. *Einstein's Monsters*, p. 47.
12. Leader, *Letters*, 7 June 1986, pp. 1021–2.
13. *Einstein's Monsters*, p. 12.
14. Ibid., p. 18.
15. Ibid., p. 19.
16. Ibid.
17. *The Pregnant Widow*, pp. 165–6.
18. *Einstein's Monsters*, p. 19

Chapter 9: Dystopian Visions

1. *VMN*, p. 227.
2. Ibid., pp. 228–9.
3. Ibid., pp. 229–30.
4. Mira Stout, 'Martin Amis: Down London's Mean Streets', *New York Times* magazine, 4 February 1990, pp. 1–13.
5. *Experience*, p. 82.

6. Ibid., p. 260.
7. *Time's Arrow*, p. 170.
8. Robert J. Lifton, *The Nazi Doctors: Medical Killing and the Psychology of Genocide* (New York: Basic Books, 1986), p. 8.
9. Ibid.
10. *Time's Arrow*, p. 142.
11. Ibid., pp. 47–8.
12. Roger Scruton, 'Books of the Year', *TLS*, 13 December 1991.
13. Rhoda Koenig, 'Holocaust Chic', *New York*, 21 October 1991, p. 117.
14. James Buchan, 'The Return of Doctor Death', *Spectator*, 28 September 1991, pp. 37–8.
15. Hannah Arendt, *Eichmann in Jerusalem: A Report on the Banality of Evil* (Harmondsworth: Penguin, 1963).

Chapter 10: The Break-Up and *The Information*

1. *Evening Standard*, 16 September 1993.
2. *Daily Mail*, 10 September 1993.
3. *Sunday Times*, 12 September 1993.
4. Ibid.
5. Ibid.
6. *Evening Standard*, 28 November 1994.
7. Laura Doan, '"Sexy Greedy Is the Late Eighties": Power Systems in Amis's *Money* and Churchill's *Serious Money*', *Minnesota Review* 34–5 (1990), pp. 69–80.
8. *TWAC*, p. 4.
9. *Experience*, pp. 158–9.

Chapter 11: A Gallery of Traumas

1. *Experience*, pp. 69–70.
2. Anthony Thwaite (ed.), *Selected Letters of Philip Larkin* (London: Faber, 1992); Andrew Motion, *Philip Larkin: A Writer's Life* (London: Faber, 1993).
3. Tom Paulin, Letter in *TLS*, 7 November 1992.
4. *Experience*, p. 366.
5. 'Action at Sea', *Sunday Telegraph* magazine, 21 January 1979.

Chapter 12: Novelist and Commentator

1. Ian Kershaw and Moshe Lewin (eds), *Stalinism and Nazism: Dictatorships in Comparison* (Cambridge, New York: Cambridge University Press, 1997).
2. *Korba the Dread*, pp. 252–4.
3. Christopher Hitchens, review of *Korba the Dread*, *Atlantic Monthly*, 20 September 2002.
4. *TSP*, p. 19.
5. 'John Pilger Takes on Martin Amis', *New Statesman*, 17 June 2002.
6. *Saul Bellow: Letters*, ed. Benjamin Taylor (London: Viking, 2010).
7. 'If Confined to a Single Word to Describe Vegas You'd Have to Settle for: Un-Islamic', *The Australian* magazine, 21 October 2006.
8. *TSP*, p. 76.
9. Liz Jensen, review of *Yellow Dog*, *Independent*, 6 September 2003.
10. Michiko Kakutani, review of *Yellow Dog*, *New York Times*, 28 October 2003.
11. Matt Thorne, review of *Yellow Dog*, *Independent on Sunday*, 31 August 2003.

12. Walter Kirn, review of *Yellow Dog*, *New York Times*, 9 November 2003.

13. Review of *Yellow Dog*, *Economist*, 25 September 2003.

14. Lewis Jones, review of *Yellow Dog*, *Sunday Telegraph*, 31 August 2003.

15. James Hynes, review of *Yellow Dog*, *Washington Post*, 23 November 2003.

16. Theo Tait, review of *Yellow Dog*, *TLS*, 5 September 2003.

17. Ludovic Hunter-Tilney, review of *Yellow Dog*, *Financial Times*, 5 September 2003.

18. *TWAC*, p. 475.

19. *Independent*, 19 February 2002.

20. M. John Harrison, 'Decline and Fall', *Guardian*, 30 September 2006.

21. *House of Meetings*, p. 194.

22. Terry Eagleton, *Ideology: An Introduction* (London: Verso, 2007).

23. Terry Eagleton, 'Rebuking Obnoxious Views Is Not Just a Personality Kink', *Guardian*, 10 October 2007.

24. *Times*, 8 July 2005.

25. *TSP*, p. 51.

26. Ibid., p. 74.

27. *The Pregnant Widow*, p. 404.

28. Leader, *Letters*, 3 August 1982, p. 947.

29. *Mail on Sunday*, 20 June 2010.

Chapter 13: Significance: Is He a Great Writer?

1. *New Writing*, ed. M. Bradbury and J. Cooke, British Council, 1992.

Bibliography

The Rachel Papers (London: Jonathan Cape, 1973).

Dead Babies (London: Jonathan Cape, 1975). Republished as *Dark Secrets* (St Albans: Triad/Panther, 1977).

Success (London: Jonathan Cape, 1978).

Other People: A Mystery Story (London: Jonathan Cape, 1981).

Invasion of the Space Invaders: An Addict's Guide (London: Hutchinson, September 1982).

Money: A Suicide Note (London: Jonathan Cape, 1984).

The Moronic Inferno and Other Visits to America (London: Jonathan Cape, 1986).

Einstein's Monsters (London: Jonathan Cape, 1987).

London Fields (London: Jonathan Cape, 1989).

Time's Arrow, or, The Nature of the Offence (London: Jonathan Cape, 1991).

Visiting Mrs Nabokov and Other Excursions (London: Jonathan Cape, 1993).

Two Stories (London: Moorhouse and Sørensen, 1994). Contains 'Denton's Death' and 'Let Me Count the Times'. Small press limited edition, total run of 326 copies.

God's Dice (London: Penguin, 1995). Contains 'God's Dice' (alternate title of 'Bujak and the Strong Force') and 'The Little Puppy That Could' (both from *Einstein's Monsters*).

The Information (London: HarperCollins, 1995).

Night Train (London: Jonathan Cape, 1997).

Heavy Water and Other Stories (London: Jonathan Cape, 1998).

The Coincidence of the Arts (Paris: Coromandel Express, 1999). Short story from *Heavy Water*, individual pages housed in a metal container, is illustrated by seven original prints by Peruvian photographer Mario Testino. Limited to fifty-five copies, each signed by M.A. and Testino.

Experience: A Memoir (London: Jonathan Cape, 2000).

The War Against Cliché: Essays and Reviews, 1971–2000 (London: Jonathan Cape, 2001).

Koba the Dread: Laughter and the Twenty Million (London: Jonathan Cape, 2002).

Yellow Dog (London: Jonathan Cape, 2003).

House of Meetings (London: Jonathan Cape, 2006).

The Second Plane. September 11: 2001–2007 (London: Jonathan Cape, 2008).

The Pregnant Widow (London: Jonathan Cape, 2010).

Uncollected Works

Fiction

'Debitocracy', *Penthouse*, November 1974, pp. 50–8, 62. Dystopian short story about a future world where sexual passion has been vanquished.

Poetry and Drama

It's Disgusting at Your Age, in *New Review*, September 1976, pp. 19–24; rpt in *The New Review Anthology* (ed. Ian

Hamilton), pp. 216–30 (London: Heinemann, 1985). One-act play that anticipates *Success*.

'An American Airman Looks Ahead', *Observer*, 5 June 1977, p. 28. Poem reflecting Amis's association with 'the Martian School'.

'Point of View', *New Statesman*, 14 December 1979, p. 954. Another 'Martian School' poem which reappears in *Other People: A Mystery*.

Produced Screenplay

Saturn 3, dir. Stanley Donen, ITC Films, 1980.

Index

Ableman, Paul   179–80
Abse, Dannie   205–6
Accidental, The (Ali Smith)   413, 420
Ackroyd, Peter   104, 136, 180
Adorno, Theodor   284
Adventures of Augie March (Saul
   Bellow)   221, 222
After Julius (Jane Howard)   54
alcoholism, sister's   22, 96, 150
Amis, Clio   333, 338, 352–3, 358–9,
   373, 374, 389–90
Amis, Fernanda   331, 333, 339,
   352–3, 373, 389–90
Amis, Hilary 'Hilly'   203–4, 290,
   321–2, 325, 326, 327, 328, 338,
   408
   and D. R. Shackleton Bailey   58,
      92–3, 96
   in London after break-up with
      Kingsley   44–5, 49, 50, 52, 57
   and Lord Kilmarnock   93, 118–19,
      126, 203–4, 350, 353
   marriage to Kingsley   1–5, 7, 9–13,
      15, 17–22, 25, 26–7, 33, 37–42

Amis, Jacob   244, 247, 263–4, 266,
   275, 296, 318, 324, 325–6,
   399
Amis, Kingsley   2, 3–4, 50, 53–5,
   58–60, 69, 70, 72, 84, 88–9, 93,
   97–8, 104–5, 115, 120, 131,
   133–4, 142, 145–6, 147–8, 150,
   156, 157–8, 159, 169–70, 170–1,
   176, 191, 196–200, 203, 204–5,
   233–4, 247, 251, 252, 259,
   290–1, 325, 333–4, 338, 364–5,
   380, 391, 405, 411
   adultery   4, 18–21, 27, 32, 37–8,
      67, 145–6, 147–8
   break-up with Hilly   37–42, 45–7,
      50, 53
   break-up with Jane   200–2
   marriage to Hilly   1, 2–13, 15,
      18–27, 30, 31, 33, 34
   Martin's care of   200–6
   parallels and contrasts with
      Martin   62–8, 76, 98–9, 100–1,
      196–8, 287–8, 290, 319, 363–4,
      426

publication of biography and
   letters   326–31, 348–50
Works:
Girl, 20   95–6, 98–9
Colonel Sun   53
I Like It Here   118
Lucky Jim   6–7, 8, 9, 61–2, 98–9,
   105, 112, 328
Lucky Jim's Politics   105
On Drink   98
Riverside Villas Murder,
   The   333–4
Stanley and the Women   204–5
That Uncertain Feeling   10
Amis, Louis   236, 296, 318, 321, 324,
   345–6, 348, 399
Amis, Martin   1, 4, 116–17, 211–14,
   216–17
1970s social life   135–45, 154–69
ageing   405–7
and Antonia Phillips   223, 225,
   225–7, 229–31, 233–8, 264–6,
   331–33
break-up with Antonia   288–93,
   296, 317, 331–33
in Brighton   60–4, 68–9
changes agent   303–6
childhood in Cambridge   30–7, 41,
   88
childhood in Princeton   25–8
childhood in Swansea   9–15,
   17–18, 20–4, 26, 28, 29
complex love-life in 1970s   124–34,
   155, 158–61
education   15–16, 28–9, 33, 43, 44,
   49–52, 56, 59–61 *see also* Oxford
European trip with Rob
   Henderson   73–7
father's biography and
   letters   326–31, 348–9

father's death   338
flat in Hogarth Road, Earl's
   Court   106–7
flat in Kensington Garden
   Square   168
flat in Pont Street, Belgravia   102,
   104, 125
as freelance interviewer/
   essayist   192–7, 206–9, 214,
   300–1
High Wind in Jamaica (film)   48–9,
   82
and Isabel Fonseca   287–8, 292,
   294, 295, 320–1, 323, 331–2,
   338–9, 346–7, 348, 351–3, 355,
   373, 383
in Israel   249
letter writing style   65–8
in London with Hilly   44–8, 49–50,
   52
in London with Jane and
   Kingsley   47–8, 53–6, 58–60,
   82–3, 90, 93–4, 96–8, 101, 124–5
looking after Kingsley   200–6
in Majorca   40–1, 73–4
Manchester University
   professorship   390, 397–401,
   406
at The Old Forge, Shilton   87–8,
   123
at Oxford   35, 61, 69, 70–3, 77–85,
   87–91
parallels and contrasts with
   Kingsley   62–8, 76, 98–9, 100–1,
   196–8, 287–8, 290, 319, 363–4,
   426
parenthood   237, 242, 244, 247,
   252, 264, 266–7, 275, 292–3,
   317, 323, 332, 351, 358
parents' break-up   40–2, 44

in Paris   176, 177–8, 191, 222
pre-Oxford social life   56–7, 58–9,
   108–10
reviews   104, 179–80, 185, 283–4,
   339, 375–7, 387
Saturn 3 (film)   175–6, 231–3
Stalinism   355–64
working in the US   193–6, 206–9,
   214
Works:
'Action at Sea'   340–1
'Bujack and the Strong Force or
   God's Dice'   245–7
'Coming in Handy'   122
Dead Babies   35–7, 40, 87–8,
   107–10, 115–16, 118–20, 140–1,
   143–4, 179
'Denton's Death'   339–40
Einstein's Monsters   242–8, 258,
   275, 292–3, 339–40, 353
Experience   14, 23, 34–5, 41–2, 47,
   53–4, 60, 65, 74–5, 77, 87, 95,
   104, 108, 112, 124, 186, 189–90,
   240, 274, 277, 305, 308, 317,
   320, 322–3, 326, 327, 331, 334,
   336–8, 348–50, 368–9, 402
Heavy Water   339–48
'Heavy Water' (short story)   340
House of Meetings   382–4, 385–9
The Information   296–303,
   306–19, 420–1
Koba the Dread   352, 353, 356,
   357, 359–64
London Fields   131, 163, 165–6,
   238, 240, 254, 255–63, 267, 270,
   296, 299, 420–1
Money   117, 216–17, 218–221,
   225, 227–31, 233, 299, 301,
   365–6, 419
My Oxford   80, 83, 87, 99

Night Train   333–5, 337, 338
*Other People: A Mystery
   Story*   182–5, 187–91, 301
'Point of View'   172
The Pregnant Widow   86, 133,
   252–4, 350, 401–5
The Rachel Papers   51, 68, 71–2,
   80–1, 97–100, 102, 104, 106,
   112, 134
'The Second Plane'   365
The Second Plane   367–8, 373,
   380, 395
'State of England'   342–5
Success   144–52, 153–5, 179–80
'Terror and Boredom: The
   Dependent Mind'   374, 395
'Thinkability'   243–4, 247–8, 254
Time's Arrow   275, 277–86, 380
*Visiting Mrs Nabokov and Other
   Excursions*   209–10
The War Against Cliché   111
'What Happened to Me on My
   Holiday'   345–8, 401
Yellow Dog   374–81, 382
see also Islam; Judaism; *New
   Statesman* (work and social life);
   nuclear disarmament; World
   Trade Centre attacks
Amis, Philip   1, 5, 9, 10, 11–12,
   13–14, 17–18, 20, 22, 26–7, 28,
   29, 31, 34–5, 43–4, 47–8, 50–1,
   52–3, 55–6, 58, 82, 95–6, 104,
   145–6, 198, 199, 200, 203–4,
   321, 350, 388, 401
Amis, Rose   22
Amis, Sally   10, 11–13, 18, 21–2, 25,
   33, 42, 44, 45, 46, 57, 93, 96, 104,
   106, 149–50, 199, 350, 388, 401
Amis, William   22, 23–4, 83
Applebaum, Anne   382, 384, 387

Ardagh, Mr (at Sussex Tutors) 60–1,
    66, 69
Arendt, Hannah 286
atheism 16–17
Atlantic Monthly 221
Ayer, A. J. 'Freddie' 83, 85, 89

Bailey, D. R. Shackleton 58, 92–3, 96
Bardwell, Hilary *see* Amis, Hilary
Bardwell, Leonard and Margery 325,
    328
Barker, Elspeth 339
Barnes, Julian 104, 111, 127, 134–5,
    138, 140, 146, 173–4, 202,
    234–5, 303, 304–5, 334, 422, 423
Barrowclough, Anne 291
Barry, John 175, 231–3
Bateson, F. W. 72
Battersea Grammar School 44,
    49–50
Baxter, Beverly 49
Behindlings (Nicola Barker) 411–12
Bellow, Saul 214–17, 221–2, 249,
    250–1, 277, 338, 368–72, 368
Bennett, Ronan 391, 393
Bergonzi, Bernard 180–1
Betjeman, John 7
Beyond Black (Hilary
    Mantel) 413–14
Blackmur, R. P. 25
Blair, Tony 341
Blond, Anthony 236
Bloom, Allan 249, 250
Bly, Robert 123, 310
book launches 104–6, 203
Booker Prize 257, 283–5, 306–7, 381
Bookseller 181
Boxer, Mark 163–4
Boycott, Rosie 176, 199–200, 234
Boyd, Alastair *see* Kilmarnock, Lord

Boyd, Jaime 119, 204
Boyd, William 308–9
Braine, John 341, 354
Brazzaville Beach (William
    Boyd) 308–9
break-up, parents' 37–40
Brighton, studies in 60–5, 68–9
Brilliant Creatures (Clive James) 168
Brooklyn 390
Brown, George Hambley 113
Brown, Tina 107, 112–16, 125,
    127–8, 155, 162, 193, 290, 398,
    401
Brown, Yasmin Alibhai 391
Buchan, James 284
Buford, Bill 181
Bursa (kebab house) 137–8, 139–40
Bury Me Standing (Isabel
    Fonseca) 294–5
Butterfield, Herbert 30
Butyrki death camp 357–8

Cambridge, Amis home in 30–7,
    40–1, 88, 147
Cambridgeshire High School for
    Boys 33–5
Cape publishers 57, 60, 102, 106,
    301, 303, 305–6
Capote, Truman 193, 214
Carey, John 70–2, 381
Cartwright, Justin 270
Caute, David 173, 174
Cecil, Lord David 72–3
Cherry (Matt Thorne) 412, 420
Chesterton Road (home with Antonia
    and boys) 234, 236–8, 264–5,
    272, 296, 399
Churchill, Winston 129
Cleary, Esmond 11
Cock and Bull (Will Self) 414–15

Cohen, Milton   92–3
Comp. Complex   140–1, 174
Conquest, Robert   4, 20, 65, 84, 95,
    104–5, 127, 142, 157–8, 159,
    170–1, 191, 201, 203, 247, 252,
    331, 354, 355, 356
Conrad, Joseph   383
Conservative Conference, Blackpool
    (1977)   164
Crook, Arthur   111

Daft, Rohan   291
Daily Express   39, 161–2, 203, 291,
    324
Daily Mail   291, 299, 331, 339, 356,
    392
Daily Telegraph   101, 392
Davies, Laing and Dick   51–2, 56
Davies, Russell   137
Dawson, Sam   15
Day-Lewis, C.   124
Day-Lewis, Tamasin   124–5
Debt to Pleasure, The (John
    Lanchester)   411
Deller, Keith and Kim   256–7
Donen, Stanley   233
Donne, John   63, 64
Dostoevsky, Fyodor   383–4
Douglas, Kirk   232
drugs   52–3

Eagleton, Terry   390–3, 397, 400–1
East Hampton, Isabel's family
    in   293, 346, 351, 385
education   15–16, 28–9, 33, 43, 44,
    49–52, 56, 59–61
Eichmann, Adolf   277–9, 286
Empson, William   111
Encounter   340
Evans, Gareth   223–4, 227

Evans, Harold   128, 193
Evening Standard   162, 203, 290–1,
    299, 303, 331, 339
Exeter College, Oxford   70, 72,
    77–82, 89
expulsion from school   50
Eyre, Richard   34, 165

Fairlie, Henry   18–20, 44
Fawcett, Edmund   346
Fawcett, Elias   345–7
Fawcett, Farah   232
Feinstein, Elaine   36
Fenton, James   84, 103–4, 105, 111,
    121, 127, 134, 136–7, 138, 139,
    143, 152–3, 159, 162, 164, 169,
    172, 191, 202, 235, 272, 362, 364
Fiction and the Fiction Industry (John
    Sutherland)   180
Flack, Karen   49
Fonseca, Isabel   130, 287–8, 292–5,
    320–1, 323, 330–3, 338–9,
    346–7, 348, 351–3, 355, 373,
    381–2, 383, 384, 389, 390, 408
Foster, Steve   240
Frye, Northrop   89–90
Fulham Road, Chelsea (Amis
    home)   44, 47–8, 50, 52–3
Fuller, Graham   154
Fuller, John and Roy   84
Furness, Mary   130–1, 158–61,
    165–6, 226, 261, 262

Gale, George   20, 30, 32, 39, 46–7,
    52, 57–8
Gale, Pat   20, 32
Garcia, Eva and Joe   10, 11–14, 24, 40
Gardnor House, Flask Walk (Amis
    home)   169, 176–7, 199, 200,
    201–2, 204, 350

Ghost Story (Toby Litt)   412–13
Gilbert, Martin   277, 355
Gorgas, Angela   167–9, 176–8, 182,
    191, 192, 198–9, 203, 223, 236,
    249, 335
Grade, Lew   175, 231
Granta   181
Graves, Robert   38, 74–5
Great Terror (Robert
    Conquest)   354–5
Greene, Graham   251
Gross, John   101, 121
Guardian   365, 366, 367, 387,
    391–3, 401
Guinness, Sabrina   164
Gulag: A History (Anne
    Applebaum)   382–3, 387

Hamilton, Ian   105, 130, 137, 138,
    139, 158, 159–60, 165, 180, 401
Hammond, Suzy   302–3
HarperCollins   306
Healey, Denis and Tim   82
Heathcoat-Amory, Bridget   163
Heller, Joseph   214
Henderson, Michael   392
Henderson, Rob   51, 56–7, 73–4, 60,
    73–7, 87, 90–1, 93–4, 102–3, 104,
    109–10, 389, 401
Hensher, Philip   392
Hewer, Rosalind   82–3, 84
High Wind in Jamaica, A (film)   48–9,
    82
Hislop, Andy   240, 241, 273, 289,
    316, 331, 333, 405
Hitchens, Christopher   17, 84, 103–6,
    107, 116, 121, 125, 127, 129,
    131, 132, 134, 136–7, 138–9,
    141–3, 147, 152–4, 157, 159–65,
    167, 168, 170, 176–7, 178, 191,

202, 204–5, 222–3, 225–7,
    228–9, 231, 235, 237–8, 240–1,
    242, 249, 258, 260–1, 266, 267,
    273, 274, 275–6, 288, 289, 292,
    303–5, 323, 338–9, 348, 350,
    355–6, 360–3, 364, 365, 368–72,
    392–3, 393
Hitchens, Peter   355–6
Hogarth Road, Earl's Court (Amis
    home)   106–7
Holbrook, Bruno (pseudonym)   114,
    122–3, 141
Holbrook, David   122
Holden, Anthony   125, 127
Hopkins, Gerard Manley   63, 64
Howard, Anthony   114, 121–2, 125,
    126, 127, 144, 152–3, 155, 161,
    170, 171, 173, 202, 335
Howard, Colin   45, 47–8, 50, 54,
    59–60, 73, 76, 83, 93, 99–100,
    101, 102–3, 108, 112, 115, 124,
    127, 145, 147, 148, 200, 201,
    239, 364–5, 392
Howard, Elizabeth Jane   37–40,
    45–8, 50, 53–4, 54, 57, 58–61, 63,
    67, 69, 71, 83, 85, 93, 95, 97, 124,
    147, 156, 176, 200, 201, 287, 392

Iffley Road, Oxford (Amis home)   89,
    90
Imlah, Mick   294
Independent   294, 339, 381, 391
Islam   366–7, 373–4, 390–7
Israel   249–50, 278, 367–9, 370
ITC Entertainment   175

Jacobs, Eric   326–7
Jamaica   49
James, Clive   103, 104–6, 127,
    131–2, 135, 137, 138–9, 152–3,

158, 159, 160, 168, 239, 262, 373–4
Jenkins, Alan 158–9, 226–7, 295
Jimenez, Natalia 346
John Harrison, M. 387
Jones, Monica 7
Jones, Penny 52
Joyce, James 410, 418–19
Judaism 249, 368–73

Kaplan, J. M. 293
Kavanagh, Julie 125–6, 127–9, 155, 185–6
Kavanagh, Pat 102, 104, 106, 168, 175–6, 202, 222, 301, 303, 304–5
Keats, John 6, 63, 64
Keitel, Harvey 232
Keneally, Thomas 284–5
Kennedy, A. L. 420
Kensington Garden Square (Amis home) 168
Kershaw, Ian 359
Kilmarnock, Lady see Amis, Hilary 'Hilly'
Kilmarnock, Lord 93, 94, 118, 126, 203–4, 326, 350, 353
Kilmartin, Terry 127, 135, 137, 139, 192, 193
Koenig, Rhoda 284
Kollek, Teddy 249, 250

Labour Conference, Blackpool (1978) 164–5
Larkin, Philip 7, 9, 20, 113, 117, 143, 201, 399–400
  correspondence with KA 1, 2, 3–4, 8, 19–20, 23, 63, 64, 65–7, 94, 176, 233, 234, 328, 329–30, 405
Lawrence, D. H. 63, 65, 366
Leader, Zachary 6, 33, 38, 39,

239–40, 258–9, 261, 289–90, 292, 307, 329, 330–1, 348, 405
Leamington Road Villa (Amis home) 237, 255, 261, 265–6, 296, 331, 333, 378
Leishman, J. B. 72
'Lemmons,' Barnet (Amis home) 82, 90, 93–4, 96–8, 101, 115, 124, 148, 169, 176
Leonard, Elmore 334
Lessing, Doris 414
Levy, Geoffrey 392
Lewin, Moshe 359
Lifton, Robert J. 276–7, 279–81, 282, 283
Lolita (Vladimir Nabokov) 211, 378
Look At It This Way (Justin Cartwright) 270

Mackendrick, Alexander 48
Madingley Road, Cambridge (Amis home) 30–7, 40–1, 88, 147
Maida Vale, London (Amis home) 48, 53
Mail on Sunday 339, 381
Mailer, Norman 206–7, 214
Majorca 33, 38, 42, 43–4, 73
Manchester Evening News 397
Manchester University 390, 397–401, 406
Mann, Sargy 55, 83, 93, 96, 100, 109, 111, 124, 146–7, 150, 239, 364
Margain, Hugo 224
'Martian Sends a Postcard Home' (Craig Raine) 172, 184–5
Martianism 172, 184–5, 187–8, 190
Marvell, Andrew 63, 64
Maschler, Tom 57, 102, 106
Maugham, Somerset 9, 111–12

McAndrew, Jean and John 26–7
McCrum, Robert 181, 406
McEwan, Ian 127, 138, 165, 181,
    191, 202, 239, 242, 265, 271–2,
    273, 307, 309, 320, 393, 422–3
McGinn, Colin 17
McKay, Peter 291–2, 294
McWilliam, Candia 167, 168
media attention 57, 203, 290–2, 303,
    321, 324, 331, 339, 349–50, 381,
    389, 391–3, 397
Mengele, Josef 279
Michie, James 8, 9
Milestones (Sayyid Qutb) 395–6
Miller, Karl 135
Milton, John 307–8
Miramax 398–9
Mitas, Chris 240–1, 274, 296, 302,
    312–13, 337–8
Mitchell, David 410, 415, 420
Montgomery, Bruce 9, 20
Moore, Dudley 113–14
Morrison, Blake 179
Motherunch's 137
Motion, Andrew 143, 308, 329, 330

Nabokov, Vera 209
Nabokov, Vladimir 27, 100, 149,
    209–11, 377
Nation 228, 370
National Portrait Gallery 168
Nazism and the Holocaust 275,
    276–86, 354–5, 356, 359–60,
    371–2
Neidpath, Lord Jamie 162–3, 165–6
New Review 105, 130, 137, 158,
    159, 180
New Statesman (work and social
    life) 65, 102, 104, 107, 110,
    113, 114, 121, 122, 126–8,

134–44, 152–3, 161, 162, 164–5,
    170–4, 178, 202, 203, 301, 340,
    341, 355, 364, 367, 372, 403
New York Times 267–8, 334
New Yorker 300, 330
Nicholson, Mavis 6, 19, 45
Nickie (Amis house guest) 31, 33, 43
North, Serena 85–6, 402
Northanger Abbey screenplay 399
nuclear disarmament 242–8, 250–4,
    258, 292–3

Observer 65, 101, 135, 137, 139,
    192, 214, 228, 256–7, 395
Old Forge, Shilton (Amis
    home) 87–8, 123
orphanage, Swansea 24–5
Orwell, George 368
Oxford and Cambridge Club 238
Oxford University 2, 3, 35, 61, 69,
    70–3, 77–85, 87–91
Ozick, Cynthia 370

Paddington Sports Club 238, 239,
    268, 312–3, 316, 329
Page, Bruce 161, 170–3
Palestine 367
Pallister, Anthony 191
Papineau, David 236, 239–40, 242,
    254, 261–2, 268, 272–3, 281–2,
    292, 307, 312, 337, 342, 343,
    345, 405
Paradise Lost (John Milton) 307
Paris 176, 177–8, 191, 222
Parkin, Patricia 306
Partington family 29–30, 321–3,
    324–6, 335–6
Penellis, Miss (primary school
    teacher) 15–16
Perpignan 76–7

Peterhouse, Cambridge 30–1
Phillips, Antonia 130, 223–7,
   229–231, 233–8, 249, 261,
   264–7, 272, 276, 288–91, 296,
   317, 331–3, 346, 347, 370, 399
Pilger, John 367
Pillars of Hercules (pub) 137, 138–9
Pinewood Studios 49, 176, 233
Pirie, David 111
Ploughman's Lunch, A (film) 165
poker 127, 239, 272, 373, 385
Polanski, Roman 179
politics 134, 152–4, 162, 164–5,
   169–71, 195–6, 213, 242, 251–2,
   275, 341–2, 354–7
   see also Islam; Judaism; Nazism;
   nuclear weapons; Stalinism;
   World Trade Center attacks
Pont Street, Belgravia (Amis
   home) 102, 104, 125
pornography 114, 122–3, 141
Pound, Ezra 63, 64
Primrose Hill (Martin's home with
   Isabel) 330, 358, 389, 390
   see also Gardnor House, Flask Walk
   (Amis home)
Prince, Peter 104
Princeton 25–8
Private Eye 114
Prudence Farmer Award 172

Quantity Theory of Insanity (Will
   Self) 414
Question Time (BBC) 393–4
Qutb, Sayyid 395–6

Raine, Craig 127, 135, 153, 169,
   172, 183–5, 406
Reagan, Ronald 193, 194–5
Reid, Christopher 172, 183–4

religion 15–17
   see also Islam; Judaism
Rodgers, Tobias 167
Ronda 92–3, 94, 118–19, 126, 353
Roth, Philip 211–12
Rothschild, Amschel 168, 177, 249,
   335
Rothschild, Anita 249
Rothschild family 163
Rothschild, Victoria 129
Rukeyser, Bill 31, 34
Rushdie, Salman 181, 239, 240, 243,
   270–4, 288, 303–4, 305, 320,
   394, 411
Russel, Nick 3

Sage, Lorna 128
Said, Edward 368–72
Satanic Verses (Salman
   Rushdie) 270–1, 303–4
Saturn 3 (film) 175–6, 231–3
Schindler's Ark (Thomas
   Keneally) 284–5
Scott, 'Bummer' 31–2
Scruton, Roger 283–4
Seale, Delilah 129, 186–7, 189, 191,
   323–4, 334, 339, 406
Seale, Lamorna 129, 186–7, 190, 191
Seale, Orlando 186, 187
Seale, Patrick 186, 187, 323
Self, Will 248, 288–9, 307, 397, 414,
   419–420
sex, subject of 21, 27, 34, 95, 133–4
Shakespeare, William 79, 91
Shamir, Yitzhak 371
Shand Kydd, Adam 177
Si and Fran (pre-Oxford
   friends) 73–4, 76, 108–9
Situation of the Novel, The (Bernard
   Bergonzi) 180–1

Slipstream (Jane Howard) 54
Smith, Ali 410, 415, 420
Soames, Emma 128–9, 129–30, 131, 156, 163, 291, 316
Soames, Jeremy 155
Soames, Mary 155–6
Soames, Nicholas 155–6, 314
Soames, Sir Christopher 155–6
Solzhenitsyn, Aleksandr 333–4, 336, 362
Somerset Maugham Prize 111–12, 118
Spectator 101, 136, 144, 179–80, 284
Spenser, Edmund 63, 64
sports 29, 135–6, 239–40, 385, 405–6
St John's, Oxford 2, 3, 70–1, 72
Stalinism 355–64
Steiner, George 285
Stewart, Lucretia 161, 165–7, 262–3
Stout, Mira 267–8, 269–70
suicide attempt, mother's 45, 148
Sunday Telegraph 193, 340
Sunday Times 9, 112–13, 128, 193, 250, 291–2, 294, 326–7, 329, 373, 406–7
Sussex Tutors 60
Sutherland, John 180, 181, 391–2, 400–1
Swansea 4, 5–6, 8, 9–16, 17–18, 20, 24, 26, 28, 29
Swansea University College 5, 6, 9
Swift, Graham 306–7
Szamuely, Tibor 354, 387–8

Taliban 373
    see also Islam
Talk (magazine) 398
Tatler 193

Taylor, D. J. 70, 181, 381
The Times 176
Thorne, Matt 412, 420
Thwaite, Anthony 176, 199, 329, 330, 340
Times Literary Supplement (TLS) 65, 101, 110–11, 118, 121, 130, 135, 137, 158, 179, 224–5, 226–7, 283–4, 288, 294, 295
Tognazzi, Ugo 177–8
Tomalin, Claire 126, 127, 335
Tomalin, Susannah 335
Treglown, Jeremy 130
Trelford, Donald 192, 193
Trilling, Diana 208–9
Trollope family 94
Trotsky, Leon 361–2
truancy 29, 44, 50
Tupper family tree 142
Tuscany 85–6, 289

United States of America 25–8, 193–6, 206–9, 214, 225–6, 275–6, 317, 346, 351, 365, 370, 373, 385, 390, 408
Updike, John 211–12
Uruguay 351–2, 381–3, 384, 389, 399

Vanity Fair 271
Vidal, Gore 139, 206, 214, 370
Vonnegut, Kurt 207–8, 214

Wain, John 20
Waldegrave, James, 13th Earl of 261
Walker, Tim 291
Walsh, John 81, 169, 266
Waugh, Auberon 'Bron' 113–14, 126
Wellfleet, Cape Cod 226, 275–6, 317, 348, 370

Wells, Alexandra 'Gully'   83, 85–9,
    93, 94, 96–7, 123, 124, 129,
    132–3, 206, 401
Wells, Dee   83, 85
West, Fred   322, 335–6
Wheen, Francis   107, 127, 135, 141,
    151–2, 153–4, 160, 161–2, 165,
    166, 170, 172, 174, 235–6, 262–3
Wollheim, Richard   224, 230–1, 238
Wood, Adolf   225
Wordsworth, Jonathan   70, 71–3,
    79–80, 81, 89, 90–1

Wordsworth, William   78
World Trade Centre attacks   365–6
Worsthorne, Peregrine   57
Wylie, Andrew   303–6, 398

Yevtushenko, Yevgeny   84
Young, Toby   292

Zanzibar (bar)   163–4